The Redbook

A Manual on Legal Style

A THOMSON COMPANY

The Redbook

A Manual on Legal Style

Bryan A. Garner

with

Jeff Newman
Tiger Jackson

ISBN 0-314-25859-0

Library of Congress Cataloguing-in-Publication Data

Garner, Bryan A.

The Redbook: A Manual on Legal Style / Bryan A. Garner

Includes bibliographical references and index.
1. Legal Composition. 2. English language—usage. 3. English language—style.
4. Law—United States—Terminology. 5. Law—United States—Language.
6. Law—United States—Methodology. 7. Printing, Practical—United States—Style manuals.

610 Opperman Drive
P.O. Box 64526
St. Paul, MN 55164-0526
1-800-328-9352

TEXT IS PRINTED ON 10%
POST CONSUMER RECYCLED PAPER

3rd reprint 2004

In memory of

Charles Alan Wright

1927–2000

Other Books Written or Edited by Bryan A. Garner

Black's Law Dictionary
(7th ed., abridged ed., pocket ed.)

A Dictionary of Modern Legal Usage

The Elements of Legal Style

The Winning Brief

Securities Disclosure in Plain English

Guidelines for Drafting and Editing Court Rules

A Dictionary of Modern American Usage

The Oxford Dictionary of American Usage and Style

Texas, Our Texas: Reminiscences of The University

A Handbook of Basic Law Terms

A Handbook of Business Law Terms

A Handbook of Criminal Law Terms

A Handbook of Family Law Terms

Table of Contents

Introduction

"The law," as William Prosser once said, "is one of the principal literary professions." Given that fact, you might expect lawyers to have a comprehensive style manual to help govern the decisions they make in their writing. Yet that has not been so until now.

It is true, of course, that there are many books on legal style. I have written more than one myself. But there never has been, for example, an exhaustive guide to capitalization, to punctuation, to bias-free language, to the use of numbers and symbols, and the like—to the thousands of sentence-level quirks that arise in legal writing.

The law has been blessed (a curmudgeon would say cursed) with citation manuals, the guides on how to cite authority. *The Bluebook* has held the field for many years, and recently the *ALWD Citation Manual* has come boldly onto the scene. They are both excellent guides, even if they can lead obsessive-compulsive personalities within the profession to fret endlessly over which commas get italicized and which ones remain roman. In this book, we have generally followed *ALWD*, but with some modifications; for example, we have kept *The Bluebook*'s traditional abbreviation forms (*Nat'l*, not *Natl.*, etc.).

But the citation manuals deal almost exclusively with citing authority, and the question inevitably arises, What about the stuff that comes in between the citations? How the sentences read is surely as important as whether the citations are in proper form. That leads us to this book, which is concerned with the form of legal sentences and their relationship to the authorities cited.

The Redbook was more than a year in the making. I began by occasionally asking practicing lawyers and law students in my advanced legal-writing courses to note three or four points that they would like answered in a manual on legal style. In a year, I had about a thousand responses. My colleagues and I grouped these into categories and began working through all the various points of style, formulating blackletter rules and supporting comments. The book gradually became something of a restatement of legal style.

Rulebooks can fossilize thinking on questions of style. In a sense, that is their purpose and their virtue. But that virtue can turn into a vice if users stop thinking about the reasons for stylistic decisions. Undoubtedly every user of this book will encounter a situation in which the better course is to depart from a rule. Yet this hardly means that the rules can be tossed aside: you need to know the rules before you can decide when to depart from them. Only then is there any hope of using the language skillfully. And that is something that everyone concerned with law should want to do.

Bryan A. Garner
Dallas, Texas
February 2002

Acknowledgments

Many superb writers and editors contributed to this book—most importantly two of my colleagues at LawProse, Inc.: Jeff Newman and Tiger Jackson, both of whom researched and drafted major segments of the book. Capitalizing on many years of experience as a journalist and graphic designer, Jeff also laid out the pages and designed the cover.

Several teachers of legal writing closely reviewed the manuscript and offered important suggestions: Bradley G. Clary of the University of Minnesota, Ruth Ann McKinney of the University of North Carolina, and Wayne Schiess of the University of Texas.

Several practicing lawyers did the same: Charles Dewey Cole Jr., Jill Dinneen, Bruce E. Fein, and Brian Melendez. I am grateful for their detailed, thoughtful suggestions. Brian Melendez especially drew on his vast legal and linguistic knowledge to contribute to every part of the book.

Terence G. Connor, Steven I. Wallach, and Judge Lynn N. Hughes made valuable contributions to Part 3, on preparing legal documents. Wilson Neely and Marvin S. Sloman reviewed § 15 (opinion letters) and improved it significantly.

David W. Schultz, a professional writer and editor and a former colleague of mine, read the entire manuscript with great acumen. So did Karen Magnuson, whose editorial judgments are second to none. To all these perceptive contributors, I am deeply grateful.

Thanks also to Richard R. Kennedy for allowing me to reproduce his appellate brief in section 19 of the book.

At the West Group, Douglas Powell saw the need for the book, and Pamela S. Siege and Louis Higgins both helped make it materialize. Heartfelt thanks to all.

This book is dedicated to the memory of one of the greatest legal writers ever: Charles Alan Wright. He cared almost as much about commas and capital letters as he did the law of federal courts, and his work was the inspiration for this book.

B.A.G.

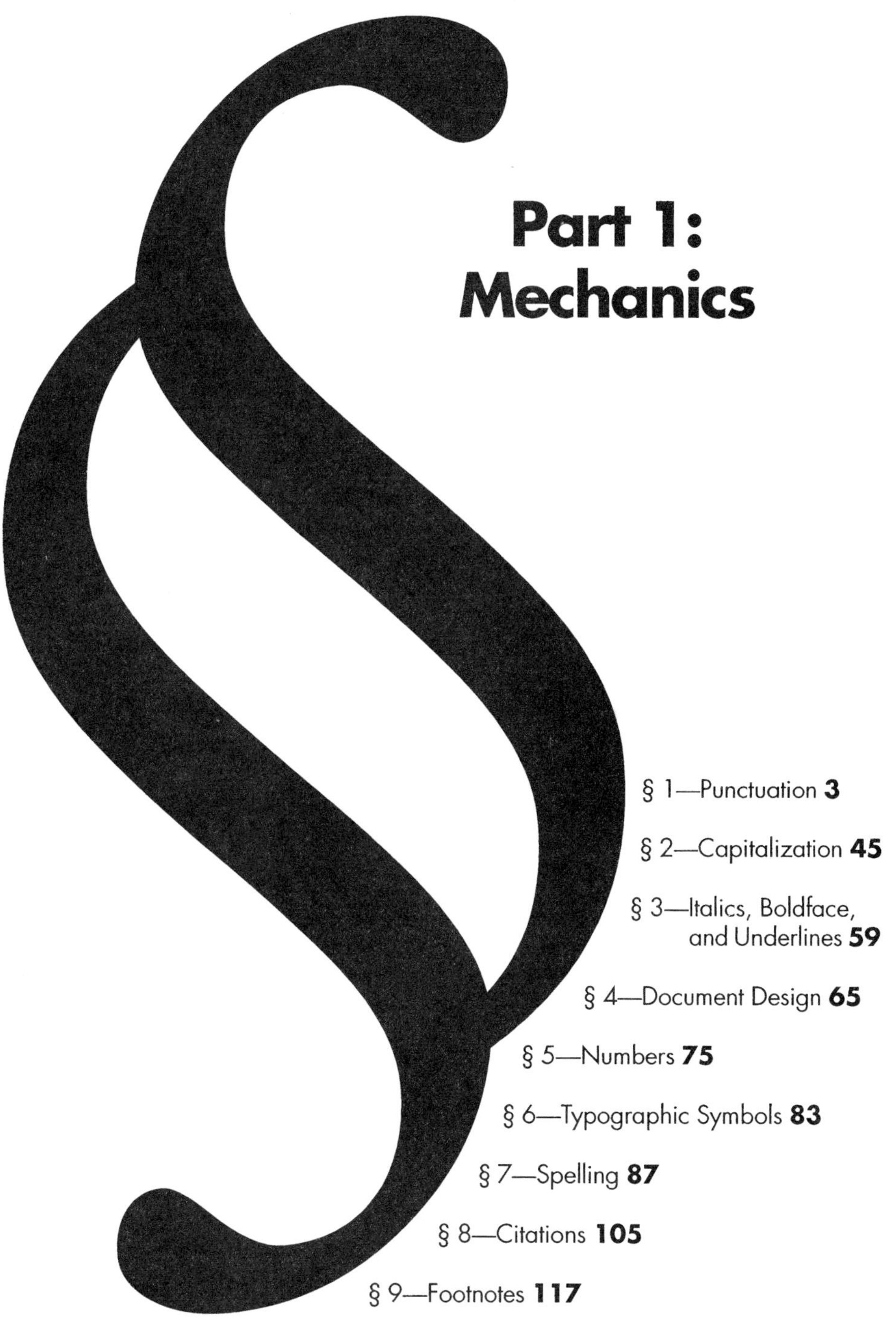

Part 1: Mechanics

§ 1
Punctuation

1.1 Punctuation marks are like traffic signs that guide readers through sentences. Although many marks are mandatory (depending on the construction), many others are optional: they can enhance clarity or shade the meaning. Some marks may substitute for others—this clause, for example, could as easily be separated from the previous one by a colon, a semicolon, or even parentheses. Each choice would result in a slightly different feel for the sentence. The em dash may suggest drama; the colon may suggest a cause–effect relationship; the semicolon may suggest that the clauses are of equal importance; parentheses may suggest that what they contain is of lesser importance.

With such variety possible, punctuation marks help convey rhetorical style. With them the writer can influence where the reader will pause and for how long, or how the reader will put the parts of a sentence together logically. Like well-placed traffic signs, they can also prevent accidents—that is, misreadings that will make a reader stop to figure out what a sentence really means.

Anyone who has trouble with punctuation should concentrate first on learning the mandatory rules, one by one. Then, after that foundation is laid, learn to use marks that add voice and flourish.

Commas

1.2 For many writers, the comma is the most troublesome punctuation mark. While some comma rules are mandatory—for example, always use them in pairs to set off midsentence parenthetical matter—others are discretionary. Even the well-known rules have a subjective element about them. When is an introductory phrase long enough to require setting off by a comma? When is a compound sentence short enough to dispense with the comma? In fact, using commas is sometimes a matter of personal style. Styles are generally grouped into two schools: *close*, or heavy on the commas, and *open*, or light on the commas. The modern trend is toward open style, but this is no license to ignore commas altogether. Use them for what they are: guideposts to help readers get through a sentence without being tripped up by miscues.

1.3 **Use a comma to separate words or phrases grouped in a series of three or more, including between the last and the next-to-last, before the conjunction.**

(a) *Serial comma.* The serial comma, or terminal separator, which is placed before the conjunction *and* or *or*, can prevent ambiguity. Generally speaking, it is always included in formal writing and often omitted in informal writing. Most magazines always use the serial comma, while most newspapers rarely do. Some writers treat it as optional—and that seems to be the trend in popular writing—but the safer practice is to use it consistently. The serial comma is never incorrect, but omitting it is sometimes quite incorrect.

Ex.: red, white, and blue

Ex.: Can you help me research this memo, draft a pleading, and schedule depositions?

Ex.: The claimed aspects of the pizzeria's trade dress included menu content, prices, pizza ingredients, and "style" or preparation. (Without the comma, the end of the sentence would be confusing.)

(b) *Complex phrases.* If phrases in a series are long, or if any of them contains internal punctuation or a conjunction, the series should be separated with semicolons rather than commas (see 1.17).

Ex.: Among the children's chores were mowing the lawn, washing the car, taking out the trash, and feeding the dog.

But: Among the children's chores were mowing, raking, and edging the lawn; washing the car; taking out the trash; and feeding the dog.

(c) *Conjunction repeated.* No comma is needed if the items are all joined by conjunctions.

Ex.: The plaintiff and the defendant and the intervenors were all ready for trial.

1.4 Use a comma to separate two independent clauses joined by a coordinating conjunction (*and, but, or, nor, for, yet, so*).

(a) *Defined.* An independent clause is one that can stand alone as a complete sentence.

Ex.: The study group called out for pizza, and the slackers packed a picnic. (Compound sentence, with a subject and a verb in each independent clause.)

(b) *Compound predicate distinguished.* Avoid using a comma to set off the second part of a compound predicate; in general, use one only if it is needed to avoid a misreading.

Not this: The study group called out for pizza, and took a quick break.

But this: The study group called out for pizza and took a quick break. (Compound predicate, with one subject and two verbs.)

An option: The study group called out for pizza and salad, and took a quick break. (The comma helps distinguish the *and* that joins two predicates from the *and* that joins two objects.)

(c) *Choice between comma and semicolon.* If one or both of the clauses are complex or contain an internal comma, a semicolon may be needed to clarify the separation of clauses (see 1.15).

Ex.: The mediation was successful thanks to the mediator's insight, persistence, and forceful personality; and, at long last, the case settled.

(d) *Comma splice.* Do not rely on a comma without a conjunction, or a comma and a subordinating word, to join two independent clauses. This error is called a "comma splice" (but see 1.16(b)).

Not this: The mediation worked, the case settled.
Not this: The mediation worked, hence the case settled.
But this: The mediation worked, and the case settled.
Or this: The mediation worked; hence, the case settled.

1.5 Use a comma to set off an introductory phrase; it is permissible, however, to omit the comma if the introductory phrase is short and the verb follows it closely.

(a) *Types of introductory matter.* Introductory matter may be a single word of transition <Obviously>, a phrase <On the other hand>, or a dependent clause <If we can agree on the price>.

Ex.: Fortunately, there were no more surprises in the eyewitness's testimony.
Ex.: Two years earlier, a similar incident had occurred in a nearby town.
Ex.: Since we have to be in Chicago next week anyway, we can take the deposition then.

(b) *Exception.* At the writer's discretion, a very short introductory phrase, usually no more than three words, may appear without a comma. Whether to use the comma will depend on how the writer expects the sentence to "sound" as it is read.

Ex.: In October another Court term will begin.
But also acceptable: In October, another Court term will begin.
But note: In fact, another Court term will begin in October.
Ex.: Soon we will all know the verdict.
But also acceptable: Soon, we will all know the verdict.

(c) *Inverted sentence.* No comma separates an introductory adverbial phrase in an inverted sentence if the verb immediately follows the phrase that modifies it.

Ex.: Sitting at the opposing counsel's table was my old mentor.

(d) *Direct address.* Use a comma to set off a word or phrase of direct address.

Ex.: Your Honor, may I approach the bench?

1.6 Use commas to set off a nonrestrictive or parenthetical phrase or clause from the rest of the sentence.

(a) *Defined.* A nonrestrictive phrase or clause is one that could be taken out of the sentence without changing the meaning. It gives additional description or information that is incidental to the central meaning of the sentence (see 10.20(b)).

Ex.: The meeting, which starts at 10 a.m., is about the Matthews case. (The time is incidental to the meaning of the sentence, so the material set off by commas is a nonrestrictive phrase. The writer has already identified the meeting being referred to.)

But: The meeting that starts at 10 a.m. is about the Matthews case. (The time is a necessary part of the sentence because it identifies which of several meetings. So "that starts at 10 a.m." is a restrictive phrase that is not set off by commas.)

(b) *Nonrestrictive appositive.* An appositive—a word or phrase next to a noun that further details or describes it—is frequently nonrestrictive (that is, it adds only incidental information). When that is so, set it off with commas.

Ex.: O'Neal, a well-respected public defender, surprised everyone by running for district attorney. (The phrase *a well-respected public defender* is nonrestrictive, so it is set off by commas.)

Ex.: Malice has a completely different meaning in one tort, defamation.

(c) *Restrictive appositive.* An appositive can be restrictive when it provides specific identification. When it is restrictive, it is not separated by commas.

Ex.: This gift is for my daughter Jane and that one for my daughter Sarah. (*Jane* and *Sarah* are restrictive appositives: each tells which daughter is meant.)

Ex.: The great jurist Learned Hand never served on the Supreme Court. (*Learned Hand* is a restrictive appositive, so no commas should separate it from *jurist.*)

(d) *Dependent clause.* A dependent clause is one that could not stand alone as a sentence. It may be restrictive (no comma) or nonrestrictive (set off by commas), depending on whether it could be taken out of the sentence without changing the meaning.

Ex.: I know what you're thinking. (*What you're thinking* is a clause because it contains a subject and a verb. It is dependent because it could not stand on its own as a sentence. And it is restrictive because it adds essential meaning to the sentence, telling *what.* So it is not separated by a comma.)

Ex.: The new mayor, who won in a landslide, takes office on January 1. (The dependent clause *who won in a landslide* is incidental to the central meaning of the sentence. So it is nonrestrictive and must be set off by commas.)

1.7 Use a comma to separate coordinate adjectives and adverbs—that is, the type that modify their target rather than each other.

(a) *Definition and tests.* Coordinate modifiers have similar meanings: together they shade the sense of the word being modified. Two traditional tests help point out coordinate modifiers: (1) reverse their order, and (2) insert the word *and* between them. If the meaning is still clear and natural-sounding, the words are probably coordinate modifiers.

Ex.: The robber coldly, methodically planned the heist. (The robber planned *methodically and coldly*, so a comma is needed.)

Ex.: Don't step on my blue suede shoes. (It would be quite odd to write *blue and suede shoes* or *suede, blue shoes*. Rather, *blue suede* as a phrase modifies *shoes*. So the phrasing must stand without a comma.)

Ex.: I still remember my little red wagon. (That the wagon is red has nothing to do with its being little—so no comma.)

Ex.: The opposing counsel was a tenacious, arrogant, brilliant lawyer. (The lawyer was *brilliant and arrogant and tenacious*, so commas separate the independent but coordinate modifiers.)

(b) *Not coordinate.* Do not use a comma between adjectives if the first adjective modifies a phrase formed by the second adjective and the noun.

Ex.: The panel will include Linda Greenhouse, the respected legal reporter. (Here, *respected* modifies the noun phrase *legal reporter.*)

1.8 Use a comma to set off a direct quotation of fewer than 50 words, unless the quoted matter is woven into the sentence itself (but see 1.23(a)).

(a) *Placement.* The comma goes between the quotation and the attribution, standing in for a period if the attribution follows the quotation.

Ex.: Judge Duggan asked, "How do you plead?"

Ex.: "If you can't afford a lawyer, the court will appoint one for you," Judge Duggan told the defendant.

Ex.: "Your trial," Judge Duggan said, "is set for July 19."

(b) *Colon as a substitute.* Where the attribution precedes the quotation, a colon may serve the same function; it is more formal.

Ex.: Judge Meir asked: "How do you plead?"

(c) *In context.* A partial quotation that is part of the sentence itself is not set off by commas.

Ex.: John swore that he "didn't see the red light."

Ex.: The judge firmly believed, as the Federal Circuit once wrote, that "[i]t is sometimes more important that a close question be settled one way or the other than which way it is settled."

1.9 Do not place a comma where it interferes with the flow of the sentence.

(a) *Phrase after conjunction or relative pronoun.* Do not use a comma after a conjunction or a relative pronoun that is immediately followed by an adverbial phrase. Although close punctuation (see 1.2) favors the comma, open punctuation does not.

Ex.: Michigan's long-arm statute may or may not grant jurisdiction; but if there is a conflict of laws, Ohio law controls.

Ex.: The court ruled that if there is a conflict of laws, Ohio law controls.

(b) *Before the predicate.* Do not put a comma between a subject and its verb unless it is required to set off nonrestrictive matter.

Not this: The issue whether the incorporation of such rules evinces a "clear and unmistakable" intent to arbitrate arbitrarily, was never decided by the New York Court of Appeals.

But this: The issue whether the incorporation of such rules evinces a "clear and unmistakable" intent to arbitrate arbitrarily was never decided by the New York Court of Appeals.

Ex.: This question, which has been the subject of much debate, has sharply divided the circuit courts. (The commas are required to set off the nonrestrictive clause.)

(c) *Before parentheses.* Do not put a comma before an opening parenthesis.

Not this: It "require[s], in varying degrees of specificity, 'a clearing system,'" (Board Op. at 3) so that must mean that claim 34 includes some clearing limitation.

But this: It "require[s], in varying degrees of specificity, 'a clearing system'" (Board Op. at 3), so that must mean that claim 34 includes some clearing limitation.

(d) *With nominal abbreviations.* Do not use a comma before *Jr.*, *III*, or the like after a personal name; but do use a comma before an academic-degree abbreviation such as *M.D.* or *Ph.D.* after a personal name, or a business-enterprise abbreviation such as *Inc.* or *L.L.P.* after a company name. Do not use a comma after any such abbreviation to separate it from the rest of the sentence.

Ex.: Dr. Martin Luther King Jr. delivered his "I Have a Dream" speech from the steps of the Lincoln Memorial on August 28, 1963.

Ex.: In a single year, Enron, Inc. went from being the seventh-largest company in sales on the Fortune 500 list to being the biggest bankruptcy filing in U.S. history.

(e) *Law-firm short form.* Abbreviate the name of a law firm with three or more named partners by using the first two names with no comma or ampersand. For a firm with only two named partners, use whatever style the firm prefers, but do not use bullets or other symbols that appear on a firm's logo.

Ex.: The Boston firm of Mintz Levin negotiated the merger. (On second reference to Mintz, Levin, Cohn, Ferris, Glovsky and Popeo. The firm uses the word *and*, not an ampersand.)

Ex.: Isaac clerked for Jones Day last summer. (Referring to Jones, Day, Reavis & Pogue of Cleveland.)

Ex.: Thelen Reid of San Francisco conducted the environmental audit. (The firm's name is Thelen, Reid & Priest.)

But: The reporter was represented by two firms, O'Melveny & Myers and Kilpatrick Stockton. (The first firm mentioned uses an ampersand in its name; the second, even though there are only two named partners, does not. A firm's preference controls.)

1.10 In a full date that is written month–day–year, put a comma between the day and the year; do not use a comma with the style day–month–year or month–year.

(a) *American style.* In the standard American format month–day–year, separate the day from the year with a comma.

Ex.: We held our breath on January 1, 2000, waiting to see if the utilities would still work.

Ex.: Your memo of November 13, 2001, has been very helpful.

(b) *Military and British style.* Do not use a comma in the format day–month–year.

Ex.: We held our breath on 1 January 2000, waiting to see if the utilities would still work.

Ex.: Your memo of 13 November 2001 has been very helpful.

(c) *No day.* Do not use a comma in the format month–year.

Ex.: The Florida recount controversy raged throughout the remainder of November 2000.

1.11 Use a comma to break down large whole numbers into sets of three digits.

(a) *Separating by threes.* Use commas to break whole numbers (not decimals) of four or more digits into groups of three. Although some writers have begun dropping the comma in four-digit numbers, this practice should be discouraged.

Ex.: 1,000

Ex.: 99,999

Ex.: 24,945,372

(b) *Exceptions.* Do not use commas in statute numbers, telephone numbers, house numbers, page numbers of fewer than five digits, years, and other serial numbers (see 5.11(b)).

Ex.: Rule 9002(a)

Ex.: 555-1212

Ex.: 6822 Magnolia Blvd.

Ex.: *Id.* at 1537

But: *Id.* at 15,442

1.12 Use a comma after the salutation in a personal letter.

(a) *Informal salutation.* The comma is an informal mark appropriate in correspondence between friends and relatives. It is also appropriate for all handwritten notes.

Ex.: Dear Mom,

(b) *Business correspondence.* For more formal uses, and especially business correspondence, use a colon (see 1.24).

Ex.: Dear Mr. Gillespie:

1.13 Consider using a comma where one or more words are omitted but understood in context.

(a) *Understood words.* A comma pause signals the reader that an obvious word or phrase, commonly the verb from the previous clause, is to be understood at this point.

Ex.: Democrats won governorships in Maine and Delaware; Republicans, in South Carolina and Nevada.

Ex.: Palestinians want statehood; Israelis, security.

(b) *Often optional.* When the meaning is clear, the comma may be omitted.

Ex.: California has 55 electoral votes, Florida 27, Vermont 3.

Ex.: Candidates are few but propositions many as voters go to the polls Tuesday.

(c) *Dramatic pause.* The comma can supply a dramatic pause for effect.

Ex.: While in office Pat had thousands of "friends"; afterward, none.

Semicolons

1.14 Except in appearance, the semicolon is not a colon at all. It would better be thought of as a "king comma," doing the work that a comma might ordinarily do if it weren't for some need for a stronger break in the sentence. When that need exists, what might have been a lowly comma before gets crowned like a checker reaching the eighth row. It's stronger than before; it has a more powerful impact on the reader. The pause is harder than any comma could deliver, though of course still not the punch of a period. And unlike a comma, a semicolon may join two independent clauses without a conjunction. Although some writers shun the semicolon, it's a versatile device in the hands of a skillful writer.

1.15 Use a semicolon to separate independent clauses if they are joined by an adverb rather than a conjunction, or if internal punctuation in either clause would otherwise create confusion (see 1.4(c)).

(a) *Common adverbs.* Some common connective adverbs are *accordingly, also, besides, consequently, further, furthermore, hence, however, indeed, instead, later, likewise, meanwhile, moreover, nevertheless, now, still, then, therefore,* and *thus.*

(b) *With comma.* The connective adverb is usually followed by a comma (in its role as introductory matter in the second clause), which alone may necessitate the use of a semicolon.

Ex.: It was almost quitting time; nevertheless, most workers planned to stay late to work on the project.

(c) *Strength of connector.* When one of the clauses contains an internal comma, another comma may not be strong enough to separate them; a semicolon may be needed, even if the linking word is a conjunction.

Ex.: Our client took great pains to answer all interrogatories quickly, honestly, and completely; so we were all upset that the other party never answered our interrogatories at all.

Ex.: Our client took great pains to answer all interrogatories quickly, honestly, and completely; in light of the goodwill we have shown, we were all upset that the other party never answered our interrogatories at all.

(d) *Coordinating conjunction.* A semicolon may be used instead of a comma to separate independent clauses connected by a coordinating conjunction; and the stronger break may be useful either to help the reader understand a complex sentence or else to indicate more of a break than a comma would provide.

Ex.: True, the President did stress in his message the need for more judges, to help the federal courts catch up with their calendars of pending cases and to cut down the frequent delays in handling litigation; and this argument, while quite warranted with respect to many lower federal courts, let Chief Justice Hughes enter the fray a little later by allowing publication of a letter in which he rather indignantly stated that the Supreme Court was "fully abreast of its work."

Ex.: Courts relying on legislative history often make no pretense that they have developed and are using a theory derived from it; and history often seems to be used only when it supports a conclusion arrived at by other means.

Ex.: The defendant's long wait was finally over; and ever so deliberately the jurors filed back into the courtroom.

1.16 Use a semicolon to separate independent clauses if there is no connecting word.

(a) *Semicolon alone.* When there is no conjunction or adverb linking two independent clauses, they should be separated by a semicolon.

Ex.: Demeanor is typically a sum total of traits and appearance; change any one and you may change the witness's credibility.

(b) *Exception.* Some authorities allow a comma instead of a semicolon when the sentence is quite short and the clauses are closely related. This exception to the prohibition against a "comma splice" (see 1.4(d)) is traditional and eminently defensible.

Ex.: The time was right, the cause was just.

Ex.: Try it, you'll like it.

1.17 Use a semicolon to separate items in a series when the items are complex or contain internal commas.

(a) *Complexity.* When elements in a series are particularly complex, the sentence may be clearer with semicolons instead of commas separating the elements.

Ex.: As commonly defined for the charge of murder, "malice" means the specific intent to kill; the specific intent to inflict serious bodily harm; the specific intent to commit a serious felony; or reckless indifference to human life.

(b) *Internal commas.* Use a semicolon to separate elements of a series of phrases or clauses if one or more of the elements contains an internal comma.

Ex.: The United States has three so-called historical bays: Chesapeake Bay, with an entrance 12 miles wide; Delaware Bay, with an entrance 10 miles wide; and Monterey Bay, with an entrance 19 miles wide.

Ex.: The campaign will stop tomorrow in Sacramento, California; Denver, Colorado; Tempe, Arizona; and Albuquerque, New Mexico.

(c) *To separate citations.* Use a semicolon to separate citations in a string.

Ex.: *U.S. v. United Mine Workers of Am.*, 330 U.S. 258, 303–04 (1947); *see also Norman Bridge Drug Co. v. Banner*, 529 F.2d 822, 827 (5th Cir. 1976); *accord Travelhost*, 68 F.3d at 961; *Petroleos*, 826 F.2d at 400.

Ex.: *Faragher*, 524 U.S. at 807; *Ellerth*, 524 U.S. at 765.

1.18 Use a semicolon to separate items in a series when the items are set off separately, as in a statute or contract.

(a) *Series lists.* It is common in drafting statutes, contracts, and other legal documents to enumerate elements in separately numbered or lettered paragraphs, with a semicolon between every two paragraphs.

Ex.: 6.1 A model or exhibit will not be admitted as part of the record of an application unless it:
(A) substantially conforms to the requirements of § 1.52 or § 1.84;
(B) is specifically required by the Office; or
(C) is filed with a petition under this section including:
(1) the petition fee as set forth in § 1.17(B); and
(2) an explanation of why the model or exhibit is necessary.

(b) *Advantages.* This "tabulated" style helps prevent various problems in legal drafting, not the least of which is unreadability.

Before: **Failure to Attend or to Serve Subpoena; Expenses.** If the party giving the notice of the taking of a deposition fails to attend and proceed therewith and another party attends in person or by attorney pursuant to the notice, the court may order the party giving the notice to pay such other party the reasonable expenses incurred by that party and that party's attorney in attending, including reasonable attorney's fees. If the party giving the notice of the taking of a deposition of a witness fails to serve a subpoena upon the witness and the witness because of such failure does not attend, and if another party attends in person or by attorney because that party expects the deposition of that witness to be taken, the court may order the party giving the notice to pay to such other party the reasonable expenses incurred by that party and that party's attorney in attending, including reasonable attorney's fees.

After: **Failure to Attend or Serve Subpoena; Expenses.** The court may order the party giving notice of a deposition to pay another party's reasonable expenses in attending, including attorney's fees, if the party giving notice fails to:
(1) attend and proceed; or
(2) serve a subpoena on the witness, who consequently does not attend.

1.19 Use a semicolon to separate an appositive or elaboration at the end of a sentence if the matter is introduced by *that is, for example, namely,* or a similar device.

(a) *Appositive matter.* Appositive matter may also be put in parentheses or set off by a dash. If it is short, a comma may suffice.

Ex.: Tenant fixtures generally fall into one of three categories; namely, trade fixtures, agricultural fixtures, and domestic fixtures.

Ex.: Tenant fixtures generally fall into one of three categories (that is, trade fixtures, agricultural fixtures, and domestic fixtures).

Ex.: Tenant fixtures generally fall into one of three categories—specifically, trade fixtures, agricultural fixtures, and domestic fixtures.

Ex.: A trade fixture is used for one purpose, namely, business.

(b) *No signal.* If appositive matter at the end of the sentence is not introduced by such a word or phrase, it should be preceded by a colon or dash instead (see 1.23(d), 1.50(c)). A semicolon would not work in this circumstance.

Ex.: Tenant fixtures generally fall into one of three categories: trade fixtures, agricultural fixtures, and domestic fixtures.

Ex.: Tenant fixtures generally fall into one of three categories—trade fixtures, agricultural fixtures, and domestic fixtures.

Colons

1.20 The colon both separates and sets up what comes next. As a separator it creates a pause roughly equivalent to that of the semicolon. But unlike a semicolon, the colon points to what comes after it, telling the reader that "here's a quotation," for example, or "here's something that reinforces what was just said," or "here's something that results from what was just said." Think of it as an arrow or a pointing finger. It's especially appropriate (and helpful) in legal writing: the purpose is quite often to draw conclusions from inferences, for example, or to lead the reader down a chain of reasoning. In some situations it is equivalent to an em dash, which may be substituted for stronger effect where appropriate.

1.21 Use a colon to join two separate but directly related clauses or phrases.

(a) *As a pointer.* A colon tells the reader that what follows the mark explains, supports, amplifies, or in some way logically flows from what precedes it.

Ex.: Things got worse in a hurry: our codefendant turned state's evidence.

Ex.: The epidemic is showing signs of abating: only four new cases were reported in the last week.

(b) *Optional nature of use.* The colon is a helpful signal to readers, but its use as a link between independent clauses is never mandatory. A semicolon could be used in either of the examples above, and all that would be lost is stylistic nuance.

Ex.: Things got worse in a hurry; our codefendant turned state's evidence.

Ex.: The epidemic is showing signs of abating; only four new cases were reported in the last week.

(c) *Phrase after colon.* What follows the colon may be either a complete clause or a simple phrase.

Ex.: Here's where we part company: over ethics.

1.22 If what follows the colon is not a complete sentence, do not capitalize the first word; if it is a complete sentence, be consistent in your decision about whether to capitalize the first word.

(a) *Phrase.* Unless some specific rule of capitalization applies, never capitalize the first word of a phrase after a colon.

Ex.: Two distinct tests of constitutionality potentially apply to Act 257: a state-law test and a federal test.

(b) *Sentence.* There are arguments for and against capitalizing the first word of a sentence that follows a colon. But when the second clause is left uncapitalized, the colon does a better job of relating the two parts of the sentence. Also, that construction parallels the form that the sentence would take if a semicolon had been used instead of a colon. Neither style is wrong, but be consistent in the style you use.

Ex.: The deponent was starting to show signs of irritability: she was tired and just wanted to go home.

Ex.: The deponent was starting to show signs of irritability: She was tired and just wanted to go home.

1.23 Use a colon to introduce a quotation, list, or statement.

(a) *Choice of punctuation.* A quotation may be introduced by a colon or by a comma (see 1.8), or it may be worked seamlessly into the sentence (in decreasing order of formality). The colon is especially appropriate for introducing block quotations, statutes, transcripts, and similar material. Though not mandatory, a term such as *following*, *as follows*, or *here* frequently accompanies the use of a colon.

Ex.: The court allowed the action to proceed, announcing the following rule adopting Section 433B of the Restatement (Second) of Torts:

> Where the conduct of two or more actors is tortious, and it is proved that harm has been caused to the plaintiff by only one of them, but there is uncertainty as to which of them has caused it, the burden is upon each such actor to prove that he has not caused the harm.

(b) *In transcripts.* Use a colon to set off the speaker's name from the text in a transcript.

Ex.:
BLAIN: Mr. Burgin, you designed the firm's accounts-receivable computer program, correct?
BURGIN: Ah, yes, I remember it well.
BLAIN: And you prepared the manual that is Defendant's Exhibit B?
BURGIN: Yes, that's right.

(c) *Numbered list.* Use a colon to introduce a numbered list. Again, separate the items with semicolons.

Ex.: Congress identified four factors as especially relevant in determining whether the use was fair: (1) the purpose and character of the use; (2) the nature of the copyrighted work; (3) the substantiality of the portion used in relation to the copyrighted work as a whole; and (4) the effect on the potential market for or value of the copyrighted work.

(d) *Appositive list.* Use a colon to introduce an appositive list at the end of a sentence—that is, a list that further explains the object of the sentence. If there are more than two elements in the list, separate them with commas or semicolons.

Ex.: The CBEST is a pass–fail examination consisting of three sections: reading, writing, and mathematics.

Ex.: Relief from liability is justified when the consenting participant meets three tests: awareness of the risk; appreciation of the nature of the risk; and voluntary assumption of the risk.

(e) *When not needed.* Never use a colon needlessly. No colon is needed to introduce a plain-vanilla predicate, such as a series of verbs, objects, or modifiers, unless the enumerated items are (1) introduced by *the following, as follows, namely,* or some similar device, or (2) set off on separate lines (as with subparts in contractual provisions). An unnecessary colon interrupts the flow of a sentence with an inappropriate pause.

Not this: That afternoon Sanders had to: make a bank deposit, pick up a loaf of bread, and get in a few sets of tennis.

But this: That afternoon Sanders had to make a bank deposit, pick up a loaf of bread, and get in a few sets of tennis.

Or this: That afternoon Sanders faced the following "chores": make a bank deposit, pick up a loaf of bread, and get in a few sets of tennis.

Not this: Procedural safeguards are essential in order to assure all parties that the technical adviser is: unbiased, impartial, and qualified.

But this: Procedural safeguards are essential in order to assure all parties that the technical adviser is unbiased, impartial, and qualified.

(f) *Formal quotation.* Use a colon to introduce a quotation in formal style; since the quotation stands alone (and is not woven into the syntax of the sentence itself), the first word is always capitalized after the colon.

Ex.: The accused showed no emotion at the arraignment, speaking only to enter a plea: "Not guilty."

Ex.: Retorted Holmes: "This case is decided upon an economic theory which a large portion of the country does not entertain."

> "Inexperienced writers often regard punctuation as a tiresome mechanical business to which little attention need be paid. There can be no greater mistake."
>
> —*M. Alderton Pink*

1.24 Use a colon after the salutation in a formal letter, and after each tag line in a memorandum.

(a) *Formality.* The colon is standard in business letters; but in personal letters a comma is more appropriate (see 1.12).

Ex.: Dear Mrs. Davis:

Ex.: Dear Mom,

(b) *British style.* American style is to always use a comma or a colon after a business salutation. British style is to use a comma for formal and informal letters or, often, no punctuation at all.

Ex.: Dear Professor Tapper

(c) *In a memorandum.* Use a colon after the tag lines on a memorandum (*To:*, *From:*, *Date:*, *Re:*, and the like) and in business reports and correspondence.

Ex.: To: All employees
From: Management
Re: Reserving vacation dates

Ex.: cc: TPM (recipients of a copy in business correspondence)

Ex.: Enclosures: Annual report

1.25 Use a colon to designate a ratio or analogy.

(a) *Ratio.* In a ratio, the colon stands for "to."

Ex.: Mix the concentrate and water in a 1:4 ratio. (Reads "1-to-4 ratio.")

(b) *Analogy.* In expressing an analogy, a single colon stands for "is to" and a double colon stands for "as." In this construction, use a space before the colon or colons.

Ex.: preponderance of the evidence : negligence :: beyond a reasonable doubt : criminal culpability

1.26 A colon is also used in several ways in citations and references, including citing the case record.

(a) *Citations.* The colon is used according to conventions between elements in a variety of constructions. In legal writing, it is used between the page number and line number (if available) in citations to the case record.

Ex.: (R. 38:12) (page 38, line 12 of the record)

Ex.: Trial Tr. vol. 1, 15:8 (June 23, 2001) (first volume of a multivolume trial transcript, page 15, line 8)

(b) *Miscellaneous uses.* The colon is used between the title and subtitle of a book or article; between chapter and verse in traditional biblical citations; between the initials of the writer and the typist in business correspondence; between the city of publication and the publisher in academic citations; between the hour, minute, and second in times; and elsewhere. Consult a specialized style or citation manual to find its correct use in a specific field.

Ex.: *Sexual Harassment: A Practical Guide to the Law, Your Rights, and Your Options for Taking Action*

Ex.: Matthew 7:7

Ex.: BAG:jwn (writer and typist in business correspondence)

Ex.: St. Paul: West Group, 2001 (in academic citations)

Ex.: 11:27 a.m.

Ex.: a record time of 3:47:21

Quotation Marks

1.27 Quotation marks come in four flavors: double and single, opening and closing. On a typewriter, a set of straight marks serves for both opening and closing quotations (" . . . "), but word processors can usually substitute the correct curly marks known as *smart quotes* (“ . . . ”). The single and double closed-quotation marks are sometimes improperly used as the symbols for *foot* and *inch*, respectively; the correct symbols are the prime (′) and double prime (″), respectively.

1.28 **Use double quotation marks around quoted material having fewer than 50 words, but not around block quotations of 50 words or more.**

(a) *Generally*. This is the standard and familiar use of the quotation mark.

Ex.: Russell said, “That delivery date is fine with me.”

Ex.: Here's what Irene said: “I don't have to pay if it's not what I ordered.”

Ex.: “Where do we go from here?” the mediator goaded the recalcitrant plaintiff. (The question mark takes the place of a comma at the end of the direct quotation.)

(b) *Block quotation*. Do not use quotation marks around a block quotation of 50 words or more. Rather, introduce the material with the proper lead-in, usually followed by a colon. Set it off from the previous text, indent it on both sides, and set it single-spaced.

Ex.: Parts of Brandeis's concurrence emphasized the need to show incitement:

> But even advocacy of [law] violation[,] however reprehensible morally, is not a justification for denying free speech where the advocacy falls short of incitement and there is nothing to indicate that the advocacy would be immediately acted on. . . . [N]o danger flowing from speech can be deemed clear and present, unless the incidence of the evil apprehended is so imminent that it may befall before there is opportunity for full discussion.

> “It's not wise to violate the rules until you know how to observe them.”
>
> —*T.S. Eliot*

(c) *Multiple paragraphs.* If matter inside quotation marks continues for more than one paragraph, do not place the closing quotation mark until the end of the matter, but place an extra opening quotation mark at the beginning of each subsequent paragraph in the quotation.

Ex.: The attorney general responded, "We are at war with an enemy that abuses individual rights as it abuses jetliners.

"Charges of kangaroo courts and shredding the Constitution give new meaning to the term 'fog of war.'" (No closing quotation marks after the first paragraph, but opening marks at the start of the second paragraph.)

1.29 Use single quotation marks around a quotation within a marked quotation, and alternate double and single quotation marks for more deeply nested quotations.

(a) *Awkwardness.* Nested quotations are awkward but frequently unavoidable. The need for them arises more often in legal writing than elsewhere, as writers quote courts that in turn quote other courts and statutes.

Ex.: "In this case there is no life expressly mentioned who can be a 'life in being.'"

Ex.: The *Chapa-Garza* court noted that "8 U.S.C. § 1101(a)(43) provides, in relevant part: '[T]he term "aggravated felony" means . . . a crime of violence for which the term of imprisonment [is] at least one year.'"

(b) *Alternative style.* Some writers prefer to use "smart" double quotation marks the first time, smart single quotation marks the second, straight double quotation marks the third, and straight single quotation marks the fourth. Rarely, if ever, should you need a fourth level of nesting.

Ex.: The *Chapa-Garza* court noted that "8 U.S.C. § 1101(a)(43) provides, in relevant part: '[T]he term "aggravated felony" means . . . a crime of violence for which the term of imprisonment [is] at least one year.'"

(c) *In block quotations.* If the main quotation is unmarked (e.g., a block quotation), a quotation within the quotation is set inside double quotation marks, and a further nested quotation is set inside single quotation marks.

1.30 Either use quotation marks around a word or phrase that is being referred to as a term, or else italicize it.

(a) *Generally.* A word used as a word (rather than for its actual meaning) is either set off by quotation marks or italicized (see 3.4). This device is more common in legal writing than general writing, largely because of its frequent use in defining terms and in using terms of art.

Ex.: Almost any person able to read was eligible for "benefit of clergy," a procedural device that effected a transfer from the secular to the ecclesiastical jurisdiction.

Ex.: As to the difference between the two phrases, counsel said there was no point in "juggling over definitions, since 'inherently' means 'inseparably' and 'imminently' means 'threateningly.'"

Ex.: The statute does not apply to honest differences of opinion. To leave no doubt on this point, Congress deliberately used the words "false" and "fraudulent."

Ex.: The meaning of "malice" depends on whether you're involved in a murder case or a libel suit.

(b) *Italic as alternative.* Italic type is an attractive alternative for this use of quotation marks, since there is no punctuation to slow down the reader's pace (see 3.4(a)).

Ex.: Even if the words were to be applied in accordance with the meaning they had when written, they could be given a broad or narrow application. In later years *among* in this context has carried the connotation of *between,* but throughout the period it has also meant *intermingled with*—a term which might preserve or obliterate the power of the states.

1.31 Use quotation marks to mean "so-called" or (more negatively) to mean "so-called-but-not-really."

(a) *Odd or informal use.* Used this way, the quotation marks can signal that the term is somehow odd, informal, or perhaps adopted by necessity—"so-called."

Ex.: Although the primordial desire for vengeance is an understandable emotion, it is a testament to the constantly evolving nature of our social and moral consciousness that the law has, in recent decades, come to regard this "eye-for-an-eye" philosophy as an improper basis for punishment.

(b) *With "so-called."* The quotation marks alone serve to signal the meaning of *so-called.* Where that term is used explicitly, the quotation marks are superfluous, and the better practice is to leave them off.

Ex.: The court further held that relief would require manual recounts in all Florida counties where so-called "undervotes" had not been subject to manual tabulation. (Either *so-called* or quotation marks alone would do the job.)

Better: In addition, the recounts in these three counties were not limited to so-called undervotes but extended to all the ballots.

(c) *With phrasal adjectives.* Do not use quotation marks around phrasal adjectives. Instead, hyphenate (see 1.57).

Not this: The defendant asked the court to lower the award, citing the "mitigation of damages" doctrine.

But this: The defendant asked the court to lower the award, citing the mitigation-of-damages doctrine.

(d) *Nicknames.* Use quotation marks around a nickname. The nickname should appear between the given name and the surname in the first citation. This device should be used only for a nickname, not for a well-known informal variation of a name.

Ex.: Richard "Racehorse" Haynes

But not: William Jefferson "Bill" Clinton

(e) *Connoting irony.* Use quotation marks around a word or phrase that is used in an ironic sense, implying that the thing it refers to is not really this at all. Used in this way, quotation marks are a signal of jest.

Ex.: Our first "Christmas tree" was a potted plant with a tin-foil star on top.

Ex.: In the years leading up to 1996–1997, Scholastic's best-selling product was *Goosebumps,* a series of "scary" children's books.

(f) *Showing disrespect.* Using quotation marks to ridicule can be a dangerous device; the reader can easily find it snide and disrespectful.

Ex.: The only "damage" this plaintiff suffered was dignitary.

1.32 Place other punctuation marks correctly in relation to quotation marks: periods and commas go inside; semicolons and colons go outside; and question marks and exclamation marks go inside only if they are part of the quoted matter.

(a) *With period or comma.* Place final periods and commas inside quotation marks. (British style is to place them outside.)

Ex.: To grant the defendant another advantage, in nonreciprocal discovery rights, would make the prosecutor's task "almost insurmountable."

Ex.: High-sounding phrases, such as "the public interest," "economic democracy," and "free enterprise," were to him mere propaganda clichés.

(b) *With semicolon or colon.* Place final semicolons and colons outside the quotation marks, even if the quoted material happens to have a semicolon or colon in that position.

Ex.: In order to formulate precise factual issues, a pleader had to state "facts," not "conclusions"; and in order that the issues be material according to the substantive law, the stating of "evidence" was condemned.

Ex.: As Archibald Cox noted, "The validity of the reporters' claim of a First Amendment privilege not to disclose sources of information was decided on the results of two inquiries": (1) were fears of sources drying up justified; and, if so, (2) does that loss outweigh the benefits of the testimony?

(c) *With question mark or exclamation mark.* A question mark or exclamation mark may go inside or outside the quotation marks, depending on whether it is part of the quotation.

Ex.: Does the parol-evidence rule play a similar role in excluding evidence of prior negotiations to interpret contract language that is "clear on its face"?

Ex.: The court session opened with the traditional cry, "Oyez! Oyez! Oyez!"

(d) *Amendment exception.* Punctuate the text of a statutory or contractual amendment exactly as it is to appear in the amended document. The usual rules of punctuation and capitalization do not apply: if a period is part of the amendment, it must go inside the quotation marks even if the main sentence continues, and it cannot itself serve as the terminal punctuation of the main sentence.

Ex.: In Rule 9027, replace "If a case under the Code is pending when a claim or cause of action is asserted in another court," with "If a claim or cause of action is asserted in another court after the commencement of a case under the Code,". (The comma inside the closing quotation mark is part of the amendment. The sentence period cannot go inside the quotation marks, as the usual rules of punctuation would require, because it is not in the text of the amendment. *If* must be capitalized even though it is not part of a complete sentence and would not be capitalized under the usual rules of capitalization.)

Ex.: In Rule 3, replace "Upon receipt of the motion and having ascertained that it appears on its face to comply with rules 2 and 3, the" with "The". (Main-sentence period goes outside the quotation marks because it is not part of the amendment.)

Ex.: Amend Fed. R. Crim. P. 32(d)(1) by replacing "The judgment must be signed by the judge and entered by the clerk." with "The judge must sign the judgment, and the clerk must enter it.". (The period must stay with the text inside both quotations, even though it does not end the main sentence after the first quotation. And a second period must go after the second quotation in order to terminate the main sentence.)

Parentheses

1.33 Parentheses are frequent fliers in legal writing: it's rare to find a page without a few pairs on it. They are required in legal citations and often show up for subordinate matter in the text. In general, they are used in pairs to enclose matter that is helpful but not essential. They therefore tend to suggest to the reader, "Take me or leave me." If the writer's purpose is to make the parenthetical content stand out rather than hide, a pair of em dashes is probably the better tool. In legal writing, don't shrink from nesting parentheses, or even having "kissing" parentheses when necessary. And, despite the practice in other styles of writing, don't use brackets as "subparentheses" in legal writing.

1.34 Use parentheses to set off extraneous matter (such as an explanation, reference, or comment) in a sentence.

(a) *Incidental to sentence.* Parentheses tell the reader that the matter they enclose is incidental to the sentence itself. They are always used in pairs.

Ex.: Only two states, Nevada (1956) and Utah (1957), had enacted statutes that specifically permitted homeschooling. (The parenthetical matter gives extra information about the content.)

Ex.: These include, among others, the opinion rules (Rules 701 and 702), the firsthand- or personal-knowledge rule (Rule 602), and the rule requiring authentication of documents (Rule 901). (The parenthetical matter refers the reader to a source.)

Ex.: This diluted Nietzscheanism had filtered into his brain through smoky night sessions with his more literate (but still not very literate) friends. (The parenthetical matter comments on the content.)

(b) *Minimizing effect.* Parentheses minimize their content (unlike em dashes, which focus attention on what they set apart). The information may be important in its own right, but the words themselves could be removed without changing the meaning of the sentence.

Ex.: In the single carton opened for examination (taken from the top tier of the last row), we noted no apparent heavy ice or frost inside the plastic bags.

Ex.: Credit-card customers (like Schnall) were invited to use "the attached Line of Credit checks to consolidate other credit-card balances."

1.35 Use parentheses to define a quick reference for a longer name.

(a) *Quick reference.* It is customary in legal writing to use shorthand references for parties, and often for statutes and other subject matter that can be abbreviated for convenience without being ambiguous.

Ex.: Columbia Gas Transmission Corporation (Columbia Gas) appeals the district court's dismissal of its declaratory-judgment action against the property owner, Deana Drain, for lack of subject-matter jurisdiction.

Ex.: The defendants, including the David J. Joseph Co. (the Company), ...

(b) *With quotation marks.* Most legal writers also use quotation marks inside the parentheses. Quotation marks may signal that what is inside them is a defined term (see 1.30). If the definition stands alone inside the parentheses, the quotation marks usually add nothing to that signal and may be omitted without sacrificing clarity. But if the reference might be ambiguous without the quotation marks, use them. And if there are other words besides *the* inside the parentheses (e.g., *collectively*), the quotation marks are usually necessary for clarity. If you use quotation marks with one reference, use them for all references to maintain a consistent style.

Ex.: Sterling manufactures and sells prescription drugs and over-the-counter ("OTC") medicines. (The quotation marks are correct but not necessary.)

Ex.: Rodger Smith worked as a technician for Longview Cable Company ("Longview"), which provided cable television service in the Longview, Texas area. (Without the quotation marks, the short name of the defendant could be confused with the city it is located in.)

Ex.: In this putative class-action suit, the plaintiffs assert various state-law claims based on an alleged scheme by the defendants, GTE Corporation and GTE South, Inc. (collectively, "GTE"), to defraud their customers into leasing telephones and paying exorbitant lease charges. (Quotation marks are needed for clarity because the parentheses contain a word other than the word being defined.)

(c) *Often not necessary.* The shortened reference is often so obvious that no parenthetical definition is needed at all. Its presence may even be distracting or irritating to some readers.

Ex.: Plaintiff–appellant Daniel Reed was severely injured in the early-morning hours of September 2, 1996, when a car ran over the tent in which he was sleeping. Reed was attending an event known as the

Burning Man Festival, held on federally owned land managed by the Bureau of Land Management ("BLM"). (*Reed* is unambiguous, so it needs no definition. But since *BLM* does not explicitly appear in the text, the writer defined it to avoid any chance of ambiguity.)

Ex.: David H. Marlin appeals the district court's grant of summary judgment to the District of Columbia Board of Elections and Ethics (Board). Marlin brought this action alleging the Board's enforcement of polling-place regulations . . . . (The writer thought it necessary to note the shortened reference to *Board*, but not to *Marlin*.)

(d) *Avoiding surplusage.* The meaning of this device is usually clear without the use of surplusage such as "hereinafter."

Not this: Appellant attempted to introduce evidence of battered women's syndrome (hereinafter referred to as BWS) in order to show that because of BWS, she believed that threats made to her by Rubio would be carried out immediately, even though an objective view of the threats would not show that to be the case. (Omit *hereinafter referred to as.*)

Not this: Janice Lee Brimberry White, as successor in interest for Susan Ann Brimberry Katzberg (hereinafter collectively referred to as "Mother"), appeals from an order granting the motion of the respondent, Richard W. Katzberg ("Father"), to modify his child-support obligations. (Omit the *hereinafter referred to as* phrase, but retain *collectively* with a comma for clarity.)

1.36 Use parentheses to set off numbers and letters that denote subparts.

(a) *Generally.* Whether written in sentence form or table form, items in a list are separated by numbers or letters in parentheses.

Ex.: A lawyer who is not competent to handle a particular legal problem has three options: (1) decline to accept the client or withdraw from representing the client; (2) become competent through study and training, if it can be done without unreasonable delay or expense; or (3) associate with counsel experienced in the area, if the client consents.

Ex.: The common-law profits were (a) turbary, the right to remove turf for use as a fuel; (b) piscary, the right to fish; (c) estovers, the right to cut timber for fuel; and (d) pasture, the right to have animals graze.

Ex.: All states, both coastal and landlocked, have the right to exercise the freedom of the high seas. This freedom includes (but is not limited to):
(1) freedom of navigation;
(2) freedom of overflight;
(3) freedom of fishing;
(4) freedom to lay submarine cables and pipelines; and
(5) freedom of scientific research.

> "To write jargon is to be perpetually shuffling around in the fog."
> —*Sir Arthur Quiller-Couch*

(b) *In pairs.* Use a set of parentheses—not a single end-parenthesis—around a number or letter used in a list.

Not this: The common-law profits were:
a) turbary, the right to remove turf for use as a fuel;
b) piscary, the right to fish;
c) estovers, the right to cut timber for fuel; and
d) pasture, the right to have animals graze.

But this: The common-law profits were:
(a) turbary, the right to remove turf for use as a fuel;
(b) piscary, the right to fish;
(c) estovers, the right to cut timber for fuel; and
(d) pasture, the right to have animals graze.

(c) *Special conventions.* Place each subsection designation of a statute, regulation, or rule in parentheses, with no space between them.

Ex.: 50 U.S.C. § 1702(a)(1)(B)

Ex.: Colo. Rev. Stat. § 38–10–117(1)

Ex.: Treas. Reg. § 301.6901–1(b)

(d) *Exception.* Follow the style of the source you are citing. Some treatises, for example, use brackets rather than parentheses for subparts.

Ex.: § 1.01[a][2]

1.37 Use parentheses in citations as prescribed by the citation manual you follow.

(a) *Idiosyncrasies.* Legal-citation style differs from academic style. In law, use parentheses for the name of the court and the date when citing a case. Also use parentheses after the citation to quote from the cited case or to explain briefly how it relates to the issue being discussed. Use a space between each set of parentheses.

Ex.: *U.S. v. Shelton*, 66 F.3d 991, 992 (8th Cir. 1995) (per curiam) (upholding, on a similar basis, the prohibition in Section 922(g) against possession of firearms by a felon) (emphasis added).

(b) *Nesting parentheses.* In legal writing it is permissible to nest several levels of parenthetical material, and it is also permissible for parentheses pointing the same way to "kiss."

Ex.: (*But see New Rock Asset Partners, L.P. v. Preferred Eq. Advancements, Inc.*, 101 F.3d 1492, 1496 (3d Cir. 1996) (quoting *Nat'l Iranian Oil Co. v. Mapco Int'l, Inc.*, 983 F.2d 485, 489 (3d Cir. 1992)).)

(c) *Space between phrases.* Never have two parentheses pointing in different ways abut each other. When you have an end-parenthesis followed by a beginning-parenthesis, as often occurs in citations, always use a space between them (see 8.14(a)).

Ex.: *Accord Childress v. City of Richmond*, 134 F.3d 1205, 1209 (4th Cir. 1998) (en banc) (Luttig, J., concurring) ("Congress may, if it chooses, override prudential standing limitations and authorize all persons who satisfy the Constitution's standing requirements to bring particular actions in federal court.").

1.38 Punctuate and capitalize parenthetical matter correctly.

(a) *Terminal punctuation.* Terminal punctuation goes outside the closing parenthesis unless (1) the entire sentence is in parentheses, or (2) the parenthetical matter requires a question mark or exclamation mark. In the latter situation, if the sentence takes the same mark, place it outside the parentheses; but if the sentence takes a period, place the question mark or exclamation mark inside the parentheses and a period outside.

Ex.: Griggs was a longtime employee of DuPont. (He was hired in 1962.)

Ex.: Griggs was a longtime employee of DuPont (having been hired in 1962).

Ex.: The trial lasted nine months (as I expected).

Ex.: The trial lasted nine months (and what a hair-puller it was!).

Ex.: The trial lasted nine months (didn't I tell you it would?).

Ex.: Did you know that the trial lasted nine months (and didn't I tell you it would)?

(b) *Capitalization.* Do not capitalize the first word in parenthetical matter—even if standing alone it would form a complete sentence—unless (1) the entire sentence is in parentheses, or (2) it is capitalized for another reason, such as a proper noun or the pronoun *I.*

Ex.: The Court applied the clear-and-present-danger test (the test was first announced by Holmes and refined by Learned Hand) to a judge's power to gag news reporters covering a trial.

Ex.: The Court applied the clear-and-present-danger test to a judge's power to gag news reporters covering a trial. (The test was first announced by Holmes and refined by Learned Hand.)

Ex.: The Court applied the clear-and-present-danger test (Holmes's legacy) to a judge's power to gag news reporters covering a trial.

Brackets

1.39 Brackets are angular parentheses, but they have their own personalities. This is especially so in legal writing, where they carry heavier editing burdens than they do elsewhere in the literary world. Brackets signal minor deletions, changes, and interpolations inside quotations, and because legal writers quote with such rigor in preserving the original text, pages can become peppered with the marks.

1.40 Bracket an editorial remark, clarification, or alteration inside a quotation.

(a) *Editorial comment.* Brackets are used the same in legal writing as in academic and business writing when the purpose is to comment on or add to the matter being quoted.

Ex.: As the court reasoned, "This approach recognizes that all activities and property require funds and that management has a great deal of [a word choice far short of "absolute"] flexibility as to the source and use of funds." (Editorial comment.)

Ex.: "The [1996] Act fundamentally restructures local telephone markets." (Addition.)

Ex.: The Clean Air Act's judicial-review provision provides that a petition for review of any "final action of the [EPA] Administrator . . . may be filed only in the United States Court of Appeals for the appropriate circuit." (Clarification.)

Ex.: Sometimes, as lawyers used to say, "*necessitas vincit legem* [necessity overcomes the law]." (Translation.)

Ex.: Doctors testified that Odle probably suffered from an organic brain disorder, which causes "defects in the way [a person] functions intellectually, socially, and emotionally." (Substitution.)

(b) *Altered quotation.* When the text is altered in any way, legal writing is strictly rigorous in showing the change—even to the point of using brackets to indicate a change in capitalization. Any alteration designed to mislead the reader is as futile as it is unethical: it is certain to be exposed.

Ex.: The Constitution "indisputably entitle[s] a criminal defendant to 'a jury determination that [he] is guilty of every element of the crime with which he is charged, beyond a reasonable doubt[.]'"

Ex.: "[I]t is not inappropriate to allow section 1981 claimants to avail themselves of Title VII discriminatory treatment standards in proving a prima facie case."

(c) [*Sic*]. Use "[sic]" to indicate that an error in quoted matter appeared in the original. The device should be used when rigorous accuracy is required, as when quoting the exact words of a statute. As a matter of etiquette, it should never be used as a snide way to highlight the errors of another writer; instead, it is better to correct those minor mistakes using brackets. An interpolated "[sic]" should not be italicized (it appears in italics above only as a tag line, to maintain an internally consistent style).

Ex.: The city ordinance in effect at the time required innkeepers to "make all reasonable accomodations [sic] for wheelchair-bound guests."

(d) *No italics for brackets.* Do not italicize brackets. In classical typography, there is no such character as an italic bracket. Although modern word-processing programs can create them, they look amateurish.

1.41 Use brackets to indicate that part of a word has been omitted or that one or more characters have been changed.

(a) *Omissions and substitutions.* Use brackets to mark omissions or substitutions of characters in words, especially to make the quotation agree in number, tense, or gender with the rest of the sentence. Use a pair of empty brackets to indicate that a character or more at the end of a word has been left out.

Ex.: The regulations in question, 14 C.F.R. §§ 121.1(a)(5) and 135.1(a)(2) (1965), applied to "commercial operator[s]," who were defined as persons operating aircraft "for compensation or hire."

Ex: We agree with the district court that the "deemed paid" language of § 904(c) can only be inferred to "relate[] . . . to the year in which the foreign tax credit will be applied."

Ex.: She noted that it was her "obligation to make certain that people receive accurate information regarding the proceedings over which [she] preside[s]."

(b) *Ellipsis distinguished.* Do not use a set of empty brackets to mark the omission of a whole word or more; use ellipsis dots instead (see 1.44). When brackets mark an omission or alteration, at least one bracket will always touch part of the word.

Not this: "When Burr lost [], he challenged Hamilton to a duel." (The word *again* is omitted.)

But this: "When Burr lost . . . , he challenged Hamilton to a duel."

(c) *Overuse.* Use this device sparingly. Too many empty brackets and bracketed substitutions clutter a quotation and dull its impact.

1.42 In legal writing—as opposed to other types of writing—do not use brackets as subordinate parentheses inside parenthetical matter.

(a) *As "subparentheses."* Although that is the practice elsewhere, in legal writing it is acceptable to nest parentheses within parentheses, so there is no need to use brackets as "subparentheses."

Not this: (When the bill was debated [1964], the ban on "sex discrimination" was considered a killer amendment that no one could accept.)

But this: (When the bill was debated (1964), the ban on "sex discrimination" was considered a killer amendment that no one could accept.)

(b) *Rephrasing or paraphrasing.* If your parenthetical contains a quotation with omissions or substitutions, consider paraphrasing to eliminate the need for brackets.

Instead of: *See* Fed. R. Bankr. P. 9006(b)(3) ("The court may enlarge the time for taking action under Rule[] . . . 4003(b) . . . only to the extent and under the conditions stated in [that] rule[].").

Try this: *See* Fed. R. Bankr. P. 9006(b)(3) (holding that the court may extend the time provisions of Rule 4003(b) only so far as allowed under the provisions of that rule).

Ellipsis Dots

1.43 Like brackets, ellipses get more use in legal writing than elsewhere. Lawyers quote a lot, and quotations often require editing and excising. There is no need to fear that ellipses will raise suspicions that the meaning has been tampered with. When you're quoting a passage, transitional words (referring to some previous sentence or paragraph) often make no sense and need to be elided. When that is so, an ellipsis is perfectly respectable—even necessary.

Many writers have trouble remembering the rules on when to use three dots and when to use four, and how to space before, between, and after the dots. Help is on the way . . .

1.44 Use three ellipsis dots to indicate the omission of one or more words inside a quotation.

(a) *Midsentence.* Use three ellipsis dots to indicate that words have been omitted in the middle of a quoted sentence. Omit any punctuation that appeared on either side of the elided matter, unless it is grammatically needed in the restructured sentence.

Ex.: "An accommodation party may sign the instrument as maker, drawer, acceptor, or indorser and . . . is obliged to pay the instrument in the capacity in which the accommodation party signs."

Ex.: "Once a plaintiff establishes a prima facie case, . . . the burden shifts to the defendant to produce rebuttal evidence." (The comma is retained.)

(b) *Paragraph omitted.* If a full paragraph or more has been omitted, center three widely spaced ellipsis dots on a separate line, then indent and continue the quotation. Use seven spaces between the dots. Note that there are other styles as well. The current edition of *The Bluebook*, for example, uses four ellipsis dots, indented as a paragraph; older editions of *The Bluebook* handled the issue differently. The recommendation here—with the three centered dots—reflects the predominant form in scholarly writing generally.

Ex.: Section 8. The Congress shall have Power to lay and collect Taxes, Duties, Imposts and Excises, to pay the Debts and provide for the common Defence and general Welfare of the United States; but all Duties, Imposts and Excises shall be uniform throughout the United States;

. . .

To make all Laws which shall be necessary and proper for carrying into Execution the foregoing Powers, and all other Powers vested by this Constitution in the Government of the United States, or in any Department or Officer thereof.

1.45 Use four dots (three ellipsis dots and a period, all identical) to indicate the omission of either (1) the end of a sentence, or (2) matter after a completed sentence when the quotation continues. Use a space before the first dot only if the matter that was omitted was the end of a sentence.

(a) *Space after last word.* If the omitted matter includes the end of a sentence, follow the last word with a hard space (see 4.13) and then four dots—three ellipsis dots plus the sentence period, with hard spaces between all dots.

Ex.: "The world will little note nor long remember what we say here . . . ." (Since *here* was not the last word of the quoted sentence, it is followed by a space, three ellipsis points, another space, and then the sentence period as the fourth dot.)

(b) *No space after last word.* If the last word ended the quoted sentence, no ellipsis is needed unless the quotation continues. If the quotation does continue, the first dot is the sentence period, so do not use a space between the word and the first of four dots (the period and three ellipsis points, with hard spaces between all dots).

Ex.: As Lincoln reminded the audience at Gettysburg, our forefathers were "dedicated to the proposition that all men are created equal." (The matter quoted is the end of the sentence, and the quotation does not continue.)

Ex.: As Lincoln memorialized the cemetery, he said, "We are met on a great battlefield of that war. . . . The brave men, living and dead, who struggled here have consecrated it far above our poor power to add or detract." (Since *war* is the last word of a sentence, it is followed immediately by a period, then a space and three ellipsis points.)

1.46 Do not use ellipsis dots at the beginning of a quotation, or where the quoted matter is worked into the syntax of the main sentence.

(a) *Start of sentence omitted.* Although the practice is common outside law, it is never permissible in legal writing to begin a quotation with an ellipsis. Instead, a bracketed capital letter will usually signal that something has been left out.

Ex.: "[G]overnment of the people, by the people, and for the people shall not perish from the earth."

(b) *In syntax.* If the quoted matter is a fragment that is worked into the structure of the main sentence, do not use ellipsis dots before or after the quotation.

Ex.: It was only "[f]our score and seven years" since the founding of the republic.

1.47 Keep the ellipsis dots standard by using hard spaces and the right typographic elements.

(a) *Hard spacing.* Use a nonbreaking ("hard") space to keep all ellipsis dots together. Use a hard space (see 4.13) between the last quoted word and the punctuation, and also between each dot.

(b) *Asterisks; bullets.* At one time, asterisks and bullets were commonly used to mark elided material. This style persists in some places: casebook editors still use it, and it is the preferred style of the U.S. Government Printing Office. But in general, writers today should use only periods as ellipsis dots.

Not this: "The offering to distribute copies * * * to a group of persons for purposes of further distribution * * * constitutes publication."

Or this: "The offering to distribute copies • • • to a group of persons for purposes of further distribution • • • constitutes publication."

But this: "The offering to distribute copies . . . to a group of persons for purposes of further distribution . . . constitutes publication."

1.48 Ellipsis dots can indicate an unfinished sentence that trails off.

(a) *Trailing off.* The ellipsis dots indicate that the partial statement was followed by silence. Three (not four) dots are always appropriate: since the sentence does not terminate, there is no period.

Ex.: The last time I saw Charlie . . .

(b) *Interruption.* In legal transcripts, terminal ellipsis dots are used to show that the speaker was interrupted. In other styles of writing, an em dash more often serves this purpose.

Ex.: Detar: I think that this was probably just an accident, okay. But there's a question . . .
Dubria: But detective . . .
Detar: But listen. Wait, wait, wait . . . let me finish, let me finish.
Dubria: Okay.

Em Dashes

1.49 The em dash (also called a "long dash") is a forceful and conspicuous punctuation mark. As wide as the typeface is tall, the em dash stands out on the page. It highlights what it either contains (when used in pairs) or separates from the main sentence. The same matter inside parentheses would be deemphasized. As a separator, the em dash often performs the pointing function of a colon, and the two marks are interchangeable in those situations. On a computer, type an em dash with a special code; on a typewriter, indicate it with two hyphens. In documents created on word processors, use a space before and after the em dash to prevent awkward line breaks—even though fine book typography omits the space. Although you may have once heard a stern warning against em dashes, they're an important part of the writer's toolbox. Just look at any page of first-rate published prose, and you're going to see one or more irreplaceable dashes.

1.50 Use an em dash—or a pair of em dashes as required by sentence structure—to give matter that is independent of the main sentence more emphasis than parentheses would provide.

(a) *Setting off words at beginning or end of sentence.* Use an em dash to separate an element that is placed at the beginning or end of a sentence and expands on another part of the sentence. In this construction the dash is similar in function to a colon (at the beginning) or parentheses (at the end), but more emphatic.

Ex.: Principle—that's what's at stake here.

Ex.: The most common problem of extra-record evidence occurs when there are ex parte contacts—communications outside the hearing and off the record from an interested party to a decision-making official.

(b) *In midsentence.* Use a pair of em dashes instead of parentheses to set off parenthetical matter—even an independent sentence—inside the main sentence. While parentheses minimize what they enclose, em dashes emphasize it. Do not use a comma, semicolon, or colon before or after the em dashes, even if one would be necessary without the interrupting matter.

> Ex.: Because an assignment for the benefit of creditors places the debtor's property out of the reach of the creditors—legal title passes to the assignee—it might seem that creditors would be able to void the assignment under a fraudulent-conveyance statute. (The comma that would have been required where the first em dash appears is no longer necessary.)

(c) *With appositive.* Use a pair of em dashes instead of commas to separate an appositive phrase, for the purpose of either (1) emphasizing it more or (2) clarifying a phrase that contains internal commas.

> Ex.: The prediction must come from "reference to a law of general application"—a state statute or the state constitution—that will deny the defendant's civil rights. (Emphasis.)

> Ex.: Aid to any of the elements of the traditional learning process—institution, teachers, or students—is an educational purpose. (Internal commas.)

1.51 Use an em dash—or multiple em dashes—in several conventions to indicate missing information.

(a) *In a transcript.* An em dash may be used instead of ellipsis dots in a transcript of dialogue to indicate an interruption or abrupt change of thought.

> Ex.: Q. Did there come a point that you decided you couldn't take it any longer?
> A. I explained to him that I was and he wouldn't—like I said, he wouldn't approve anything.

(b) *In dates.* Use an em dash after the birth year in a biographical reference to indicate that the person is still alive.

> Ex.: David Foster Wallace (1962—).

(c) *Expunction.* Use two em dashes with no space between them to replace part of a word or name. This device is most often used to elide all but the first letter of a word or a name, usually either to expunge an obscenity or to preserve a person's anonymity.

> Ex.: "How do I get this d—— thing to work?"

> Ex.: Mr. H—— informed the police of the robbery plans.

(d) *In citations.* In legal citations, use two em dashes with no space between them to indicate reporter volume and page numbers that have not yet been determined. An underline may also be used for this purpose.

> Ex.: *Roe v. Flores-Ortega,* —— U.S. ——, 120 S. Ct. 1029, 145 L. Ed.2d 985 (2000). (Two em dashes.)

> Ex.: *Roe v. Flores-Ortega,* ____ U.S. ____, 120 S. Ct. 1029, 145 L. Ed.2d 985 (2000). (Underlines.)

(e) *Same author.* Use three em dashes with no spaces between them to indicate the repetition of an author's name in an alphabetical bibliography.

Ex.: Kilpatrick, James J. *The New York Times Style Book for Writers and Editors.* Edited by Lewis Jordan. 3d ed. New York: McGraw–Hill, 1962.

———. *The Writer's Art.* Kansas City: Andrews, McMeel & Parker, 1984.

(f) *To be supplied.* In a transcript, use three closed em dashes to indicate a speaker's pause while waiting for another person to "fill in the blank."

Ex.: Q. So the ship sailed on the ninth of ———? When was it?
A. March.
Q. The ninth of March. Thank you.

En Dashes

1.52 The en dash is half the length of the em dash. It is helpful where a hyphen is too short to do the job. On a computer, you make an en dash with a special code. On a typewriter, users must substitute a hyphen: for that reason the en dash was long confined to the publishing world. Today, outside publishing, it often goes unused, its duties still assumed by the hyphen.

1.53 Use an en dash to designate a span from one value to another, but avoid it to stand for *to* if the word *from* is used.

(a) *To show a range.* The en dash typically connects dates, page numbers, and the like.

Ex.: The American Civil War (1861–1865)

Ex.: *Schneider Nat'l Carriers, Inc. v. Carr,* 903 F.3d 1154, 1158–59 (7th Cir. 1990)

(b) *Not mixed with words.* When used to span two numerals, an en dash stands in for the phrase *from . . . to* or *between . . . and.* When the word *from* or *between* is used with an en dash, the construction does not "read" correctly after the understood terms are supplied.

Right: Randolph served in the Continental Congress 1779–1782.
Wrong: From 1779–1782 Randolph served in the Continental Congress. (Make it *From 1779 to 1782 . . . .*)

1.54 Use an en dash to join two like terms.

(a) *To show equality.* The en dash signals that the two things joined are of equal importance.

Ex.: The Taft–Hartley Act

Ex.: attorney–client privilege

(b) *To show duality.* The conjunctive en dash works better than a slash (which is more often disjunctive) to join two equal roles or offices held by one person (see 1.81(e)).

Ex.: a talented playwright–director

Ex.: the newly elected secretary–treasurer

1.55 Follow the established convention within a given jurisdiction to use the en dash to join sections or chapters and subparts.

(a) *By convention.* Usage varies greatly on how en dashes are incorporated into legal-numbering systems.

Ex.: 42 U.S.C. § 2000e–5(e)(1)

Ex.: UCC § 2–102

Ex.: Pub. L. No. 99–508

(b) *To distinguish.* If a designation is alphanumeric (e.g., 42 U.S.C. § 1396a), use an en dash to distinguish the subparts.

Ex.: 42 U.S.C. § 1396a–2

(c) *Ambiguity.* If a designation already contains an en dash or hyphen, use the word *to* rather than an en dash to indicate a range.

Ex.: N.M. Stat. Ann. § 30–18–13(a) to (g)

Hyphens

1.56 The hyphen gives writers more trouble than any other punctuation mark except the comma. And like the comma, the hyphen generates some controversy. Fortunately, finding out when to hyphenate within a word is easier than finding out when to use a comma: just look up the word in a dictionary. Unfortunately, a dictionary is of no help when trying to master the phrasal adjective: after all, the number of such phrases is infinite.

1.57 Hyphenate a phrasal adjective that appears before a noun or pronoun unless it falls within one of several narrow exceptions.

(a) *Basic rule.* A phrase functioning as an adjective in front of a noun or pronoun should ordinarily be hyphenated (hence, *failure-to-warn claim* but *failure to warn*). Otherwise, some readers will not instantly know which noun in the phrase is *the* noun (in the example above, *claim*) and which one functions as an adjective (in the example above, *failure*).

Ex.: A third-year associate is handling the case. (Writing *a third year associate* would cause a brief miscue.)

Ex.: From the flag-salute cases to the released-school-time cases to the peddling-of-religious-propaganda cases, the Court usually came out, in a close vote, on the side of free religion.

Ex.: Even more than his go-right-ahead encouragements to Congress and his stop-right-there strictures to state legislatures, the assured audacity with which Marshall lifted his own branch of the federal government from neglect and contumely to respect and power helped fashion a cohesive, consolidated nation.

(b) *Need for clarity.* Some style guides recommend hyphenating phrasal adjectives only when needed for clarity. But while some phrasal adjectives may be clear to the writer and to most readers, the absence of hyphens will cause some readers to misstep midway through the sentence. So the better practice is always to hyphenate.

Ex.: The defendant made an assumption-of-the-risk argument. (Without the hyphens, a reader would at first think the defendant made an assumption.)

Ex.: Our claim falls into a well-settled area of law. (Without the hyphen, the reader would at first see the claim falling into a well.)

Ex.: The court employed a likelihood-of-confusion test.

(c) *After the noun.* If a phrasal adjective does not precede the noun it modifies, do not hyphenate it unless it is a standard phrase that is invariably hyphenated, such as *cost-effective*, *drug-free*, *risk-averse*, and *short-lived*. In general, these hyphenated fixed phrases will be listed in a dictionary, but most other phrases needing hyphens will not be.

Ex.: The defense of assumption of the risk requires proof of actual notice of the danger.

Ex.: The rule of law we base our claim on is well settled.

But: Our exhilaration was short-lived.

And: A portion of each donation is tax-exempt.

(d) -ly *adverbs.* Do not hyphenate a phrasal adjective that begins with an *-ly* adverb unless the phrase is longer than two words.

Ex.: Our case got a badly needed boost when a corroborating witness came forward.

Ex.: A poorly prepared brief can mean the difference between winning and losing.

But: A poorly-thought-out argument can be worse than no argument at all.

And: A not-so-highly-regarded advocate can sometimes make stunningly good arguments.

(e) *Proper nouns.* Do not hyphenate a proper noun used as an adjective. If the phrase contains additional words besides the name, hyphenate between the name and the other word; but if the construction is awkward, recast the sentence.

Ex.: The *State Street Bank* decision paved the way for business-method patenting. (No hyphens for *State Street Bank.*)

Ex.: The rookie litigator wore a Brooks Brothers suit to a Malibu Beach reception.

Ex.: Our firm was defending a Pulitzer Prize-winning reporter against a $10 million libel suit.

(f) *Foreign phrases.* Do not hyphenate an obviously foreign phrase used as an adjective.

Ex.: The defendant challenged the court's in rem jurisdiction.

Ex.: A hearing is set for Wednesday on McFadden's habeas corpus petition.

Ex.: The judge threw out the case, saying that the plaintiff had failed to state a prima facie case.

Ex.: Any retroactive enhancement statute would amount to a constitutionally prohibited ex post facto law.

(g) *With multiple elements.* When a phrasal adjective or a compound word contains an understood word because it is paired with a similar phrase, use a suspension hyphen with the separated element.

Ex.: The Court found that the statute was both over- and underinclusive.

Ex.: More to the point are the numerous early- and mid-19th-century decisions expressly sustaining warrantless arrests for misdemeanors not involving any breach of the peace.

Ex.: The rookie was a Nebraska-born and -raised athlete.

1.58 Use a hyphen with numbers to join two-word spelled-out numbers from 21 to 99 and to write fractions unless one of the numbers is already hyphenated.

(a) *With numbers.* Use a hyphen between the tens place and the ones place when spelling out two-word numbers from 21 to 99.

Ex.: The Twenty-sixth Amendment lowered the voting age to 18.

(b) *With fractions.* Use a hyphen to separate the numerator from the denominator when writing out fractions (when using numerals, see 1.81(a)).

Ex.: Constitutional amendments require ratification by three-fourths of the states.

(c) *An exception.* But when the fraction being written out itself uses a hyphenated number, omit the hyphen that separates the two parts of the fraction.

Ex.: Ninety-nine and forty-four one-hundredths percent pure.

1.59 Use a hyphen to break a word between syllables.

(a) *For line breaks.* When necessary, a word may be broken between lines. Avoid awkward breaks, which can occur when one of the parts is a separate word standing alone; avoid leaving fewer than three letters on each line; and avoid hyphenating at the end of more than two consecutive lines.

Ex.: Coverage A provides comprehensive general liability insurance for bodily injury to cover malpractice claims.

(b) *For syllabification.* Use hyphens to indicate where a word breaks into syllables.

Ex.: The word breaks di-ver-si-fi-ca-tion.

(c) *Between syllables only.* The break must always be between two syllables. If you're not confident, use a current dictionary to check syllabification.

1.60 Use a hyphen to show that you are referring to a prefix, suffix, letter, or letters in a word, and to show that a word is being spelled out.

(a) *Part of a word.* Use a hyphen to show how part of a word or number relates to the omitted part.

Ex.: In law, the prefix *quasi-* often describes a judicial fiction; for example, a *quasi-contract* is not really a contract at all.

(b) *For spelling*. Use hyphens to indicate that a word is being spelled out.

Ex.: The jury spelled relief j-u-s-t-i-c-e.

1.61 In general, avoid using a hyphen after a routine prefix—but there are exceptions.

(a) *Generally*. Modern usage omits most hyphens after prefixes, even when it results in a doubled letter.

Exs.: *misspell* / *nonstatutory* / *overindulgence* / *preempt* / *reelect*

(b) *Exceptions*. But there are many exceptions, often necessitated by doubling letters. Generally, if the compound word without a hyphen would be confused with another word, would be difficult to pronounce, or would be just too ugly to live with, it will retain the hyphen.

Exs.: *re-create* / *anti-intellectual* / *co-op* (but *cooperative*)

(c) *With proper noun*. A hyphen is needed when the root word is a proper noun or a noun phrase (see 7.6(b), (g)).

Exs.: *un-American* / *anti-Semitic* / *pre-Columbian*

Ex.: *pro-free-trade*

(d) *With certain prefixes*. A hyphen is almost always needed after the prefixes *all-*, *ex-*, and *self-*, and with the various legal terms formed with *quasi-*.

Exs.: *all-encompassing* / *ex-convict* / *self-serving* / *quasi-contract*

Periods

1.62 The period was the earliest and is today the most common punctuation mark. (It sometimes seems scarce in legal writing.) It is one of three terminal punctuation marks, the others being the question mark and the exclamation mark. Besides its use to end a sentence, the period also marks abbreviations, separates list designators from contents, and acts as the decimal point in numbers. A period is identical to an ellipsis dot.

1.63 Use a period to end a sentence that is a declaratory statement, an indirect question, or a request.

(a) *Generally*. The period is the standard terminal punctuation unless a question mark or an exclamation mark is called for.

Ex.: It does not follow from the fact that Wong could gain access to the website that he was a "party" to its contents. (Declaratory statement.)

Ex.: We must consider for the first time whether the Americans with Disabilities Act requires an employer to violate the seniority provisions of a collective bargaining agreement to accommodate a disabled employee. (Indirect question.)

Ex.: Please speak louder. (Request.)

(b) *Matter of interpretation*. Which terminal punctuation to use can sometimes be a close call. For example, a request phrased in the form of a question may be spoken as a polite request; if no reply is invited, if the voice does not rise as it does when one asks a question, then a period may be more appropriate than a question mark.

Ex.: Would you hand me the dictionary.

(c) *With exclamation mark.* It is a judgment call when the intensity of a sentence rises to the level to justify an exclamation mark.

Ex.: Stop it.

Ex.: Stop it!

(d) *With declaratory sentence.* Note that either a declaratory statement or, more commonly, a command may merit an exclamation mark. But the use of that mark in legal writing (except in quotations) is rarely appropriate.

1.64 Use periods after letters or numbers in an outline or list.

(a) *Outline style.* In traditional outline style, a period should always follow the letter or number.

Ex.: I. Introduction
    A. First theme
        1. First support for first theme . . .

(b) *Decimal numbering system.* If you're using a decimal numbering system, avoid a period after the last number.

Ex.: 1.1 Term of Employment

(c) *Parentheses or period.* In a list, prefer parentheses around the letter or number; otherwise, use a period after the letter or number. But do not use both.

Ex.: Limitations on involuntary bankruptcy petitions:

1. Creditors may not file under Chapter 9, 12, or 13.
2. Insurance companies, banks, farmers, and charities are protected.
3. The petition must usually be filed by three creditors.

1.65 Use a period after a heading only if the heading is run in with text or is a complete sentence.

(a) *No period with labels.* If the heading is a simple label, do not end it with a period.

Ex.: Statement of Facts (no period unless heading is run in with text)

(b) *Period with sentences.* If the heading is a complete sentence, it takes a period (or other terminal punctuation).

Ex.: The plaintiff suffered no physical injury, and this state does not recognize a tort for negligent infliction of emotional distress. (Period after heading. In context, the heading would be set in boldface.)

(c) *Read-in tags.* Use a period after a read-in tag line (such as the *Read-in tags* that precedes this sentence) to separate it from the sentence, even if the tag itself is not a complete sentence.

(d) *Consistency.* Be consistent: each heading at the same level should be either a phrase or a sentence.

1.66 Use a period after most abbreviations, but not after most contracted abbreviations.

(a) *Generally.* An abbreviation is a shortened form made by leaving off letters, usually at the end of the word.

Ex.: "Co." for "Company" in *Thompson Coal Co. v. Pike Coal Co.*

Ex.: "a.m." for *ante meridiem* (or "in the morning") in "9 a.m."

Ex.: "Ph.D." for "Doctor of Philosophy"

(b) *No periods.* By convention, some abbreviations do not take periods.

Ex.: "mm" for "millimeter" in "35 mm camera"

Ex.: "mph" for "miles per hour" in "55 mph"

(c) *Contractions contrasted.* A contracted abbreviation is made by substituting an apostrophe for one or more missing letters (see 1.78). But some contracted forms (such as *Mr.* and *Mrs.*) are traditionally spelled with a period (although in British English *Mr* and *Mrs* predominate).

Ex.: "it's" for "it is"

Ex.: "can't" for "cannot"

Ex.: "ma'am" for "madam"

But: "Dr." for "Doctor"

(d) *ALWD abbreviations.* The *ALWD* citation manual uses a new system of abbreviation that is a hybrid of *The Bluebook*'s contractions and general conventions. It eliminates the apostrophe altogether and adds a period after the contracted form.

Ex.: "Association"	*Bluebook*: Ass'n	*ALWD*: Assn.
Ex.: "Commissioner"	*Bluebook*: Comm'r	*ALWD*: Commr.
Ex.: "Department"	*Bluebook*: Dep't	*ALWD*: Dept.
Ex.: "International"	*Bluebook*: Int'l	*ALWD*: Intl.
Ex.: "National"	*Bluebook*: Nat'l	*ALWD*: Natl.

(e) *With state names.* Use a period with an abbreviated state name in text. Do not use a period after the two-letter postal abbreviation, which should be capitalized (both letters) and used only in addresses.

Ex.: We moved from Nashville, Tenn., to Palo Alto, Calif., in 1995.

Ex.: Send the package to me at 3201 State Street, Nashville, TN 37221.

1.67 Avoid periods after letters in an acronym or initialism unless a different style is specified.

(a) *Modern style.* The modern trend is to write both acronyms (initial letters pronounced as words, e.g., NASA) and initialisms (those pronounced as the letters themselves, e.g., IBM) without periods.

Exs.: LSAT / AFL–CIO / SCOTUS / WWW / USCA

(b) *Conventions.* Demands of style, including citation conventions, may dictate a different approach.

Exs.: U.S. (United States) / U.S. (*United States Reports*)

Question Marks

1.68 The question mark gives writers little trouble. The only problem may be its use inside a sentence to flavor a word, phrase, or clause: it's odd to see a "terminal" punctuation mark that doesn't terminate the sentence. But that construction is generally too casual for legal writing anyway.

1.69 Use a question mark to end an interrogative sentence.

(a) *And indirect questions.* Distinguish an interrogative sentence (a direct question) from a declarative sentence containing an indirect question.

Ex.: Is this your gun? (Interrogative.)

Ex.: I asked you if this is your gun. (Declarative.)

(b) *In compound sentence.* In a compound sentence, the nature of the second clause decides the terminal punctuation.

Ex.: I asked you once, is this your gun?

Ex.: Is this your gun?—tell me the truth.

(c) *And declaratory form.* Note that a sentence may have an interrogative meaning but a declaratory form. It is the sense that matters, not the form.

Ex.: You went back to the office the morning after being fired?

(d) *With interrogative tag.* A tacked-on question at the end of a declaratory sentence requires a question mark to end the entire sentence.

Ex.: It's hot in here, isn't it?

Ex.: You are going to answer my questions, aren't you?

(e) *With multiple endings.* Use a question mark after multiple endings to a question; do not capitalize the beginnings of subsequent ending phrases.

Ex.: Does the biggest share of the blame go to Congress? the President? the people?

1.70 Use a question mark after a questioning word, phrase, or clause contained in the main sentence but separated from it by parentheses or em dashes.

(a) *Capitalization.* Unless the interrogative material is a complete sentence, do not capitalize the first word unless it is a proper noun, the pronoun *I*, or the first word of the main sentence (see 2.5).

Ex.: This improper (illegal?) activity must end.

Ex.: The easement—You know it's a legal easement, don't you?—gives your neighbor the right to use that road across your property.

Ex.: When?—that's all my client wants to know.

(b) *No second terminal punctuation.* When the independent matter falls at the end of an interrogative sentence, the question mark of the main sentence serves to mark the inserted matter as well (see 1.38(a)).

Ex.: Who will be next to fall for the illegal scheme (will the pyramid collapse before then)?

1.71 Use a question mark in parentheses to indicate uncertainty about what immediately precedes it.

(a) *Dates.* This device is most often seen with dates or numbers.

Ex.: Murray was born on July 17(?), 1757, in Philadelphia.

(b) *Not terminal punctuation.* Used this way, the question mark cannot serve as terminal punctuation for the main sentence.

Ex.: The doctrine today is recognized only in Louisiana (?).

Exclamation Marks

1.72 It's hard to imagine a situation in legal writing in which an exclamation mark would be justified, except for a direct quotation (and even then its use might be considered editorializing unless the quotation appeared in print). When it is used, keep the following conventions in mind.

1.73 Use an exclamation mark to end a sentence that expresses a demand, surprise, danger, stress, or some other intense emotion.

(a) *Generally.* This is the usual use of the exclamation mark.

Ex.: Police! Open up! (Demand.)

Ex.: To arms! To arms! The British are coming! (Surprise or danger.)

Ex.: You've got to be kidding! (Stress.)

(b) *In place of question mark.* It is sometimes appropriate to use an exclamation mark instead of a question mark after an emotional question.

Ex.: How can you say that!

1.74 Use an exclamation mark after an exclamatory interjection.

(a) *Generally.* Common exclamatory interjections are *oh!*, *hah!*, *whew!*, and the like, as well as countless profanities. But phrases may be interjections as well.

Ex.: So! Now you're changing your story?

Ex.: For the love of Pete! Why didn't you tell me that before?

(b) *No mark with vocative "O."* The vocative *O*—used to call or invoke something—does not take an exclamation mark by itself, although it may be part of an exclamation that does.

Ex.: O Canada

Ex.: O Rising Dawn

Ex.: O tempora! O mores!

1.75 An exclamation mark in parentheses may indicate feigned shock at or mockery of what immediately precedes it.

(a) *Referent.* Use the positioning of the parenthetical device to indicate what it refers to: if it abuts a word with no space between them, it refers only to that word; otherwise, it refers to the preceding phrase or clause.

Ex.: The defendant was too generous(!) not to share the opportunity with friends. (The exclamation mark suggests that the writer did not think the defendant's true motive was generosity at all.)

Ex.: Because the environmentalist plaintiffs had not bought tickets to the endangered territories they sought to defend (!), the Supreme Court ruled that they did not have standing to sue. (The exclamation mark suggests that the writer found the Court's reasoning to be absurd; it refers to the preceding clause, not just to the word *defend.*)

(b) *Editorial protest.* An exclamation mark is sometimes used, especially in nonlegal writing, following an oddity or misspelling in a quotation. In legal writing use "[sic]" instead.

Not this: "I heard footsteps cranching(!) in the snow."

But this: "I heard footsteps cranching [sic] in the snow."

Apostrophes

1.76 Like the hyphen, the apostrophe punctuates a word rather than a sentence. It has two main purposes: to form a possessive and to indicate omitted letters in a contracted abbreviation. It is also sometimes used to form the plural of letters, numbers, abbreviations, and words used as words (rather than for their meaning). In form, it is identical to the single closing quotation mark. It is improperly used as the symbol for the measurement *foot,* which should be designated by a prime (′). Note that many word processors' "smart quote" feature will incorrectly insert an opening single quotation mark instead of an apostrophe at the beginning of a word or number; one way to trick it is to type a dummy letter first (even another apostrophe), type the correct apostrophe, then delete the dummy letter.

1.77 Use an apostrophe to form the possessive case.

(a) *Generally.* The formation of possessives is dealt with more extensively elsewhere (see 7.11–7.15). In general, if the word does not end in *-s,* form the plural by adding *-'s.* If it is singular and ends in *-s,* add *-'s* unless the result would be hard to pronounce. If it is plural and ends in *-s,* add *-'.*

Ex.: *Blackstone's Commentaries*

Ex.: a witness's testimony

Ex.: Moses' laws

Ex.: the octopuses' tentacles

(b) *Possessive pronouns.* Do not use an apostrophe to form the pronoun possessive *hers, its, theirs, ours, yours,* or *whose.* And watch for the sound-alike contractions *it's, there's,* and *who's.*

1.78 Use an apostrophe to mark a contraction: it represents omitted letters (or numbers in a date).

(a) *Generally.* Contracted abbreviations are common in case-name citations, and for that alone they are used more frequently in legal writing than elsewhere. For example, *Department* is contracted to *Dep't* in *Bluebook* style (but to *Dept.* in *ALWD* style).

Ex.: *D.C. Fed'n of Civic Ass'ns v. Volpe.* (The apostrophes replace *eratio* in *Federation* and *ociatio* in *Associations* in this *Bluebook*-style citation.)

(b) *In dates.* In informal writing, an apostrophe marks the elision of numerals in a date, where the century is understood.

Ex.: The senator was first elected in '88. (The apostrophe replaces *19* in *1988*.)

(c) *In formal writing.* The use of common contractions (e.g., *isn't*) has long been shunned in formal prose. That taboo is disappearing, however: consider how stilted the interrogative *is it not?* sounds.

Ex.: Contractions aren't the taboo they once were in formal writing. (The apostrophe replaces the *o* in *are not*.)

1.79 Use an apostrophe (followed by *s*) to form the plural of letters, single-digit numbers, symbols, and some abbreviations.

(a) *Incorrect and correct uses.* This form is commonly misused as applied to names (e.g., *the Smith's* should be *the Smiths*). But it is correct in those limited instances when the writer needs to refer to letters and numbers as such.

Ex.: Mind your *p*'s and *q*'s.

Ex.: How many 0's are there in a million? (Better: *How many zeros . . .*).

(b) *With lowercase abbreviations.* This form is often used with lowercase abbreviations. With capitalized abbreviations, multiple-digit numbers, and dates, the preferred plural is a simple *-s*.

Ex.: What kind of mpg's does this model get?

Ex.: You will escort the VIPs to the head table.

Ex.: The new attorney general cut his legal teeth as a Detroit prosecutor in the 1980s.

Ex.: Lows tonight will be in the upper 30s.

> "Most problems of punctuation, aside from the easy one of finding what is permissible, may be reduced to questions of (1) clearness, (2) management of emphasis, and (3) movement, including economy and variety."
>
> —*George Summey*

Slashes

1.80 The slash (also called *virgule*, *solidus*, or *diagonal*) has few uses in formal writing except with dates and fractions. It is best known as the star character in two grammatical abominations: *and/or* and *he/she*. It is especially unfit for legal writing because it is inherently ambiguous: its function may be conjunctive <secretary/treasurer> or disjunctive <a buy/sell decision>.

1.81 Use a slash in a limited number of grammatical conventions; where alternative punctuation is appropriate, avoid the slash.

(a) *Fractions.* Use a slash to separate the numerator from the denominator in a fraction when using numerals (but use a hyphen when the numbers are spelled out: see 1.58(b)).

Ex.: Each of the eight grandchildren received 1/16th of the estate.

(b) *Dates.* Use a slash to separate the month, day, and year in the informal short-date style; a hyphen works just as well.

Ex.: The 11/7/2000 election would not be "over" for another month.

Or: The 11-7-2000 election would not be "over" for another month.

(c) *Abbreviations.* Use a slash to denote an abbreviation when convention so dictates.

Ex.: Recruiting Attorney, c/o Dewey Cheatum & Howe, Harvard Square, Cambridge, MA 02139 (*in care of*)

Ex.: d/b/a (*doing business as*)

Ex.: Do it w/o delay. (*without*)

Ex.: $4,000/year raise (*per*)

(d) *Alternatives.* Use a slash in some paired words to indicate alternatives (*either/or*).

Ex.: After two days of talking about the evidence, the jurors' guilty/not-guilty vote had not changed.

Ex.: Under the program, students take some courses on a pass/fail basis.

(e) *Double offices.* Use a slash to indicate double roles (*both/and*); an en dash works as well, and should be preferred (see 1.54(b)).

Ex.: Phelps was elected secretary/treasurer.

Or: Phelps was elected secretary–treasurer.

Ex.: Schwarz is the firm's top mediator/negotiator.

Or: Schwarz is the firm's top mediator–negotiator.

(f) *Line breaks.* Use a slash to indicate a line break in poetry.

Ex.: Yet, still we can turn inside out / Old Nature's Constitution, / And bring a Babel back of *names*—/ Huzza! for REVOLUTION!

(g) *Examples.* A slash is used to separate examples of word usage.

Exs.: Oxymorons—e.g., jumbo shrimp / soft rock / random order

Bullets

1.82 Bullets are an attractive way of presenting a list of roughly equal elements. They work just as well in legal writing as they do in journalism and elsewhere. As with any other type of list, a bulleted list may consist of single words, phrases, or complete sentences, as the examples below illustrate. And, as with any other list, the elements must be parallel in form.

1.83 Use bullets to create visual appeal in setting out important lists.

(a) *With colon.* Use a colon to introduce a bulleted list.

Ex.: Student publications that generate lawsuits fall into three categories:

- school-sponsored newspapers;
- nonschool or underground newspapers written and distributed by students; and
- materials distributed by students at school but written and published by nonstudents.

(b) *Plain bullets.* For bullets, stick with solid round dots smaller than the size of a lowercase *o*; avoid squares, triangles, diamonds, and fancy art.

(c) *Hanging indent.* Use hanging indents to make the bullets stand out, and set a small tab margin so that each bullet will be the equivalent of about two characters away from the text.

(d) *Indent list.* Indent the bullets to at least the point on the page where a paragraph indent is, or perhaps slightly to the right of that point.

(e) *Single-spacing.* Single-space within bulleted points; double-space between them.

Ex.: In this factual setting, several policies supported the district court's dismissal without prejudice:

- The dismissal removed the case from the district court's docket pending the agency appeal.
- The dismissal also preserved the resources of the court and the parties by preventing further discovery and litigation on claims that might not survive the reissue.
- In addition, the dismissal eliminated any prejudice to the accused infringer from the bare existence of the infringement suit.
- Finally, the dismissal without prejudice left undisturbed the patentee's opportunity to enforce any patent claims surviving the reissue.

1.84 Avoid bullets if the subparts marked by them will need to be cited.

(a) *Cannot be cited.* Bullets are often inappropriate in legal drafting because elements cannot be pinpointed in a later citation.

(b) *Numbers or letters instead.* Instead of a bulleted list, use a numbered or lettered paragraph form in drafting.

§ 2
Capitalization

2.1 The modern trend is toward less capitalization: most commonly, capitals either (1) begin a sentence or a complete quotation or (2) designate a proper noun or the pronoun *I*. But in legal writing, as in other specialized writing, some words are capitalized by convention: *Court*, for example, to designate the U.S. Supreme Court, the high court of any jurisdiction, or the court that is hearing your case.

Legal writing also makes liberal use of defined terms, typically designated in parentheses and perhaps quotation marks immediately after the first use of the full name. A contract may refer throughout to *Buyer* and *Seller*, for example. Once defined, the term becomes a proper noun and is capitalized.

Capitalization is important in headings as well. The use of all caps in a short, centered heading might signal the beginning of a main section. The hierarchy of subheadings may be signaled in a variety of ways, and some writers like to use different styles of capitalization to signal subheadings. Even so, outline-style numbering is much easier for the reader to understand than variations in capitalization; the two techniques may be especially helpful in tandem.

Some writers overuse capitalization for emphasis, but that is not good style. All-caps text is less legible than lowercase text, so the message *("read this!")* conflicts with the medium *("don't read this!")*.

2.2 Use lowercase unless a rule calls for capitalization.

(a) *Down-style vs. up-style*. Although styles of capitalization have varied over time, the prevailing trend among professional editors is toward a down-style—one in which words are capitalized sparingly. Up-style, by contrast, capitalizes many words (even, in headings, most or all of them). Down-style is easier to read: only words that require emphasis, according to standards set by rule, get emphasized. In legal writing, there is an unfortunate tendency toward contagious capitalization. It is a reversible condition.

(b) *Quotations exception*. If a quoted passage contains an oddly capitalized word, you may choose to reproduce it precisely as in the original (but see 1.40(b)).

> Ex.: "No Person shall be a Senator who shall not have attained the Age of thirty Years, and been nine Years a Citizen of the United States, and who shall not, when elected, be an Inhabitant of that State for which he shall be chosen." U.S. Const. art. I, § 3, cl. 3.

(c) *Consistency*. Make decisions about capitalization based on logic and, with a name, the preference of that person or company. But once you have decided whether to capitalize, be consistent within a piece of writing.

2.3 Capitalize the first word in a sentence.

(a) *Names*. If a name that is not usually capitalized <von Braun; de la Rosa> or is idiosyncratically capitalized <e.e. cummings; iMac> appears at the beginning of a sentence, the first character should be capitalized.

Ex.: De la Rosa will race with Team Jaguar.

Ex.: IMac rumors were circulating before the trade show opened.

(b) *Sentence in a sentence.* The first word of a sentence inside a sentence is often capitalized, unless it is enclosed in parentheses.

Ex.: We agreed to the settlement—It was more than we had expected, after all!—and shook hands.

But: We agreed to the settlement (it was more than we had expected, after all!) and shook hands.

2.4 Capitalize the first word of a direct quotation if it is a full sentence and formally introduced; do not capitalize if it is a partial sentence, is grammatically woven into the main sentence, or is introduced by the conjunction *that*. Do not capitalize an indirect quotation.

(a) *Direct quotation.* The first word of a quoted sentence retains its initial capitalization. If the quotation is split by an attribution, the second part is not capitalized.

Ex.: When he was arrested, the defendant blurted out, "Man, some other dude did it!"

Ex.: "The only thing we have to fear," Roosevelt exhorted the nation, "is fear itself."

(b) *Partial sentence.* Do not capitalize a direct quotation that is not a complete sentence.

Ex.: When arrested, the defendant claimed "some other dude" did it.

Ex.: Fear itself, Roosevelt said, is "[t]he only thing we have to fear."

(c) *Sentence parts.* Do not capitalize part of a direct quotation that is woven into the syntax of the sentence, unless another capitalization rule applies.

Ex.: The manager was always "in a conference," or had "just stepped out of the office," according to the secretary.

(d) *Following "that."* Do not capitalize a quoted sentence if it follows the conjunction *that* in the main sentence.

Ex.: When he was arrested, the defendant blurted out that "some other dude did it!"

Ex.: Roosevelt exhorted the nation that "[t]he only thing we have to fear is fear itself."

(e) *Indirect quotation.* Do not capitalize an indirect quotation unless another capitalization rule applies.

Ex.: The secretary said that the manager was in a conference.

Ex.: My supervising partner said I should reread both depositions.

(f) *Capitalization of original.* Use brackets to change the capitalization of the first word of a quotation if it is changed from the original (see 1.40(b)).

Ex.: Churchill warned: "[A]n iron curtain has descended across the continent."

2.5 Capitalize the first word in a direct question, even if it does not begin the sentence.

(a) *Direct question.* Because a direct question is a sentence apart from any sentence it may be contained in, the first word must be capitalized. The question may be set up by a comma, an em dash, or a colon. If a colon is used, the decision whether to capitalize will depend on whether what follows is a direct question or a declaratory statement (including an indirect question).

Ex.: And the petitioners' silence on this point raises another question: On what authority do they further ask for a setoff against the judgment?

Ex.: I need to call my lawyer—What's that number again?

Ex.: It makes you wonder, How can the State prove intent?

(b) *Indirect question distinguished.* Because an indirect question is a declaratory statement, it does not call for a question mark and its first word should not be capitalized.

Ex.: I need to ask my lawyer how I should plead.

Ex.: She asked whether we had been anywhere near the scene of the crime.

2.6 Capitalize proper nouns—usually, the names of people and places or the titles of statutes, books, articles, and the like.

(a) *Old writings.* Formerly, as in the U.S. Constitution, important nouns were mostly capitalized at the writer's discretion. But this convention has long been defunct, and today only proper nouns are capitalized in text.

(b) *Common and proper nouns.* If a word or phrase may be either a proper noun or a common noun, capitalize it only when the context calls for a proper noun. Otherwise, make it lowercase.

Ex.: Oregon's legislature passed the Married Women's Property Act in 1866. (The article *the* signals that the phrase is being used as a proper noun, the name of a specific statute.)

Ex.: Seven states have passed a married women's property act in the past five years. (The article *a* signals that the phrase refers to a class of statutes.)

(c) *Trademarks.* Trademarked names of products are considered proper names. Do not use trademark symbols in text (see 6.6).

Ex.: Coca-Cola

Ex.: Dumpster

(d) *Artwork.* Capitalize the title of an artistic work.

Ex.: Whistler's Mother

Ex.: Toccata and Fugue in D Minor

(e) *Midword capitals.* Use midword capitals if that is the style of a company or product name. But if a company logo uses all capitals and is not made up of initials, revert to initial capitals.

Ex.: WordPerfect (follow company preference)

But: EXXON (use Exxon)

(f) *Proper-noun phrases.* When two proper nouns share the last word, which itself is normally a common noun, and the two are combined into one phrase with the final word plural, do not capitalize the shared word. It is often advisable, however, to repeat the singular noun.

Ex.: Main and Elm streets

Ex.: the Judiciary and Rules committees

Ex.: the Federal Energy Regulatory and Federal Maritime commissions

Better: the Federal Energy Regulatory Commission and the Federal Maritime Commission

(g) *Headings.* In an up-style heading (see 2.2(a)), capitalize a word in a hyphenated phrase if it would be capitalized standing alone (see 2.10(b)).

Ex.: The Law-of-the-Case Doctrine as Applied in the Second Circuit.

2.7 Capitalize short-form proper nouns.

(a) *Full and short names.* Legal writers frequently refer first to a full name and then to a shortened name. The shortened form is a common noun, but it refers to a specific governmental entity or officer—or to a corporate entity. When that is so, the noun should be capitalized.

Ex.: Farmers Home Administration (on later reference, the Administration)

Following are some of the nouns that most frequently fall into this category:

Academy	Commissioner	District	School
Administration	Committee	Division	Secretary
Administrator	Commonwealth	Federation	Service
Association	Company	Foundation	State
Authority	Cooperative	Government	Subcommittee
Board	Corporation	Hospital	Superintendent
Bureau	Council	Institute	System
City	County	Institution	Township
College	Department	Partnership	Union
Commission	Director	Railroad	University

(b) *Specific governmental acts.* When you're referring to a particular governmental act that contains one of the following words, and you're using the word as a short form on a subsequent reference, capitalize:

Act	Charter	Pact	Resolution
Amendment	Code	Proclamation	Statute
Article	Doctrine	Regulation	Survey
Bill	Ordinance	Report	Treaty

(c) *The term "rule."* Capitalize *rule* when referring to a particular rule by number, but not when the number is absent.

Ex.: Rule 32

Ex.: The rule also specifies what type sizes are permitted.

2.8 Follow established conventions in capitalizing adjectives formed from proper nouns.

(a) *Exclusively proper nouns.* Capitalize adjectives derived from words that exist only as proper nouns.

Ex.: American

Ex.: Holmesian

Ex.: Marxist

(b) *Nonexclusive nouns.* When a word does not exist exclusively as a proper noun, the adjective derived from it is lowercase.

Ex.: congressional (*but* Congress)

Ex.: constitutional (*but* U.S. Constitution)

Ex.: presidential (*but* the President)

(c) *Nonexclusive adjectives.* Some proper adjectives are used in phrases that have an independent common meaning; these are usually set in lowercase, depending on established usage. For instance, one person may write *french fries* while another person writes *French fries.* Both are correct. Consult a current dictionary to see whether a usage has become standardized. If both capitalized and noncapitalized forms are in use, choose one and apply it consistently throughout your writing.

Ex.: Brussels sprouts (or brussels sprouts)

Ex.: Buffalo wings (or buffalo wings)

Ex.: diesel fuel

Ex.: plaster of Paris (or plaster of paris)

2.9 Capitalize defined terms.

(a) *Convention.* The established convention in legal writing is to capitalize defined terms to show that they've been defined and that they're being used as defined.

Ex.: George P. Whitley ("Seller") agrees to sell John Inman ("Buyer") a 1968 Volkswagen Minivan ("Van") for the sum of $1,000. Buyer agrees that the Van is offered for sale "as is," with no warranties expressed or implied by Seller.

Ex.: In August 1996, the Agency's administrative law judge ("ALJ") terminated the suspensions. The ALJ, however, declined to void the suspensions *ab initio*, and the Secretary affirmed this decision.

> "It is only half-culture that despises simplicity."
>
> —*John F. Genung*

(b) *Syntax.* Distinguish between the use of a word as either (1) a defined term, used as a proper noun and capitalized, or (2) a common noun, set lowercase and typically signaled by an article. Define terms in a way that will preserve natural usage on subsequent references.

Ex.: First National Bank (FNB) agrees to lend . . . . Further, FNB agrees . . . .

Ex.: First National Bank ("the Bank") agrees to lend . . . . Further, the Bank agrees . . . .

Ex.: The Buyer further agrees to pay the Seller an additional $25 late charge if any payment remains unpaid 10 days after the Due Date.

(c) *Emphasis and clarity.* Capitalization makes a defined term stand out. It may also help to avoid ambiguity if a similar term is used in the writing.

Ex.: On Saturday the Developer promised that the house would be completed in the following week.

Ex.: Photographs that would have documented the storm damage were lost by the developer.

2.10 Capitalize up-style headings (see 2.2(a)).

(a) *Noncapitalized words.* Do not capitalize an article or a short conjunction or preposition (four letters or shorter) unless it is the first or last word in the heading (or in a line of a multideck title). The *to* in an infinitive is also lowercase.

Ex.: False Statements on Stock Performance

But: False Statements Regarding Stock Performance

Ex.: Defendant Made a Misleading and Actionable Misstatement of Fact

Ex.: Dissolution and Winding Up (capitalize the last word)

(b) *Hyphenated and open compounds.* The first element is always capitalized. The following element is usually capitalized, unless (1) it is an article, a preposition, or a coordinating conjunction of fewer than five letters, or (2) the first element is a prefix and the second element is not a proper noun or proper adjective. If a heading ends with a compound, other than one with a hyphenated prefix, the final element is capitalized.

Ex.: Run-of-the-Mill Cases in Property Law

Ex.: Self-defense Arguments in Tort Cases

Ex.: Pre-Christian Legal Systems

Ex.: Remedies for Quasi-contracts

Ex.: Strategic Run-Arounds to Be Dealt With

2.11 Capitalize acronyms (each character)—that is, words formed from the initials of other words.

(a) *False acronyms.* Do not capitalize all the characters in so-called false acronyms—words in which the characters do not stand for other words.

Ex.: *fax* or *Fax* (if otherwise requiring a capital), but never *FAX*.

(b) *Proper-name acronyms.* Some writers use an initial capital followed by lowercase letters if the acronym is pronounced phonetically as a word and has more than four letters. But unpronounceable acronyms (called *initialisms*) are always written in all caps. The better style is to always use all caps with acronyms.

Ex.: UNICEF (or, less commonly, Unicef)—the word is sounded out.

Ex.: Nasdaq (always sounded out, and commonly written caps and lowercase).

Ex.: NAACP—the letters are sounded out.

(c) *Noncapitalized acronyms.* Some acronyms have become common words. These are always lowercase unless a rule requires them to be capitalized (e.g., as part of a title).

Ex.: laser (light amplification by stimulated emission of radiation)

Ex.: radar (radio detecting and ranging)

2.12 Capitalize the word *court* in reference to (1) the highest tribunal in any jurisdiction, once it has been identified, whether it is the United States Supreme Court or a state supreme court, and (2) whatever court you are addressing, even if it is the lowest court within its jurisdiction.

(a) *Lower courts.* When referring to any other court by a partial name, or to lower courts in general, the word *court* is not capitalized.

Ex.: federal court

Ex.: probate court

Ex.: trial court

(b) *Deference.* To show deference, capitalize the word *court* when referring to any tribunal that you happen to be addressing.

Ex.: This Court will be deciding a question never before ruled on in this jurisdiction. (In addressing a trial court.)

2.13 Capitalize a geographic term that denotes a defined region or area, but not one that merely describes direction or position.

(a) *Compass points.* Use lowercase for a compass point, unless it is part of a proper name or used for a proper name.

Ex.: north, south, east, west

Ex.: The American South

Ex.: Northwest Passage

Ex.: the West (i.e., NATO)

Ex.: the south of France

(b) *Positions.* Similarly, a term that merely indicates position is capitalized only if it is part of a proper name.

Ex.: Central Park

Ex.: Left Bank (Paris)

Ex.: right fork of the Colorado River

(c) *Descriptive or identifying terms.* A term that does not apply to only one entity or is not commonly used as a proper name is lowercase.

Ex.: South American continent

Ex.: tropic of Cancer

Ex.: polar regions

(d) *Political divisions.* Unless it is part of a proper name, a political-division term, such as *state, county, city,* or *republic,* is not capitalized.

Ex.: the Chelmsford city limits

Ex.: New York City

Ex.: New England states

Ex.: State of Maine

(e) *Topographical names.* When a topographical name is used descriptively, it is lowercase. But it is capitalized when used as part of a name or as a geographical denotation.

Ex.: Hudson River Valley

Ex.: the watershed valley of the Hudson River

Ex.: Florida peninsula

Ex.: Rocky Mountains

Ex.: Mississippi Delta

Ex.: the continent (referring to any continent)

Ex.: the Continent (referring specifically to the European Continent)

2.14 Capitalize calendar terms that are proper nouns, but not those that are generic terms.

(a) *Days and months.* Capitalize the proper names of the days of the week and the months of the year, but not generic names.

Ex.: Tuesday, November 2, 2004

Ex.: a May–September romance

Ex.: working for the weekend

(b) *Seasons.* Do not capitalize the names of the seasons (but see 2.17(c)).

Ex.: the spring semester

Ex.: my winter coat

Ex.: in summer 2002

(c) *Holidays.* Holidays, whether secular or religious, are always capitalized.

Ex.: Good Friday

Ex.: the Fourth of July

Ex.: New Year's Day

> "Well did the Chinese say that when a piece of paper blows into a law-court, it may take a yoke of oxen to drag it out again."
>
> —*F.L. Lucas*

2.15 Capitalize every title of honor or respect.

(a) *Title before name.* A civil, religious, military, professional, or noble title that immediately precedes a person's name is always capitalized.

Ex.: Chairman Kaga

Ex.: General Schwarzkopf

Ex.: King Faisal

Ex.: Judge Judy

(b) *Title not before name.* To indicate preeminence or distinction, a title that immediately follows a person's name or that substitutes for a name is capitalized if it identifies a head or assistant head of state, a head or assistant head of an existing or a proposed national governmental unit, a diplomatic title, or a ruler or prince. Otherwise, a title is not capitalized.

Ex.: Tony Blair, Prime Minister of the United Kingdom

Ex.: the Vice President

Ex.: Clerk of the Supreme Court

Ex.: assistant secretary of state

Ex.: the Chargé d'Affaires

Ex.: Don Glazier, president of AdLuc Technologies

(c) *Titles in second person.* Titles, especially honorifics, in the second person are always capitalized.

Ex.: Your Honor

Ex.: Madam Chair

Ex.: Mr. Secretary

(d) *Job titles.* Nonprofessional job-related titles are usually descriptive and not capitalized.

Ex.: baseball player Mark McGwire

Ex.: coach of the Texas Tech football team

Ex.: LaWanda Anton, presiding juror

(e) *Parties.* In legal writing, the terms *plaintiff* and *defendant* are sometimes used as titles for the litigants. If either term is used instead of a party's name and is not preceded by *the*, capitalize the title. The better style is to identify the plaintiff and defendant and use their names.

Ex.: When Plaintiff asked Defendant where the car was, Defendant claimed . . . .

Ex.: When the plaintiff asked the defendant where the car was, the defendant claimed . . . .

Better: When Ms. Burke asked Mr. McArthur where the car was, Mr. McArthur claimed . . . .

(f) *Other cases.* When discussing other cases, do not capitalize words such as *plaintiff, defendant,* and *court* (unless it is the high court of a jurisdiction).

Ex.: The court denied the defendant's motion for a judgment as a matter of law.

2.16 Capitalize a word or phrase that denotes an important epoch or historical event.

(a) *Generally.* Epochs and events can be historical, political, cultural, or economic, and used with or as proper names.

Ex.: Prohibition

Ex.: Roosevelt's New Deal

Ex.: the Renaissance

Ex.: South Sea Bubble

(b) *Numerical designations.* Unless it is part of a proper name, the numerical designation of a period is lowercase.

Ex.: twentieth century

Ex.: Fourth Dynasty Egypt

(c) *Generic terms.* Phrases such as *golden age* and *colonial period* are frequently applied to more than one distinct point in time, so they are usually not capitalized.

Ex.: the golden age of film

Ex.: India's colonial period

But: the Bronze Age

2.17 Capitalize the name of anything personified.

(a) *Proper-name substitutes.* Common nouns and adjectives used in popular descriptive epithets for a person are capitalized.

Ex.: the Old Pretender (James II of England)

Ex.: the Father of Our Country (George Washington)

Ex.: the Great Emancipator (Abraham Lincoln)

(b) *Fictitious names.* A common noun may be combined with a human name to create a fictitious or unidentified person.

Ex.: Jim Crow

Ex.: John Barleycorn

Ex.: Jane Doe

(c) *Vividness.* A vivid personification is capitalized to distinguish it from its ordinary usage, especially if it is an abstraction that is given human qualities (see 2.14(b)).

Ex.: We are all architects of Fate.

Ex.: When Spring waves her wand, Winter is banished.

2.18 Capitalize to show irony or mockery.

(a) *Emphasis.* In some contexts, capitalizing gives a special stress to a word or phrase.

Ex.: After three years of battling the law-school dragon, the lawyer-candidate is confronted by the Dreaded Bar Exam.

Ex.: The defendant wants to blame everything on the Big Bad Government.

(b) *Caution.* Use this device sparingly. A few instances heighten the effect, but overuse dulls the impact.

2.19 Avoid all-caps writing.

(a) *History.* Typewriters and typesetters had limited options for typefaces that would make portions of a writing stand out. Because word processors can produce varied typefaces, it is not necessary—or desirable—to use all caps.

(b) *Difficulty with all caps.* A passage written in all caps is hard to read because the uniform size of the characters makes them indistinct.

Ex.: AS A SPECIFIC BARGAIN INDUCEMENT FOR CREDITOR TO EXTEND CREDIT TO DEBTOR AND AFTER HAVING THE OPPORTUNITY TO CONSULT COUNSEL, EACH PARTY HEREBY EXPRESSLY WAIVES THE RIGHT TO TRIAL BY JURY IN ANY LAWSUIT OR PROCEEDING RELATING TO THIS AGREEMENT OR ARISING IN ANY WAY FROM THE OBLIGATIONS.

(c) *Initial caps.* A short passage written with initial capitals may be marginally easier to read. But even capitalizing initial letters has drawbacks: the capitals are distracting, and it becomes hard to identify defined terms (see 2.9). Reserve this style for headings only.

Ex.: As a Specific Bargain Inducement for Creditor to Extend Credit to Debtor and After Having the Opportunity to Consult Counsel, Each Party Hereby Expressly Waives the Right to Trial by Jury in Any Lawsuit or Proceeding Relating to This Agreement or Arising in Any Way from the Obligations.

(d) *Limited capitals.* The same passage written with initial capitalization using the rules in this chapter is much clearer.

Ex.: As a specific bargain inducement for Creditor to extend credit to Debtor and after having the opportunity to consult counsel, each party hereby expressly waives the right to trial by jury in any lawsuit or proceeding relating to this Agreement or arising in any way from the Obligations.

(e) *Different typeface.* Instead of using all caps, you might make a critical passage in a contract stand out by changing the typeface. For example, if you're using a serif type such as Times Roman, try using a boldface sans-serif typeface such as Arial to draw attention to an important provision. You could also set the type in a larger size.

Ex.: **As a specific bargain inducement for Creditor to extend credit to Debtor and after having the opportunity to consult counsel, each party hereby expressly waives the right to trial by jury in any lawsuit or proceeding relating to this Agreement or arising in any way from the Obligations.**

(f) *Limited all caps.* If you must use all caps, limit them to one line.

Ex.: PLAINTIFF'S SUMMARY JUDGMENT MOTION MUST BE DENIED.

2.20 Use caps and small caps when a citation-system rule or other directive requires them or when the usage is conventional.

(a) *Abbreviations.* Some abbreviations are conventionally set in caps and small caps. The most common are for the time of day and for eras. If uncertain whether an abbreviation should be set in small caps, consult a general style guide, such as the current edition of the *Chicago Manual of Style.*

Ex.: A.D. 1776

Ex.: 33 B.C.

Ex.: 2002 C.E.

(b) *Never in main text.* Most law reviews that follow *Bluebook* style use caps and small caps, roman type, and italics in citations (which appear in footnotes). Caps and small caps are never used in the main text, except perhaps for short headings.

(c) *Periodical titles.* In a *Bluebook*-style law-review citation, no matter what kind of periodical is cited (e.g., newspaper, magazine, journal), its name is set in caps and small caps. An article name is italicized. In *ALWD* style, the name of a periodical is set in ordinary roman type.

Ex.: *Bluebook*: 83 MINN. L. REV. 1337.

Ex.: *ALWD*: 83 Minn. L. Rev. 1337.

Ex.: *Bluebook*: NEWSWEEK, Jan. 8, 1996.

Ex.: *ALWD*: Newsweek, Jan. 8, 1996.

Ex.: *Bluebook*: 135 CONG. REC. H1811.

Ex.: *ALWD*: 135 Cong. Rec. H1811.

(d) *Book titles.* In a *Bluebook*-style law-review citation, book titles are set in caps and small caps. The title of a shorter work within a collection is italicized. In *ALWD* style, a title is italicized and an author's name is set in ordinary roman type. *ALWD* style also includes the publishing information, but *Bluebook* style does not. For an encyclopedia (such as *Corpus Juris Secundum* or *American Jurisprudence*), *ALWD* style is to set the title in roman type, with no publishing information other than the year.

Ex.: *Bluebook*: BLACK'S LAW DICTIONARY (7th ed. 1999).

Ex.: *ALWD*: *Black's Law Dictionary* (Bryan A. Garner ed., 7th ed., West 1999).

Ex.: *Bluebook*: HANS J. WOLFF, ROMAN LAW 45 (1951).

Ex.: *ALWD*: Hans J. Wolff, *Roman Law* 45 (University of Oklahoma Press 1951).

Ex.: *Bluebook*: 60 AM. JUR. 2D *Patents* § 1003 (1987).

Ex.: *ALWD*: 60 Am. Jur. 2d *Patents* § 1003 (1987).

> "It is easy enough to say that a person should live in such a way as to avoid the perfect infinitive after the past conditional, but it is another matter to do it."
>
> —*James Thurber*

(e) *Authors.* In a *Bluebook*-style law-review citation, the name of a book's author is set in caps and small caps, even if only a shorter work within the book is cited. But if the author of the shorter work is not the author of the book, the author's name is set in ordinary roman type. In *ALWD* style, an author's name is always set in ordinary roman type, and a title is italicized. For a shorter work within a book, *Bluebook* style is to italicize the signal *in*, but *ALWD* style is roman.

Ex.: *Bluebook*: KARL LLEWELLYN, THE BRAMBLE BUSH 56 (1930; repr. 1951).
Ex.: *ALWD*: Karl Llewellyn, *The Bramble Bush* 56 (1930; Oceana Publications repr. 1951).
Ex.: *Bluebook*: CLARENCE DARROW, *The Skeleton in the Closet* 235, *in* VERDICTS OUT OF COURT (Arthur & Lila Weinberg eds., 1963).
Ex.: *ALWD*: Clarence Darrow, *The Skeleton in the Closet* 235, in *Verdicts Out of Court* (Arthur & Lila Weinberg eds., Quadrangle Books 1963).
Ex.: *Bluebook*: Felix Frankfurter, *The Case of Sacco and Vanzetti* 115, *in* 2 THE WORLD OF LAW (Ephraim London ed., 1960).
Ex.: *ALWD*: Felix Frankfurter, *The Case of Sacco and Vanzetti* 115, in *The World of Law* vol. 2 (Ephraim London ed., Simon & Schuster 1960).

(f) *Law-review citations.* In a *Bluebook*-style law-review citation, the titles of uniform acts, model codes, statutes, rules of evidence or procedure, and the like are set in caps and small caps. In *ALWD* style, use italics for restatements of the law, and ordinary roman type for everything else.

Ex.: *Bluebook*: RESTATEMENT (SECOND) OF TORTS § 918 (1979).
Ex.: *ALWD*: *Restatement (Second) of Torts* § 918 (1979).
Ex.: *Bluebook*: UNIF. PROBATE CODE § 2–706 (amended 1993).
Ex.: *ALWD*: Unif. Probate Code § 2–706 (amended 1993).
Ex.: *Bluebook*: FED. R. CIV. P. 11.
Ex.: *ALWD*: Fed. R. Civ. P. 11.

2.21 Follow any special rules that may require caps and small caps.

(a) *Court rules.* Some courts prescribe caps and small caps for certain purposes. For example, a style guide for the state courts of Arkansas recommends using caps and small caps when quoting from a transcript.

Ex.: ATTORNEY: Did you see the accident at the intersection?
WITNESS: I sure did.
ATTORNEY: Can you describe what you saw?
WITNESS: I'd just noticed the light was green so I could cross, when a truck raced across my path and then I heard the crash.

(b) *Government rules.* Some departments, agencies, and the like may have citation rules dictating the use of caps and small caps. For example, the first rule in the Public Utility Commission of Texas Citation Guide requires Texas statutes to be cited in caps and small caps.

(c) *Practitioners' usage.* Caps and small caps are not customarily used for citations in legal memoranda or court documents.

(d) *Judicial opinions.* Judicial writers sometimes use caps and small caps for citations, especially of statutes and rules of evidence and procedure, but there is no uniformly accepted stylistic rule. For example, courts in Texas and Virginia use caps and small caps for the titles of periodicals, but New York and Oregon courts do not. And Texas courts use caps and small caps for rules of evidence and procedure, but Virginia courts do not.

(e) *Punctuation.* Only punctuation that is part of the citation or abbreviation is set in caps and small caps. So, for example, a book author's name is in caps and small caps, but a comma that follows the name is in normal roman type.

> "Never set headlines using capital initials and lowercase on every word—unless your intention is to create visual hiccups. This is a bad and outmoded convention left over from nineteenth-century newspapering days."
>
> —*Jan V. White*

§ 3
Italics, Boldface, and Underlining

3.1 Writers use a variety of devices to make text stand out in a document: italic type, boldface type, underlining, even quotation marks and capitalization. There are really only two reasons for making text stand out: to emphasize it or because some style convention directs it. Hence, in legal writing, we set one word or phrase in a quotation in italics so that the reader will immediately see how it relates to the argument at hand, and we set case names in italics just because that's how lawyers do it.

When it comes to using italics or any other device for emphasis, there is no greater rule than this: less is more. The conservative use of special type makes its appearance more special. Its liberal use not only dilutes its impact, but irritates the reader as well. That's something an advocate can't risk.

In general, italic type is appropriate in text, while boldface type is appropriate for headings. Underlining is a holdover from the typewriter era and should be avoided altogether.

3.2 Use italics (preferably not underlining) to show emphasis.

(a) *Styles compared.* Underlining is a holdover from the typewriter era, when underlining and capitalization were the only ways to show emphasis. Italic type is clean and legible, whereas computer underlining is obtrusive and can be hard to read because it typically obliterates the descenders on the letters *f*, *g*, *j*, *p*, *q*, and *y*.

Not this: DeShaney v. Winnebago County Dep't Soc. Servs., 489 U.S. 189 (1989).

But this: *DeShaney v. Winnebago County Dep't Soc. Servs.*, 489 U.S. 189 (1989).

(b) *Exception.* Break the rule when necessary for unusual emphasis: that is, when a page is crammed full of italicized citations, a word or two in italics is not going to stand out. In that narrow circumstance, underlining may be justifiable.

(c) *In quotation.* It is usually not necessary to follow the style of the source when quoting: if the original used underlining for emphasis, for example, it is unobjectionable to substitute italics to serve the same purpose. Only if there is some question about what the styles mean (such as when both italics and underlining appear in the source) must the writer either follow the style of the original or else explain the changes in a parenthetical note after the quotation.

3.3 Use italics for foreign words and phrases that have not been anglicized.

(a) *Uneven application.* The rule on italicizing foreignisms is one that everyone seems to agree with, but no one agrees on where to draw the line. The surest guide is *Black's Law Dictionary* (7th ed. 1999): check it to see whether phrases such as *prima facie* and *de novo* should be italicized. The appearance of the headwords will tell you.

Ex.: The district court's grant of summary judgment is reviewed *de novo*, drawing all factual inferences in favor of the non-moving party. (2d Cir. opinion)

But: We review de novo the denial of Rhoad's request for judgment as a matter of law. (4th Cir. opinion)

(b) *Common understanding.* The determining factor is whether the word or phrase is commonly understood. But commonly understood by whom? A lawyer would know the meaning of *de novo*, for example, but most nonlawyers would not.

Ex.: The district court granted Plaintiff *in forma pauperis* status, and sua sponte dismissed his case as frivolous.

Ex.: By definition, a dictum is an unnecessary statement made by a majority. An *ipse dixit* labeling of a statement as a "holding" does not make it so.

Ex.: This maxim is often cited by modern devotees of a turbulently changing common law—often in its Latin form (*cessante ratione legis, cessatet ipsa lex*) to create the impression of great venerability.

3.4 Use italics to signal that a letter, word, or phrase is being used as a term—when it is being defined, for example—rather than for its meaning.

(a) *Or quotation marks.* Quotation marks may also be used for the same purpose (see 1.30(b)), but italics do not interrupt the flow of a sentence as much as punctuation does.

Ex.: A *parody* is an imitation of a serious piece of literature, music, or composition for humorous or satirical effect.

Ex.: The district court, finding the term *incentive compensation* ambiguous, denied Bock's motion for summary judgment.

Ex.: The word *nevertheless* appears three times in the paragraph.

(b) *In hypotheticals.* In legal writing the parties in hypothetical situations often have the italicized names *A* and *B*.

Ex.: *A* conveys Blackacre to *B* "and his heirs, forever."

3.5 Use italics for case names.

(a) *Legal convention.* In legal writing, case names are invariably emphasized, either by setting them in italics or by underlining them. Some practition–ers and legal-writing instructors still prefer underlining, arguing that it makes the case names stand out more than italicizing does. But for the reasons discussed in 3.2(a), italics are the better choice. Italicize the full case name, including the parties' names and *v.*, *in re*, or *ex rel.* (but not the comma following the parties' names). On later references the case is usually referred to by one party's name alone, but as a reference to the case itself the name is still italicized.

Ex.: *Allen v. United States,* 164 U.S. 492 (1896).

Ex.: South Carolina has adopted a statute that governs circumstances in which an *Allen* charge is prohibited.

Ex.: *In re Winship,* 397 U.S. 358, 361 (1970).

Ex.: The Court held that this instruction ran afoul of *Winship.*

(b) *Informal names.* A few notable sets of cases developing a landmark doctrine are referred to collectively. In these phrases, the word *cases* is also capitalized and italicized.

Ex.: the *Slaughter-House Cases* (emasculating the Privileges or Immunities Clause of the Fourteenth Amendment)

Ex.: the *Civil Rights Cases* (holding that the Fourteenth Amendment reaches only state action)

(c) *In text.* Follow the same italic style in text and in footnotes. This style agrees with that of *ALWD*, but *The Bluebook* prescribes using italics for a case name in a footnote only if the name is grammatically part of the sentence.

Ex.: In *Elkins v. United States,* the Supreme Court affirmed the Fourth Amendment prohibition of unreasonable searches. (Grammatically part of the sentence.)

But: The trial was not "just a few hours long," Bose Corp. v. Consumers Union of U.S., Inc., 466 U.S. 485, 500 (1984). It lasted six weeks. (Grammatically not part of the sentence, so not italicized under *Bluebook* style.)

Better: The trial was not "just a few hours long," *Bose Corp. v. Consumers Union of U.S., Inc.,* 466 U.S. 485, 500 (1984); it lasted six weeks. (To maintain a consistent style through the document.)

3.6 Use italics for the titles of books and other publications, and (only in legal writing) for the titles of articles (but see 2.20).

(a) *Books.* Italicize titles of books, both in text and in footnotes.

Ex.: *Webster's Third New International Dictionary* 675 (1993).

Ex.: Copyright protection was sought for a work titled *Selden's Condensed Ledger of Bookkeeping Simplified,* which explained a new system of bookkeeping.

(b) *Articles.* In legal writing, italicize titles of articles. (This differs from the style in general writing, whereby article titles are set in roman and put inside quotation marks.)

Ex.: Hans Jonas, *Philosophical Reflections on Experimenting with Human Subjects,* 98 Daedalus 219 (1969).

(c) *Periodicals.* Do not italicize the names of periodicals.

Ex.: Jacoby, Handlin & Simonson, *Survey Evidence in Deceptive Advertising Cases Under the Lanham Act,* 84 Trademark Rep. 541 (1994).

3.7 Use italics for citational signals.

(a) *Purpose.* Italics draw the reader's attention to the signal and give the signal emphasis.

Ex.: *See* Peter T. Kilborn, *Feeling Devalued by Change, Doctors Seek Union Banner,* N.Y. Times A1 (30 May 1996).

Ex.: *Cf. Hill v. Lockhart,* 474 U.S. 52, 58 (1985).

(b) *Signals as sentence elements.* If the introductory signal is an ordinary English word or phrase used in syntax, do not italicize it.

Ex.: For a point-by-point analysis, see David L. Marcus, *Is the Submarine Patent Torpedoed?,* 70 Temple L. Rev. 521, 572–84 (1997).

3.8 Use italics to report subsequent history in a citation.

(a) *Subsequent history.* A complete citation includes a mention of actions taken on further appeals. The procedural information is italicized.

Ex.: *United States v. Valensia,* 222 F.3d 1173, 1182 (9th Cir. 2000), *cert. granted, judgment vacated, remanded,* —— U.S. ——, 121 S. Ct. 1222 (2001).

Ex.: *United States v. Alpine Land & Reservoir Co.,* 503 F. Supp. 877 (D. Nev. 1980) ("*Alpine Decree*"), *aff'd as modified,* 697 F.2d 851 (9th Cir.) ("*Alpine I*"), *cert. denied,* 464 U.S. 863 (1983).

(b) *Other information.* Additional notes, such as the type of opinion (e.g., concurrence, dissent, en banc) and the judge's name, are not italicized.

Ex.: Our court has similarly observed that, in North Carolina, "allegations of ineffective assistance of counsel *generally* are properly raised on collateral review." *Smith v. Dixon,* 14 F.3d 956, 966 (4th Cir. 1994) (en banc) (emphasis added).

3.9 When a word or phrase within italicized matter should itself be italicized, make it roman.

(a) *Toggle.* The purpose of italic type is to make the word or phrase stand out from its surroundings. If the surroundings are all italic, then roman type stands out.

Ex.: Donna Clarke & Bruce Bower, *Due Process in Texas Fails to Meet* Goldberg v. Kelly *and* Mathews v. Eldridge *Standards,* 2 Tex. Tech J. of Tex. Admin. L. 135, 136 (2001).

(b) *Context.* A writer sometimes needs to show some flexibility with this rule. For example, if roman type does not adequately distinguish the word or phrase, underlining or using all caps is occasionally justified (see 3.2(b)).

3.10 Do not italicize a punctuation mark after italicized matter unless it is a part of the matter itself.

(a) *Trailing punctuation*. Most often in legal writing, a comma will follow italicized matter, as it does in a case citation. Always use roman type for a comma, period, closing parenthesis, or any other punctuation mark that is not part of the italicized matter itself.

Ex.: A junior inventor "may be entitled to a patent even though an earlier inventor discovered first if that earlier inventor is held to have abandoned, *without divulging the secrets of the invention*." (The closing period and quotation marks are not italicized.)

Ex.: (*See, e.g.*, *Dix-Seal Corp. v. New Haven Trap Rock Co.*) (The comma after *see, e.g.* is not italicized, nor is the closing parenthesis mark after *Co.*)

(b) *Exception*. Punctuation that is part of a title is italicized, even if it closes the citation or sentence as well.

Ex.: Timothy Jost discusses the dilemma in his article *The American Difference in Health Care Costs: Is There a Problem? Is Medical Necessity the Solution?*

3.11 Despite all the earlier rules, be careful not to overuse italics.

(a) *Effective when rare*. When used judiciously, italicizing for emphasis can be effective.

Ex.: In the first suit, Defendant Employer was nonsuited without prejudice, but the district court entered a final order dismissing Defendant Employee *with prejudice*. Under established caselaw, a final order against an employee acts as res judicata to a subsequent suit against an employer.

(b) *Ineffective when overused*. Italicizing for emphasis is most effective when used in quoted matter to point out relevance to the issue at hand. It is less effective when used to emphasize the writer's own words. It is ineffective—even counterproductive—when overused.

Not this: A *reasonable person* in the seller's position would provide a warning *after* the time of sale *only* when the seller *knows* that the product poses a *substantial risk of harm*.

But this: A reasonable person in the seller's position would provide a warning after the time of sale only when the seller knows that the product poses a *substantial* risk of harm.

Not this: But the interest that can protect a power of attorney must be an interest in the subject matter itself and *must be coupled in the same person* such that *the agent may exercise his power in his own name*.

But this: But the interest that can protect a power of attorney must be an interest in the subject matter itself and must be coupled in the same person such that the agent may exercise his power *in his own name*.

(c) *Other techniques.* Use word order and stronger word choices rather than italic type to convey emphasis. Tighten quotations to just the part that you want to emphasize. Place what is being emphasized at the end or the beginning of its sentence for natural emphasis.

Ex.: After-sale warnings justify their costs only if the risk of harm is sufficiently great.

(d) *Emphasis.* When italic type appears for emphasis in quoted matter, always append a parenthetical note explaining whether the emphasis was in the original or has been added. While *The Bluebook* advises adding a notation only if emphasis has been added, an explicit comment removes any question about the source.

Ex.: They pointed out that Nev. Rev. Stat. § 533.085 protects "the right of any person to take and use water . . . where appropriations have been *initiated* in accordance with law prior to March 22, 1913." (Emphasis added.)

Ex.: Of the criminal liability created in 18 U.S.C. § 111, the Supreme Court has found "it plain that Congress intended to protect *both* federal officers and federal functions . . . [and] [e]nsure a federal forum for the trial of offenses involving federal officers." *U.S. v. Feola*, 420 U.S. 671, 679 (1975) (emphasis in original).

3.12 Reserve boldface type for headings.

(a) *For separation.* Boldface type breaks up text. It is best used for headings, where it provides a vertical break between sections and subsections.

(b) *Not in text.* Using boldface type in text dilutes its functionality as a separator. It can confuse the reader about what degree of emphasis the writer intended for bold and italic type.

3.13 Use italics for names of ships, spaceships, and other vessels.

(a) *Not for designation.* But do not italicize the designation before the name.

Ex.: The SS *Ioannis P. Goulandris* had chartered to carry olive oil, cheese, and tobacco from the western Greek port of Piraiévs to the United States via the Strait of Gibraltar.

(b) *Reserved use.* The names of craft that travel by water (e.g., submarines, barges) or through the air (e.g., dirigibles, balloons, jets) are traditionally italicized. The names of noteworthy railroad engines (e.g., *The Flying Scotsman*) are sometimes italicized, but there is no consistency in usage. Local rules or guidelines may require that the names of other things be italicized.

> "In legal affairs . . . it is often possible as well as necessary to insist that particular words be used in particular ways."
>
> —*Irving Lee*

§ 4
Document Design

4.1 Word processors have changed lawyers' work environment tremendously since the late 1980s. For better or worse, they have made a designer out of every user. Even following the same set of court rules and writing the same kind of document, two lawyers—one knowledgeable in document design and one not—can end up with documents that look quite different: one can be pleasant-looking, the other offputting. So it's important for writers to be aware of what makes for good (and bad) design and why.

4.2 Follow court rules in formatting all documents to be filed in court.

(a) *Meticulous formatting.* Be rigorous about observing applicable rules on margins, spacing, typeface, type size, and page limits in court rules. Clerks of court often check these elements before accepting a brief for filing.

(b) *Typographical tricks.* Never use tricks such as "squeezing" type to thwart the court's formatting or page-limit rules.

Typeface

4.3 Choose a readable typeface that is appropriate for the document.

(a) *Definitions.* Typefaces, called *fonts* on computers, fall into three general categories: *serif, sans serif* (pronounced /sanz SEHR-uf/), and *decorative.* The letters of a serif typeface, such as the one used here, feature "feet" and other finishing strokes that enhance the readability of text. For ordinary paragraphs, serif type is the most legible type because the serifs subtly differentiate characters. That is why almost every book and magazine publisher uses a serif typeface in text. The letters of sans-serif type, such as that used in this book for examples and bold headings, have no such finishing strokes (*sans serif* simply means "without serifs"). Sans-serif type is considered more legible than serif type in single lines of type and in very short passages. It is appropriate in what is known as "display type," as in headings and callouts, and in small sizes, such as that used in classified ads and in tabular matter such as stock prices and sports scores. For text, however, a serif typeface is usually a better choice. Never use a decorative typeface such as scripts, Old English, or a comic face, which may be appropriate for ads but have no place in professional writing.

Exs. (serif):	Times Roman	Garamond
Exs. (sans serif):	Helvetica	Gill Sans
Exs. (decorative):	*Chancery*	Comic Sans

(b) *Variations.* Typewriters once limited one's options: a legal writer might emphasize words either by using all caps or by underlining. Word processors allow writers to choose bold and italic styles of most typefaces, making for a more sophisticated format. But writers must learn to use these tools with care, choosing an appropriate type style and using its variations only when doing so serves a good purpose.

(c) *Courier.* The typewriter-style typeface Courier is *monospaced,* so that every letter takes the same amount of horizontal space, whether it's a lowercase *i* or a capital *W.* The visual effect is cruder than that of a proportionally spaced typeface—which explains why no publisher today would print a book with it. A proportionally spaced typeface such as Times Roman or Garamond is easier to read because the words form more recognizable units. More words fit comfortably on a line, and therefore on a page, than with Courier (compare the type samples below). The only good reason to continue using Courier is if the judge to whom your document is addressed prefers the old typewriter style, as some do.

Ex.: This is set in 12-point Times Roman.

Ex.: `This is set in 12-point Courier.`

4.4 Do not use more than two typefaces in a document.

(a) *Mixing styles.* A serif typeface is the better choice for body copy because it enhances readability. The safest practice is to stick to one typeface throughout a document, using its roman, italic, bold, and bold italic styles as needed. But a bold sans-serif typeface can provide a sharp contrast and help headings stand out from the text. Never combine two different typefaces of the same category (serif or sans serif) in the same document.

Ex. (both heading and text in Times Roman):

STANDARD OF REVIEW

All issues raised are matters of law, to be reviewed de novo.

Ex. (heading in Arial and text in Times Roman):

STANDARD OF REVIEW

All issues raised are matters of law, to be reviewed de novo.

(b) *Ransom-note effect.* Having too many different typefaces on a page produces a piecemeal, cut-and-paste appearance that becomes distracting. In the example below, the heading is in Arial Bold, the text in Times Roman, and the quotation in Garamond Italic.

Ex.:

History of the Boundary Line

The boundary of the property in issue was established more than 250 years ago. By royal decree in 1740, King George II of England declared:

> *That the Dividing Line shall pass up thro the Mouth of Piscataqua Harbour and up the Middle of the River . . . . And that the Dividing Line shall part the Isles of Shoals and run thro the Middle of the Harbour between the Islands to the Sea on the Southerly Side . . . .*

Even though the United States achieved independence a few decades later, the courts have continued to recognize royal land grants in the chain of title.

4.5 Use an appropriate type size.

(a) *Readability.* Although many readers say that they prefer 12-point type, it is somewhat small for an 8½-by-11-inch page with one-inch margins and double-spacing. If you have a choice, use 13-point type. The national standard for federal appellate briefs is 14-point type (see Fed. R. App. P. 32(a)(5)). For headings, 14-point type is acceptable, but anything larger seems loud and aggressive. On the other hand, anything smaller than 10-point type looks like the proverbial "fine print," designed *not* to be read.

Ex.: This Heading Is Like Shouting. (16 point)

Ex.: This heading is not so overwhelming. (14 point)

Ex.: This is the standard type size for text. (13 point)

Ex.: You're not supposed to be reading this fine print. (8 point)

(b) *Size.* Typefaces vary in apparent size, even if they are the same point size (see examples below). The difference is the *x-height*—that is, how large the lowercase letters are. Between two typefaces, the one with the bigger x-height is generally easier to read at small sizes, while the one with the smaller x-height generally fits more characters on a line. Typefaces also vary in how condensed the letters are. If you need to fit more text into a document, and if court rules permit, try changing the typeface.

Ex.: This is a sentence set in 13-point Garamond.

Ex.: This is a sentence set in 13-point Times Roman.

Ex.: This is a sentence set in 13-point Century.

(c) *Headings.* The best practice is the easy one: stick to one type size throughout the document. Headings may be set in a slightly larger point size than text, but never larger than 14 point. Subheadings should be the same size as the text; if they are bold and in a contrasting typeface, they may even be slightly smaller.

White Space

4.6 Use white space purposefully.

(a) *Definition and purpose.* White space is all the area on a page where no words appear. Whatever increases meaningful white space usually also enhances a document's appearance and readability. By "meaningful white space" is meant the margins and the space around headings, block quotations, bulleted items, and the like. It does not include the randomly inserted blank lines that occur in double-spacing.

(b) *Focal point.* White space directs the reader's eyes and gives them a resting place. It also allows the reader some breathing room to digest the message.

(c) *Contrast.* The empty space between textual elements makes words stand out as they become easier to distinguish. The contrast helps prevent a monotonous flow of prose.

(d) *Organization.* A writer can group information and clarify relationships among points by using white space. A greater distance between passages implies separation, as between points of argument, whereas proximity implies connection, one idea leading into the next.

(e) *Comprehension.* Just as a long sentence or a long paragraph is difficult to read, so too is a long block of text. By using white space and subheadings to break up copy into shorter "bites," a writer can help the reader absorb the information better.

4.7 Leave a little more room in margins than you are required to.

(a) *Readability.* When a court rule sets a margin width (e.g., one inch on all sides), the specified width is usually a minimum and not an absolute width. Greater margins enhance readability by creating more white space and preventing lines from becoming too long. Unless a rule disallows it, use 1.1-inch margins for 13-point type, or 1.2-inch margins for 12-point type.

(b) *Notes.* A larger margin allows space for readers to make notes alongside a passage. Narrow margins make the text appear crowded and tend to produce a less professional, less valuable appearance.

(c) *Extra space at bottom.* When margins are equal on all four sides, the text may appear to slide down the page. Making the bottom margin a little bigger than the side margins avoids this effect.

(d) *Gutters.* If the document will be bound, add an extra half-inch to the gutter margin. If the document is printed on one side of the paper only, add the extra space to the left side of the page. If the document is printed double-sided, add the extra space to the "inside" margin.

4.8 Use indents of a quarter of an inch or so; use the tab key or automatic paragraph formatting to keep them consistent.

(a) *Purpose.* Indents add white space and give shape and definition to a paragraph (see 4.14). They also make lists, long quotations, and other elements stand out.

(b) *Length.* Although an odd custom of a "double indent" (an indent of an inch or more) is common within the legal profession, the custom has nothing to recommend it. The maximum indent should be half an inch, the default on word processors and typewriters both.

(c) *Block quotations.* Block quotations must have a left-margin indent. Unless they appear in a narrow column of type, they should also have an equal-sized right-margin indent.

(d) *Uniformity*. Use the indent key or automatic paragraph formatting to keep indents uniform (see 4.15). With most typefaces, the spacebar produces variable-width spaces, which can lead to alignment problems.

4.9 On documents such as contracts (as well as other documents in which subparts are numbered and lettered throughout), use hanging indents cascading from the left side.

(a) *Purpose of hanging indents*. Progressive indents on the left side neatly display the interrelationship of parts and subparts.

(b) *Length of indents*. To make this convention work, create small indents equivalent to only a space or two. This way, the progressive indents will not move so far to the right that too few characters will fit on a line.

Ex.: B. Under the Equal Credit Opportunity Act, a creditor's notification of adverse action must include:
1. a statement of the action taken;
2. notice of the provisions of the ECOA;
3. the name and address of the federal agency that regulates compliance; and
4. either
(a) a statement explaining why the action was taken; or
(b) a disclosure of the applicant's right to receive such a statement.

Justification

4.10 Avoid full justification; set text flush left.

(a) *Difficulty reading*. Except in the hands of a skillful typographer, fully justified text can actually be hard to read. Because the text is forced to both edges of the body, it may produce several problems with type: (1) the spacing between letters may be stretched to make the edges even; (2) rivers of white space may appear, necessitating editing to correct; and (3) the text may appear to be "sliding down the page" unless margins are adjusted. These problems are common in fully justified text but rarely occur with flush-left text. The uneven right margin on a page of flush-left copy also gives visual clues that help the reader find the beginning of the next line.

(b) *Avoiding rivers*. A river is a flow of white space produced by word spaces that appear near each other on consecutive lines of text. Rivers appear more often in fully justified text than in flush-left text because the word processor must increase the space between words and letters to make the text stretch evenly between the margins. Rivers also appear when the line length is too long or too short. Rivers can be corrected either by changing the margin width (wider is usually better) or by editing the text so that the word spaces no longer align.

4.11 Reserve centering and flush-right alignments for special uses.

(a) *Centering.* Centering is sometimes appropriate for titles and captions of documents, for main headings, and for page numbers. Although some writers prefer to center all headings, the more common practice is to set them flush left.

(b) *Flush right.* There are few appropriate uses for flush-right alignment. Some legal writers set the court name and case number flush right in the style of pleadings and motions. More often, a text block (such as the name and address of the attorney filing the document) must appear on the right side of the page. But the lines within the block are left-aligned, so use tabs rather than flush-right alignment. Page numbering is the only other appropriate use for flush-right text, although page numbers may also be centered.

Horizontal Spacing

4.12 Use even forward-spacing in your documents: one space between words and one space after punctuation marks (including colons and periods).

(a) *Typewriter limitations.* The custom during the reign of the typewriter was to insert two spaces between sentences. The reason was that typewriter typefaces are monospaced, like the Courier typeface on computers: every letter takes the same amount of horizontal space, whether it's a lowercase *i*, a capital *W*, or a space. That is fine for lining up columns of numbers but lousy for creating legible text. Continue the custom only if you use a typewriter or the Courier typeface.

(b) *Word processors and flexibility.* On a computer, you almost certainly have typefaces with proportional spacing. Letters fit together snugly, words are more legible as discrete entities, and spaces stand out. Because double-spacing between sentences looks odd in typeset copy, many word-processing programs automatically replace two spaces with one. Additionally, if you use two forward spaces and justify the right margin, a line may break between the spaces and end short of the right margin.

4.13 Use a hard (nonbreaking) space to avoid breaking lines at inappropriate places.

(a) *Hard space.* Get to know your word processor's hard-space function and use it in places where you do not want a line to break.

(b) *Importance.* The hard space is especially important in legal writing, where by convention a space separates citation symbols such as § and ¶, as well as abbreviations such as *cmt.* and *p.*, from the number that follows.

Ex.: § 1983

Ex.: cmt. a

Ex.: pp. 24–32

(c) *Ellipses.* Use hard spaces before and inside (but not after) a series of ellipsis dots to ensure that the dots will be evenly spaced and will stay together on one line.

Ex.: "in Order to . . . secure the Blessings of Liberty"

4.14 Mark the beginning of a paragraph by tab-indenting its first line; in a single-spaced document, leave an extra line between paragraphs.

(a) *Indenting.* Indent the first line of each paragraph.

(b) *New section.* You may choose not to indent the first paragraph of each section. The reasoning behind this book-style typesetting convention is that the purpose of the indent or extra space is to show the reader where a new paragraph starts; at the beginning of a section, it is obvious where the paragraph starts. Once again, however, this practice is more common in publishing houses than in law offices.

(c) *Intervening space.* Add a half-line or full line of space between paragraphs in a single-spaced document such as a letter or a memo. Word-processing programs can do this automatically, or you can add an extra hard return between paragraphs.

(d) *Block style.* Block-style formatting—with extra space between paragraphs but no indents—is discouraged in legal writing. The style causes problems when some copy such as a long quotation is itself indented: it becomes impossible to tell whether what follows is a continuation of the previous paragraph or a new paragraph.

4.15 To ensure that the indentation is consistent throughout the document, use a tab instead of the spacebar for indenting.

(a) *Paragraph indents.* With proportional typefaces, the width of a spacebar's space is fixed in flush-left copy but variable in fully justified copy. Using the spacebar to indent paragraphs in justified copy will result in paragraph indents that vary noticeably. It wastes time and looks amateurish—use the tab settings instead for ease and consistency.

(b) *Aligning columns.* Unless you're using Courier (a practice to be discouraged), it is futile to try to align multiple columns using the spacebar. Even with Courier or another monospaced typeface, any copy change will ruin the alignment. Instead, learn to use the word-processing tools: tab and table settings are there precisely to avoid alignment problems.

4.16 Avoid adjusting a typeface's spacing or width.

(a) *Spacing.* Word-processing software lets the user change the spacing between letters and between words. Reducing the space results in denser copy, while increasing it makes the copy airier.

(b) *Width.* Word-processing software also lets the user compress and expand the horizontal width of a type's characters.

(c) *Limitations.* While it may at first sound tempting to use spacing and width to obviate a court's page-limit rules, avoid that temptation. Text that is set too tight and letters that are condensed too much are hard to read. Besides, it violates the spirit (and possibly the letter) of court rules and risks annoying the judicial reader. Even worse consequences, such as sanctions, are possible.

Vertical Spacing

4.17 Prefer single-spaced documents in-house, but for court filings always follow rules and customs that require double-spacing.

(a) *Advantages of single-spacing.* Surprisingly to some people, single-spaced copy is more reader-friendly than double-spaced copy. Not only is the manuscript almost half the length, but the structure of the writing shows better when the copy is single-spaced. Headings stand out better because the extra spacing around them is not diluted by extra white space between every two lines. Paragraphs are less intimidating: a double-spaced paragraph of 400 words can take up a full page.

(b) *Disadvantages of double-spacing.* Double-spacing prevents sentences from standing out. It results in fewer paragraphs and fewer headings on a page, making it harder to follow the writing's structure. While the extra white space is convenient for an editor (see 4.18), it hinders readability because it is dispersed throughout the page.

(c) *Court rules.* Despite the advantages of single-spaced copy, court rules often require that briefs and other filings be double-spaced. Strictly adhere to any such rules.

4.18 Double-space draft documents to make them easier to edit.

(a) *Editing ease.* Double-spacing leaves room for corrections and edits to be written between lines of type. A marked-up page will be much less cluttered than a page of single-spaced copy; the marks will be easier to follow, and only half as many will appear on a page.

(b) *Triple-spacing.* A draft that will be heavily edited may need to be printed out triple-spaced.

4.19 Avoid awkward page breaks.

(a) *Headings.* Make sure that a heading is followed by at least two lines of text before a page break, or else force a page break before the heading.

(b) *Widows and orphans.* Avoid any page break that leaves a single line of a paragraph at the top or bottom of a page. This can be done automatically by setting the "widows and orphans" or "keep together" preferences in your word-processing program.

Headings

4.20 Make the hierarchy of headings clear to the reader by using a combination of outlining tags, capitalization style, type style, and type size.

(a) *Outlining tags.* Use a conventional outlining style, being certain that it matches any table of contents in the document. The traditional outlining style <I–A–1–(a)> is most recognizable and is used almost universally in judicial opinions and most other types of expository prose in law.

Ex.: I. The Contract-Interpretation Claims
A. Applicable Legal Principles
1. The Determination of Ambiguity Is a Question of Law

(b) *Decimal tags for legal drafting.* In transactional documents and other types of legal drafting, a modified decimal-numbering system is generally easiest to follow, since virtually every paragraph is numbered. For the recommended form, see 20.3(d).

(c) *Capitalization.* In general, all caps is acceptable only for a major section heading that is a short phrase and never more than one line. For all other headings and subheadings, use up-style (see 2.10)—or even sentence format if the heading is bold.

(d) *Type style.* Using boldface type—or even a boldface sans-serif face with a serif body type—is a good way to make sure that headings stand out from the text.

(e) *Type size.* It is acceptable to set main headings in 14-point type, even if the body copy is smaller. But the slight change in size is hardly noticeable to the reader.

(f) *Combining techniques.* Most legal writers use more than one technique to create a hierarchy of headings. A typical choice is boldface caps for a main heading, boldface initial caps for the next level, and boldface italics for subheadings, all with outlining tags.

(g) *Number of levels.* Limit the number of heading levels to no more than four; use just three if possible. The more levels there are, the harder it is for the reader to recognize where in the outline of the argument a heading fits.

(h) *Progressive indents.* Avoid the practice, common in legal writing, of using progressively larger left-side indents to signify the hierarchy of headings. It is especially inappropriate because lower-level headings tend to become longer, yet with this technique they are forced into many short lines crowded onto the right-hand side of the page.

4.21 Except for short top-level section headings, which may be centered, prefer headings to be set flush left and single-spaced, with a tight hanging indent.

(a) *Centering.* Main section headings, such as "STATEMENT OF FACTS," are best set centered on one line in boldfaced caps.

(b) *Flush left.* All headings except main section headings are best set flush left, especially if they are longer than one line.

(c) *Single-spaced.* Even if the text of a document is double-spaced, always single-space headings.

(d) *Hanging indent.* Use a narrow hanging indent between the outline tag and the text of a heading.

4.22 Use headings and subheadings to create white space and to help the reader follow the structure of the argument. Use a little extra space above a main heading to indicate a major break.

(a) *Reader cues.* The white space around headings and subheadings will make the structure of your document more visible. It will help readers see your organizational structure and give them a moment to rest and think about the point they have just read before continuing to the next one.

(b) *Spacing of headings.* Use an extra line or half-line of space above headings; the distance helps cue readers to expect a change of subject.

(c) *Subheadings.* Easy-to-notice subheadings break long text blocks into a series of smaller, bite-sized chunks. They make long messages easier to read. Use subheadings liberally—every few paragraphs—to help readers find what they're looking for. Do not put extra space above them; reserve that technique for main headings (see 4.6(d)).

> "Simple prose is clear prose. And simple prose, if smooth and rhythmical, is readable prose. Let your ideas alone do the impressing. If they look banal to you, there's only one remedy: upgrade them. Don't try to camouflage their weakness with razzle-dazzle rhetoric. You'll razzle-dazzle yourself right into a bog of bull."
>
> —*John R. Trimble*

§ 5
Numbers

5.1 Deciding whether to use numerals or to spell out numbers in text is usually a matter of setting a style and sticking with it. There is no right and wrong; consistency is all any reader can ask for. But there are some general principles.

First, the most formal writing prefers to spell out numbers: on a wedding invitation, for example, even the year, the date, and the time of day are spelled out. Legal writing is formal, and many lawyers follow the academic-writing convention of spelling out numbers up to 100.

But that style is in tension with the modern trend of using numerals for all but the smallest numbers. Most newspapers, for instance, spell out numbers only up to 10. The popular trend has one overwhelming advantage over the academic tradition: it's much easier to read numerals than spelled-out numbers.

5.2 **Be consistent about when to use numerals and when to spell out numbers in text—preferably spelling out one to nine and using numerals for 10 and above.**

(a) *Main conventions.* The two main style conventions are to spell out numbers of either one or two digits—that is, either up to nine or else up to 99—and to use numerals for larger numbers. The practice applies to ordinal numbers (first, second, 23d) as well as cardinal numbers (one, two, 23).

Ex.: Edward Shelley had two sons: Henry was his first son and Richard his second.

Ex.: No interest is good unless it must vest, if at all, not later than 21 years after some life in being at the creation of the interest.

(b) *Other conventions.* Other conventions also exist, including (1) spelling out numbers below 11 (or 101), and (2) spelling out numbers through 12 (common with ordinal street names). If your organization or practice area prefers a particular convention, then follow it. Whatever style you decide on, use it consistently.

(c) *Numerals in citations.* The style applies only to numbers in text; numbers in citations are always written as numerals unless they are part of a title.

(d) *In titles.* Repeat a title as it is written, regardless of what convention you use for your own text.

Ex.: She was reading *The 7 Habits of Highly Effective People.*

Ex.: Gabriel Garcia Marquez, *One Hundred Years of Solitude* 56 (1998).

5.3 If one item of a kind should be in numerals, then use numerals for all items of that kind in the immediate context.

(a) *In series.* If one item in a series should be in numerals, use numerals for all the items.

Ex.: The convicted robber drew concurrent sentences of 8, 8, and 12 years for the three incidents.

(b) *In proximity.* Even if not strictly in series, numbers that denote the same type of thing should usually be in the same format. But be reasonable and ignore this guidance if the result would be absurd.

Ex.: In 1960 there were 5 lawyers in this county; today there are 125.

Ex.: You can't see the next town, which is just five miles down the road, but you can see the sun, which is 93 million miles away.

5.4 If two numbers that are not of the same kind appear next to each other, one (usually the first) should be spelled out to avoid confusion.

(a) *First number.* Usually, it is the first number that must be spelled out.

Ex.: The package contained fifty $20 bills. (Normally, we would write *50.*)

(b) *Second number.* But if the second number is an ordinal or part of an adjective phrase, it may be spelled out instead.

Ex.: We have 256 one-L students this year. (But: We have three 1L representatives on the Student Bar Association.)

Ex.: The team's roster swelled with 17 second-round draftees.

Ex.: We are honoring fifteen 4.0-GPA graduates today.

5.5 Avoid beginning a sentence with a number; if you must use a number to begin a sentence, spell it out.

(a) *Start of sentence.* No matter what numbering convention you use, always spell out a number at the beginning of the sentence.

Ex.: Eleven months and 29 days later, the plaintiff filed this suit.

(b) *Years.* Avoid starting a sentence with a year; if you must, spell it out.

Not this: 1935 saw the passage of the Social Security Act.

Better: Nineteen thirty-five saw the passage of the Social Security Act.

Best: The Social Security Act passed in 1935.

(c) *Citation.* The caveat against starting a sentence with a number holds even if the number is part of a citation. Rewrite around the problem.

Not this: 18 U.S.C. § 2511(2)(a)(i) authorizes the company to monitor employee e-mail in order to enforce company policy.

But this: Federal law authorizes the company to monitor employee e-mail in order to enforce company policy. 18 U.S.C. § 2511(2)(a)(i).

Or this: Federal law authorizes the company to monitor employee e-mail traffic in order to enforce company policy.[5] (Citation in footnote.)

5.6 Use numerals for statute, volume, chapter, and section numbers; in tables; in dates and times; for money; with units of measurement; in decimals; and in names of roads, military divisions, and the like.

(a) *Count and series.* In general, numerals are used with count nouns and where the numbers appear in series.

Ex.: Title 28 of the U.S. Code

Ex.: § 1983

Ex.: Chapter 11

Ex.: July 4, 1776 (but *the Fourth of July* as the holiday)

Ex.: 5:15 p.m. (but *five o'clock shadow*)

Ex.: $6.99

Ex.: 6%

Ex.: 32°F

Ex.: 1.414

Ex.: I-95

(b) *Exceptions for names.* Some names contain numerals or spelled-out numbers; others are spelled out by convention. Use the preferred name despite any style rule to the contrary.

Ex.: 1st Infantry Division (but *The Big Red One*)

Ex.: First Division, Army of Northern Virginia

Ex.: the Fourteenth Amendment (by convention)

Ex.: the Eleventh Circuit

(c) *Other exceptions.* By convention, the ordinal designations of centuries and of amendments to the U.S. Constitution are spelled out.

Ex.: twentieth century

Ex.: Fourteenth Amendment

5.7 Spell out a large number that is used as an exaggeration or an idiomatic phrase.

(a) *Exactness not implied.* Using numerals may suggest a precision that is absent when words such as *hundreds* are used loosely.

Ex.: Although the plaintiff claims he was in great pain, he drove past a hundred doctors' offices before stopping at one.

Ex.: I've told you a thousand times.

(b) *In slogans.* The same is true with slogans: because exactness is not implied, spelling out is more appropriate than using numerals.

Ex.: President Bush the senior presented awards to many of the "thousand points of light" for their volunteer work.

Ex.: McDonald's boasts of "billions and billions served."

5.8 For a number in the millions or more (especially if precision is not required), round it off and spell out *million, billion,* etc.

(a) *Comprehension.* Smaller numbers are much easier to work with, for both the reader and the writer.

Ex.: A Middleton County jury awarded the plaintiff $210,000 in compensatory damages and slapped a $2 million punitive-damages verdict on the defendant.

(b) *Rounding off.* If more precision is called for, round off the number to one or (at most) two decimal places.

Ex.: Congress allocated $2.6 billion for research on the secret project.

(c) *Dollar sign and word.* If the number is money, use either a symbol in front of the number or the corresponding word after the amount, but not both.

Not this: $1 trillion dollars

But this: $1 trillion

(d) *When precision counts.* If precision is required, give the exact number.

Ex.: The Franks sold the property in 1995 for $1,147,900.

5.9 In legal writing, spell the ordinal numerals *2d* and *3d,* not *2nd* and *3rd.*

(a) *Legal convention.* This legal convention applies as well to larger numbers ending in 2 and 3.

Ex.: *Lee v. Bankers Trust Co.*, 166 F.3d 540 (2d Cir. 1999).

Ex.: The law was passed by the 92d Congress.

(b) *General convention.* Outside legal contexts, use the generally accepted spellings, *2nd* and *3rd.*

Ex.: The picketers joined hands and recited the 23rd Psalm as police began to make arrests.

Ex.: The musical is playing in a theater on 42nd Street.

(c) *Other ordinals.* All other ordinals, such as 1st, 4th, etc., follow the normal conventions.

Ex.: The law was passed by the 101st Congress.

5.10 Be careful not to allow any ambiguity when writing numbers.

(a) *"K" and "M."* In business writing, $25K may be understood to mean $25,000 and 2M to mean 2 million. But in other trade usages, *M* stands for *thousand* (its value as a Roman numeral). Since there is a possibility of ambiguity, numerical abbreviations should never be used in legal writing.

(b) *Billion and larger.* Be explicit when referring to numbers of a billion and larger; although the U.S. definition is dominant in the world of finance, British usage has traditionally set the value of a billion at 1,000 times greater than the number denoted by American usage (what Americans call a trillion), and a trillion at the value that Americans call a quintillion.

5.11 Use a comma to separate large whole-number digits into sets of three, from the right; but do not use commas in room numbers, telephone numbers, highway numbers, military time, years, or other serial numbers, or in page numbers and paragraph numbers shorter than five digits.

(a) *For thousands.* While some style guides make the comma in a four-digit number optional, it has to be used sometimes (e.g., in a table that contains one or more numerals of five digits or more). To maintain a consistent style, the better choice is to use the comma all the time.

Ex.: 1,000 clowns

Ex.: 93,000,000 miles

(b) *Exceptions.* Do not use commas in serial-type numbers, such as rooms, addresses, phone numbers, road numbers, years, product serial numbers, and the like (see 1.11(b)).

Ex.: 1600 Pennsylvania Avenue

Ex.: Room 1408

Ex.: 555-1212

Ex.: Farm Road 2222

Ex.: AM 1520

Ex.: 1700 hours

Ex.: A.D. 2002

Ex.: 123-45-6789

(c) *Citation numbers.* Do not use a comma in a page number or paragraph number unless the number contains five or more digits.

Ex.: 799 F.2d 1219

Ex.: *Id.* at 1537

Ex.: *Id.* at 15,442

(d) *Not in decimals.* Do not use commas after a decimal point.

Ex.: 3.14159

5.12 Use an en dash (or a hyphen) to signal an inclusive range of numbers; avoid the word *from* or *between* in front of the numbers (see 1.53).

(a) *Using "from" and "between."* The punctuation often stands for *from . . . to* or *between . . . and*, and it includes both numbers. Use either the mark or the words; avoid *from* and *between* with the mark.

Ex.: The discussion can be found on pages 25–27.

Ex.: The United States fought in World War II from 1941 to 1945.

Ex.: Nixon's 1969–1974 tenure was marked by diplomatic achievements and domestic controversy.

(b) *Unit of measurement.* When expressing a range of numbers in legal writing, it is acceptable to use a unit of measurement once, following the numerals. But it is not acceptable to use a numerical term in the same way, because the result is ambiguous.

Ex.: The plot was 140 by 210 feet.

Ex.: The project is expected to cost $30 million–$40 million. (Not *$30–$40 million.*)

(c) *Or hyphen.* An en dash is better than a hyphen for this purpose, but either mark is acceptable.

5.13 Be careful about using apostrophes with numbers.

(a) *Plurals.* A numeral's plural is formed by adding *-s* alone.

Ex.: The top scorers included three 143s, four 157s, and one 161.

Ex.: 1920s

Ex.: The robber was described as in his 40s.

(b) *Possessives.* Although it is an uncommon form, possessive numbers must and do use apostrophes.

Ex.: We look back at 1941's Day of Infamy for guidance.

5.14 Elide to two digits the second number in a range of pages if the numbers are three or more digits long; but do not elide numbers in a range of sections or paragraphs, a range of measurements, or a span of years (see 8.12).

(a) *Rules.* Legal style does not allow the elision of two-digit page numbers. Larger numbers are elided to two digits.

Ex.: 893 F.2d at 1106–07 (not 1106–7)

Ex.: 56 Fed. Reg. at 42,997–99

But: 56 Fed. Reg. at 42,997–43,000

(b) *Not with measurements.* Unlike page numbers, which are referred to only from the smaller number to the larger, measurements may go from the lesser to the greater or vice versa. Elision is never appropriate because of the possible ambiguity.

Ex.: The high temperatures reached 115–119 degrees. (Not *115–19 degrees.*)

(c) *Sections and paragraphs.* Retain all digits in ranges of sections and paragraphs.

Ex.: 42 U.S.C. §§ 12701–12714

Ex.: Miller Aff. ¶¶ 101–102

(d) *Not with years.* By convention, do not elide the second number in a span of years.

Ex.: Andrew Johnson (1808–1875)

5.15 Use the simplest appropriate forms for times, dates, and money.

(a) *Unless needed for accuracy.* Do not use the minutes to write an even hour—or the cents to write an even dollar amount—unless the extra numbers are needed for accuracy or to match a related reference nearby.

Ex.: Krol left his house at 6 a.m. to drive to work.

Ex.: Krol was out of the house from 6:00 a.m. until he returned from work at 3:45 p.m.

Ex.: The 911 call was placed at 3:47 p.m.

Ex.: A $10 bill was left on the counter.

Ex.: The check was for exactly $10.37.

(b) *Relative time references.* When the date is important, make sure that the complete date is stated explicitly. But once it is established, avoid repeating the year, or even the month, on every subsequent reference. Narrative phrases such as "two weeks later" are more helpful to the reader than a series of dates.

5.16 When spelling out numbers, hyphenate only the two-word numbers below 100; do not use *and* except when expressing cents.

(a) *Hyphen alone.* Do not use *and* to join parts of a whole number.

Ex.: She wrote the check for one hundred seventy-three dollars.

Ex.: Two hundred seventy electoral votes are needed to win.

(b) *With "and."* Use *and* to join the whole part of a number with a fraction.

Ex.: She wrote the check for one hundred seventy-three and 47/100 dollars.

Ex.: The LP spins at thirty-three and a third rpm.

5.17 Hyphenate fractions unless one of the terms is itself hyphenated (see 1.58).

(a) *Generally.* Hyphenate fractions regardless of whether they are serving as nouns or adjectives in the sentence.

Ex.: Two-tenths of a mile of skid marks led to the accident site.

Ex.: A two-thirds majority is needed to override a veto.

(b) *Big fractions.* Do not hyphenate between the numerator and denominator of a fraction if either of those terms itself contains a hyphen.

Ex.: The manufacturer has long claimed that its soap is "ninety-nine and forty-four one-hundredths percent pure."

> "The real reason for good usage in writing is that if you do not achieve it, your educated reader will be thinking of you, not of the point you're trying to make."
>
> —*John W. Velz*

5.18 Use Roman numerals sparingly and according to convention.

(a) *Successors.* Roman numerals are used in names, to differentiate successors. Do not use a comma to separate the number from the name unless that is the person's preference.

Ex.: Loudon Wainwright III

Ex.: Pope John Paul II

(b) *Outlines.* Roman numerals are also used in traditional outlines.

Ex.: IV. Statement of Facts

(c) *Front matter.* Use lowercase Roman numerals (*romanettes*) to number pages in the front matter of a book.

Ex.: The foreword begins on page ix.

(d) *Miscellaneous uses.* Roman numerals are also used in various other ways, according to convention.

Ex.: Super Bowl XXXVI

Ex.: MCMXXXIV (dates in movie credits)

> "If you can't always cut the baloney and write in plain English, just do it whenever you can. Choose the simple, concrete word over the mushy, complicated one every time you can."
>
> —*Patricia T. O'Conner*

§ 6
Typographic Symbols

6.1 The section sign (§) and paragraph sign (¶) see more use in legal writing than anywhere else. Other symbols are used less frequently in legal writing than in general writing.

A symbol is effective only if the reader instantly recognizes it. For that reason alone, you would be hard-pressed to find a section or paragraph mark in the mass media. Yet lawyers see them every day.

It is this instant recognition that makes a symbol work for the writer. How much easier is it to recognize *$2.57* than *two dollars and fifty-seven cents, 28%* than *28 percent* or *twenty-eight percent, 75°F* than *75 degrees Fahrenheit* or *seventy-five degrees Fahrenheit*?

Some legal stylists insist that section and paragraph symbols should be restricted to citations only, and should never appear in text. But where they help the reader and do not violate any other rules (such as appearing at the beginning of a sentence), they are helpful shortcuts.

6.2 When referring to a specific section or paragraph number, use the symbol § (section) or ¶ (paragraph) in text and citations, unless the symbol would start a sentence.

(a) *Legal convention.* In legal writing, the symbols § and ¶ are as recognizable as the symbols % and $ are in popular writing. Because their use facilitates rather than inhibits comprehension, the symbols are stronger than the spelled-out terms. Always use a nonbreaking space, or "hard space," between the symbol and the number that follows (see 4.13).

Ex.: The Cooperative contends, however, that despite the apparently absolute language of § 823(f), the statute is subject to additional, implied exceptions, one of which is medical necessity.

Ex.: This dispute arises under ¶ 36 of the contract, governing periodic payments for supplies and materials.

(b) *Beginning sentence.* Always spell out the word when it begins a sentence.

Ex.: Section 1983 was enacted by Congress as part of the Ku Klux Klan Act of 1871.

Ex.: Paragraph 52 is a liquidated-damages clause, but ¶ 53 provides for injunctive relief.

6.3 Pluralize a typographic symbol by doubling it. So when referring to two or more sections or paragraphs, use the double symbol §§ or ¶¶.

(a) *In citations.* Form the plural of a symbol used in a citation by doubling the symbol. If the symbol is a letter followed by a period (such as *p.* or *n.*), double the letter and retain the period.

Ex.: Weil contended that Jalyn's actions infringed its trademark rights in violation of §§ 32(1)(a) and 42 of the Lanham Act.

Ex.: p. 36 (singular); pp. 36–42 (plural)

Ex.: pp. 36 ff.

Ex.: n. 14 (singular); nn. 14–15 (plural) (In *Bluebook* style, n.14 and nn.14–15.)

(b) *Exception with subsections.* Use a single symbol to cite multiple subsections within the same section.

Ex.: § 42(1)(a), (2), (5)(b).

(c) *Sequences.* Because *et seq.* refers to multiple sections or paragraphs, it requires the plural form §§ or ¶¶. But the use of *et seq.* is poor form that is forbidden in legal citation (*Bluebook* Rule 3.4(b)) and elsewhere (*Chicago Manual of Style*, 14th ed., § 17.9). Cite the whole reference instead.

6.4 Use the symbols $, ¢, %, and ° with numerals in text; spell out the word when used alone.

(a) *Commonly understood.* When used with numerals, the symbols for dollars, cents, percentages, and degrees are more easily comprehended than the spelled-out terms they stand for. The symbol should be preferred in text. Do not use a space between the symbol and the figure.

Ex.: My torts casebook cost $70.

Ex.: I ate a 99¢ hot dog for lunch.

Ex.: Becca got 40% of the vote in the Student Bar election.

Ex.: It must be 100° outside.

> "The kind of writing instruction most of us have gotten in school is exactly the reverse of what we need. Instead of teaching us how to communicate as clearly as possible, our schooling in English teaches us how to fog things up. It even implants a fear that if we don't make our writing complicated enough, we'll be considered uneducated."
>
> —*John L. Beckley*

(b) *Spelling out.* When the number is spelled out, as when it falls at the beginning of a sentence or when it is used inexactly, the word that the symbol stands for must also be spelled out.

Ex.: Seventy dollars is a lot to pay for a schoolbook.

Ex.: Ninety-nine cents isn't cheap for a hot dog if you have to kick in another buck for antacids.

Ex.: Forty percent of the vote was enough to get Becca into a runoff.

Ex.: The locals say that hundred-degree temperatures are normal for this time of year.

(c) *Range.* When a range is expressed by two numerals, repeat the symbol.

Ex.: The company enjoyed a 15%–20% increase in sales in each of its first three years.

Ex.: Price cuts ranged from 25¢ to 40¢ per unit.

Ex.: The more powerful chip increased internal heat by 2°–4°F.

(d) *Foot, inch marks.* Do not use "smart quotes" for foot and inch symbols. The correct marks are the prime and double-prime (′ for foot, ″ for inch). As an acceptable substitute, you may use straight "typewriter-style" quotation marks (' for foot, " for inch).

Best: The skid marks were measured at 8′4″.

Acceptable: The skid marks were measured at 8'4".

Unacceptable: The skid marks were measured at 8’4”.

(e) *"At" symbol.* Use the @ ("at") symbol only in e-mail addresses.

Ex.: attorney@lawfirm.com

6.5 Use an ampersand only in a business name.

(a) *Not a general substitute.* The ampersand is not acceptable as a general substitute for the word *and* except in the most informal writing, such as hastily handwritten notes. But it is required when writing of a business or firm that includes it in its formal name.

Ex.: Procter & Gamble

Ex.: Pulaski Bank & Trust Co.

Ex.: ATMP Oil & Gas

Ex.: Thompson & Knight, P.C.

(b) *In case names.* An ampersand may substitute for *and* in a party's abbreviated name, even if the word *and* is otherwise spelled out.

Ex.: Scrooge and Marley, L.L.P.

Ex.: *Scrooge & Marley, L.L.P. v. Cratchit*

6.6 Do not use a trademark or copyright symbol in text.

(a) *Purpose.* The purpose of intellectual-property symbols is to let the owner put the public on notice that the work is protected. There is no legal requirement that the symbol be reproduced every time the protected mark appears in copy, and to do so would be distracting. The trademarked word should be capitalized, but no symbol should be used.

Ex.: Hard Rock owns the rights to a variety of Hard Rock trademarks.

Ex.: Handmacher–Vogel, Inc. owns Registration No. 554,949, comprising the word "Weathervane," coupled with the representation of a weathervane, for women's suits.

(b) *Significance.* The ® symbol signifies that the trademark or servicemark is registered. The ™ symbol signifies an unregistered trademark, and the ℠ symbol signifies an unregistered servicemark.

(c) *Copyright notice.* The copyright symbol © should be used only in a copyright notice line, not in text. The U.S. Copyright Office accepts either of the following forms for the notice:

Ex.: © 2002 by West Group

Ex.: Copyright 2002 by West Group

> "One can no more write good English than one can compose good music merely by keeping the rules. On the whole they are aids to writing intelligibly, for they are in the main no more than the distillation of successful experiments made by writers of English through the centuries in how best to handle words so as to make a writer's meaning plain."
>
> —*Sir Ernest Gowers*

§ 7
Spelling

7.1 The very thing that makes English such a rich language also makes its spelling so difficult. Words have entered modern English from many sources and different systems of spelling. They have brought their own pronunciations, too, so phonetics is often an unreliable spelling aid.

The result of this mishmash is that for every "rule" of spelling there are usually many exceptions. Still, there are some basic rules of spelling that come in handy over and over again. And there are more general guidelines as well, such as for compounding words and using hyphens with certain prefixes.

But when it comes to spelling, there is no alternative to looking it up in a dictionary. No writer should hesitate to do so if there is any doubt about the correct spelling of a word. After all, misspelled words in a legal document signal an unacceptable sloppiness that can quickly undermine the writer's credibility.

General Principles

7.2 Always use your computer's spell-checker, but never rely on it.

(a) *Generally.* Get to know your computer's spell-checker, and especially how to add to and edit its custom dictionaries. Words (and names) that your computer flags over and over again—but that you know are spelled correctly—should be added to a custom dictionary.

(b) *Self-check.* Make a habit of checking your spelling every time you enter new copy or edit existing drafts. The best routine is to save the file one last time (having saved regularly while working on the document), then run the spell-check, and finally close the file, saving changes.

(c) *Proofreaders.* Do not rely solely on the computer's spell-checker; it's no substitute for human eyes. Invariably, the more eyes that see a draft, the better. Your work product reflects your level of professionalism, and neglectful errors signal anything but rigorous work habits.

(d) *Autocorrection.* By the same token, be cautious about allowing your word-processing software to make automatic corrections. There's always a "failure rate" with lists of automatic substitutions, and the practice can introduce errors.

7.3 Use an up-to-date dictionary; preferably, everyone in an organization should use the same one.

(a) *Current edition.* Language changes, especially when it comes to compound words and new terms. Buy the current edition of a good dictionary and stick to it as your standard. *Merriam-Webster's Collegiate Dictionary* and *Webster's New World Dictionary* are the best. *The American Heritage Dictionary* and the *New Oxford American Dictionary* are also first-rate. For legal terminology, consult the unabridged *Black's Law Dictionary* (7th ed. 1999).

(b) *Uniformity.* It's a good office policy to have a standard dictionary that everyone uses. This is an inexpensive and easy way to ensure consistency in office writings.

7.4 Keep a list of the words you have trouble with; update it regularly and keep it handy.

(a) *Troublesome words.* We all struggle with certain words. Keep a file of your own troublesome words on your computer. If you have to look up a word more than once, add it to the list.

(b) *Ease of reference.* Sort the list in alphabetical order, and keep a printout handy beside your computer or in your desk. Not only is consulting your personal crib sheet faster than consulting a dictionary, but the effort you take to add a word to the list will itself help you learn the spelling once and for all.

7.5 Know the elementary spelling rules.

(a) *"I" before "e."* We all remember the rule: "*i* before *e*, except after *c*, or when sounded like *a*, as in *neighbor* and *weigh*" <piece> <conceive>. But there are many exceptions: *codeine, counterfeit, either, feisty, foreign, forfeit, height, heir, leisure, neither, protein, seize, sovereign, weird*; words from the French such as *caffeine*; and words from the German such as *braumeister, poltergeist,* and *stein.*

(b) *Silent "-e" and suffixes.* Drop the silent *-e* at the end of a word before adding a suffix that starts with a vowel <refine–refinery–refinement>.

- By convention (and to keep the rule consistent), consider the silent *-e* dropped even if its replacement is still silent <refined>.
- If the silent *-e* is preceded by a vowel, the *-e* is dropped even if the suffix starts with a consonant <argue–argued–argument>.
- The most common exceptions to the rule crop up (1) where the silent *-e* is preceded by a soft *-c-* or *-g-*, in order to preserve the pronunciation <commence–commencement> <manage–management> (but the rule is preserved where the pronunciation is not threatened, as the *-dg-* accomplishes in *abridgment, drudgery,* and *judgment*); (2) where the

form might be confused with other words <dyeing> <singeing>; (3) where the word ends in *-ee*, *-ye*, or *-oe* <freeing (but *freed*)> <eyeing (but *eyed*)> <canoeing (but *canoed*)>; and (4) where the word ends in *-ie* <lie–lying (but *lied*)> <die–dying (but *died*)>.

(c) *"-y" ending and suffixes.* When adding a suffix to a word that ends in *-y* preceded by a consonant:

- if the suffix is *-ing*, just add the suffix <burying>; but
- if the suffix is anything else, change the *-y* to *-i* <buried> <buries>.

(d) *Doubling consonants.* Double the final consonant before adding a suffix if:

- the word ends with a single consonant (other than *-w* or *-x*) preceded by a single vowel; and
- it is a single-syllable word, or if it is a multisyllable word and the final syllable is accented both before and after the suffix is added (hence *referred* but *reference*); and
- the suffix begins with a vowel <commit–committee–commitment> <defer–deferral–deferment> *but* <travel–traveler–traveling> (accent on first syllable); <deal–dealer–dealing> (final consonant preceded by two vowels).

(e) *"-ic" ending and suffixes.* Add a *-k-* to a word ending in *-ic* before appending a suffix that starts with a vowel <trafficker> <panicky> <picnicking> *but* <frolicsome> (suffix starts with a consonant).

7.6 Avoid hyphens with most prefixes and suffixes (but see 1.61).

(a) *Modern trend.* While there are exceptions—and you should consult a dictionary if in doubt—the modern trend is away from hyphenating prefixes. For most words, that principle carries even if the prefix ends with the same letter that begins the main word <nonnative> <neoorthodoxy> <reelect> .

(b) *Proper nouns.* A hyphen is always required when joining a prefix to a proper noun <pro-American> <pre-Columbian> <inter-European>.

(c) *Mandatory prefixes.* A hyphen is almost always required with the prefixes *self-* <self-serving> (the exception to the exception is *selfsame*), *all-* <all-consuming>, *ex-* <ex-governor>, and *quasi-* <quasi-contract>.

(d) *For clarity.* A hyphen may be needed to prevent a misreading <pre-sent> <re-lease> <un-ionized>.

(e) *With numerals.* A hyphen is used between a prefix and a date or other numeral <post-2000> <sub-0° F>.

(f) *Proper names.* A hyphen is used to combine two proper names into a single label <Italian-American>. But an en dash is used instead when the purpose is to indicate equal status <Taft–Hartley Act> (see 1.54(a), 7.19).

(g) *With hyphenated phrases.* A hyphen is used to join a prefix to a phrasal adjective <non-life-threatening> <pro-right-to-work>. Although some typesetters use an en dash after the prefix in such a phrasal adjective, the result looks overfussy and confuses some readers.

(h) *Suffixes.* Generally, do not use a hyphen between a word and its suffix. Two exceptions are: (1) when the result would otherwise repeat the same letter three times <childlike; *but* quill-like>, and (2) with the suffix *-wise* in an adjective <penny-wise> but not in an adverb <otherwise>.

Plurals

7.7 Form the plural of most regular nouns by adding *-s* or *-es*.

(a) *Basic rule.* The simple plural form is the suffix *-s* <facts> <suits>.

(b) *Sibilant endings.* When the word already ends in *-s* or another sibilant sound (*-z*, *-x*, *-sh*, *-ch*):

- if the word ends in a consonant, add *-es* <boxes> <benches>; or
- if the word ends in a silent *-e*, drop the *-e* and add *-es* (note that the *-e* is now pronounced) <cases> <judges>.

(c) *"-y" ending.* If the word ends in *-y* preceded by a consonant, change the *-y* to *-i* before adding *-es* <jury–juries>. A common exception: *monies* is considered a passable but poor substitute for *moneys.*

(d) *"-o" ending.* If the word ends in *-o*, check a dictionary if you're not sure of the plural form because there are many exceptions.

- Generally, if the final *-o* is preceded by a vowel, add *-s* to form the plural <trios> <zoos>; by a consonant, add *-es* <heroes> <tomatoes>.
- But many consonant-*o* words take *-s* alone <bozos> <silos>—many musical terms fall under this exception <pianos> <solos>.
- Many words can take either form <mottos–mottoes> <lassos–lassoes>—and some can take even a third form <buffaloes–buffalos–buffalo>.
- Words that appear in the plural as often as in the singular tend to take the *-oes* ending <dominoes> <peccadilloes>.
- Foreign terms, proper names, and shortened terms tend to take the *-os* ending <gazebos> <Cheerios> <limos>.

(e) *"-f" or "-fe" ending.* If the word ends in *-f* or *-fe* (but not *-ff*), change that ending to *-v* and add *-es* <scarf–scarves> <knife–knives>. But this rule also has many exceptions <roof–roofs> <safe–safes>, so unless you're sure of the spelling, consult a dictionary.

(f) *Irregular words.* If the word is irregular, the plural may be formed by changing vowels <foot–feet> <woman–women>, and sometimes consonants <mouse–mice>; for a few words, by adding *-en* <ox–oxen> or *-ren* <child–children>; and, for even fewer words, by doing both <brother–brethren>.

(g) *Proper names.* For proper names, follow the rule for regular forms, but do not change a final *-y* to *-i* <the Dalys> <four Marys>. By convention, a few exceptions exist <the Rockies>. Do not make the common error of using an apostrophe to form the plural of a name.

7.8 Check the spelling of the plural forms of foreign terms; in most instances, prefer the anglicized form if one is available.

(a) *"-is" ending.* Many foreign terms that end in *-is* form the plural by changing the ending to *-es* <crisis–crises> <parenthesis–parentheses>.

(b) *"-um" ending.* Many foreign terms that end in *-um* form the plural by changing the ending to *-a* <bacterium–bacteria> <medium–media>. But most of these words have become anglicized and now have regular plural forms <forum–forums> <stadium–stadiums>. Many can take either form <curriculum–curricula–curriculums> <memorandum–memoranda–memorandums>, often according to the field they are used in. When in doubt, use the regular English form ending in *-s*.

(c) *"-us" ending.* Many foreign terms that end in *-us* form the plural by changing the ending to *-i* <alumnus–alumni> <radius–radii>. But most of these words have become anglicized and now have regular plural forms <focus–focuses> <prospectus–prospectuses>. Many can take either form <cactus–cactuses–cacti> <fungus–funguses–fungi>, often according to the field they are used in. A few foreign terms that end in *-us* form the plural without any change in form <apparatus–apparatus>. Still others change the ending to *-era* or *-ora* <opus–opera> <genus–genera>. Of these, some are anglicized and accept the standard plural form as well <corpus–corpora–corpuses>. Avoid incorrect classical forms such as *octopi* (the correct English plural is *octopuses*, the classical plural being *octopodes*).

(d) *"-a" ending.* Many foreign terms that end in *-a* form the plural by changing the ending to *-ae* <alumna–alumnae> <alga–algae>. But most of these words have become anglicized and now have regular plural forms <cornea–corneas> <encyclopedia–encyclopedias>. Many can take either form <formula–formulas–formulae> <antenna–antennas–antennae>, often according to the field they are used in.

(e) *"-on" ending.* Many foreign terms that end in *-on* form the plural by changing the ending to *-a* <phenomenon–phenomena> <criterion–criteria>. These words sometimes confuse writers because the plural form, which dominates in usage, looks like the singular form described in 7.8(d), so there is a mistaken tendency to add an *-s* to the already plural form to derive, e.g., *phenomenas*, a nonword.

(f) *"-ex" or "-ix" ending.* Many foreign words that end in *-ex* or *-ix* form the classical plural by changing the ending to *-ices* <index–indices> <appendix–appendices>; but it is usually preferable to use the anglicized *-es* form <indexes> <appendixes>.

(g) *"-eau" ending.* A few foreign terms that end in *-eau* form the plural by changing the ending to *-eaux*, but they may take the regular anglicized plural form as well <bureau–bureaux–bureaus> <tableau–tableaux–tableaus>.

(h) *Retained forms.* Other foreign terms retain their form from the Italian <graffito–graffiti>, Greek <stigma–stigmata>, Hebrew <cherub–cherubim>, and other languages.

7.9 In general, form the plural of a compound noun by pluralizing the main element.

(a) *Equivalents.* If both elements of the compound are nouns of roughly equal importance, and especially if the word is closed (not written as two words or hyphenated), pluralize the last element <handcuffs> <county jails>.

(b) *Noun and modifier.* But if the open compound comprises a noun followed by a modifier, the noun takes the plural form (this often occurs in legal terms taken from the French) <attorneys general> <mothers-in-law> <notaries public> <attorneys-at-law>.

(c) *Noun and particle.* If the compound is a noun with a preposition particle, the noun usually takes the plural form <passers-by> <hangers-on>.

(d) *Verb and particle.* But if the nominal compound is a verb with an adverb particle, the plural form falls at the end of the word <runoffs> <sit-ins>.

(e) *Particle first.* And if the particle precedes the noun or nominal verb, the plural falls at the end of the word <undercurrents> <overruns>.

(f) *"-ful" ending.* Pluralize words ending in *-ful* by adding *-s* to the end of the suffix <handfuls>; but if the full adverb *full* is used instead, pluralize the noun <hands full>.

7.10 Follow a consistent style in forming the plurals of letters, words used as words (rather than for their meaning), numbers, and abbreviations.

(a) *Letters.* Form the plural of a single lowercase letter by setting the letter in italics and appending an unitalicized *-'s* <*p*'s and *q*'s>.

(b) *Words as words.* Form the plural of a word used as a word (rather than for its meaning) by italicizing the word and appending an unitalicized *-s* or *-es* <there are three *word*s in that sentence>.

(c) *Numbers.* Form the plural of numbers by adding *-s* without an apostrophe <the 1990s> <afternoon temperatures in the 70s>. Note that some style manuals recommend using *-'s* in these constructions, but the modern trend is toward the simpler style.

(d) *Initialisms.* Form the plural of acronyms and initialisms; words that began as acronyms; and capitalized, unpunctuated abbreviations by adding *-s* (with no apostrophe) <IOUs> <IPOs> <lasers> <CDs>.

(e) *Abbreviations.* Form the plural of abbreviations that require periods or that consist of all lowercase letters by adding *-'s* <J.D.'s> <r.p.m.'s> <pdf's>.

(f) *Citations.* Form the plural of one-letter abbreviations in citations (*l.* for line, *n.* for note, *p.* for page, *v.* for volume) by doubling the letter <pp. 10–12> <nn. 4–7>.

(g) *Measurements.* Do not change the form of measurement abbreviations used in the plural <10 yd> <4 mi>.

Possessives

7.11 Add *-'s* to the end of a word to form the possessive of (1) a singular noun, or (2) a plural noun that does not end in an *s* or *z* sound.

(a) *Basic rule.* This is the general rule <boy's> <girl's> <children's> <women's>.

(b) *Sibilant endings.* It holds true for singular nouns even if the base word ends in *-s* or even *-ss* <witness's>, and is preferred even when it results in a triple sibilant sound <princess's>.

(c) *Names.* Except for some ancient names (see 7.11(e)), the rules do not change just because the word is a proper noun <Chris's> <the Cortezes'>.

(d) *Test.* If you are tempted to use a lone apostrophe rather than *-'s* on a singular possessive because the base word ends in a sibilant sound, try putting the word at the end of an answer with the noun understood. For example, if you are tempted to write, "This accident was caused by Mr. Jones' negligence," think how you would answer the question, "Whose negligence caused this accident?" Your answer would surely be, "Mr. Jones's." So write instead, "This accident was caused by Mr. Jones's negligence."

(e) *Ancient names.* Some ancient multisyllabic names that end in a sibilant sound take the apostrophe only <Jesus'> <Moses'> <Socrates'>.

(f) *Singular name, plural form.* Singular names that are plural in form also take just the apostrophe <American Airlines' profits (but *American's profits*)> <the Court of Appeals' decision> <the *New York Times*' staff>.

(g) *"For —— sake."* Idioms combining a word ending in a sibilant sound with the word *sake* use either the apostrophe alone <for convenience' sake> or nothing at all <for goodness sake> .

(h) *Organizations.* Some organizations use a plural rather than a possessive form <Young Lawyers Association>.

7.12 Add an apostrophe to the end of a word to form the possessive of a plural noun that ends in an *s* or *z* sound.

(a) *Basic rule.* This is the general rule <boys'> <girls'> <Bushes'>.

(b) *Exception.* A very narrow exception arises with irregular-form plurals, even though they end in an *s* sound <mice's> <geese's>.

7.13 Do not use apostrophes with possessive pronouns.

(a) *Confused with contractions.* Apostrophes are a frequent cause of misspellings when the pronoun gets confused with a contraction <its (possessive) vs. it's (contraction for "it is")> <their (possessive) vs. they're (contraction for "they are")> <whose (possessive) vs. who's (contraction for "who is")>.

(b) *Simple test.* One test is to always sound out the words that the contraction stands for when you use the word. If the contraction is wrong, use the other form instead.

7.14 With phrases, form the possessive on the last word.

(a) *Last word.* The possessive form must go immediately before the word it modifies to prevent a misunderstanding <the school board's decision> <the Twin Cities' ball club>.

(b) *Contrasted with compound plurals.* Note how this rule differs from the rule for forming plurals of some compound words. For example, the plural of *attorney general* is *attorneys general,* but the possessive is *attorney general's.* Likewise, the plural is *sons-in-law,* but the possessive is *son-in-law's* (see 7.9(b) & (c)).

(c) *Awkwardness.* If the phrasing is awkward, recast the sentence <instead of *the assistant attorneys general's offices,* write *the offices of the assistant attorneys general*>.

7.15 Use the same rules for numbers and abbreviations.

(a) *Number examples.* <2001's top story> <the 76ers' season>.

(b) *Abbreviation examples.* <the NAACP's boycott> <the VIPs' table>.

> "Spelling and pronunciation are not fully comparable . . . . People have been speaking English far longer than they have been writing it. And, of course, each of us learned first to speak and only later to write. Writing, though based on speech, is a somewhat artificial and stripped-down version of it."
>
> —*Barbara Wallraff*

Compounds

7.16 A compound word joins two or more words to express a single thing. Frequently used compounds become a permanent part of the language <rooftop> <farmhouse>, but many others are writers' temporary constructions that will probably never see widespread use <cyberlag> <waffle-textured>. These latter constructions can't be found in any dictionary, so how do we know whether to spell them as separate words ("open"), hyphenated, or as a single word ("closed")? A few principles can guide us, but there are no hard-and-fast rules.

Compound words tend to evolve over time and with general acceptance, from the open form <whistle blower> to the hyphenated form <whistle-blower> to the closed form <whistleblower>. All three forms of *whistleblower* are currently in use (the one-word form being best).

A similar problem arises when words are strung together to modify another word. These strung-together-to-modify-another-word constructions are called phrasal adjectives. In this paragraph, for example, the *strung*-phrase poses no problem in the first sentence because the words are in natural word order. In the second sentence, though, they act as a single unit to modify the word *constructions*. Without the hyphens, the reader would have a hard time sorting out the sentence. No dictionary could anticipate every possible combination of words that could make up such a phrase, and lexicographers purposely omit most such nonce phrases.

Again, though, there are some principles that can guide a writer in handling them.

7.17 A compound formed by two nouns of equal importance is likely to be closed.

(a) *Pronunciation clue.* One clue is how the compound is pronounced. If the stress is clearly on the first word, the compound is more likely to be closed <workday> <bedspread> <classmate>. If the words carry the same stress, the compound is more likely to be open <ball game> <home page> <iron ore>.

(b) *Evolving use.* Watch for evolving use: from two words, to a hyphenated form, to a single compound. For example, in 1998–1999 *web site* was picked by writers 81% of the time (according to a Westlaw news survey). But by 2001 that open form was in a statistical tie with the single word *website.* The same evolution can be seen with other words, such as *database*, *lawnmower*, and *healthcare*.

(c) *Human suffixes.* A compound formed with *man*, *woman*, or *person* is usually closed <fireman> <policewoman> <spokesperson> <busboy> <*but* flower girl> (but see 12.3(o)).

7.18 The combination of an adjective and a noun is usually open.

(a) *Generally.* Since this is the normal word order, there is little reason to join the terms <red dog> <hot pad> <deep freeze>.

(b) *Distinct meaning.* On the other hand, when the two words take on a distinct meaning, they are often combined: a *hot bed* signifies something completely different from a *hotbed.* The same principle applies to many other words <blueprint> <shorthand> <drywall>.

7.19 When words of equal importance are joined, use an en dash (see 1.54(a)).

(a) *Duality.* One common use of this construction is to show a double role or office <writer–philosopher> <secretary–treasurer>.

(b) *Measurement.* Another use of this construction is to join two unlike units of measurement when they are multiplied together <4 column–inches> <33 foot–pounds>. No en dash is used where like units of measure are multiplied together <1,200 square feet> <4 metric tons>.

(c) *Hyphen acceptable.* A hyphen is often used instead of the en dash for these constructions, but the en dash is stronger at showing equivalence between the terms that are joined.

7.20 When a noun is joined with a preceding preposition or adverb, the compound is usually closed.

(a) *Independent meaning.* Often these words have significance independent of their components <upswing> <downtown> <overview> <underwear>.

(b) *No independent meaning.* But when the independent significance is weaker, the words are often open or hyphenated <down payment> <off-season>.

7.21 When a noun is joined to a gerund, it is usually hyphenated.

(a) *Temporary terms.* This is especially true of temporary phrases—phrases coined on the fly rather than established in common usage <wheat-growing> <trip-planning> <charity-giving>.

(b) *Permanent terms.* But it is true of many permanent phrases as well <double-dealing> <ballot-stuffing> <house-raising>.

(c) *Closed terms.* Many such gerund phrases have become closed compounds <lawmaking> <housecleaning> <birdwatching>, especially terms that have secondary significance apart from their component terms <babysitting> <handwriting> <stonewalling>.

(d) *Open terms.* A few such phrases remain two words <data processing> <bill collecting> <lawn bowling>. But even such a phrase takes a hyphen when used to modify another noun <data-processing department>.

7.22 When a verb is coupled with a preposition or adverb, it is open, but a noun derived from the same form is either closed (usually) or hyphenated.

(a) *Phrasal verbs.* This construction is called a phrasal verb; the term after the verb is called a particle, and it gives the verb a different meaning than the verb would have standing alone <hold up> <take off> <break down>.

(b) *As closed nouns.* Many of these phrasal verbs can be used as one-word nouns <holdup> <takeoff> <breakdown>. But some cannot <get over> <move on> <take up>.

(c) *Short particles.* When the particle is very short (two letters), the resulting noun is sometimes hyphenated <break-in>, but not always <breakup>.

7.23 When a verb is joined to a preceding preposition or adverb, the resulting word is closed; words formed this way do not serve as nouns.

(a) *Effect of closing.* Coupling a particle to a verb in that order results in a word with a meaning distinct from the original verb <uphold> <undermine> <oversee>.

(b) *Noun formation.* To form a noun, such a word must take on the *-ing* gerund ending <upholding> <undermining> <overseeing>.

7.24 A verb formed from a compound noun often takes the same form as the noun.

(a) *Closed.* If the noun is solid, the verb is almost always solid as well <rubberneck> <railroad> <handcuff>.

(b) *Hyphenated.* If the noun is open or hyphenated, the verb is usually hyphenated <rubber stamp (*n.*) – rubber-stamp (*vb.*)>.

(c) *Adjective–noun phrase.* If an adjective–noun phrase is used as a verb, the verb is hyphenated even though the noun phrase would be open <strong-arm> <bad-mouth> <soft-pedal>.

> "Now it is true, very true, that a vice president should know how to spell *potato*. On the other hand, to hear TV news reporters who can barely get through two sentences without committing some atrocious assault on the English language waxing superior over a misspelled word is also slightly dizzying."
>
> —*Dorothy Rabinowitz*

7.25 For many other terms, no reliable principles apply; use a current dictionary to check the spelling.

(a) *Possessive noun–noun.* When a noun is joined with another noun in the possessive case, the result may be open <dead-man's float>, hyphenated (more commonly) <bird's-eye>, or closed (rarely) <menswear>. When the words are joined, the apostrophe is lost <hairsbreadth>.

(b) *Agent noun.* When a noun is joined to a verb and used as an agent noun (with an *-er* or *-or* suffix), the result is usually hyphenated <page-turner> <vote-getter> <fund-raiser>. These words seem to take awhile to close <bookkeeper> <copyeditor> <globetrotter>. And alternative spellings are common <copy editor> <fundraiser>.

(c) *Verb–particle.* When the *-er* or *-ing* form of a verb is coupled with a trailing preposition or adverb, the resulting noun is usually hyphenated <looker-on *but* onlooker> <runner-up> <dressing-down>, and the first word usually takes the plural form <lookers-on> <runners-up>, but not always <dressing-downs>. Yet some similar terms do not follow these principles <passerby (or *passer-by*)–passersby (or *passers-by*)>.

(d) *Longer phrases.* Longer phrases may or may not be hyphenated when used as nouns <know-it-all> <son of a gun>.

(e) *Letter plus noun.* A noun coupled with a letter may or may not be hyphenated <A-line dress> <B movie> <C clef> <D-Day>.

> "When Dava Sobel finished an early chapter in her best-selling book *Galileo's Daughter*, she dutifully ran it through the Microsoft Word spell-checking program on her computer. A good thing, too. Microsoft objected to Sobel's insistence that the Galilei clan spent so much time in Tuscany. Word suggested she change *Tuscany* to *Tucson*. 'I think Galileo would have loved Tuscon,' Sobel said. 'but that's a different book.'"
>
> —*Dick Teresi*

American vs. British Spelling

7.26 Be aware of variations in American and British spelling. For the most part, the differences fall into one of several categories.

(a) *"-ize" vs. "-ise."* In American spelling, the action suffix used in changing a noun into a verb is spelled with a *-z-*. British spelling often uses an *-s-* instead, although the *-z-* spelling is sometimes acceptable as well.

Ex.: Am. spelling: analyze | Br. spelling: analyse
Ex.: Am. spelling: apologize | Br. spelling: apologise
Ex.: Am. spelling: burglarize | Br. spelling: burglarise
Ex.: Am. spelling: capitalize | Br. spelling: capitalise
Ex.: Am. spelling: characterize | Br. spelling: characterise
Ex.: Am. spelling: mobilize | Br. spelling: mobilise
Ex.: Am. spelling: organize | Br. spelling: organise
Ex.: Am. spelling: realize | Br. spelling: realise
Ex.: Am. spelling: recognize | Br. spelling: recognise
Ex.: Am. spelling: standardize | Br. spelling: standardise

(b) *"-or" vs. "-our."* Some nouns that end in *-or* in American spelling end in -*our* in British spelling; this rule does not apply to agent nouns such as *payor* and *creditor.*

Ex.: Am. spelling: behavior | Br. spelling: behaviour
Ex.: Am. spelling: demeanor | Br. spelling: demeanour
Ex.: Am. spelling: labor | Br. spelling: labour
Ex.: Am. spelling: misdemeanor | Br. spelling: misdemeanour
Ex.: Am. spelling: neighbor | Br. spelling: neighbour
Ex.: Am. spelling: rumor | Br. spelling: rumour

(c) *Doubling the final "-l."* American and British spelling rules differ over how to add a suffix to a word that ends in a single vowel and the letter *l*. In American writing the *l* is doubled only if the word is accented on the final syllable. In British spelling the *l* is almost always doubled.

Ex.: Am. spelling: counselor | Br. spelling: counsellor
Ex.: Am. spelling: labeled | Br. spelling: labelled
Ex.: Am. spelling: libelous | Br. spelling: libellous
Ex.: Am. spelling: traveled | Br. spelling: travelled

Some words that end in *-ll* in American spelling end in a single *-l* in British spelling. When these words take on a suffix, it looks as though the spelling rule is turned on its head, but it is the spelling of the root word that accounts for the apparent anomaly.

Ex: Am. spelling: enrollment (enroll) | Br. spelling: enrolment (enrol)
Ex: Am. spelling: installment (install) | Br. spelling: instalment (instal)

Even that does not explain some forms, though.

Ex.: Am. spelling: skillful | Br. spelling: skilful (skill)
But: Am. spelling: willful | Br. spelling: wilful (will)

(d) *"-ter" vs. "-tre."* Many words that end in *-er* in American spelling end in *-re* in British spelling.

Ex.: Am. spelling: caliber — Br. spelling: calibre
Ex.: Am. spelling: center — Br. spelling: centre
Ex.: Am. spelling: meter — Br. spelling: metre
Ex.: Am. spelling: theater — Br. spelling: theatre

(e) *"-dge" words.* In American spelling, most words that end in *-dge* drop the final *-e*. before adding a suffix. In British spelling the *-e* is retained.

Ex.: Am. spelling: abridgment — Br. spelling: abridgement
Ex.: Am. spelling: acknowledgment — Br. spelling: acknowledgement
Ex.: Am. spelling: judgment — Br. spelling: judgement

(Note that *acknowledgement* is an acceptable but not the preferred American spelling, and that *judgment* is standard in British legal writing.)

(f) *Hyphenated forms.* Compound words and words with prefixes are more likely to be hyphenated in British spelling than in American spelling.

Ex.: Am. spelling: bookkeeper — Br. spelling: book-keeper
Ex.: Am. spelling: cooperate — Br. spelling: co-operate
Ex.: Am. spelling: neoclassical — Br. spelling: neo-classical

(g) *"-ogue" words.* Many words that end in *-ogue* commonly drop the final *-ue* in American spelling, but not in British spelling. But it is never an error to retain the *-ue*, and that is the preferred form in legal writing.

Ex.: Informal Am. spelling: catalog — Br. spelling: catalogue
Ex.: Informal Am. spelling: dialog — Br. spelling: dialogue
Ex.: Informal Am. spelling: travelog — Br. spelling: travelogue

(h) *Miscellaneous.* Many other words are spelled differently in American writing and British writing, but do not fall into easy categories. In legal writing, keep in mind particularly the American and British spellings of *offense* (*offence*), *defense* (*defence*), *specialty* (*speciality*), *pretense* (*pretence*), and the noun *license* (*licence*).

Ex.: Am. spelling: airplane — Br. spelling: aeroplane
Ex.: Am. spelling: aluminum — Br. spelling: aluminium
Ex.: Am. spelling: check — Br. spelling: cheque
Ex.: Am. spelling: connection — Br. spelling: connexion
Ex.: Am. spelling: draft — Br. spelling: draught
Ex.: Am. spelling: fulfill — Br. spelling: fulfil
Ex.: Am. spelling: gray — Br. spelling: grey
Ex.: Am. spelling: jail — Br. spelling: gaol
Ex.: Am. spelling: jewelry — Br. spelling: jewellery
Ex.: Am. spelling: maneuver — Br. spelling: manoeuvre
Ex.: Am. spelling: plow — Br. spelling: plough
Ex.: Am. spelling: skeptic — Br. spelling: sceptic
Ex.: Am. spelling: spelled — Br. spelling: spelt
Ex.: Am. spelling: story — Br. spelling: storey

Common Misspellings

7.27 Be wary of common misspellings. Below are the correct spellings of the most frequently problematic words in the language.

absence
accessible
accidentally
acclaim
accommodate
accomplish
accumulate
achievement
acknowledgment
acquaintance
acquire
acquittal
ad
address
admissible
adviser
align
all right
a lot
amateur
analogous
apparatus
appearance
arctic
argument
ascent
atheist
athletics
auxiliary
balance
balloon
barbecue
barbiturate
bargain
basically
battalion
beggar
beginning
belief
believe
beneficial
biscuit
bouillon
boundary
Britain
buses
business
calendar
camouflage
canceled
cancellation
cantaloupe
carousel
category
cemetery
changing
chief
cigarette
collectible
colonel
colossal
column
commingle
commission
commitment
committee
competent
conceivable
condemn
conference
conferred
connoisseur
conscience
conscientious
consciousness
consensus
consistent
continuous
controlled
controversy
coolly
corollary
correspondence
counseled
counselor
counterfeit
courteous
courtesy
criticize
deceased
decedent
deceive
deductible
defendant
deference
deferred
definitely
dependent
descendant
description
desiccate
desirable
desperate
develop
development
difference
dilemma
disappearance
disappoint
discernible
discipline
disingenuous
dissatisfied
dominant
drunkenness
ecstasy
efficiency
egregious
eighth
eligible
eliminate
embarrass
eminent
emperor
encouragement
enforceable
enroll
entirely
entrepreneur
equipped
equivalent
especially
exaggerate
exceed
excel
excellent
existence
exorbitant

expedite
expense
experience
fallacy
familiar
fascination
feasible
February
feisty
fiery
finally
financially
flammable
fluorescent
fluoride
forcibly
foreign
foresee
foreword
forfeit
formerly
forty
fourteen
fourth
frantically
fundamentally
gauge
generally
goodbye
government
governor
grammar
grandeur
gray
grievous
gruesome
guarantee
guerrilla
guidance
handkerchief
happily
harassment
height
heinous
hemorrhage
heroes
hierarchy
hoarse
homogeneous
hoping
hors d'oeuvre
humorous
hygiene
hypocrisy
hypocrite
ideally
idiosyncrasy
ignorance
imaginary
immediately
imminent
implement
imprimatur
inadvertent
incidentally
incredible
incumbent
independence
independent
indicted
indispensable
inference
innovate
innuendo
inoculate
insurance
intellectual
intelligence
interesting
interference
interrupt
irrelevant
irresistible
jealousy
jewelry
judgment
kaleidoscope
knowledge
labeled
laboratory
laid
led
legitimate
leisure
length
liaison
license
lieu
lieutenant
lightning
likable
likelihood
likely
limousine
liquefy
loneliness
lose
lovely
luxury
magazine
maintain
maintenance
manageable
management
maneuver
marriage
marshal
mathematics
maybe
medicine
medieval
mediocre
memento
mileage
millennium
millionaire
miniature
minuscule
minute
mischievous
missile
misspelled
mortgage
mosquito
mousse
movable
murmur
muscle
mustache
mysterious
narrative
naturally
necessary
necessity
neighbor
nickel
nineteenth
ninety
ninth
noticeable
nowadays
nuisance
obedience

obstacle
occasion
occasionally
occurred
occurrence
official
omission
opinion
opponent
opportunity
oppression
optimistic
origin
outrageous
overrun
paid
panicky
pantomime
parallel
paralyze
paraphernalia
parliament
particularly
pastime
pavilion
peaceable
peculiar
penetrate
perceive
performance
permanent
permissible
permitted
perseverance
persevere
persistence
personnel
physician
picnicking
piece
pilgrimage
pitiful
plagiarism
plaintiff
playwright
pleasant
poinsettia
possess
possession
possessive
possibility
possible
possibly
potato
potatoes
practically
prairie
precedence
preceding
preference
preferred
prejudice
preparation
prerogative
prescription
prevalent
primitive
principal
principle
privilege
probably
procedure
proceed
proceedings
prominent
pronunciation
propaganda
psychological
publicly
pursue
quandary
questionnaire
queue
quizzes
realistically
recede
receipt
receive
recognize
recommend
reconnaissance
reference
referral
referring
relevant
relieving
religious
remembrance
reminiscence
renaissance
repetition
rescission
resemblance
restaurant
restaurateur
rheumatism
rhyme
rhythm
ridiculous
sacrilegious
safety
salable
satellite
scary
scenery
schedule
scurrilous
secede
seize
seizure
sense
sentence
separate
separation
sergeant
several
severely
shepherd
sincerely
sizable
skiing
soliloquy
sophomore
souvenir
sovereign
specifically
specimen
specious
strategy
strength
stubbornness
subtle
succeed
success
sufficient
supersede
supplement
suppress
surprise
surreptitious
surround
surveillance
susceptible

suspicious
syllable
symmetrical
synonymous
temperature
tendency
themselves
therefore
thorough
though
threshold
through
tomorrow
totaled
tournament
tourniquet
trafficking
tragedy
transferable
transferred
traveled
treatise
tries
truly
twelfth
tyranny
ukulele
unmistakable
unnecessary
until
usable
usually
vacuum
valuable
vengeance
vilify
villain
violence
Wednesday
weird
wherever
wholly
withhold
yacht
yield

> "[A newspaper's] story identified Intel Corp., the Pentium's maker, as Until Corp. . . . Software giant Microsoft Corp. became Microvolts Corp. . . . Ron Leckie, vice president of marketing for Megatest Corp., was identified as Ron Lackey, vice president of Megadeaths Corp. . . . After spending three hours looking for a hacker, the newspaper concluded its own spell-checker program was to blame. Each name changed in the story matched the first choice in the spell-checker program."
>
> —*Scott McCartney*

§ 8
Citations

8.1 Citations identify original and supporting sources, show the significance of the information cited, and help readers find the sources either to verify or to conduct further research. Citations often demonstrate that a proposition has been thoroughly researched, or that a principle of law is heavily supported by authority. But overusing citations for no substantive legal reason merely clouds the writer's point. And incorrect citations can impair a writer's credibility and call an argument's validity into question—they may even lead to sanctions.

8.2 Choose a citation system and stick to its essential conventions throughout a particular writing.

(a) *Bluebook.* The oldest and most comprehensive system available is *The Bluebook: A Uniform System of Citation,* which is widely used by law reviews, courts, and law firms. But *The Bluebook*'s comprehensiveness makes it complex. Explanations of some citing forms are not clear, and many are not illustrated. New editions, published approximately every five years, sometimes include changes that are illogical or inconsistent with earlier editions. Most judges and their clerks were raised on *The Bluebook.*

(b) *ALWD.* A relatively new system (introduced in 2000 by the Association of Legal Writing Directors) is the *ALWD Citation Manual.* It has been adopted by many law schools and law journals, some moot-court competitions, and some courts. Written in plain English, it contains useful quick-format guides and informational sidebars. Rules have fewer exceptions than in *The Bluebook* system. But *ALWD* is less comprehensive than *The Bluebook* (e.g., *ALWD* lacks detailed guidance on citing foreign sources of law).

(c) *Maroonbook.* Since 1989, the *University of Chicago Manual of Legal Citation* (better known as the *Maroonbook*) has offered brief guidance on citing legal materials. The rules are not prescriptive, and flexibility is encouraged. But this manual has not been widely adopted. It is the least comprehensive system. The citation forms are unpunctuated, which produces a half-finished appearance and sometimes introduces ambiguity. The *Maroonbook* does not encourage consistency from one legal writing to another—even those by the same author.

(d) *State style manuals.* Some states, such as California and North Dakota, have their own state-specific style manuals. These are usually mandatory for court documents, and may be required by in-state legal publications. Other states, such as Delaware, allow writers to use either the state-specific citation manual or a general citation system.

8.3 If court rules, journal guidelines, or any other directives conflict with the citation system, the directives control. Ignore anything to the contrary in the citation system.

(a) *Courts.* Some jurisdictions, such as California, North Dakota, and Texas, have their own citation rules. Many states, such as Delaware, supplement the general systems with more detailed systems for citing state legal materials. Some courts strictly require attorneys to use a specific citation system, such as *The Bluebook.* For examples of judicial strictness and consequences of disobedience, see *Billing v. City of Norfolk,* 848 F. Supp. 630, 635–36 (E.D. Va. 1994), and *Cotter v. Helmer,* No. 88 Civ. 5710 (PKL), 1990 WL 103980, at *8 n. 5 (S.D.N.Y. July 17, 1990).

(b) *Law journals.* Law journals usually prefer one citation system and require its use for all submissions. For instance, the *University of Chicago Law Review* requires *Maroonbook* form, and the *Harvard Law Review* requires *Bluebook* form. But law journals may also have supplemental or contradictory guidelines, especially for electronic-form submissions. For example, although the *American Indian Law Review* requires writers to use *The Bluebook,* it contradicts *The Bluebook* by requiring writers (1) to use boldface type where *The Bluebook* requires small caps, and (2) to provide emphasis by underlining instead of italicizing.

8.4 Learn the fundamental rules of how to cite authority. But do not get so lost in the minutiae that you forget why they exist: to help the reader check your research.

(a) *Basics.* Among the essential rules that a legal writer needs to know are (1) the formats for citing cases, constitutions, statutes, regulations, rules of evidence and procedure, books, articles, and legal encyclopedias; (2) the rules about using signals; and (3) the methods of citing electronic materials (usually websites, legal databases, and materials on CD-ROM). Litigators additionally need to know how to cite evidence and case documents (especially those from the earlier stages of a case).

(b) *Trivia and nonsense.* Although you want your documents to conform to a consistent style, do not get too hung up on the minutiae. Do not spend a lot of time trying to find out whether a certain period should be roman or italic. Do not let a citation manual dictate what typeface you use, especially if it seems to suggest Courier (but *do* follow court rules). And although you want to produce the correct form of a citation, do not allow a citation manual to dictate whether you put citations in text or in footnotes.

8.5 Cite the record unobtrusively.

(a) *Basics.* Unless otherwise specified by court rules, a basic pinpoint citation to the appellate record (or *transcript* or *appendix*) requires only the volume number (if the record consists of more than one volume), an abbreviation for *record*, and the page number. The citation may be offset with brackets or parentheses.

Ex.: R. 34 / (R. 34) / [R. 34] (All ways to cite page 34 of the record.)

(b) *Page and line.* If the page's lines are numbered, the precise line can be pinpointed after the page number and a colon.

Ex.: R. 34:28 / (R. 34:28) / [R. 34:28] (All ways to cite line 28 of page 34 of the record.)

(c) *Overcitation.* Many legal writers write needlessly lengthy descriptive references to the record.

Ex.: After the statement "XYZ asked the court to dismiss the case, but ABC opposed this request."

Not this: ABC's Memorandum in Opposition to Plaintiff's Motion for Judgment on the Pleadings and for Dismissal, January 30, 2001, record page 87.

But this: R. 87. (The place in the record where the statement's supporting or documentary information can be found.)

8.6 Choose which precedents to cite based on authority, hierarchy, freshness, and clarity of reasoning. Avoid string citations.

(a) *Authority.* Always cite precedent from the jurisdiction you are writing for, if available. Controlling authority is always stronger than merely persuasive authority from another jurisdiction.

(b) *Hierarchy.* Within the jurisdiction you are writing for, cite authority from the highest court, if available; citation to a higher court is always stronger than citation to a lower court.

(c) *Freshness.* Prefer more recent citations, if available. But if a seminal case is well known for developing the proposition you are arguing, cite that landmark case more prominently than its progeny.

(d) *Reasoning.* Regardless of its precedential value, consider discussing (rather than merely citing) a case that will give your reader a clear and well-reasoned discussion of some doctrine, public policy, comparison of judicial approaches, or other point of law that is especially important to your argument.

(e) *Number of citations.* One or two citations are sufficient if the law is controlling or well established. Citing a string of lower-court citations adds no weight to an appellate court's decision. Neither does citing a string of authorities that repeat a well-established point of law (e.g., the constitutional right to remain silent).

(f) *No controlling authority.* If there is no controlling law but several authorities are in agreement, weave that information into the text and include exemplary citations in footnotes. Ex.: "The First,[1] Fourth,[2] Fifth,[3] Seventh,[4] Tenth,[5] and Eleventh[6] circuits have all held . . . ."

8.7 Use abbreviations as required in the first full citation.

(a) *First citation.* The first reference to an authority should always be a full citation.

(b) *Lists.* Each citation system provides a list of common abbreviations for state names, titles, frequently used words, and so on. For example, *Pennsylvania Central Transportation Company* becomes *Pa. Cent. Transp. Co.* Similarly, Rule 16 of the Federal Rules of Criminal Procedure becomes Fed. R. Crim. P. 16.

8.8 Use short-form citations after the first full citation.

(a) *Clarity.* A short-form citation is less complete than its long form. It must clearly identify the source referred to. For example, *Pa. Cent. Transp. Co. v. New York City*, 366 N.E.2d 1271, 1273 (N.Y. 1977) becomes *Pa. Cent. Transp. Co.*, 366 N.E.2d at 1273.

(b) *Distinctive name.* Prefer the first party's name for the short-form (pinpoint) citation; but if the first party (1) is a governmental entity, (2) is a frequent litigant, or (3) has a name similar or identical to that of a party in another citation, use the second party's name instead. So *State v. Campbell*, 798 So. 2d 524, 530 (Miss. 2001), becomes *Campbell*, 798 So. 2d at 530; *Sierra Club v. Whitman*, 268 F.3d 898, 903 (9th Cir. 2001), becomes *Whitman*, 268 F.3d at 903; and *Pickering v. Sacavage*, 642 A.2d 555, 557 (Pa. Commw. Ct. 1994), and *Rolen v. Pickering*, 628 So. 2d 850, 852 (Ala. Civ. App. 1993), become *Sacavage*, 642 A.2d at 557; and *Rolen*, 628 So. 2d at 852.

8.9 Use pinpoint citations whenever possible.

(a) *Purpose.* Pinpointing the precise location of source material, meaning the precise page number and perhaps even the footnote number, enables researchers to locate the support for your position, especially if the source material is lengthy or the reference is to a footnote. Take, for instance, *Hawaii v. Mallon*, 950 P.2d 178, 240 (Haw. 1998). That opinion includes a 110-page dissent. If you cite the dissent without pinpointing the page, it is unlikely that a researcher will take the trouble to find it.

(b) *Pinpoint citation to first page.* In legal writing, it is customary to give a pinpoint citation to the first page by repeating the reference to the first page.

> Ex.: Richard A. Posner, *Against Footnotes*, 38 Ct. Rev. 24, 24 (2001).
>
> Ex.: Maureen B. Collins, *Legal Writing Can Be a Scream*, 88 Ill. B.J. 725, 725 (2000).

(c) *Paragraphs.* If a decision has numbered paragraphs, and no rules direct otherwise, cite the paragraph number.

> Ex.: *Grand Casino Tunica v. Shindler*, 772 So. 2d 1036, 1038 ¶ 8 (Miss. 2000).

(d) *Credibility.* Failing to pinpoint a reference impairs a writer's credibility because the failure makes it difficult, even impossible, to determine an argument's or proposition's validity. Good research is identified openly. Poor research is presented obscurely.

8.10 Use *id.* carefully.

(a) *Function of "id."* The term *id.* (the abbreviation for *idem*, "the same") is a special short-form citation. It means that the immediately preceding authority is cited again. If the authority is the same, but a different page is referred to, the short form becomes "*id.* at (page number)."

(b) *Multiple authorities.* If the preceding citation contains several authorities, it is unclear whether *id.* refers to the collective contents of the preceding citation or only a specific authority there. Rather than using *id.*, repeat the relevant citation in short form.

(c) *And "ibid."* This term (the abbreviation for *ibidem*, "in the same place") serves the same function as *id.* but appears mostly in nonlegal writing. Instead of *ibid.*, use *id.*—the customary legal form.

8.11 Avoid *infra, supra, op. cit., loc. cit.,* and similar abbreviations to refer to a citation that appears elsewhere in the writing.

(a) *Definitions.* All of these references direct the reader to a source cited elsewhere in the work. *Infra* tells the reader that the citation will be found later in the footnotes or text. The others indicate that a reference has already been cited above.

(b) *Usage.* These abbreviations are used for internally cross-referencing citations. If these cross-references do not adequately identify the source material, readers must search for the first full citation. For instance, if a citation merely states, "*See* Anti-Cybersquatting Consumer Protection Act, *supra*," a reader must needlessly search the earlier pages of the document to find the "Anti-Cybersquatting Consumer Protection Act, 15 U.S.C. § 1125."

(c) *Law reviews.* Most journals and law reviews allow cross-referencing in footnotes if (1) repetition of a lengthy footnote is avoided, (2) the cross-referenced footnote is nearby, and (3) only a few cross-references are used. Some journals prefer that writers use English words (e.g., *above, below*) instead of the Latin signals *infra, supra,* and others—or simply identify the cross-referenced footnote (e.g., *See n. 52).*

(d) *Footnotes.* When used in footnotes, these distracting internal cross-references to citations in other footnotes force a reader to stop and flip through a document's pages to find and read the other notes, then search for the original point.

8.12 When citing sequential pages, sections, paragraphs, or similar elements, use an en dash (see 5.14). If you elide page numbers of three or more digits, always leave two digits.

Ex.: pp. 107–09

But: pp. 1196–1204

Ex.: § 34(a)–(d)

Ex.: ¶¶ 20–28

8.13 When citing a plurality, concurring, or dissenting opinion, include the type of opinion in parentheses immediately after the citation before any parenthetical. Identify the author of a concurrence or dissent.

(a) *Plurality opinion.* It is usually unnecessary to name the writer of a plurality opinion, but it is permissible.

Ex.: *Waters v. Churchill*, 511 U.S. 661, 664 (1994) (plurality opinion).

Ex.: *Davis v. Bandemer*, 478 U.S. 109, 132 (1986) (White, J., plurality opinion).

(b) *Concurrence or dissent.* The writer of a concurrence or dissent is always identified in a brief parenthetical.

Ex.: *Waters v. Churchill*, 511 U.S. 661, 682 (1994) (Souter, J., concurring).

Ex.: *New St. Ice Co. v. Liebmann*, 285 U.S. 262, 311 (1932) (Brandeis, J., dissenting).

(c) *Unsigned opinion.* Unsigned opinions are usually given somewhat less weight than those attributed to specific judges. If an opinion's author is unidentified, use the phrase *per curiam* in parentheses.

Ex.: *Thornton v. Phillips County, Alaska*, 240 F.3d 728, 729 (8th Cir. 2001) (per curiam).

(d) *Full-court hearing.* If an opinion was issued after a hearing by a full court in a tribunal that usually hears cases in panels consisting of fewer than all the judges, use the phrase *en banc* in parentheses (after the court and year but before any other parenthetical information).

Ex.: *Nicini v. Morra*, 212 F.3d 798, 810 (3d Cir. 2000) (en banc).

Ex.: *Kordenbrock v. Scroggy*, 919 F.2d 1091, 1110–11 (6th Cir. 1990) (en banc) (concluding that there was "substantial possibility" that the jury construed its instructions to "mean that mitigating as well as aggravating circumstances could be found only if the jury was unanimous").

8.14 Space parenthetical explanations or quotations correctly in relation to the rest of the citation.

(a) *Spacing.* If a citation is followed by one or more sets of parenthetical information, leave a space between back-to-back parentheses (see 1.37(c)).

Ex.: *Metro. Coal Co. v. Howard,* 155 F.2d 780 (2d Cir. 1946) (involving warranty for barge).

Ex.: *Cowan v. Doering,* 545 A.2d 159, 168 (N.J. 1988) (Clifford, J., dissenting) (commenting on a mentally disturbed plaintiff).

(b) *Punctuation.* If a parenthetical does not contain a complete sentence, do not include terminal punctuation inside the parenthetical. Either a period or a semicolon (if another citation follows) always goes immediately after the citation's last closing parenthesis.

Ex.: *In re Oakwood Mobile Homes, Inc.,* 987 S.W.2d 571, 574 (Tex. 1999) (declaring that neither adhesion contracts nor arbitration clauses are per se unconscionable); *Ex parte Davis,* 17 S.W.3d 360, 371–72 (Tex. App. 2000) (considering procedural unconscionability of arbitration clause in adhesion contract).

Ex.: *Phillips v. Wash. Legal Found.,* 524 U.S. 156, 173 (1998) (Souter, J., dissenting) ("property in interest income follows ownership of the principal on which the interest is earned, and the Court treats any income generated by a client's funds like income that the client could derive directly through a method of money management or investment that costs more than it produced") (citation omitted).

8.15 If parenthetical matter is given with a citation, it should appear before the subsequent history.

(a) *History.* If a source (e.g., a case or statute) has been modified in any way after coming into existence, its history and the effect on its value as authority must be shown. The history is never enclosed in parentheses.

Ex.: *Runyon & Son, Inc. v. Davis,* 605 So. 2d 38, 47 (Miss. 1992), *overruled on other grounds by Richardson v. APAC-Miss., Inc.,* 631 So. 2d 143, 152 (Miss. 1994).

(b) *Additional citation.* A case with a subsequent history often requires an additional citation to identify the source of the history.

Ex.: *Conoco Inc. v. Dep't of Justice,* 521 F. Supp. 1301, 1305–06 (D. Del. 1981) (declaring that FOIA exemption for "intra-agency" memorandums or letters was applicable to handwritten notes), *aff'd in part, rev'd in part & remanded on other grounds,* 687 F.2d 724 (3d Cir. 1982).

> "Easy talking, difficult hearing. Easy writing, hard reading."
>
> —*Edward N. Teall*

8.16 Use the correct signal to show the relationship between a textual statement and the material cited.

(a) *Basics.* The correct signal depends on the citation system you are using. Use signals consistently. Following are the introductory signals and their meanings:

- *No signal.* If the cited authority states the definition or proposition in the text, or directly supports the stated proposition, no signal of any kind is used.
- *See.* The cited authority implicitly supports the proposition in some way. For instance, the supported proposition may logically flow from the cited authority, or the authority's dicta may suggest the proposition.
- *Cf.* The cited authority provides an analogy that supports the stated proposition. Because the authority usually directly supports a different proposition, a parenthetical explaining the analogy is often necessary.
- *E.g.* The cited authority is one of many authorities that similarly state or support the proposition. This signal is combined with other signals when the authorities do not directly support the proposition.

  Ex.: *See generally, e.g.,* Walter F. Murphy, *Elements of Judicial Strategy* (1964).

  Ex.: *But cf., e.g., Chisholm v. Georgia,* 2 U.S. 419, 478 (1793) (opinion of Jay, C.J.).
- *Compare . . . with.* Two possibilities: (1) The cited authorities support or illustrate the stated proposition but do so in different ways. (2) The authorities offer alternative analyses of the proposition and arrive at different conclusions.
- *Contra.* The cited authority directly contradicts the stated proposition.
- *But see.* The cited authority implicitly contradicts the proposition in some way. For instance, the authority may show that the proposition is limited or contradicted by some factors or in some circumstances.
- *But cf.* The cited authority provides an analogy that contradicts the stated proposition. A parenthetical explaining the analogy is often necessary.
- *See generally.* The cited authority provides useful background information related to the proposition but does not necessarily support or contradict the proposition.

Signals occasionally used:

- *Accord.* The cited authority, which is not mentioned in the text, states or directly supports the proposition. This signal usually introduces one or more case citations.

  Ex.: *McIlroy v. PaineWebber, Inc.*, 989 F.2d 817, 821 (5th Cir. 1993). *Accord Nat'l Post Office v. U.S. Postal Serv.*, 751 F.2d 834 (6th Cir. 1985)).

  Ex.: *NSBA v. Rothery*, 619 N.W.2d 590, 593 (Neb. 2000). *Accord NSBA v. Howze*, 618 N.W.2d 663 (Neb. 2000); *NSBA v. Mefferd*, 604 N.W.2d 839 (Neb. 2000).

- *See also.* The cited authority, which is not mentioned in the text, provides additional supporting material. Because it might not directly support the proposition, a parenthetical may be necessary to explain the authority's relevance.

(b) *Older legal materials.* Because of changes in citation standards, signals used in writings from different years may be unreliable. For instance, *The Bluebook* redefined *cf.* six times in 39 years. In 1947, *cf.* signaled an authority containing parallel propositions but materially different facts. In 1955, it signaled an authority that expressed a proposition, possibly only analogous, that lent some support to the writer's statement, conclusion, or opinion of law. Today its meaning is as given above.

(c) *Modern resources.* Signals may not be identical across current citation systems. For instance, under the *Bluebook* system, *but see* means that an authority "clearly supports" a contrary proposition; under the *ALWD* system, it means that the authority either contains dicta contrary to the writer's proposition or implicitly contradicts the proposition; under the *Maroonbook* system, it either directly or indirectly contradicts the writer's proposition.

(d) *Undefined signals.* Not all signals are used in all systems. For instance, *The Bluebook* uses the signal *accord*, which does not appear in either the *ALWD* or the *Maroonbook* system. *The Bluebook* and *ALWD* both use *contra*, *e.g.*, and *cf.*; the *Maroonbook* does not. The *Maroonbook* uses *consider* and *contrast . . . with*, neither of which appears in *The Bluebook* or *ALWD*.

> "It is foolish to use technical terms when scientific precision is unnecessary, and where the meaning may be as well expressed in words intelligible to the unlearned."
>
> —*Henry Bradley*

8.17 Do what you reasonably can to condense citations.

(a) *Abbreviations.* As often as possible, use abbreviations for case names, judicial reporters, compilations of statutes and regulations, and other commonly consulted sources.

Not this: *Federal Reporter (Second Series)*
But this: *F.2d*

(b) *Short-form citations.* After the first full citation, use the appropriate short form (see 8.8).

(c) *Redundancies.* If the reporter name identifies the deciding court, do not identify the court again in the parenthetical before the date.

Ex.: *Waggener v. Leggett*, 246 Miss. 505, 509 (1963).

8.18 Use parallel citations only when court rules say to or some other rule makes them mandatory.

(a) *Generally.* If parallel citations are not required, do not use them. Choose just one form as dictated by your citation system or any overriding directives.

Not this: *Coleman v. Gulf Ins. Group*, 41 Cal. 3d 782, 718 P.2d 77, 226 Cal. Rptr. 90 (1986).
But this: *Coleman v. Gulf Ins. Group*, 41 Cal. 3d 782 (1986).
Or this: *Coleman v. Gulf Ins. Group*, 226 Cal. Rptr. 90 (Cal. 1986).
Or this: *Coleman v. Gulf Ins. Group*, 718 P.2d 77 (Cal. 1986).

(b) *Punctuation.* Always separate parallel citations with commas.

Ex.: *Brown v. Bd. of Educ.*, 349 U.S. 294, 75 S. Ct. 753, 99 L. Ed. 1083 (1955).

(c) *Undesirability.* Parallel citations are more difficult to read than single citations, and they unduly separate sentences and parts of sentences. They inflate the authorities without giving them any additional weight.

8.19 Use a parenthetical if the note will elucidate the citation.

(a) *Clarification.* If a source directly supports your statement or proposition, no parenthetical is generally necessary. But if several unrelated points are discussed on the page cited, parentheticals may be helpful.

(b) *Multiple sources.* If several sources support a single statement but on different bases, use parentheticals to distinguish the citations.

Ex.: [5] *Peay v. BellSouth Med. Assistance Plan*, 205 F.3d 1206, 1211–12 & n. 4 (10th Cir. 2000) (concluding that personal jurisdiction in ERISA case requires adequate contacts with the particular state); *Bd. of Trustees v. Elite Erectors, Inc.*, 212 F.3d 1031, 1035 (7th Cir. 2000) (deciding that personal jurisdiction in ERISA case is established by adequate contacts with United States as a whole).

(c) *Specificity.* A narrow parenthetical can help pinpoint the specific information in a source.

Ex.: *Addressograph Multigraph Corp. v. Zink,* 329 A.2d 28, 33 (Md. 1974) (defining incidental and consequential damages following a breach of warranty under UCC § 2–715). (The contextual information helps the researcher to quickly locate the information on the page.)

(d) *Obscurity.* A vague or broadly worded parenthetical diminishes the value of a citation. For example, a parenthetical stating "discussing contract law" does not show that the source supports a textual proposition concerning the rights of a third-party beneficiary.

(e) *Form.* A parenthetical explanation should (1) begin with a present participle (*holding, affirming, reversing, overruling,* etc.), (2) consist of a direct quotation, or (3) be a combination of both.

Ex.: *Boos v. Barry,* 485 U.S. 312, 318 (1988) (recognizing public-issue signs to be classic examples of free speech).

Ex.: *Schenck v. Pro-Choice Network,* 519 U.S. 357, 377 (1997) ("Leafletting and commenting on matters of public concern are classic forms of free speech that lie at the heart of the First Amendment.").

Ex.: Andrew Siegel, "Steady Habits" *Under Siege: The Defense of Federalism in Jeffersonian Connecticut,* in *Federalists Reconsidered,* at 207 (Doron Ben-Atar & Barbara B. Oberg eds., 1998) (discussing "the strong republicanism of the Connecticut Federalists on the eve of the 'infamous' Hartford Convention").

8.20 Never trust the citations in another document; always verify from original sources.

(a) *Electronic shortcomings.* The citation forms provided by electronic legal databases typically include all the parallel citations. But never assume that the citation given in an electronic source conforms to the standards of a given legal-citation system. For that matter, never assume the word-for-word accuracy of the electronic text; although most online versions of print materials are fully accurate, there are inevitable lapses. So whenever you can, confirm citations against print versions.

(b) *Inaccurate information.* Legal materials may be retitled, codified, renumbered, or amended. A citation in another document may no longer be a good one.

(c) *Older legal materials.* The older the source material, the less likely it is that the internal citations will be consistent with current citation norms.

Ex.: (from a 1941 citation)
Anderson v. Dunn, 6 Wheat. 204, 227, 5 L.Ed. 242.

Ex.: (as it would appear today)
Anderson v. Dunn, 19 U.S. 204, 227 (1821).

(d) *Sanctions.* Improper citations can result in sanctions ranging from a rebuke (e.g., *Howard v. Oakland Tribune*, 245 Cal. Rptr. 449, 451 n. 6 (Ct. App. 1988)) to a heavy fine (e.g., *Hurlbert v. Gordon*, 824 P.2d 1238, 1245 (Wash. Ct. App. 1992)) to suspension (e.g., *In re Shepperson*, 674 A.2d 1273, 1274 (Vt. 1996)).

8.21 Before you submit your writing to anyone else, double-check your citations to be sure that the citation form and subsequent history are correct.

(a) *Updates.* Cases, statutes, and regulations are especially likely to be modified in some way that either needs to be reflected in a parenthetical or requires changing the citation's form.

Ex. (vacated opinion, published three months after the original decision):
United States v. Faasse, 227 F.3d 660, *opinion vacated*, 234 F.3d 312 (6th Cir. 2000).

Ex. (recodified statute):
Act of April 6, 1995, 74th Leg., R.S., ch. 20, § 1, sec. 152.006, 1995 Tex. Gen. Laws 113, 142–43 (amended and recodified 1999) (current version at Tex. Fam. Code Ann. §§ 152.206, 152.307 (Vernon Supp. 2001)).

Ex. (amended regulation):
1989, No. 68, §§ 4, 5 (amending 23 V.S.A. §§ 1203(d), 1205).

(b) *Sanctions.* A court may impose sanctions for failure to cite good authority or controlling authority.

Ex.: *Smith v. United Transp. Local 81*, 594 F. Supp. 96, 101 (S.D. Cal. 1984) (attorney based entire argument on vacated authority).

Ex.: *Glassalum Eng'g Corp. v. 392208 Ontarion Ltd.*, 487 So. 2d 87, 88 (Fla. Dist. Ct. App. 1986) (counsel neglected to shepardize questioned authority that would have led to controlling authority).

8.22 If your chosen legal-citation system does not explain how to cite some materials, such as electronic or Internet sources, consult a recently published nonlegal manual of style.

(a) *Nonlegal style.* The leading text on matters of nonlegal style is the current edition of the *Chicago Manual of Style*. Keep an up-to-date edition handy.

(b) *Clarity.* When special circumstances make legal-style conventions unworkable, choose clarity over convention. For instance, if there is a commonly understood or otherwise logical abbreviation for a word in a lengthy citation, use that abbreviation.

> "Every legal writer is presumed to be a liar until he proves himself otherwise with a flock of footnotes."
>
> —*Fred Rodell*

§ 9
Footnotes

9.1 Footnotes are a scholar's mark. They establish the foundation on which the writer has built new ideas and revised or replaced old ones. A dearth of footnotes may suggest that a writer (1) is unfamiliar with the literature on the subject, (2) fears that readers will be repelled by too many footnotes, or (3) is withholding due credit so that the ideas expressed will appear more innovative. Because footnotes are also resources and steppingstones for others who are interested in delving deeper into the subject, appearance and content are also important. There is no magic ratio of footnotes to text, but guiding factors include the purpose of the writing, the intended audience, the subject matter, and the content. The appearance of footnotes is almost as important as the information they contain.

9.2 Follow whatever prescriptions are set down in court rules, journal guidelines, or any other controlling directives.

(a) *Court rules.* There is no consistency among courts' preferences for footnote style. For example, U.S. Tax Court Rule of Prac. & Proc. 23(d) prescribes 12-point type for footnotes, but U.S. Supreme Court Rule of Prac. & Proc. 33 prescribes 9-point type.

(b) *Law reviews.* Some law reviews require footnotes to conform to a local system of citation (e.g., the *Texas Law Review* and most other law reviews in that state follow the *Texas Rules of Form*). Others provide detailed guidelines to supplement a general citation system. For example, the *American Indian Law Review* advises writers to use *Bluebook* form, and also requires some terms to be spelled out in the text but expressed as symbols in footnotes (contrary to *Bluebook* style).

9.3 Unless you're required to do otherwise, put footnotes in smaller type than the text, and single-space them.

(a) *Typeface.* Unless court rules, journal guidelines, or other directives state differently, follow the typeface conventions set forth in your chosen legal-citation system.

(b) *Type size.* Unless an express directive provides otherwise, a footnote should be about two points smaller than the body's text (perhaps 11-point type for 13-point text). Avoid minuscule footnotes. They may create the impression that you are trying to obscure poor research or evade page limits (see 9.8).

9.4 Use sequential numbering for footnotes throughout the writing.

(a) *Documents and articles.* To accord with legal-citation rules, footnotes that appear in a brief or a law-review article must be consecutively numbered throughout the work. This is true whether the work contains hundreds of footnotes or just a few.

(b) *Books and treatises.* In a longer scholarly writing such as a book or treatise, the writer may choose to restart the footnote numbers at the beginning of each chapter or section.

(c) *Arabic numerals.* Although nonlegal sources with very few footnotes may use a nonnumerical footnoting system, legal writers prefer numerals—even if only one footnote appears in the writing. (For a curious exception, a solitary footnote marked with an asterisk, see *Westinghouse Elec. Corp. v. NLRB*, 809 F.2d 419, 425 (7th Cir. 1987).)

9.5 Put the superscript number after all punctuation marks except a dash and, sometimes, a closing parenthesis.

(a) *Dash.* Separating the superscript from the related clause or sentence can cause confusion. The em dash highlights what immediately precedes it. If the citation is separated from the emphasized clause, the relationship between the sources listed in the footnote and the statements is obscured. For instance, if both statements are supported by caselaw, a reader cannot distinguish whether a cited case supports both statements or only one.

> Ex.: It is a well-established common-law principle that mere "fighting words" are not sufficient provocation to justify an assault[8]—yet some appellate courts have found that a victim's vaguely worded insults invite a defendant's violent response.[9]

(b) *Parentheses.* The superscript is placed outside an end parenthesis if the superscript refers to what is before the opening parenthesis as well as the contents of the parentheses. Otherwise, place the superscript inside the closing parenthesis.

> Ex.: The monitor was visible to everyone in the courtroom (except for one juror who was asleep)[1] throughout the daylong hearing. (Reference is to everything before and within parentheses.)

> Ex.: A reasonable consumer should be able to see that a bottle contains a foreign substance as large as a mouse (unless the bottle is opaque[7]), and complain to the vendor, not a court. (Reference is to contents of parentheses only.)

(c) *Quotation marks.* The superscript is placed outside closing quotation marks.

> Ex.: Paraphrasing Justice Oliver Wendell Holmes, the court declared that "it must be assumed that a jury does its duty, abides by cautionary instructions, and finds facts only because those facts are proved."[2]

9.6 Never use more than one superscript in the same place.

(a) *Lack of clarity.* When two superscripts appear side by side, their purposes are unclear. They may refer to different sources for different propositions or to the same proposition in multiple sources (see 9.7). Or they may refer to contradictory sources.

(b) *Contrary information.* It is not necessary to footnote a contradictory source separately. Use a signal to distinguish the sources cited, and if necessary use parentheticals.

Not this: [3] *Crawn v. Campo*, 643 A.2d 600, 605 (N.J. 1994) (holding that standard for liability in recreational sports injury cases is recklessness, not ordinary negligence).

[4] *But see Lestina v. West Bend Mut. Ins. Co.*, 501 N.W.2d 28, 33 (Wis. 1993) (adopting negligence standard to determine whether recreational-sports participants are liable for their conduct).

But this: [3] *Crawn v. Campo*, 643 A.2d 600, 605 (N.J. 1994) (holding that standard for liability in recreational sports injury cases is recklessness, not ordinary negligence). *But see Lestina v. West Bend Mut. Ins. Co.*, 501 N.W.2d 28, 33 (Wis. 1993) (adopting negligence standard to determine whether recreational-sports participants are liable for their conduct).

9.7 Consolidate multiple sources into one footnote when possible.

(a) *Full support.* Resources that apply generally to a statement or proposition should appear in the same footnote. It is not usually necessary to provide a separate footnote for every source, even if several are specifically referred to.

Ex. (text): Many leading legal minds—Blackstone, Darrow, and Dworkin among them—have spoken out about capital punishment.[4]

Ex. (footnote): [4] Ronald Dworkin, *Freedom's Law* 300–01 (1996) (discussing how the Eighth Amendment bars capital punishment); Clarence Darrow, *Clarence Darrow on the Death Penalty* 39 (1991) (noting that although the defendant has killed, that itself is no justification for the state taking life; stating that "I would hate to live in a state that I didn't think was better than a murderer"); 4 William Blackstone, *Commentaries on the Laws of England* 18–19 (1765) (calling for restrictions on death penalty).

(b) *Distinctions.* If a clause in the sentence applies to some but not all of the cited sources, place one superscript at the end of the clause and another at the end of the sentence.

Ex.: One legal scholar has argued that a fine is sufficient punishment,[5] but another asserts that confinement motivates offenders to reform.[6]

9.8 Never use footnotes to evade page-limit restrictions.

(a) *Ethics.* This ploy is easily detected, is widely frowned on, and brings your integrity into question.

Ex.: *See, e.g., Anderson v. Alpha Portland Ind., Inc.*, 836 F.2d 1512, 1521 (8th Cir. 1988) (caustically observing that plaintiff's counsel violated the spirit of the page-limit rules by overusing single-spaced footnotes).

(b) *Sanctions.* Attempting to circumvent court rules can draw severe sanctions, such as:

- a public reprimand

  Ex.: *Lake County Riverboat L.P. v. Ill. Gaming Bd.*, 730 N.E.2d 524, 534 (Ill. App. Ct. 2000) (scolding attorneys for using voluminous single-spaced substantive footnotes in minuscule type).

- damages

  Ex.: *Cattellier v. Depco, Inc.*, 696 N.E.2d 75, 79 (Ind. Ct. App. 1998) (ordering attorney to pay opposing counsel's fees as damages and penalty for using smaller type than rules required).

- a lost award

  Ex.: *Varda, Inc. v. Ins. Co. of N. Am.*, 45 F.3d 634, 640 (2d Cir. 1995) (denying usual award of appeal costs because most of brief's facts and argument were contained in single-spaced, page-long footnotes).

- fines

  Ex.: *Westinghouse Elec. Corp. v. NLRB*, 809 F.2d 419, 425 (7th Cir. 1987) (unnumbered footnote) (levying a $1,000 fine on attorneys who used single-spaced footnotes to condense 70 pages into 50).

  Ex.: *Kano v. Nat'l Consumer Coop. Bank*, 22 F.3d 899, 899 (9th Cir. 1994) (imposing a $1,500 fine after noting that attorney was aware of rules and nonetheless used noncompliant footnotes in two briefs).

- the striking of a brief

  Ex.: *TK-7 Corp. v. Estate of Barbouti*, 966 F.2d 578, 579 (10th Cir. 1992) (striking brief for compressing nine pages of text into illegitimately shrunken footnotes).

- waiver of appeal

  Ex.: *Cattellier v. Depco, Inc.*, 696 N.E.2d 75, 80 n. 5 (Ind. Ct. App. 1998) (warning that repeated rule violations could bring appeal's dismissal).

9.9 Minimize substantive footnotes.

(a) *Purpose.* Do not expect readers to look at your footnotes. Besides being time-consuming, many readers find looking up and down the page tiring and distracting.

(b) *Camouflage.* If you use a lot of substantive footnotes, it might look as though you are (1) trying to hide your argument's true merits from an opponent, (2) hedging your arguments, (3) hiding your inability to organize a coherent discussion, or (4) self-indulgently exploring trivialities.

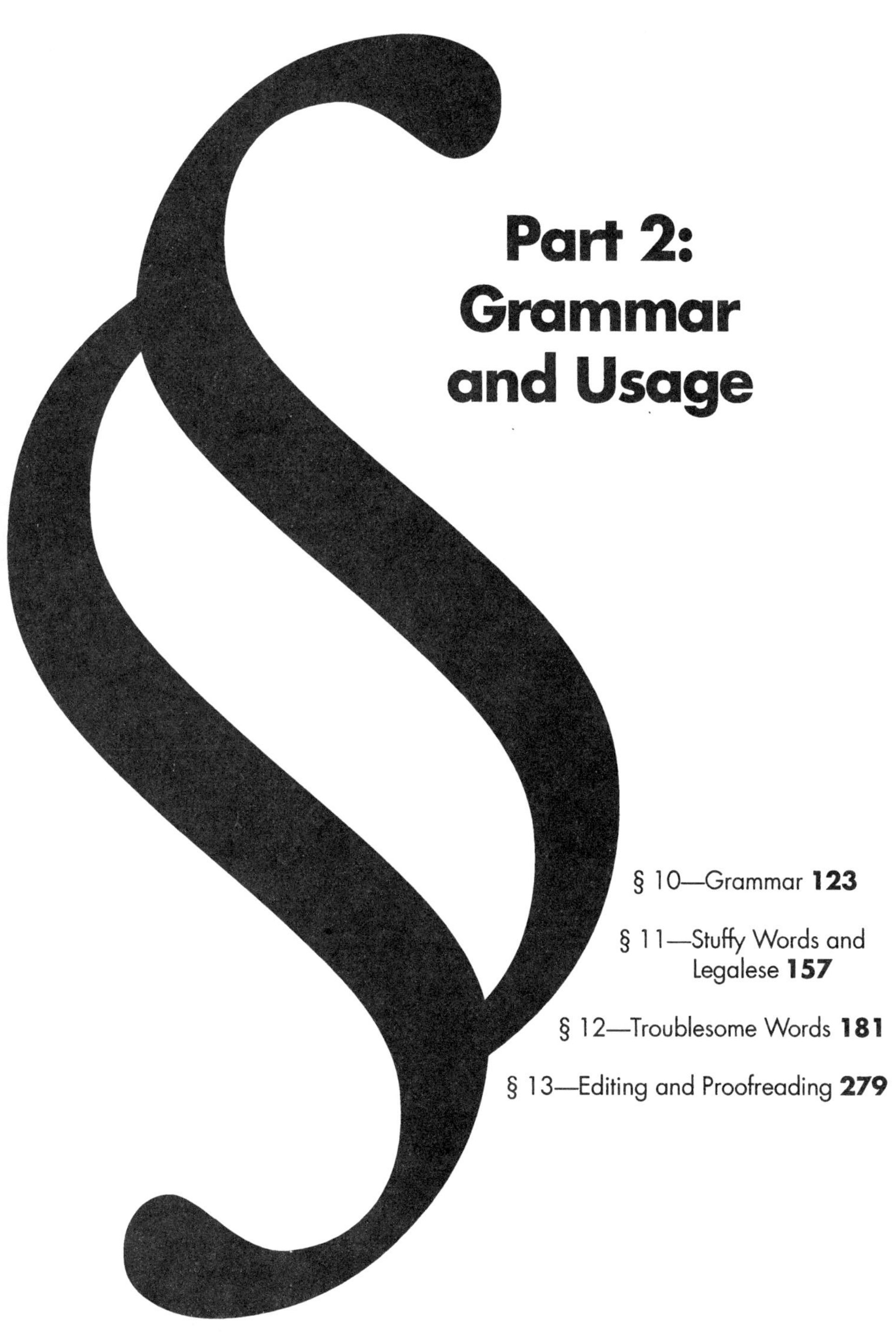

Part 2: Grammar and Usage

§ 10
Grammar

10.1 Grammar is the system of using words to build sentences. These sentence-builders are classified into parts of speech. A single word may act as different parts of speech in different sentences, depending on its role in the sentence. The word *name*, for example, may function as a noun <my name is Jordan>, a verb <name this tune>, or an adjective <name brand>. *More* may function as an adjective <get more exercise> or an adverb <study more diligently>. *Out* may be a noun <three outs retire the side>, a preposition <go out the side exit>, an adverb <it's nice out>, or an adjective <out box>. In modern usage, *out* may also be a verb <you had no right to out him>.

The rules of grammar are entirely functional in their operation: the word's function in the sentence is what matters, not what part of speech the word is usually classified as. By understanding how the various parts of speech work together, writers develop the skills needed to express new ideas in new ways—and still be confident that the message will be communicated to the reader.

Unfortunately, grammar also bears a legacy of bad writing advice. The pedantic "rule" to never split an infinitive, for example, is a superstition that just won't die. So too that a preposition is a taboo part of speech to end a sentence with. And forget the idea that a conjunction should never start a sentence. Any writer can benefit from unlearning such baseless nonsense.

Nouns

10.2 A noun is a name. It may be generic (a "common noun") <street> or specific (a "proper noun") <Wall Street>. It may name a person <lawyer> <Clarence Darrow>, a place <courtroom> <Washington, D.C.>, or a thing, either tangible (a "concrete noun") <reporter> <Federal Reporter 3d> or intangible (an "abstract noun") <public good> <Good Samaritan doctrine>.

A noun may appear in any of three cases: nominative (as a subject or its complement), objective (as an object or its complement), or possessive. But in English, only the possessive case has a change in spelling.

A noun also has properties of number (singular or plural), gender (masculine, feminine, or neuter), and person (first, second, or third). Its spelling usually changes for number, rarely changes for gender, and never changes for person.

A participle, a phrase, or an entire clause may function as a noun in a sentence <seeing is believing> <the Old Man of the Mountain is in New Hampshire> <that we must act quickly should surprise no one>. For that matter, any word or even a letter or number is a noun when used as a word <the word *please* contains two *e*'s>.

A noun may function as some other part of speech. For example, it may function as an adjective in a noun phrase <the litigation team>, and in the possessive case a noun is always adjectival in function <the judge's robe>. Or, especially in loose usage, it may function as a verb <to office downtown>. Some nouns used as verbs may become standard over time <to premiere on Broadway>, but unless they are well accepted you should avoid them in formal writing.

10.3 Ensure that related nouns agree in number.

(a) *Concrete nouns.* Concrete nouns that relate to each other in the sentence must agree in number.

Ex.: Both lawyers waited till the last minute to file their briefs. (Not *brief.*)

(b) *Abstract nouns.* Use a singular abstract noun with a plural concrete noun if the use is idiomatic.

Ex.: Three witnesses promised to testify, and they all kept their word.

But: Family members gathered while the rescue went on; quietly they shared their fears.

10.4 Indicate joint possession by making only the final noun in the series possessive; indicate separate possession by making each noun in a series possessive.

(a) *Joint possession.* When only the final noun in the series is possessive, the indication is that the thing is owned collectively by each of those named in the series.

Ex.: The study group will meet at Jim and Monika's house tonight to review for the final. (Jim and Monika share possession of the house.)

(b) *Individual possession.* When each noun in the series is possessive, the indication is that each owns a separate thing.

Ex.: The group looked at Jim's and Monika's class notes before discussing the model exam question. (Jim and Monika have separate class notes.)

10.5 Use the possessive case with a noun when the sense is a measurement of time or value; but consider recasting the sentence with a phrasal adjective instead.

(a) *As measurement.* In this construction, the possessive is shorthand for an *of*-phrase.

Ex.: The tenant gave the landlord 30 days' notice. (The sense is *notice of 30 days.*)

Ex.: Perot charged that there wasn't a dime's worth of difference between the two major parties. (The sense is *the worth of a dime.*)

(b) *Old-fashioned.* The possessive construction for time can sound somewhat archaic, and wording the phrase is usually a straightforward edit.

Ex.: Each party was required to give a 30-day notice.

10.6 Use the double-possessive construction (*of* ——*'s*) with a noun to shift perspective to the object: the focus is on the object's relationship to the subject of the preposition, not the other way around.

(a) *Redundancy.* This construction (also known as the *double genitive*) is logically redundant: *of* is possessive and *'s* is possessive. But it is deeply rooted in English idiom. It is mandatory with personal pronouns—we might write about *a friend of Keisha* but never *a friend of her* (see 10.18(a)).

Ex.: Jacob was a friend of Mike's. (The focus is on Mike's attitude toward Jacob, not the other way around.)

Ex.: This line of questioning of Mr. Clark's has nothing to do with any issue before this court.

(b) *To avoid ambiguity.* The construction can sometimes be useful to prevent ambiguity. But there is often a superior alternative to the double possessive.

Ex.: This is a painting of Helen's.
Distinguish: This is a painting of Helen.
Better: This is Helen's painting.
Or. This painting belongs to Helen.

(c) *Reword.* Even where no ambiguity is possible, a simple edit may result in a more natural-sounding sentence.

Correct: A friend of Amy's stopped by.
Better: One of Amy's friends stopped by.

10.7 Ensure that an appositive agrees with and directly follows the noun or noun phrase that it identifies or supplements; if it is nonrestrictive, set it off with commas, parentheses, or em dashes.

(a) *Defined.* An appositive is a noun or noun phrase that further identifies or further describes another noun or noun phrase (its referent).

Ex.: Susan B. Anthony's father belonged to the Society of Friends, a religious group that recognized the equality of men and women. (The phrase *a religious group that recognized the equality of men and women* is the appositive of *Society of Friends*. It is nonrestrictive, so it is set off from the rest of the sentence, here by commas.)

Ex.: The philosopher Jeremy Bentham is considered the founder of Utilitarianism. (*Jeremy Bentham* is the appositive of *philosopher*. It is restrictive, so it is not set off.)

Ex.: Unless they represent the government, amici curiae must obtain the court's leave (permission) to file a brief. (*Permission* is the appositive of *leave*. It is nonrestrictive, so it is set off, here by parentheses.)

(b) *Agreement.* An appositive must agree in number, gender, case, and person with its referent.

Not this: John C. Calhoun's career, vice president under both John Quincy Adams and Adams's archrival Andrew Jackson, was unique in American history. (The possessive *Calhoun's* cannot serve as the referent to the nominative appositive *vice president.*)

But this: John C. Calhoun, vice president under both John Quincy Adams and Adams's archrival Andrew Jackson, had a career unique in American history. (Both referent *Calhoun* and appositive *vice president* are in the nominative case.)

Ex.: Truman bypassed two sitting justices, Robert Jackson and Hugo Black, and nominated as chief justice his treasury secretary, Frederick Moore Vinson. (*Justices* and *Jackson and Black* agree in number, as do *secretary* and *Vinson.*)

(c) *If nonrestrictive.* If an appositive is nonrestrictive—if it explains something more about its referent but does not exclusively identify it—set it off by commas (usually), parentheses (to decrease emphasis), or em dashes (to increase emphasis).

Ex.: John McCain, an Arizona senator, found unlikely allies among liberal Democrats.

Ex.: John McCain (R-Ariz.) found unlikely allies among liberal Democrats.

Ex.: John McCain—a conservative Republican senator—found unlikely allies among liberal Democrats.

But: The conservative Republican senator John McCain found unlikely allies among liberal Democrats. (No commas or other setoff punctuation because *John McCain* is necessary to the meaning of the sentence: it restricts the universe of *conservative Republican senators* that the sentence may refer to.)

10.8 Be careful about irregular plurals.

(a) *Irregular forms.* Most English nouns form their plurals by adding an *-s* or *-es*. But many words have irregular plural forms. Some change a vowel; some change a consonant; some add an *-en* or *-ren* (see 7.7(e) and (f)).

Ex.: foot – feet

Ex.: mouse – mice

Ex.: man – men

Ex.: woman – women

Ex.: life – lives

Ex.: child – children

(b) *Romance syntax.* Especially in law, many terms that have entered the language from Law French retain the noun–adjective syntax; it is the noun part that takes the plural form (see 7.8).

Ex.: notary public – notaries public

Ex.: attorney general – attorneys general

Ex.: court-martial – courts-martial

(c) *Foreign terms.* Many foreign words retain their original plural forms; others have been anglicized so that they take the English *-s* or *-es*; still others take both forms, sometimes for different meanings of the word (see 7.8).

Ex.: alumnus – alumni

Ex.: antenna – antennae (insects) – antennas (cars)

Ex: medium – media (journalists) – mediums (clairvoyants)

(d) *Same form.* Some words keep the same appearance for the singular and plural; this is especially true of game animals.

Ex.: deer – deer

Ex.: fish – fish

Ex.: caribou – caribou

(e) *Confused singulars.* Some words look plural in form but are actually singular; many of them are often mistakenly used with plural verbs. For example, *kudos* and *bona fides* are both singular nouns, not plural.

Pronouns

10.9 A pronoun is a word that stands in for a noun. That noun is usually an antecedent—that is, a word that appears before the pronoun and that the pronoun refers to. A few pronouns—such as *you*, *I*, *everyone*, and *nothing*—do not require antecedents because the reference is obvious. Interrogative pronouns do not require antecedents because the reference is unknown. And because indefinite pronouns are undefined, most do not take antecedents.

Pronouns are classified by their function as:

- personal (*I, me, you, he, him, she, her, it, we, us, they, them*);
- possessive (*my, mine, your, yours, his, her, hers, its, our, ours, their, theirs*);
- reflexive–intensive (*myself, yourself, himself, herself, itself, ourselves, yourselves, themselves*);
- demonstrative (*this, that, these, those*);
- interrogative (*who, whom, whose, which, what*);
- relative (*who, whom, whose, what, when, where, why, which, that*, and many combined forms with the suffixes *-ever* and *-soever*);
- indefinite (including *all, another, any, both, each, either, every, few, many, most, much, neither, nobody, none, no one, nothing, one, ones, other, others, several, some*, and compound forms with the suffixes *-one, -body*, and *-thing*); or
- reciprocal (*each other, one another*).

A pronoun has the same number, person, and gender as its antecedent, but its case is determined by its use in the sentence. In general, these properties matter more with pronouns than nouns because pronouns can vary considerably in form according to those properties (e.g., *they, them, their, theirs*).

Particular problems arise with agreement in number, person, and gender between the pronoun and its antecedent, and with confusion about where to use the nominative or objective case.

10.10 Make the grammatical antecedent of a pronoun the noun that (1) precedes the pronoun most closely, and (2) agrees in number, gender, and person with that pronoun.

Number

(a) *Generally.* Use a pronoun that agrees in number with its antecedent.

Not this: The company found that they could not meet the demand.

Not this: The company found that itcould not meet the demand.

(b) *From antecedent.* A pronoun is singular or plural according to the number of the noun or pronoun it refers to.

Ex.: The *parties* entered the mediation session reluctantly, but by early afternoon *they* appeared to be more cooperative.

Ex.: The parties entered the mediation session reluctantly, but by early afternoon *each side* decided that *it* should cooperate.

(c) *Conjunctive compound antecedent.* A pronoun that refers to two or more antecedents joined by *and* is plural.

Ex.: *The district attorney and the defense counsel* announced that *they* were ready for trial.

Ex.: *The 12 jurors and the bailiff* developed a bond during *their* time together.

(d) *Disjunctive compound antecedent.* A pronoun that refers to two or more singular antecedents joined by *or* or *nor* is singular.

Ex.: Neither *the prosecution nor the defense* had *its* case ready for trial.

Ex.: Tell *Walter or Bill* to file the petition when *he* goes to the courthouse this afternoon.

(e) *Disjunctive with mixed antecedents.* If antecedents of mixed number are joined by *or* or *nor*, the pronoun should agree with the closest antecedent; but because it is jarring to encounter a singular pronoun with a potentially plural antecedent, it is much better to put the plural antecedent last, if possible (see 10.26(d)).

Ex.: If you find *my keys or my pen*, bring *it* to me.

Better: If you find *my pen or my keys*, bring *them* to me.

Ex.: Either *the trial judge or the three appellate judges* will decide this issue, so we will leave it up to *them*.

(f) *Two or more adjectives.* If a singular antecedent is modified by two or more adjectives and used in a comparative way, the pronoun will be plural to reflect the plural sense of the multiple adjectives combining with the singular noun.

Ex.: French, Quebecois, and Louisiana law reflect their Roman roots.

Ex.: Criminal and tort law differ significantly in their definitions of *assault*.

(g) *Singular indefinite pronoun.* As an antecedent, a clearly singular indefinite pronoun (*another*, *each*, *either*, *every*, *much*, *neither*, *nobody*, *no one*, *nothing*, *one*, *other*, and combining forms) takes a singular pronoun.

Ex.: There's *something* about Mary. I don't know what *it* is.

Ex.: *Everyone* is free to take *his or her* business elsewhere.

(h) *Plural indefinite pronoun.* As an antecedent, a clearly plural indefinite pronoun (*both, few, many, others, several*) takes a plural pronoun.

Ex.: Counsel clients thoroughly; *most* don't understand *their* rights, and *few* know all *their* options.

Ex.: In the jury room, *several* still held out. *They* didn't believe that the plaintiff was being honest.

(i) *Other indefinite pronouns.* Some indefinite pronouns may be singular or plural (*all, any, more, most, none*); as antecedents, they take either a singular or a plural pronoun, depending on their context in the sentence. *None* is notable: as a condensation of *not one* or *no one*, it would appear to be singular in form; but in use it is often plural. Both uses are correct, the singular being both rarer and more emphatic.

Ex.: *Some* of the money *is* mine. I want *it.*

Ex.: *Most* of the coins *are* mine. I want *them.*

Ex.: *None* of the circuits *are* eager to extend the doctrine.

Or: *None* of the circuits *is* eager to extend the doctrine.

(j) *Collective nouns.* A collective noun poses a special problem: if the action or state expressed by the predicate is collective, the pronoun is singular; but if it is individual, the pronoun is plural. In British usage, collective nouns usually take a plural pronoun.

Ex.: The *crowd* rose to *their* feet as the ball-carrier broke into the clear.

Ex.: The *team* gave *its* all in the come-from-behind win.

(k) *Relative pronouns.* A relative pronoun takes on the number, person, and gender of its antecedent and passes them on to any pronouns that in turn refer to the relative pronoun.

Ex.: It is I who am responsible for my fate. (*Who* becomes first-person singular and takes the *be*-verb *am* and the personal pronoun *my.*)

Ex.: It is she who is responsible for her fate. (*Who* becomes third-person singular feminine and takes the *be*-verb *is* and the personal pronoun *her.*)

Ex.: It is they who are responsible for their fate. (*Who* becomes third-person plural and takes the *be*-verb *are* and the personal pronoun *their.*)

Gender

(l) *Generally.* Use a pronoun that agrees in gender with its antecedent.

(m) *Third-person singular.* A personal pronoun in the third person may be masculine (*he, him, his*), feminine (*she, her, hers*), or neuter (*it, its*) in gender; it must match the gender of its antecedent.

Ex.: Taft never forgot *Learned Hand's* "disloyalty," and many believe that this act cost *Hand his* first chance to serve on the Supreme Court.

Ex.: By this time, *she* was known as *Red Emma*, and *she* was followed by detectives wherever *she* went.

Ex.: The *Tractatus* played a crucial role in making the common law more uniform. In 14 books *it* covered each of the 80 distinct writs used in the king's courts.

(n) *Gender-neutral masculine.* It is no longer customary to use a masculine form as a gender-neutral inclusive (that is, with the understanding that the feminine is included as well). See 12.4(n) and (o) for tips on how to avoid constructions that readers may consider sexist.

Ex.: The respondent has 20 days to file an answer. (Not *his answer.*)

(o) *Singular "they."* In formal writing, do not use *they, them,* or *their* as a gender-neutral third-person singular.

Ex.: *Everyone* should bring *his or her* own laptop computer to the software-training class. (Not *their own laptop computer.*)

Better: *All* participants should bring *their* own laptop computers to the software-training class.

(p) *Neuter by default.* Where gender is indefinite or irrelevant, use the neuter terms.

Ex.: Well, John Marshall has made his *decision.* Let him enforce *it.*

Ex.: It was as though *time itself* stood still.

But: It was as though *Justice herself* wept.

Person

(q) *Generally.* Use a pronoun that agrees in person with its antecedent.

Not this: Every lawyer needs a good moral compass, or else you may wind up facing disciplinary proceedings. (Shift from third-person antecedent to second-person pronoun.)

But this: As a lawyer, you need a good moral compass, or else you may wind up facing disciplinary proceedings.

Or this: Lawyers need good moral compasses, or else they may wind up facing disciplinary proceedings.

(r) *Distinguished.* A first-person pronoun refers to the speaker (*I, me, we, us, my, mine, our, ours, myself, ourselves*); a second-person pronoun refers to the person being spoken to (*you, your, yours, yourself, yourselves*); a third-person pronoun refers to someone or something else (*he, him, she, her, it, they, them, his, her, hers, its, their, theirs, himself, herself, itself, themselves*).

Ex.: *Tom Clark* had been a Texan Democrat all *his* life and a politician–prosecutor for most of it, *his* six years on the Court not excluded.

Ex.: *I* can't find *my* glasses.

Ex.: *Mr. Watson,* come here. I want *you.*

10.11 Make pronoun references unambiguous.

(a) *Multiple antecedents.* If another noun of the same number, person, and gender comes between the intended antecedent and the pronoun, the sentence may be ambiguous; it will probably be awkward even if there is no reasonable misunderstanding.

Ex.: The plaintiff's attorney handed the affidavit to the clerk; she then asked the judge to enter it into evidence. (*She* might be either the *clerk*—the closer noun and the grammatical antecedent—or the *attorney*.)

Better: After handing the affidavit to the clerk, the plaintiff's attorney asked the judge to enter it as evidence. (The pronoun *it* is unambiguous since it could not refer to any of the three people that precede it in the sentence.)

(b) *Repeated pronoun.* Do not use the same pronoun to refer to more than one antecedent in close proximity, especially in the same sentence.

Not this: Ayoka had left her purse at the office, so Robin lent her $10 of her own money.

But this: Ayoka had left her purse at the office, so Robin lent her $10.

(c) *Explicit antecedent.* The antecedent must appear in the sentence; it cannot be merely implied.

Ex.: Having grown up in a law-oriented family, Karen always wanted to become one herself. (There is no explicit antecedent for *one*. Replace *one* with *a lawyer*.)

(d) *Noun antecedent.* Possessive nouns function as adjectives. In formal writing, an adjective cannot serve as an antecedent; also, the noun it is modifying may be the grammatical antecedent in the sentence.

Ex.: The car's exhaust system needs work, but otherwise it runs fine. (The grammatical antecedent of *it* is *system*, not *car*. Replace *it* with *the car*.)

Ex.: We took John's car because he was going to drive anyway. (Because *John's* serves as an adjective in the sentence, in the strictest grammar it cannot be the noun antecedent of *he*.)

(e) *Antecedent first.* In formal writing, do not use a pronoun before its antecedent in a sentence. Otherwise, it may be unclear what the pronoun refers to.

Not this: Because they were afraid of the expense and the uncertain outcome, the plaintiffs agreed to the settlement offer.

But this: Because the plaintiffs were afraid of the expense and the uncertain outcome, they agreed to the settlement offer because they.

Or this: The plaintiffs agreed to the settlement offer because they were afraid of the expense and the uncertain outcome.

10.12 Use the nominative case for a subject or a predicate nominative.

(a) *Generally.* The nominative-case pronouns are *I*, *we*, *you*, *he*, *she*, *it*, *they*, *who*, and *whoever*.

Ex.: They will make the first offer. (Subject.)

Ex.: Who am I? (*Who* and *I* are in the nominative case.)

Ex.: You! Get over here! (Direct address.)

(b) *As predicate nominative.* A predicate nominative is a noun or pronoun that follows a linking verb and refers to the subject. When a personal pronoun is used as a predicate nominative, the choice between the nominative and objective case can be tricky: the nominative case, while correct, sounds stilted. It is usually better to rephrase the sentence.

Ex.: This is she. (Predicate nominative.)

Better: Speaking.

10.13 Use the objective case for (1) the direct or indirect object of a verb, and (2) the object of a preposition.

(a) *Generally.* The objective-case pronouns are *me, us, you, him, her, it, them, whom,* and *whomever.*

Ex.: How will this ruling affect us? (Direct object.)

Ex.: Give me an example. (Indirect object.)

Ex.: To whom is the letter addressed? (Object of a preposition.)

Ex.: Let this be a lesson to you and me. (Not *you* and *I*.) (Compound object of a preposition.)

(b) *Determined by function.* When a pronoun appears in a clause, its function in the clause—not the clause's function in the sentence—determines the case of the pronoun.

Ex.: The contract will go to whoever submits the lowest bid. (Not *whomever*: *whoever* is the subject of the dependent clause, so it is nominative.)

10.14 Use the correct case and order when using a first-person pronoun with a noun or another personal pronoun in a compound phrase.

(a) *First person last.* By custom, the first-person pronoun comes last in such a phrase.

Ex.: Ralph and I will take the deposition. (Not *I and Ralph*.)

Ex.: Just between you and me, I think they're ready to settle. (Not *between me and you*.)

(b) *Hypercorrection in first person.* It is a common error to "overcorrect" and use the nominative case where the objective case is required in a compound construction with the first-person personal pronoun. One way to check is to speak the sentence using only the questionable pronoun.

Ex.: Just between you and me, I think they're ready to settle. (Not *between you and I*.)

Ex.: It's time for her and Abbie to get over their differences. (Not *for she and Abbie*.)

10.15 In formal writing, use the nominative case after *than* if the pronoun would be nominative in the understood clause that follows *than*.

(a) *As a conjunction.* In formal writing, restrict *than* to its traditional use as a conjunction. The pronoun takes its case from its function in the resulting clause, even if most of the clause is understood rather than expressed. If the pronoun is the subject or the predicate nominative of the clause, it should be in the nominative case.

Ex.: You know that better than I. (The understood clause is *than I do.*)

Ex.: I regard her more highly than he. (Understood is *than he does.*)

Ex.: I regard her more highly than him. (Understood is *than I regard him.*)

(b) *As a preposition.* In speech and in informal writing, the idiomatic use of *than* as a preposition with a pronoun in the objective case is accepted.

Ex.: You know better than me how patent law works.

Ex.: I deserve to win this case more than her.

10.16 In formal writing, use the nominative case for a pronoun used as a predicate nominative, renaming the subject after a linking verb.

(a) *Formal usage.* In formal writing, the rules of grammar are followed more strictly. If the wording sounds pompous, it is usually better to recast the sentence.

Ex.: It was I who testified in your behalf.

Ex.: The witness spoke with Mrs. Harrison almost every day; he knew right away that the caller was she. (Better: . . . *he knew right away that she was the caller.*)

(b) *Informal usages.* In speech and in informal writing, the use of the objective case is often idiomatic and unobjectionable.

Ex.: It's me.

Ex.: Is that her?

10.17 Use the possessive case of a pronoun to show ownership, attribution, measure, or some similar relationship.

(a) *Generally.* The possessive pronouns are *my*, *mine*, *your*, *yours*, *his*, *her*, *hers*, *its*, *our*, *ours*, *their*, and *theirs*.

Ex.: Can a third party get its voters to the polls?

Ex.: You have to get your facts right.

(b) *No apostrophe.* None of the possessive pronouns uses an apostrophe; confounding the possessive *its* with the contraction *it's* (meaning *it is*) is the most common spelling error in the language.

Ex.: It's important that achievement receive its reward.

(c) *Absolute possessives.* There are two ways to show possession with possessive pronouns: the simple possessive <that is *your* car> and the absolute possessive <that car is *yours*>. The form is the same for some pronouns <*his–its*> but different for others <*her–hers*>.

Ex.: That is *his* wallet. / That wallet is *his*. (Same form.)

Ex.: That is *her* briefcase. / That briefcase is *hers*. (Different forms.)

(d) *With a gerund.* Use the possessive case for a pronoun or noun that is paired with a gerund (i.e., an *-ing* verb functioning as a noun), but the objective case if it is paired with a present participle.

Ex.: We're counting on his speaking at the convention. (It is the *speaking* that is being counted on, not *him.*)

Ex.: Our schedule shows him flying to the convention on the 15th. (*Him flying to the convention on the 15th* is what the schedule shows.)

Ex.: There is no use in your testifying. (*Testifying* is useless, not *you.*)

10.18 Use the double-possessive construction (*of* —) with personal pronouns.

(a) *Mandatory with pronouns.* In this idiomatic construction (also called the *double genitive*), the use of a noun in the objective case is defensible (see 10.6) and even preferred by some authorities. Not so with personal pronouns: the use of the objective case is always a glaring error.

Ex.: He was a friend of mine. (Obviously not *a friend of me.*)

Ex.: Telling the truth was never a strong point of yours.

(b) *To intensify.* This construction can have an intensifying connotation, frequently negative, when the prepositional phrase follows a demonstrative pronoun (*this, that, these, those*) and a class noun.

Ex.: That boy of hers is always getting into trouble.

Ex.: This interrogatory of yours is just a burdensome fishing expedition.

Ex.: Who could ever forget that moving speech of his?

10.19 Use the relative pronoun *who* to refer to people only (although *whose* may refer to things as well); *which* to refer to things or animals only; and *that* to refer to either people or things (or both).

(a) *"That" with people.* While *who* is often the better choice when referring to people, *that* is perfectly proper as well, especially when referring to groups of people taken collectively. It is mandatory to use *that* when referring to people and things combined.

Ex.: The senators who had voted against the bill celebrated their victory.

Ex.: It was the Senate that killed the bill.

Ex.: It was the farm-state Republicans who killed the bill.

Ex.: It was a handful of lobbyists and their bankrolls that turned public opinion against the bill.

(b) *"Which" with things.* Do not use *which* to refer to people; if the clause is nonrestrictive, use *who.*

Ex.: The class of plaintiffs is composed of former customers of the bankrupt company, many of whom lost their entire savings. (Reference to people, so *of whom* rather than *of which.*)

Ex.: A bloc of East Coast senators who had supported the bill tried to bring it up for another vote. (Reference to people—*senators.*)

Ex.: A bloc of East Coast senators, which had supported the bill, tried to bring it up for another vote. (Reference to a thing—*bloc*.)

(c) *"Whose" with things*. It is permissible to use *whose* to mean *of which*.

Ex.: The Capitol dome, whose completion was celebrated in 1882, will be restored next year.

10.20 For relative pronouns referring to anything other than people, use *that* to introduce a restrictive clause, *which* to introduce a nonrestrictive clause.

(a) *Restrictive clause*. A restrictive (or defining) clause is one that is essential to the meaning of the sentence. In the preceding sentence, for example, the clause *that is essential to the meaning of the sentence* is essential to the meaning of the sentence, so it is a restrictive clause. It identifies the type of *one* (clause) that this sentence is about from the universe of all clauses. Use *that* or *who* to introduce a restrictive clause, and do not set off the clause from the rest of the sentence by commas.

Ex.: A union that did not allege any injury from the disqualification of its officer immediately upon conviction lacked standing to challenge the statute imposing the disqualification. (The clause *that did not . . . conviction* restricts the universe of *union*s that the sentence is about.)

Ex.: A defendant who claims mootness because it has stopped the challenged acts bears a heavy burden to show that the wrongful behavior will not recur. (The clause *who claims . . . acts* restricts the universe of *defendant*s that the sentence is about.)

(b) *Nonrestrictive clause*. A nonrestrictive clause, which is also called a nondefining clause, can be removed without changing the essential meaning of the sentence. In the preceding sentence, *which is also called a nondefining clause* is a nonrestrictive clause because the essence of the sentence is unchanged if the clause is removed. It does not restrict the number of *nonrestrictive clause*s that the sentence is about from the universe of all nonrestrictive clauses. Use *which* or *who* to introduce a nonrestrictive clause. Set off the clause from the rest of the sentence—usually by commas, but by parentheses to minimize or by em dashes to emphasize the matter.

Ex.: The plaintiff asked to substitute the state officer as a defendant in place of the state, which had been dismissed on Eleventh Amendment grounds. (The clause *which had been dismissed . . . grounds* does not restrict the universe of *state*s that the sentence is about.)

Ex.: Lawyers—who are officers of the court—should never overlook jurisdictional questions that courts expect the parties to raise first. (The clause *who are officers of the court* does not restrict the universe of *lawyer*s that the sentence is about.)

> "There seems to be a wave of incapacity for grammar, comparable to the phenomenon of a crime wave."
>
> —*Edward N. Teall*

(c) *"That" as restrictive.* By rule, *that* is used to introduce a restrictive clause only; it is always an error to use *that* to introduce a nonrestrictive clause.

Ex.: Courts may attempt to control prejudicial publicity by restricting the information that (not *which*) trial participants can give to the press both before and during a trial. (Restrictive clause.)

Ex.: In *Nebr. Press Ass'n v. Stewart,* the Court held that pretrial gag orders on the press, which (never *that*) amount to prior restraints, are unconstitutional. (Nonrestrictive clause.)

(d) *"Which" as nonrestrictive.* By convention, *which* is reserved for introducing a nonrestrictive clause. It's not an outright blunder to use *which* to introduce a restrictive clause. It's even necessary in a few contexts, such as *that which* and *by which* constructions <*that which* does not kill me makes me stronger>. But it usually sounds slightly pompous.

Ex.: The fighting-words doctrine, which (never *that*) is often relied on by governments to justify regulations, has not been a dispositive ground of decision in many Supreme Court cases. (Nonrestrictive clause.)

Ex.: Fighting words are words which (prefer *that*) by their very utterance inflict injury or tend to incite an immediate breach of the peace. (Restrictive clause.)

(e) *No commas with restrictive clauses.* Never use commas to set off a restrictive clause.

Ex.: Erroneous statements are inevitable in free debate; they must be protected if free expression is to have the breathing space that it needs to survive. (Never a comma after *space.*)

10.21 Use reflexive and reciprocal pronouns with care.

(a) *Reflexive for objective.* Do not use *myself* as a stuffy substitute for the simple *I* or *me.*

Ex.: John and I (not *myself*) want you to draft our wills.

Ex.: The letter was addressed to Jane and me (not *myself*).

(b) *When object is also subject.* Use the reflexive pronoun for the object when the object is the same as the subject.

Ex.: I cut myself while gathering the papers. (*Myself* reflects *I.*)

Ex.: They had to see it for themselves. (*Themselves* reflects *they.*)

Ex.: Keep it to yourself. (*Yourself* reflects the understood subject, *you.*)

(c) *When subject is repeated emphatically.* Use the reflexive pronoun as an intensive when the subject or object is mentioned twice.

Ex.: Abby herself wanted to try the case.

Ex.: Truth itself is the first victim of war.

(d) *"Each other" and "one another."* Use the reciprocal pronoun phrase *each other* to refer to two nouns, *one another* to refer to more than two.

Ex.: The twin brothers supported each other throughout law school.

Ex.: Members of the victim's family consoled one another as the detective testified.

Verbs

10.22 Verbs are words of action or linking. They form the basis for the predicate of the sentence: that which the subject does, is, or is like. English has drawn on German, Latin, Norse, and French for many verbs we use today. The result is a diverse language, but also a lack of uniformity and a perplexing abundance of exceptions to the general rules of grammar.

Verbs have properties of voice (active and passive), mood (indicative, subjunctive, and imperative), tense (present, past, and future, with alternative perfect, progressive, and perfect–progressive aspects of each), number (singular and plural), and person (first, second, and third).

Verbs have five forms: two present-tense forms (the stem and the third-person singular), present participle, past tense, and past participle. Most regular verbs form the third-person singular by adding *-s* or *-es* to the stem, the past tense and past participle by adding *-ed* to the stem, and the present participle by adding *-ing* to the stem. But there are spelling variations according to the ending of the stem. Some examples will illustrate the rules:

- normal *fold–folds–folded–*[*has*] *folded–folding*
- silent *-e* *race–races–raced–*[*has*] *raced–racing*
- consonant + *-y* *bury–buries–buried–*[*has*] *buried–burying*
- vowel + consonant *hop–hops–hopped–*[*has*] *hopped–hopping*

There are many exceptions to the last pattern. Words that are not accented on the last syllable, for example, usually do not double the final consonant before adding a suffix. And American and British spellings differ on many words.

Irregular verbs follow no standard rules in forming their past tense and past participle, although their present participle is formed in the same way as that of regular verbs. When in doubt, consult a dictionary. Here are a few of the irregular verbs in the English language (showing the traditional inflection of stem, past tense, and past participle):

- *begin–began–begun*
- *break–broke–broken*
- *bring–brought–brought*
- *eat–ate–eaten*
- *fly–flew–flown*
- *go–went–gone*
- *hurt–hurt–hurt*
- *lay–laid–laid*
- *lie–lay–lain*
- *mean–meant–meant*
- *set–set–set*
- *sit–sat–sat*
- *steal–stole–stolen*
- *swear–swore–sworn*
- *take–took–taken*

Some verbs have alternative past-tense forms (e.g., *learned* or *learnt*, *strived* or *strove*, *sank* or *sunk*) or past-participle forms (e.g., *proved* or *proven*, *sunk* or *sunken, shrunk* or *shrunken*). A good dictionary will show the preferred form and also usage appropriate to the variants—e.g., differences between the past-tense verb <the plaintiff has proved negligence> and the past-participial adjective <the defendant's negligence is a proven fact>.

Tense, voice, and mood are indicated by using one of the four main verb forms, either alone or with one or more *be*-verbs (*am, are, is, was, were, be, being, been*), auxiliary verbs (*can, could, shall, should, will, would, have, has, had, may, might, must, do, does, did*), or both. Quasi-auxiliary verbs (e.g., *ought to, used to, need to, dare to*) may also add nuance.

Irregular forms and subject–verb agreement are two of the most common problems that writers have with using verbs.

10.23 Use a singular verb after a singular subject.

(a) *Generally.* Use a singular verb with a subject composed of a singular noun or a singular phrase or clause.

Ex.: Nothing is forever.

Ex.: To settle for less than my client has actually paid in medical bills is out of the question. (The entire infinitive phrase *to settle . . . bills* is the subject; it is singular in number.)

Ex.: Denying aliens entry into the country is called *exclusion.* (The gerund phrase *denying aliens . . . country* is the subject; it is singular.)

(b) *Distractions.* Do not be distracted by a prepositional phrase that comes between the subject and verb, or by a predicate nominative or a complement of the other number.

Ex.: A panel comprising seven lawyers, four judges, and three nonlawyers is going to study the community's pro bono needs. (*panel . . . is*)

Ex.: Only one in six of the city's registered voters is expected to participate in the off-year election. (*one . . . is*)

Ex.: Your audience is three judges on the appellate panel. (*audience is*)

Ex.: Quick and painful comes the 12 jurors' decision. (*decision . . . comes*)

Ex.: Furthermore, a faction on the committees that recommended the reforms—after five public hearings and four months of debate—is now talking about opposing the majority report. (*faction . . . is*)

(c) *Dependent clauses.* Do not be distracted by separate agreements within dependent clauses, whose subjects and verbs must agree independently of the main clause.

Ex.: Not one of those people who think they know everything thinks very hard. (*Thinks* agrees with *not one; think* agrees with *who,* which in turn takes the plural attribute of *people;* and *know* agrees with *they.*)

(d) *Compound but singular in meaning.* When a compound subject is singular in meaning, it will take a singular verb. This occurs more often with compound phrases and clauses than with compound words because the construction more often describes steps in a singular process.

Ex.: Black tie and tails is the designated attire.

Ex.: Cream cheese and olive is her favorite sandwich spread.

Ex.: To forsake my client and to settle for less than my client has actually paid in medical bills is out of the question. (The two infinitive phrases refer to the same action, so the sense is singular in number.)

(e) *Compound referring to one thing.* When the compound words refer to a singular thing, the verb will be singular.

Ex.: The hammer and sickle was the Communist Party's insignia. (The singular determiner *the* before *hammer* is a clear signal that the phrase is singular in meaning.)

Ex.: A philanthropist, author, and scholar is with us tonight. (*Philanthropist, author,* and *scholar* all refer to the same person.)

(f) *Illusory compounds.* When a singular subject is joined with other nouns or pronouns by prepositions such as *together with, as well as, along with, but not,* and the like, the subject is still singular and the matching verb should also be singular. The resulting phrase is nonrestrictive and set off with commas.

Ex.: Senator Briley, along with several colleagues, continues to oppose the redistricting plan.

Ex.: The attorney general, not to mention the secretaries of state and defense, supports using the military tribunals.

Ex.: Tawana, but no other students, insists that class never end early.

(g) *Idioms with indefinite pronouns.* Use a singular verb with a compound construction of the singular indefinite pronouns *anyone and everyone, anybody and everybody,* and *anything and everything.*

Ex.: The sergeant said that anything and everything is being done to locate the suspects.

Ex.: Anyone and everyone who calls in to the new phone system gets put on hold immediately.

(h) *Idioms with "each" and "every."* Use a singular verb with compounded singular subjects modified by the indefinite pronoun *each* or *every;* these pronouns relate individually to the verb, so the use of a singular verb is idiomatic (but see 10.23(c)).

Ex.: Every Tom, Dick, and Harry who applies is accepted. (The phrase *every Tom, Dick, and Harry* takes the singular verbs *applies* and *is accepted,* even though the phrase *Tom, Dick, and Harry* alone would take the plural verbs *apply* and *are accepted.*)

Ex.: Tom, Dick, and Harry each applies and is accepted.

(i) *Idiom with "many a."* Use a singular verb with the plural indefinite pronoun *many* as a subject when *many* is followed by *a* and a singular noun.

Ex.: Many a law student has frozen up when finals come around.

> "Grammar is to most of us an elusive mystery, maddening as a mosquito."
>
> —*Robert Palfrey Utter*

(j) *Phrases of measurement.* Use a singular verb with a noun phrase that is plural in form (or appearance) but singular in meaning; especially watch out for mass-noun phrases of measurements, names and titles in plural form, and similar traps.

Ex.: Ten blocks is too far to walk in this rain.

Ex.: A hundred dollars is more than I am willing to pay.

Ex.: Thirty minutes is the standard lunch break here.

Ex.: The Boy Scouts of America has taken a lot of criticism lately.

Ex.: *Seventy-six Trombones* is always a fitting selection for any parade.

Ex.: The United States is a common-law nation.

Ex.: General Motors is up 3%.

Ex.: Politics makes strange bedfellows.

Ex.: Her bona fides is not an issue.

10.24 Use a plural verb after a plural subject.

(a) *Generally.* Use a plural verb with a plural subject and most compound subjects.

Ex.: People demand justice.

Ex.: Property and procedure were my first-year downfalls.

(b) *Conjunctive compound.* A conjunctive-compound subject will usually be plural (but see 10.23(d)–(e)).

Ex.: The plaintiff and the defendant agree to the continuance.

Ex.: What your client wants and what my client wants are two different things. (The two phrases joined by *and* make a plural subject, agreeing with the plural verb *are.*)

(c) *With "each."* Use a plural verb with a plural subject even if the subject is modified by the indefinite pronoun *each*: if the subject is plural rather than a compound of singular nouns or pronouns, then the addition of *each* after the subject does not create the singular-sense idiom described in 10.23(h). Instead, *each* functions as an adverb.

Ex.: The candidates each have two minutes for an opening statement.

(d) *Plural indefinite pronouns.* Use a plural verb with the plural indefinite pronoun *both, few, many, others*, or *several* as the subject.

Ex.: We have two options. Both are problematic.

Ex.: Many are called, but few are chosen.

(e) *With class adjectives.* Use a plural verb with an adjective that is used as a noun to represent a class with the adjective's attribute. Unlike a collective noun, which denotes a singular entity that comprises individual members, a collective adjective represents no singular entity, but rather the assemblage of individual members.

Ex.: The meek stand to inherit the earth.

Ex.: The fragile are protected by the eggshell-skull doctrine.

(f) *Plural-form nouns.* Use a plural verb with a noun that has a plural form and sense.

Ex.: Were these scissors the murder weapon?

Ex.: My running pants are in the wash.

Ex.: The scales of justice are a powerful symbol.

Ex.: The odds are against us.

10.25 Use the context of the sentence to determine whether a singular or plural verb is needed with certain subjects.

(a) *With count pronouns.* Use the context of the sentence to determine the number of the verb when the subject is an indefinite pronoun of count (*all, any, more, most, some*), a numerical fraction, or a noun of partition (e.g., *fraction, part, portion*) or multitude (e.g., *bunch, number, variety*). When the meaning is a part of a singular whole or a mass noun, use a singular verb. When the meaning is a number or a share of more than one thing (a count noun), use a plural verb.

Ex.: Most of the new law students tense up when finals come around.

Ex.: Most of the first-year class tenses up when finals come around.

Ex.: But two-thirds of the tense students perform well.

Ex.: But two-thirds of that group performs well.

Ex.: Unfortunately, a portion of the tensed-up students fail to understand the call of the question.

Ex.: Unfortunately, a portion of that group fails to understand the call of the question.

Ex.: A number of students stress out over finals.

Ex.: A variety of study aids are available.

(b) *With collective nouns.* Use the context of the sentence to determine the number of the verb when the subject is a collective noun; use a singular verb if the action itself is collective, but use a plural verb if the action is individual. The American preference is to use collective nouns (e.g., *committee, staff, team*) as singular, and to specify individuals (e.g., *committee members*) when individual action is implied. In some sentences the distinction between group and individual action will be clear. But often the meaning will be susceptible of either interpretation, and the word choice will be based merely on which form sounds better. Where that is so, consistency of choice within the document is more important than which choice is made.

Ex.: The jury deliberates on a verdict. (A singular, collective action.)

Ex.: The jury eat pizza for lunch. (Plural, individual actions.)

Ex.: The band plays *The Star-Spangled Banner.* (Clearly collective.)

Ex.: The band warm up their instruments. (Clearly individual.)

Ex.: The faculty (*is? are?*) divided on the issue of affirmative action. (The action can be construed as collective or individual.)

(c) *With singular-form nouns.* When a noun has the same form in both numbers, use the correctly numbered verb according to the subject's number.

Ex.: The series on the history of common law runs on Wednesday nights.

Ex.: Two series on the history of common law run simultaneously.

Ex.: A leaping fish breaks the surface.

Ex.: Two leaping fish break the surface.

(d) *With foreign nouns.* With a foreign-derived noun, use the correctly numbered verb according to the subject's number. Foreign-derived nouns ending in *-a* can be especially troublesome because they may be singular <amoeba, encyclopedia, minutia> or plural <criteria, data, media>. *Data* and *media* are often used as singular nouns in casual use, but in formal writing they should be used as plurals. To further complicate matters, the singular terms may form plurals with the Latin *-ae* <minutiae> or the English *-s* <encyclopedias>, or both, alternatively <*amoebae, amoebas*>. And the plural terms may take the singular ending *-um* <medium> or *-on* <criterion>. When in doubt, check a dictionary.

Ex.: Local media are covering this case closely.

Ex.: The Yale alumna is taking a job with Dow Chemical.

Ex.: The data are clear on this point.

Ex.: The minutiae of the disputed facts of this case make the legal principles hard to extract.

(e) *With "-ics" words.* Use the context of the sentence to determine the number of the verb when the subject is the name of a science or discipline ending in *-ics*. Words such as *economics* and *statistics* may refer in the singular to the discipline itself, or in the plural to the practical application of the discipline.

Ex.: Economics is central to any management curriculum.

Ex.: The economics of this project are going to require some public funding.

Ex.: Ceramics is a great hobby.

Ex.: These ceramics are from the pre-Columbian era.

(f) *In relative clauses.* Use the antecedent of a relative pronoun to determine the number and person of the verb in the relative clause.

Ex.: The book that contains the story is checked out. (*That* is third-person singular, properties that it assumes from *book*, so it takes the corresponding verb, *contains.*)

Ex.: The books that contain the story are checked out. (*That* is third-person plural, properties that it assumes from *books*, so it takes the corresponding verb, *contain.*)

Ex.: Wasn't it you who were responsible? (*Who* is second person, a property that it assumes from *you*, so it takes the corresponding *be*-verb, *were.*)

10.26 If the subject is a disjunctive compound (joined by *or* or *nor*), the verb should agree with the element of the compound closest to the verb; if the compound contains both singular and plural elements, try to place the plural subject closest to the verb.

(a) *With singular subjects.* Use a singular verb with two or more singular subjects joined by *or* or *nor.* It does not matter whether the subject is composed of words, phrases, or clauses.

Ex.: Neither the prosecution nor the defense is ready for trial.

Ex.: Either two associates or I am taking Stone's deposition tomorrow. (The verb *am* agrees both in number and in person with the nearer subject, *I.* But the sentence sounds awkward.)

(b) *Singular in meaning.* If the compound subject denotes a thing that is singular in meaning, or describes the same thing, use a singular verb.

Ex.: To plead it or to try it is the decision you face. (It's a singular decision with two options.)

Ex.: To be or not to be is Hamlet's dilemma. (It's a singular dilemma.)

(c) *With mixed elements.* If the compound subject contains singular and plural elements, use a verb that agrees with the closest subject.

Ex.: Either trade-secret law or patent law, but not both, protects any single invention.

Ex.: Neither the jurors nor the judge seems sympathetic to our argument.

(d) *Plural element last.* If possible, put the plural subject last to make the sentence less jarring (see 10.10(e)).

Ex.: Neither the judge nor the jurors seem sympathetic to our argument.

10.27 Minimize the passive voice.

(a) *How formed.* The passive voice consists of a *be*-verb (or sometimes a form of *get*) combined with the past participle of a transitive verb. Intransitive verbs (those that do not take a direct object) cannot form the passive voice. The *be*-verb may be understood rather than expressed. A *by* prepositional phrase often accompanies the construction; when it does not appear, it can be understood from the context (see 10.43(c), 13.3(b)).

Ex.: State immunity cannot be abrogated under the Fourteenth Amendment unless it is shown that the states have engaged in a pattern of patent infringement. (The sentence has two passive constructions: *immunity cannot be abrogated* and *it is shown.*)

Ex.: Before the 1976 Act, sound recordings had no copyright protection and could be reproduced by "pirates" with relative immunity from federal copyright laws. (The *could be reproduced* construction is followed by a *by* prepositional phrase.)

Ex.: Consider it done. (Either *to have been* or *having been* is understood before the past participle *done* in this oblique passive construction.)

Ex.: I heard it suggested that we raise our offer. (Some *be*-verb is understood before *suggested.*)

(b) *Where appropriate.* The passive voice is often criticized as weaker than the active voice. The criticism is justified by general overuse of the passive voice. Writers should watch for it and prefer the active voice unless there is good reason not to. But, as the first two sentences of this paragraph show, the passive voice is appropriate in some places, especially (1) where the actor is unknown or unimportant, and (2) where the emphasis is on the recipient of the action instead of the actor.

Ex.: The jury awarded the plaintiff $55,000. (Active voice.)

Ex.: The plaintiff was awarded $55,000. (Passive voice.)

10.28 Use the subjunctive mood to express a wish, a demand, a requirement, an exhortation, or a statement contrary to fact—as well as in a number of fixed idioms.

(a) *Generally.* The subjunctive mood is peculiar in form and function. It is little used except in a few fixed phrases. A verb in the subjunctive mood has no third-person-singular (*-s*) variation; *be* is used rather than *am*, *are*, and *is* <if I be honest>; and *were* is used instead of *was* <if he were honest>. The present tense may be used to express would-be conditions in the past <truth be told, their objection should have been sustained>, and the past tense to express would-be conditions in the present <I would not do that if I were you>.

Ex.: Be that as it may, the suit has already been filed. (*Be that as it may* is a fixed phrase in the subjunctive mood.)

Ex.: If you be honest you will admit liability for the accident. (The stilted sound of *if you be honest* reflects the archaic nature of the subjunctive mood. But changing it to *if you were honest* changes the tone from "you can be honest" to "you are dishonest.")

(b) *"That"-clause of need.* Use the subjunctive mood in *that*-clauses of request, demand, and requirement. If a *be*-verb is required, use *be* (regardless of person and number) and the past or present participle, regardless of when the action takes place. If no *be*-word is required, use the present-tense stem alone, regardless of when the action takes place.

Ex.: We insist that we be allowed to review the document before it is admitted into evidence. (*Be allowed to review* is subjunctive, expressing a request.)

Ex.: Rule 11 requires that lawyers use good faith in making and responding to discovery requests. (*Use* is subjunctive, expressing requirement.)

Ex.: The retiring judge told about being a first-year law student whose torts professor insisted that he study harder or face certain failure. (*Study* is present-tense subjunctive, expressing a demand.)

Ex.: The foundation requires that a scholarship recipient be enrolled full-time to maintain eligibility. (*Be enrolled* is subjunctive, expressing a requirement.)

(c) *To express a wish.* Use the past-tense subjunctive mood with the word *were* (regardless of person and number) to indicate a wish. Use the past tense to indicate a present-time wish.

Ex.: I wish Maria were more certain about her decision. (*Were* is subjunctive; the indicative verb would be *was*. The past-tense form attains a present-time meaning in the subjunctive mood.)

Ex.: Don't you wish you were a fly on the jury-room wall?

Ex.: I wish I were in Dixie.

(d) *Exhortations and things contrary to fact.* Use the subjunctive mood in clauses starting with *if*, *as if*, or *as though* to express exhortations and things contrary to fact (including suppositions and illusions as well as impossible things).

Ex.: If we were to offer $75,000, would you take it?

Ex.: Any reasonable official would have known that a choke hold was excessive force, but the officer acted as if immunity would protect him.

Ex.: The cross-examination seemed as though it were never going to end. (An illusion: *were going to end* is subjunctive.)

Ex.: Long live rock 'n' roll! (An exhortation: *may* is understood, so the meaning is *may rock 'n' roll live long*.)

(e) *Fixed idioms.* Use the subjunctive mood as it occurs in many fixed phrases.

Ex.: If I were you . . . .

Ex.: If need be . . . .

Ex.: So help me God . . . .

10.29 Connect every participial phrase to its subject.

(a) *At start of sentence.* If a participial phrase begins the sentence, its subject should be the noun, pronoun, or noun phrase that most closely follows it. A participial phrase that modifies any other potential subject is called a misplaced participle. One that has no subject at all in the sentence is called a dangling participle.

Ex.: In keeping with constitutional policy, the Supreme Court has defined a "writing" as any physical rendering of fruits of creative intellectual or aesthetic labor. (The subject of *in keeping with constitutional policy* is *the Supreme Court*.)

Ex.: Described in dissent as "the Dred Scott decision of copyright law," *Williams & Wilkins Co.* appears not to have given serious consideration to the effect of defendants' practices on plaintiff's potential market. (The subject of *described . . . law* is *Williams & Wilkins Co.*)

(b) *Close to subject.* If a participial phrase does not start a sentence, it should modify the noun, pronoun, or noun phrase that most closely precedes it.

Ex.: The Court has held there to be no First Amendment immunity for a TV station charged with misappropriating a performer's human-cannonball act by videotaping the entire act and broadcasting it on a news program. (The subject of *charged . . . program* is *TV station*.)

Ex.: Because "malice" is a term of such variable meaning, some courts, influenced no doubt by the prima facie tort theory, have abandoned the concept altogether and speak rather of justifiable and unjustifiable interference. (The subject of *influenced . . . theory* is *courts*.)

(c) *Misplaced and dangling modifiers.* If the phrase is misplaced (not clearly connected to the word it modifies) or dangling (having no word to modify), edit the sentence.

Before: Often used in early America, experts suggest that shaming punishments may have a promising future in the modern criminal-justice system. (The phrase *often used in early America* is misplaced because it does not modify the nearest noun, which is *experts.*)

After: Often used in early America, shaming punishments may have a promising future in the modern criminal-justice system, experts suggest.

Better: Experts say that shaming punishments, often used in early America, may have a promising future in the modern criminal-justice system.

10.30 Omit auxiliary or main verbs in compound predicates, but only if the auxiliary and main verbs match grammatically for each predicate.

(a) *For style reasons.* Elision of repeated words makes for concise and effective prose.

Ex.: In the last sixty years the role of the common-law judge has been revolutionized in the civil world and amplified in the criminal. (The auxiliary *has been* is understood before the second main verb *amplified,* just as *world* is understood after *criminal.*)

Ex.: We can and should reform our judicial-selection process. (The main verb *reform* is understood after *can.*)

(b) *Parallel constructions.* But the parallel must be exact.

Not this: The invention must be refined to a point at which a prototype has or could be made.

But this: The invention must be refined to a point at which a prototype has been or could be made.

10.31 Use the past tense to describe what a court did in a case. Otherwise, when discussing the law, generally use the present tense.

(a) *Present tense as default.* Prefer the present tense for legal writing unless there is a good reason to use another tense.

Ex.: I argue that Cardozo was an authentic legal pragmatist in the tradition of Oliver Wendell Holmes and, especially, John Dewey.

Ex.: Clarence Darrow is a folk hero, an American legend.

(b) *Past tense for case history.* One good reason for using the past tense is for stating the facts and relating the procedural history of the case, both of which happened in the past. But use the present tense when discussing the law.

Ex.: Abdille was born in Somalia in 1967 and was orphaned at an extremely early age. He never learned the identity of his parents and hence could not trace his clan lineage. (Past tense to discuss history.) Clan lineage is a central feature of social and political life in Somalia, and an individual's inability to identify himself with a particular clan can be a substantial, perhaps life-threatening, impediment. (Present tense to discuss law or, as here, custom.) Abdille sought asylum and withholding-of-removal relief both from Somalia and from South Africa. (Past tense to discuss procedural history.)

Adjectives

10.32 An adjective is a word that describes, specifies, or in some other way modifies a noun. (Grammatically, an adjective may be attached to a pronoun, but it is still detailing the person, place, or thing that the pronoun is standing in for.) It may describe the noun <flowery> <mellow> <persnickety> or delimit the noun <three> <the> <Paul's>.

Many adjectives are independent words in their own right, such as *good, bad, red, green, short, tall, fast*, and *slow*. Many others are developed by adapting nouns and, less often, verbs with suffixes such as *-able* <laughable>, *-ed* <zippered>, *-ful* <youthful>, *-ial* <presidential>, *-ic* <Icelandic>, *-ish* <boyish>, *-like* <lifelike>, *-ous* <glamorous>, and *-y* <toothy>. All participles are inherently adjectival <a perfected interest> <a fishing expedition>.

A number of words can serve in the same form as either an adjective or an adverb, such as *better, best, much, less, near*, and *far*.

A phrase or clause may also serve as an adjective in a sentence.

Adjectives lend color and texture to writing. But their overuse weakens prose: good writers rely on nouns and verbs to tell the story and make the argument.

10.33 Use the comparative form as a measure of quality between two things and the superlative form as a measure of quality among three or more.

(a) *Regular forms*. As a rule, for most one-syllable and many two-syllable adjectives, use the suffix *-er* to form the comparative and *-est* to form the superlative. If the word ends in *-e*, drop the *e*. If the word ends in *-y*, change the *y* to *i*. If the word ends in a *-d* or *-t* preceded by a single vowel, double the final consonant.

Ex.: mean–meaner–meanest

Ex.: eerie–eerier–eeriest

Ex.: toothy–toothier–toothiest

Ex.: mad–madder–maddest

(b) *Irregular forms*. Watch for irregular words, which form their comparative and superlative in unpredictable ways.

Ex.: bad–worse–worst

Ex.: good–better–best

Ex.: many–more–most

Ex.: much–more–most

(c) *With "more–most," "less–least."* For other two-syllable and longer adjectives (including those formed with suffixes other than *-y*), form the comparative by using the adverb *more* or *less*, and the superlative by using the adverb *most* or *least.*

Ex.: maroon – more maroon – most maroon

Ex.: youthful – more youthful – most youthful

Ex.: condescending – less condescending – least condescending

(d) *Class comparison.* Use *other* or *else* when using the comparative form to rank something against the rest of its class; otherwise, you are making an illogical comparison.

Ex.: Tamesha made better grades than anyone else in her class. (Without *else* the comparison is between Tamesha and, among others in her class, Tamesha herself. And Tamesha's grades can't be better than Tamesha's grades.)

Ex.: Tamesha made better grades than any other first-year law student in the school. (Without *other* the sentence implies that Tamesha is not a first-year law student.)

(e) *Double comparatives.* Never use a double-comparative or -superlative construction; that is, the comparative or superlative form with *more, most, less*, or *least.*

Ex.: Isn't there a more superior (read *a superior*) authority?

10.34 Use an adjective, not an adverb, as a subject complement (predicate adjective) after a linking verb or a verb of sensory perception.

(a) *With linking verbs.* Some writers who would never be tempted to write *she is prettily* trip over *be*-verbs, linking verbs (such as *seem*), and verbs of becoming (such as *become, turn out, prove to be*, and *grow*).

Ex.: Your brief turned out good. (Not *well.*)

Ex.: The deal went bad when one backer reneged. (Not *badly.*)

(b) *With verbs of sense or becoming.* Verbs of sensory perception (such as *appear, feel, look, smell, sound*, and *taste*) call for a predicate adjective. But sometimes an adverb sounds tempting, as in the common error *I feel badly for you*. A test for whether an adjective or an adverb is needed is to substitute a *be*-verb to see if the sentence makes sense: *I am badly* fails the test.

Ex.: I feel bad about your loss.

Ex.: A cup of coffee sounds good about now.

10.35 Do not use an adverb of comparison with an absolute adjective.

(a) *No qualifiers.* An absolute (or uncomparable) adjective is one whose quality cannot be changed. The best example is *unique*: something either is or is not "one of a kind." Nothing can be more or less "one of a kind" than something else, so *more unique* and *less unique* are illogical. Other examples of absolute adjectives are *absolute*, *complete*, *false*, *fatal*, *final*, *irrevocable*, *sufficient*, and *void*.

(b) *"Almost" and "nearly."* Something may be closer to an absolute quality than another thing. So it is not wrong to say that an edited manuscript is "more nearly complete," for instance, or that an injury is "almost fatal."

10.36 Use dates as adjectives sparingly.

(a) *Full dates as adjectives.* Using all three elements—plus a comma—can become unwieldy, so use the construction sparingly. An *of*-phrase is traditionally preferred to using a date as an adjective. When a date is used as an adjective, omit the otherwise-mandatory comma after the year. Although some style guides call for one, the second comma has the undesirable effect of halting the reader when no pause is intended—it does not correspond to any pause in speaking the words.

Ex.: your July 23, 2001 letter

Ex.: the April 12, 2002 accident

Better: the accident of April 12, 2002

(b) *Short dates as adjectives.* Using a short date—such as a year or a month and day—as an adjective may tighten a sentence.

Ex.: the 2004 campaign

Ex.: the May 3 hearing

10.37 In some phrases and idiomatic constructions, use an adjective after the word it modifies.

(a) *Legal terms.* In law, several terms from Law French retain their Romance "postpositive" syntax, in which the adjective follows the noun. Even terms whose words have been replaced with their English counterparts retain that arrangement.

Ex.: court-martial

Ex.: notary public

Ex.: attorney general

Ex.: the body politic

Ex.: the city proper

(b) *Pronouns.* An indefinite pronoun often takes a postpositive adjective.

Ex.: Are you looking for anything special?

Ex.: If someone attractive asks, I'll be on the patio.

(c) *Stilted phrasing.* The words *things* and *matters* may take postpositive adjectives, but the result may sound stilted.

Ex.: In matters procedural, Professor Wright admitted of no equal.

Ex.: She urged her students to fight for all things just and true.

10.38 Use the definite article *the* to signal a specific person, place, or thing; use the indefinite article *a* or *an* to signal a generic reference.

(a) *Placement.* The article goes first in any phrase, ahead of any descriptive adjective. It is not hyphenated as part of a phrasal adjective unless it falls in the middle.

Ex.: a better-than-ever offer

Ex.: a top-of-the-morning greeting

(b) *Determining "a" or "an."* Use *a* before a word beginning with a consonant sound, *an* before a word beginning in a vowel sound.

Ex.: a humbling wait to hear a one-hour talk at a historical society

Ex.: an unambiguous statement about a universal truth

Ex.: an SEC position offered to a UCLA graduate

Adverbs

10.39 If nouns are the *who*-words of a sentence, and verbs are the *what*-words, adverbs are the *when-*, *where-*, *why-*, and *how*-words. They modify verbs to explain more about the action (e.g., we must move *quickly*), adjectives to clarify that attribute (e.g., we need a *fully* developed theory), and other adverbs to calibrate their degree of modification (e.g., we must move *very* slowly). They also join with prepositions and verbs to form phrases <e.g., chalk *up* another victory; get *down* to brass tacks).

As with adjectives, a phrase or clause may also serve an adverbial role in a sentence. This often occurs with introductory temporal phrases (e.g., *On Monday,*) and clauses (e.g., *Once we select a jury,*). But mid- and end-sentence phrases are also common <we drove to the capital [*where?*] in Julia's car [*how?*] Wednesday [*when?*] to testify [*why?*] at a hearing [*where?*]>.

An adverb is typically formed by adding the *-ly* suffix to an adjective <madly> <insanely>, changing *-y* to *-i* as needed <sleepily> <toothily>. But many adverbs do not end in *-ly*, and it is wrong to add the unnecessary suffix <thus [never *thusly*]> <doubtless [never *doubtlessly*]>.

Often, an adverb could fit into a sentence in more than one place (as with *often* in this sentence). At other times, there will be only one proper position for the adverb (as with *only* in this sentence). Placement can have rhetorical effect or even change substantive meaning.

A simple ("adjunctive") adverb modifies a single word in the sentence (e.g., may I speak *frankly*?). A sentence ("disjunctive") adverb modifies the sentence itself <e.g., *frankly,* my dear, I don't give a damn>.

A conjunctive adverb joins two clauses and indicates the relationship between them (e.g., Kym got the papers signed; *afterward*, she filed them with the clerk). Many kinds of relationship can be expressed this way: *likewise*, *otherwise*, *therefore*, *however*, *for instance*, *in other words*, and *meanwhile*, to name a few.

An interrogative adverb likewise modifies the entire clause (e.g., *where* did that come from?).

10.40 Place an adverb in its strongest position, often at the beginning of a sentence or inside a verb phrase.

(a) *After first auxiliary.* The strongest position for an adverb that modifies a verb phrase is right after the first auxiliary verb. Since 1762, grammarians have consistently held that this is the most natural and robust placement for an adverb. (Notice *have consistently held* in the preceding sentence.)

Ex.: We *should not have let* Duckworth testify.

Ex.: Harlan *may yet prove* not so orthodox a Justice as many suppose.

Ex.: Mental derangement sufficient to invalidate a will *is generally said* to consist in one of two forms.

(b) *Split infinitive.* When the verb phrase containing the adverb is an infinitive (*to* plus a verb, such as *to dismiss*), the result is what has sometimes been condemned as a "split infinitive" (e.g., *to summarily dismiss*). Avoid this construction if you are not comfortable with it, but use it if the word order strengthens both the infinitive and the adverb.

Ex.: In the proposed budget, the President wants *to more than double* spending on domestic security.

Ex.: "*To boldly go* where no one has gone before."

(c) *Temporal adverb.* The strongest position for a temporal adverb or adverbial phrase that precedes the action of the main verb in time or logic is at the beginning of the sentence.

Ex.: *After developing a useful, nonobvious, and new invention,* the inventor may claim a patent.

Ex.: *Before distributing the estate,* most jurisdictions authorize relatively liberal periodic payments of cash to the surviving spouse, dependent children, or both.

(d) *Contrast at start of sentence.* Likewise, the strongest position for an adverb or adverbial phrase that contrasts one sentence with what went before is also at the start of the sentence. This provides a transition between sentences.

Ex.: *On the other hand,* a broad construction of "relatives" would encompass a group too broad to be ascertainable as a private trust.

Ex.: *Conversely,* the promise must be made and accepted as the conventional motive or inducement for furnishing the consideration.

Ex.: *Still,* there was a strong trend at work: New York passed its first law in 1848, and by 1850 about 17 states had granted married women some legal capacity to deal with their property.

(e) *Emphasis at end of sentence.* Sometimes the strongest position for an adverb is at the end of the sentence, for emphasis.

Ex.: If the plaintiff could prove any actual monetary damages that resulted from this minor incident, my client would pay them *happily.*

Ex.: While a single below-average evaluation might have justified some disciplinary action when it was issued, it doesn't look like anything more than a pretext for discriminatory firing *a year later.*

10.41 Place emphatic adverbs such as *only, so, very, quite,* and *just* immediately before whatever they modify.

(a) *Placement of "only."* The word *only* is probably misplaced more often than any other modifier in English writing. It emphasizes the word or phrase that comes immediately after it; therefore, when it comes too early in the sentence, it actually plays down what it should emphasize.

Ex.: The "sweat-of-the-brow" doctrine only demanded (read *demanded only*) that the author demonstrate the investment of some "original work" into the final product.

Ex.: The prankster intended only to scare the victims, not to hurt them.

(b) *Idiomatic placement.* The idiomatic use of *only* before the verb, regardless of what it is modifying, works in spoken English because the meaning is usually clear from the speaker's inflection. But in writing that placement is often ambiguous.

Ex.: To be registered, a trademark actually must (read *must actually*) be used to identify and distinguish goods or services.

Prepositions

10.42 A preposition is so called because it is usually positioned before a noun, pronoun, or nominative phrase or clause and relates its subject to another word in the sentence.

The relationship is commonly one of space <in, on, under, beside> or time <before, after, during, until>, but it also may express possession <of, for, by>, description <with, like, as>, or circumstance <about, against, aboard>. The resulting prepositional phrase may serve as an adjective or adverb (or, less commonly, a noun), depending on its function in the sentence.

Prepositions can be simple <in, of, for> or complex <in accordance with, on behalf of, with respect to>. Complex prepositions are often a source of wordiness and overblown style: prefer the simple forms where possible (see 11.2(c)). At other times they are unavoidable <across from, out from under>.

In addition to the common prepositions, several prepositions have the form of a verb's present participle <considering, regarding, barring>.

The use of prepositions is highly idiomatic: there are no infallible rules to guide the writer in deciding which preposition to use with a particular word. See 12.4(3) for a list of terms often used in legal writing, along with prepositions that fit them for different uses. For other terms, check a dictionary.

10.43 To combat verbosity, minimize prepositional phrases.

(a) *Buried verbs.* Uncover buried verbs used with prepositional phrases. Verbs are often buried in noun forms ending in *-tion*, *-ment*, *-ance*, *-ity*, *-sure*, and the like. Restoring the verb typically eliminates a stuffy prepositional phrase and adds action to the sentence (see 13.3(c)).

Before: A subpoenaed attorney has the opportunity to object to the disclosure of arguably privileged material.

After: A subpoenaed attorney can object to disclosing arguably privileged material.

Before: The contract obligated the employer to make contributions to the pension fund.

After: The contract obligated the employer to contribute to the pension fund.

(b) *One-word replacements.* Some prepositional phrases can be replaced with an adverb <with all diligence = quickly>, an adjective <with blue eyes = blue-eyed>, or a term of possession or agency <of the company = the company's>. In all such cases, the sentence will be shorter and cleaner (see 13.3(d)).

Before: Some are convinced that punishments of the scarlet-letter type have the potential for more effectiveness than prison sentences for many offenders, especially for offenders who are nonviolent.

After: Some are convinced that scarlet-letter punishments could have more effect than prison sentences for many offenders, especially nonviolent ones.

(c) *Active voice.* Eliminate *by* prepositional phrases by changing from the passive to the active voice where appropriate; the sentence will be stronger and shorter (see 10.27, 13.3(b)).

Before: The legislation was fiercely debated by both sides, each offering its own bill.

After: Both sides fiercely debated the legislation, each offering its own bill.

(d) *As a cause of bloat.* Some prepositional phrases are necessary. But their overuse—especially in *of*-phrase strings—is a leading cause of clogged prose. Some can be simply eliminated without losing any meaning.

Ex.: Although the automaker recently reported a second-quarter loss of $1.3 million, the CEO of the company expects to end the year with a modest profit. (*Of the company* adds nothing to the sentence and should be omitted.)

Before: "Maximizing profits" means terminating the employment of any physician whose use of ancillary services cuts too deeply into the profit margin.

After: "Maximizing profits" means terminating any physician whose use of ancillary services cuts the profit margin too deeply.

10.44 When possible, omit a repeated preposition or object in favor of a compound construction.

(a) *Compound object.* Where a preposition is repeated with a different object, it is usually better style to use the preposition once with a compound object.

Ex.: Commercial speakers have extensive knowledge of the market and their products. (Rather than *of the market and of their products.*)

Ex.: The creditor may use the note to pay its own debts, sell to another creditor, or post as security for its own obligations. (Rather than repeating *to* before each infinitive phrase.)

(b) *Ambiguity.* If a compound object may confuse the reader, repeat the preposition instead.

Ex.: The defendant may meet the burden of coming forward with evidence by an independent showing or by reference to the presentence report. (Not *by an independent showing or reference to the presentence report* because a misreading would result.)

(c) *Compound prepositions.* When the object is repeated, it is usually better style to use compound prepositions with the single object.

Ex.: An easement of necessity gives the plaintiff the right to get on and off the landlocked property.

Ex.: The indictment charges the defendant with shoplifting a shirt from Wal-Mart on or about the night of July 3.

Conjunctions

10.45 A conjunction joins two or more words, phrases, clauses, or sentences. It may coordinate one element with another as equals <her LSAT score was high, *but* her GPA was average>, or subordinate one element to another <*although* her GPA was average, her high LSAT score got her accepted>.

Correlative conjunctions are used in pairs to introduce equal or alternative elements <both–and> <either–or> <neither–nor> <not only–but also>.

Adverbs and adverbial phrases may also be used as conjunctions <consequently> <with the discovery phase of the lawsuit complete>.

10.46 Use a coordinating conjunction to join like elements.

(a) *Definition.* The main coordinating conjunctions are *and, but,* and *or;* also common are *nor, for, yet,* and *so.* They join clauses of equal stature.

(b) *Punctuation.* Follow punctuation rules (see 1.3–.4, 1.15(d)) when using a coordinating conjunction to join like elements.

Ex.: "Last Words" is not vulgar, lewd, obscene, or plainly offensive. (Joining equal words.)

Ex.: Analysis of the "substantially limits" prong requires an individualized inquiry, guided by three considerations articulated by the EEOC: (1) the nature and severity of the impairment; (2) its duration; and (3) the expected long-term impact. (Joining equal phrases.)

Ex.: Felix explained that a § 1031 permit was conditioned upon the provision of adequate insurance and bond, and that in light of Steele's recent bankruptcy, the City was concerned with his ability to provide adequate security. (Joining equal clauses.)

Ex.: A coowner may waive his right to refuse to join a suit to enforce the patent. But Horphag did not waive this right. (Equal sentences.)

10.47 When appropriate, use a coordinating conjunction to begin a sentence to emphasize contrast (*but*, *yet*), additional support for a proposition (*and*), an alternative (*or*), or a logical conclusion (*so*).

(a) *Start of sentence.* Although this device should not be overdone, the occasional use of a coordinating conjunction to begin a sentence is an effective rhetorical device.

Ex.: But if appellants alleged that such a policy actually existed—without knowing whether it did or not—they would risk violating Rule 11.

Ex.: Yet those bargains would not be void. At the most, they would be voidable if the buyer chose to challenge the seller.

Ex.: And thus we are confronted with the question, "What possible analogy could have been found between a wrongful act producing harm and a failure to act at all?"

(b) *Stuffiness.* The use of *for* in the same construction is archaic and sounds stuffy.

Ex.: For to hesitate is to lose.

10.48 Use a subordinating conjunction to join a dependent clause to the main clause of a sentence.

(a) *Definition.* A dependent clause is one that cannot stand alone, but only because the subordinating conjunction itself makes it an incomplete statement. The conjunction makes the entire clause modify the main clause, usually in an adverbial function.

Ex.: Although Jarvis invested this money in legitimate mutual funds, he knew that he was potentially endangering Hager's solvency by encouraging Hager to invest with Penn Central. (*Although . . . funds* cannot stand on its own, but only because of the subordinating conjunction, *although*.)

(b) *To show relationships.* The conjunction shows a time, place, or manner relationship to the main clause, or a logical connection to the main clause.

Ex.: "Blue Laws" came to life in part thanks to labor, because unions wanted a shorter workweek and Sunday laws were a useful instrument. (The second, subordinate clause explains why (*because*) the first, main clause is true.)

Ex.: When a case came before Holmes in which he had to choose between the realist critique of his youth and his settled judicial doctrine, he chose orthodoxy. (The first, subordinate clause tells *when* the second, main clause is true.)

> "The half-educated . . . do not suspect that the immense majority of grammars which were in use in our schools until very recently abounded in unfounded assertions about our language and laid down rules without validity."
>
> —*Brander Matthews*

10.49 Make sure that correlative conjunctions frame sentence parts that match each other grammatically.

(a) *Definition.* Correlative conjunctions may join like elements <both–and> <either–or> <whether–or>, express a connection in logic <although–yet> <if–then> <since–therefore>, or express a sequence in time <once–then> <when–then>.

> Ex.: These examples indicate the controversy that exists *both* between *and* within states as to the permissibility of scarlet-letter punishments.

(b) *Parallelism.* The elements must be the same part of speech, and if they are phrases or clauses they must be parallel in structure as well.

> Ex.: In this case, *although* we agree that the Department regulation mainly affects economic interests, *it is also clear that* the regulation implicates both Publisher's and Prisoner's First Amendment rights.

> Ex.: Under the Open Meetings Law, the public is *not only* entitled (read *entitled not only*) to attend governmental meetings, *but also* to be given notice of the time, place, and subject matter of those meetings. (Nonparallel structure.)

Interjections

10.50 Use interjections sparingly, if at all.

(a) *Definition.* Interjections are words or phrases that are, by definition, "thrown into" a sentence. They stand alone with no connection to any other word or phrase in the sentence. They most often express exclamation <oh!, as if!, damn!> and stand alone with an exclamation mark. They may also be placed within a sentence, separated by commas <oh, uh, well>.

(b) *Limited use.* Except for *Oyez! Oyez! Oyez!* and direct quotations, interjections have little place in most legal writing.

> "All I know about grammar is its infinite power. To shift the structure of a sentence alters the meaning of the sentence, as definitely and inflexibly as the position of a camera alters the meaning of the object photographed. Many people know about camera angles now, but not so many know about sentences."
>
> —*Joan Didion*

§ 11
Stuffy Words and Legalese

11.1 Just because you know what *malum prohibitum* means or what a *habendum clause* does is no reason to use such language at the dinner table. A lawyer should keep in mind that the purpose of communication is to communicate, and this can't be done if the reader or listener doesn't understand the words used.

Some lawyers also tend to use words in peculiar ways, using *same* as a pronoun, for example <plaintiff accepted the deed as written and signed same>, and peppering contracts and resolutions with *whereas*es and *wherefore*s. Some critics suggest that the impenetrable language serves the same purpose that mumbo-jumbo has always served: to keep the public in the dark and to protect a trade monopoly.

But the trend today is toward the use of plain language and away from the stuffiness and jargon-laced prose that characterized much legal writing in the past. It's a welcome trend, and one that writing coaches universally encourage.

Pompous Style

11.2 Use the simplest, most straightforward words that you can.

(a) *Plain English.* Language lovers often go through predictable phases of growth: first learning exotic new words and later avoiding them in favor of plain and clear terms. Using simple words and phrases instead of stuffy ones results in a more natural style.

(b) *Simple substitutes.* Choose simple words over fancy ones. Below is a necessarily limited list of dressed-up words and their simpler alternatives.

Instead of this:	Try this:
abutting	next to
accede to	allow; grant
accordingly	so
acquainted with	know
acquire	get
additional	more; extra; added; other
adjacent to	next to
administer (medicate)	give
administer	run; operate; manage; handle
advantageous	useful; helpful
advert to	refer to
advise	tell [unless you're giving advice]
afford	allow
all or part	any; some or all
alter	change
ameliorate	improve
apparent	plain
appellation	name
approximately	about
ascertain	find out; make sure
assist; assistance	help
attain	reach; get; win; make
attempt	try; seek
attributable to	due to; because of
augment	increase
augmentation	increase

Instead of this:	Try this:
authored	wrote
automobile	car
cognizant	aware
commence	start; begin
comment	say
conceal	hide
concept	idea; plan
concerning	on; about; for
condign	fitting; deserving
conflagration	fire
conjecture	guess
consequently	so; thus
constitute	make up; form; be
consummate	utmost; best; top
contiguous to	next to
contumacious	contemptuous
couched	phrased
demonstrate	show
desideratum	wish; aim; goal
deteriorate	get worse; run down
dichotomy	split
directive	order
disadvantage	drawback
discontinue	stop
divers	various; several
domesticate	tame
dwell	live
dynamic	forceful
educator	teacher
elapse	pass; go by
elect to	choose to
elucidate	explain
eminently	highly
emphasize	stress; point up
endeavor	try
enthused	enthusiastic; excited
envisage	foresee; see; predict; look for
equanimity	poise
erroneous	wrong; incorrect; mistaken
erstwhile	former; formerly; once; one-time
eschew	avoid
essayed	tried; did
eventuality	event; possibility
eventually	in the end
evidencing	showing
evince	show

Instead of this:	Try this:
examination	exam; test; check; checkup
exceedingly	highly
excessively	too; unduly
exclusively	only
expenditure	cost; expense; payment
experiment	test
extended	long
extinguish	put out
facilitate	help; ease; make easier
favorable	good
following	after
forward	send
frequently	often
fundamental	basic; main
furthermore	further
gainsay	deny
gratuitous	needless; free
impact	affect; influence
implement	carry out; set up
inaugurate	begin; start
inception	start; beginning
incongruous	unfitting; incoherent
inconsiderable	slight; small; little
indebtedness	debt
indicate	say; mention; write; hint; suggest
indication	sign
indisposed to	reluctant to
individual	person
inform	tell
infringe on	infringe
inimical	adverse; hostile
initial	first; early
injudicious	unwise
instant [adj.]	this
intimate [vb.]	hint
intransigence	stubbornness
inundate	flood
inure (get used to)	adjust; accustom
inure (of a benefit)	mature; vest
kindly	please
lengthy	long
locality	place; town; city; village; county
modify; modification	change
multitudinous	many
narrate	tell

Instead of this:	Try this:
necessitous	needy
nevertheless	even so; still; but
notwithstanding	despite
numerous	many
obligate	bind
occupation	job; work; business
occur	happen
odor	smell
oftentimes; ofttimes	often
opportune	convenient; handy; proper
orientate	orient
originate	start; come from
outcome	result
overall	whole; entire; total
overly	unduly; too
paradigm	model
partially	partly
participate	take part; go along; be one of
possibility	chance
practically	almost; nearly
precede	go before; come before
predecease	die before
presently	now; soon; in a moment
procure	get
prosecute (a business)	do; carry on; conduct (business)
purchase	buy
regarding	about

Instead of this:	Try this:
relocate	move
render	make; leave
request	ask
requisite	needed; required
reside	live
residence	house; apartment; address
respecting	for
schism	split
segment	part
significance	meaning; point
simultaneously	at the same time
subsequent	later
subsequently	later; after that; afterwards; then
substantial	large
substantially	largely; much
supposition	belief; thought; idea
surmise	guess
susceptible of	
(a meaning)	open to
(a threat)	prone to; vulnerable to
thrice	three times
transmit	send
ultimately	in the end
unto	to
utilize	use
vehicle	car; truck; motorcycle; etc.
vend	sell
wherewithal	means, money, ability

(c) *Paring down phrases.* By trimming your sentences you will make your prose tighter and more persuasive (see 13.3(e)). Wordy phrases are the biggest source of undergrowth and the first place to look when you trim your drafts. Below are some common phrases used in legal writing and their simpler substitutions.

Instead of this:	Try this:
acquire knowledge	learn
adequate number of	enough
a large amount of	a lot of; much
a large number of	many
a small amount of	some; a little
a small number of	a few
am in receipt of	have
as a consequence of	because of
as a means of —ing	to —
as previously stated	again

Instead of this:	Try this:
as regards	about; regarding
at no time	never
at the place where	where
at the present time	now
at the time that	when; once
at the time when	when
at this juncture	now
at this point in time	now
because of the fact that	because; since
be determinative of	determine

Instead of this:	Try this:
by means of	by
by necessity	necessarily
by reason of	because of
cause injury to	injure
commensurate with	equal to; appropriate for
despite the fact that	although
due to the fact that	because
during such time as	while
during the course of	while
enclosed please find	enclosed is; I enclose; here is
excessive amount of	too much
excessive number of	too many
for the purpose of —ing	to —
for the reason that	because; since
for this reason	so; thus
have knowledge of	know
in a — manner	—ly (with many adjectives)
in accordance with	under; according to
in addition to	besides
inadequate amount of	too little
inadequate number of	too few
in an effort to	to
inasmuch as	because; since
in back of	behind
in conjunction with	with; along with
in connection with	regarding; about; for
in excess of	more than
in favor of	for
in furtherance of	furthering; to advance
in lieu of	instead of
in light of the fact that	because; since
in order that	so
in order to	to
in proximity to	near
in reference to	about
in respect to	respecting
in the amount of	for
in the course of	while; during
in the event of	if
in the event that	if

Instead of this:	Try this:
in the instant case	here; now
in the near future	soon
in the neighborhood of	around
in the vicinity of	near; around
is able to	can
is applicable	applies
is authorized to	may
is binding on	binds
is required to	must
is unable to	cannot
it is certain that	certainly; surely
it is probable that	probably
it would appear that	apparently
make a decision	decide
make an inquiry	ask
make an observation	comment; observe; watch
make reference to	refer to
notwithstanding the fact that	although
on a daily basis	daily
on behalf of	for
on the ground that	because; since
on the part of	by
period of time	period; time
pertaining to	on; about
previous to	before
prior to	before
pursuant to	under; according to
reach a resolution	resolve
subsequent to	after
sufficient amount of	enough
sufficient number of	enough
take into consideration	consider
the majority of	most
to the detriment of	harming; prejudicing
undertake an effort	try
under the provisions of	under
until such time as	until
with reference to	about
with regard to	about; regarding
with respect to	about; regarding
with the exception of	except for

> "You are no less a lawyer for being understandable."
>
> —*Christopher T. Lutz*

(d) *Avoiding legalese.* Some legal writers cling to legalisms as if they were life preservers. Too often, the result is that the client is confused and the judge is amused at best, irritated at worst. Good legal writers favor words that their intended readers—especially clients—will understand. Below is a list of legalisms and plain-English translations.

Instead of this:	Try this:
ab initio	from the start
aforementioned	this; that; named earlier
aforesaid	this; that; named earlier
albeit	although; though
anent	concerning
antecedent to	before
anterior to	before
apprise	tell; inform
arguendo	for the sake of argument
aver	state
bestow	give
bona fide; bona fides	good faith
case at bar	here; this case
case sub judice	here; this case
cestui que trust	beneficiary (of a trust)
child en ventre sa mere	fetus; unborn child
de son tort	by (his or her) own wrongdoing
ex contractu	in contract (law); contractual
ex delictu	in tort (law)
execution (of a will, contract)	signing
ex hypothesi	hypothetically
feral	wild
fora	forums
forthwith	immediately; now; at once
gravamen	crux; gist; burden
henceforth	from now on
henceforward	from now on
herein	here
heretofore; hitherto	up to now; until now; till now
in esse	in being
in haec verba	in these words; verbatim
instant case	this case
instanter	at once
inter alia	among other things
inter alios	among other people
inter partes	between parties
inter se	among themselves
lessee; leasee	tenant
lessor; leasor	landlord
mesne	intermediate
messuage	house, buildings, and land
negative [vb.]	negate
non compos mentis	insane
notwithstanding	despite; in spite of; even though
pray	request; ask for
remise	release; surrender
residue	rest; remainder
res nova	case of first impression
said [adj.]	the; this; that
same [pron.]	it [or the antecedent]
save	except
seisin	title; possession
shall	must
simpliciter	simply; considered by itself
style	name
subjoin	attach
such [adj.]	the; this; that
sui generis	one of a kind; unique
sui juris	legally competent
tabula rasa	clean slate
testament	will
testifier	witness
thence	from this; from that; from there
thenceforth	from then on
thenceforward	from then on
thereafter	afterwards; from then on
thereat	there; at it
therefor	for it; for them

Instead of this:	Try this:
therefrom	away; from it; from that
therein	there; in it
thereof	of it
thereout	from it; from that; from them
theretofore	up to then; until then; till then
thereupon	then
these presents	this document
thitherto	up to then; until then; till then
to wit	namely
vel non	or not; or the lack of it
vendee	buyer
vendor	seller
viz.	namely; that is
whence	from where
whensoever	whenever; at all
whereat	where
wherein	in which; where; when
whomsoever	whomever
whosoever	whoever

(e) *Useless verbiage.* Many terms and phrases continue to drift along in legal writing like so much deadwood in a stream. There is no reason anymore for writing "know all men by these presents." Watch out for the words and phrases below, and do not be afraid to dismiss them with prejudice.

aforementioned
aforesaid
as a matter of fact
as such
as to
basically
clearly
comes now
for all purposes
for your information
further affiant saith [or sayeth] not
hereby
hereinafter referred to as [*just place the defined term in parentheses*]
in any way
in connection with
in the above-styled and -numbered cause
in the final analysis
in the process of
it being the case that
it goes without saying that
it is apparent [clear] that
it is important to bear in mind that
know all men by these presents
needless to say
on the matters set forth herein
overall
the fact [of the matter] is
the fact that
veritable
whereas
wherefore, premises considered
witnesseth
would show that

> "I am particularly careful to avoid jargon, and to write simply and clearly. For certain types of writing a high level of technicality is unavoidable; but in general it is the second-rate intellect that cultivates a pretentious vocabulary and a solemn and portentous style."
>
> —*Richard A. Posner*

(f) *Synonymia.* The doublet and triplet phrase common in Middle English still survives in legal writing. That's probably the worst possible soil for it to grow in because those who interpret legal writing are impelled to strain for distinctions so that no word is rendered surplusage. Yet that is exactly what all but one word (and often *any* one word) in each of the following phrases is.

Doublets
act and deed
agree and covenant
agreed and declared
aid and abet
aid and comfort
all and singular
all and sundry
amount or quantum
annoy or molest
annulled and set aside
answerable and accountable
any and all
appropriate and proper
attached and annexed
authorize and empower
betting or wagering
bills and notes
bind and obligate
by and between
by and under
by and with
canceled and set aside
cease and come to an end
cease and desist
cease and determine
chargeable and accountable
covenant and agree
custom and usage
deed and assurance
deem and consider
definite and certain
demises and leases
deposes and says
desire and require
do and perform
dominion and authority
due and owing
due and payable
each and all
each and every
ends and objects
escape and evade
exact and specific
execute and perform
false and untrue
final and conclusive
finish and complete
fit and proper
for and in behalf of
fraud and deceit
free and clear
from and after
full and complete
full faith and credit
full force and effect
good and effectual
good and tenantable
goods and chattels
have and hold
indemnify and hold harmless
keep and maintain
kind and character
kind and nature
known and described as
laid and levied
leave and license
legal and valid
liens and encumbrances
made and signed
maintenance and upkeep
make and enter into
make and execute
means and includes
messuage and dwelling-house
mind and memory
name and style
new and novel
nominate and appoint
null and of no effect
null and void
object and purpose
order and direct
other and further
over and above
pains and penalties
pardon and forgive
part and parcel
peace and quiet
perform and discharge

power and authority
premeditation and malice aforethought
repair and make good
restrain and enjoin
reverts to and falls back upon
sale or transfer
save and except
seised and possessed of
sell or transfer
separate and apart
separate and distinct
set aside and vacate
shall and will
shun and avoid
similar and like
sole and exclusive
son and heir
successors and assigns
supersede and displace
surmise and conjecture
terms and conditions
then and in that event
title and interest
total and entire
touch and concern
true and correct
truth and veracity
type and kind
uncontroverted and uncontradicted
understood and agreed
unless and until
uphold and support
used and applied
various and sundry
will and testament

Triplets

cancel, annul, and set aside
form, manner, and method
general, vague, and indefinite
give, devise, and bequeath
grant, bargain, and sell
grants, demises, and lets
hold, possess, and enjoy
lands, tenements, and hereditaments
make, publish, and declare
name, constitute, and appoint
ordered, adjudged, and decreed
pay, satisfy, and discharge
possession, custody, and control
promise, agree, and covenant
ready, willing, and able
remise, release, and forever discharge
remise, release, and forever quitclaim
repair, uphold, and maintain
rest, residue, and remainder
right, title, and interest
signed, sealed, and delivered
situate, lying, and being in
vague, nonspecific, and indefinite
way, shape, or form

Terms of Art

11.3 Unless the context requires otherwise, use legal terms according to their specialized sense as terms of art.

(a) *Terms of art.* Some words are "terms of art" for lawyers—that is, they express certain legal ideas that are scarcely expressible otherwise. Examples are *habeas corpus* and *res ipsa loquitur*, both of which have a rich legal history. They are not really used outside law.

(b) *Ordinary words with special legal senses.* Many everyday words take on new meanings when used in a legal context. Following is a collection of words that law students must relearn. They mean one thing to most people but often something completely different to a lawyer.

abstract. *Common meaning:* an adjective describing something that is theoretical rather than concrete. *In law:* a noun referring to a concise summary of a writing <abstract of title>.

acceleration. *Common meaning:* a speeding up. *In law:* the calling due of a mortgage or other loan, or the cutting off of an interest in property due to the failure of an estate.

accounting. *Common meaning:* the analysis of a company's financial condition. *In law:* also, a cause of action to settle accounts, recover money owed, or compensate for a breach of contract.

action. *Common meaning:* movement. *In law:* a legal proceeding <action to quiet title>.

adhesion. *Common meaning:* the sticking together of two things. *In law:* an adjective describing a contract that gives one party no bargaining power.

admiralty. *Common meaning:* a high rank in the navy. *In law:* maritime law, or an adjective describing any court that is hearing a suit in maritime.

affirmation. *Common meaning:* confirmation that something is true, or a motivational statement. *In law:* a secular counterpart to an oath <do you swear or affirm . . . ?>.

alibi. *Common meaning:* any excuse to avoid blame for something. *In law:* the specific defense of proving that the defendant was somewhere else when the crime was committed.

allowance. *Common meaning:* money, especially a weekly stipend from one's parents. *In law:* money set aside for a purpose; a court's compensation for the services of a fiduciary such as a trustee; or a tax deduction <oil-depletion allowance>.

alter ego. *Common meaning:* a second identity; a very close friend. *In law:* A fraudulent corporation being used to disguise the dealings of its owner while providing the owner protection from liability.

ancient. *Common meaning:* very old, as of the Roman Empire and earlier. *In law:* about 20 years old, for purposes of authenticating a writing to be introduced as evidence, or establishing an easement restricting both landowners from removing a shared stone wall.

answer. *Common meaning:* a reply to a question. *In law:* a response to either a pleading or a request for discovery <respondent has 20 days to file an answer>.

appearance. *Common meaning:* what you look like. *In law:* attendance in a courtroom, especially for purposes of establishing personal jurisdiction.

appropriation. *Common meaning:* money allocated for a certain purpose, especially by a legislature. *In law:* private property taken away, especially by a court, or the privacy tort of making commercial use of another person's name or likeness.

artisan. *Common meaning:* a skilled craftsperson. *In law:* a contractor or mechanic <artisan's lien>; or, in patent law, "a person of ordinary skill in the art," be it industrial design or biochemistry.

assault. *Common meaning:* a physical attack. *In law:* at common law (but not under modern penal statutes), the act of putting someone in reasonable fear of a physical attack or offensive touching (i.e., battery).

assignment. *Common meaning:* a task or an appointment to a position. *In law:* the transfer of one person's legal interest in property to another person <assignment of account>, or an appellant's charge that the trial court made a mistake <assignment of error>.

assumption. *Common meaning:* something taken for granted. *In law:* the taking on of the debt or liability of another person <assumption of a loan> <assumption of risk>.

attachment. *Common meaning:* one thing stuck to another thing, or affection for another person. *In law:* seizure of property to secure or satisfy a money judgment <attachment of wages>.

author. *Common meaning:* a person who writes a book, article, or the like. *In law:* for copyright purposes, the creator of almost any creative work, such as a painting, sculpture, choreography, or computer software.

avoid. *Common meaning:* to dodge or elude something. *In law:* to make something void, such as to make a contract unenforceable or to annul a marriage.

bankrupt. *Common meaning:* an adjective describing an insolvent person. *In law:* as easily, a noun for the debtor.

bargain. *Common meaning:* something bought at a discounted price; a good buy; to dicker over a price. *In law:* an agreement between two people for the exchange of promises or performances <benefit of the bargain>.

basis. *Common meaning:* the fundamental principle on which other things stand. *In law:* the amount that a taxpayer has invested in a capital asset, as used in calculating gains and losses for tax purposes.

bill. *Common meaning:* a statement of an amount owed. *In law:* a pleading to a court of equity, similar to a complaint or pleading in a court of law <bill of exceptions>; a proposed statute.

blackletter. *Common meaning:* (as two words) a thick Gothic or Old English typeface. *In law:* an adjective designating a well-settled principle of law <blackletter law>.

bona fide. *Common meaning:* genuine; real. *In law:* done in good faith <bona fide effort at mediation>.

camera. *Common meaning:* a device for taking photographs. *In law:* a judge's chambers, in the phrase "in camera."

caption. *Common meaning:* text under a picture in a publication. *In law:* the identification of a lawsuit by the parties' names, the court, the docket number, and the cause of action.

chose. *Common meaning:* selected. *In law:* (pronounced /shohz/) an item of personal property; also, a thing, whether tangible or intangible (such as a right).

churning. *Common meaning:* stirring up, as with water, or turning cream into butter. *In law:* the wrongful practice of a professional, especially a stockbroker, in performing unnecessary work for a client in order to pad the fee.

code. *Common meaning:* a system of encryption for transmitting secret messages. *In law:* an organized system of statutes or regulations <United States Code>.

color. *Common meaning:* a hue. *In law:* the appearance of authority or a right <under color of state law>.

colorable. *Common meaning:* capable of being colored. *In law:* apparently true and valid <a colorable claim on an estate>, or intentionally deceptive <a colorable transfer of property to avoid taxes>.

common. *Common meaning:* shared; familiar; inferior; vulgar. *In law:* a right to use the property of another, such as the common areas of a rental property.

community. *Common meaning:* collectively, people who live in a distinct area or who share a common interest. *In law:* also, in community-property states, the marriage itself <fraud on the community>.

competency. *Common meaning:* competence; an area of competence. *In law:* narrowly, the mental ability to understand one's circumstance and to make decisions in order to assist in one's own defense; a competency hearing determines whether a defendant can be put on trial.

complaint. *Common meaning:* a grievance. *In law:* the plaintiff's initial pleading in a civil lawsuit, or a formal charge against a criminal defendant.

composition. *Common meaning:* an arrangement of things, such as an essay or a piece of music. *In law:* an agreement by creditors to accept less than everything the debtor owes them.

compound. *Common meaning:* to increase in value, as interest on invested money; or to make worse, as an error. *In law:* also, to forgo prosecuting a criminal defendant in exchange for a bribe <compounding a felony is itself a felony>.

conclude. *Common meaning:* to finish; to deduce. *In law:* also, to formalize an agreement <conclude a contract>; to bar or estop <the admission concluded our main line of defense>.

condemn. *Common meaning:* to denounce. *In law:* to pronounce a criminal defendant guilty; to take private property for a public purpose; to declare a structure uninhabitable; to declare food or water unfit for human consumption.

connive. *Common meaning:* to conspire. *In law:* more specifically, to look the other way while a wrong is being done, while under a duty to stop or report it <the night manager connived at the pilferage of other employees>.

consideration. *Common meaning:* respect; kindness; thought. *In law:* something of value or a legal detriment promised in exchange for another person's contractual promise or performance.

consortium. *Common meaning:* a collection of companies working together toward a common goal. *In law:* a family member's companionship, love, help, and (of a spouse) capacity for sexual relations, the loss of which may provide a cause of action in tort for the other spouse.

construction. *Common meaning:* the building of a structure. *In law:* the construing of a writing, especially a statute, will, contract, or deed <the plaintiff offers a strained construction of the agreement>.

constructive. *Common meaning:* positive; promoting further development. *In law:* irrebuttably established by operation of law <constructive knowledge>; established by a legal fiction in order to craft a remedy <constructive trust>.

continuance. *Common meaning:* the state of remaining in the same state; a sequel. *In law:* postponement of a trial or other judicial proceeding until another date.

contort. *Common meaning:* (accent on the second syllable) to twist out of shape, especially one's body. *In law:* (accent on the first syllable) a cause of action that includes aspects of contract law and tort law.

contribution. *Common meaning:* a donation. *In law:* the right of a tortfeasor who has paid more than a proportionate share of a judgment to recover the excess from other liable defendants.

conversion. *Common meaning:* the changing from one form into another, or adopting a new religion. *In law:* the act of treating the property of another as one's own, as by possessing it or disposing of it.

conveyance. *Common meaning:* a means of transportation. *In law:* the transfer of interest in real property from one person to another, or the document by which the transfer is accomplished.

cover. *Common meaning:* a lid or blanket. *In law:* the purchase of goods to replace those not supplied because of a breach of contract, with the right to recover costs in excess of the contracted price.

curator. *Common meaning:* a museum manager. *In law:* (in some jurisdictions) a guardian or conservator.

cure. *Common meaning:* to restore physical health. *In law:* to restore legal "health," as by remedying defects in a title or by replacing nonconforming goods rejected by the buyer.

damages. *Common meaning:* more than one type or incident of damage. *In law:* the money that a defendant is ordered to pay a plaintiff to compensate for the damage caused.

dedication. *Common meaning:* commitment; the addressing of something (e.g., a book) to someone. *In law:* a gift of private property for public use, such as a public road or park.

defective. *Common meaning:* inoperable or dangerous due to a flaw in design or manufacture. *In law:* also, describing an insufficiency in a legal process <defective service of notice>.

demean. *Common meaning:* to debase someone or oneself. *In law:* in the term's original sense, as used in the lawyer's oath of office, "to behave" (here, to behave oneself in an upright manner); that archaic sense lives on in the word "demeanor."

demise. *Common meaning:* death. *In law:* a lease (either the document or the legal relationship); the conveyance of a decedent's property to another person, either through a will or by intestacy; or a conveyance by lease, as distinguished from a devise.

demur. *Common meaning:* to object on moral grounds (or confused with the adjective for *coy*, "demure"). *In law:* to admit all the facts in a plaintiff's petition, but deny that they state a claim on which relief can be granted (today's demurrer is most often called a motion to dismiss).

depose. *Common meaning:* to dethrone a monarch. *In law:* to take someone's testimony in a sworn deposition; to testify.

determine; determinable; determination. *Common meaning:* all have to do with deciding something. *In law:* all have to do with ending (terminating) something, usually an interest in property <fee simple determinable> <cease and determine>.

detour. *Common meaning:* a rerouted street. *In law:* not a frolic (see below), but an employee's minor departure from business for personal reasons; the employer remains liable for the employee's torts on a detour.

devise. *Common meaning:* to think up a scheme for doing something. *In law:* to pass on property to someone through a will; or, as a noun, that property, the provision in the will, or the will itself.

digest. *Common meaning:* a book of articles and stories condensed from another source and republished. *In law:* a systematic collection of case excerpts, arranged by legal subjects and the propositions that the case holdings support.

dignitary. *Common meaning:* a person of rank. *In law:* describing a type of tort that compensates the plaintiff for an insult or humiliation rather than for a personal injury or property damage <invasion of privacy is a dignitary tort>.

dilution. *Common meaning:* the watering down of a liquid. *In law:* a weakening by a variety of means, such as by gerrymandering (voting power), selling more stock (per-share value), or using a famous name for an unrelated product (trademark distinctiveness).

disability. *Common meaning:* a debilitating physical condition. *In law:* a legal incapacity, such as being a minor and therefore unable to contract.

discovery. *Common meaning:* the finding of something new. *In law:* pretrial investigation of information held by the other party, by compulsory questioning of parties, witnesses, and documents.

disinterested. *Common meaning:* not interested (as many people understand the word). *In law:* having no personal or financial interest at stake, and therefore able to render a fair and impartial decision.

disposition. *Common meaning:* demeanor or inclination. *In law:* the distribution of an estate according to either instructions in a will or an intestacy statute; also, a final determination in a proceeding.

distress. *Common meaning:* anguish. *In law:* seizure of property to secure a debt; the property seized; a court order for such a seizure <distress sale>.

domicile. *Common meaning:* one's home. *In law:* the jurisdiction (especially the state) in which a person intends to stay, even if currently residing elsewhere, or where a corporation either is incorporated or has its main place of business.

entail. *Common meaning:* to require. *In law:* to limit the ability of heirs to divest real property by specifying that title pass to the offspring (or just sons or daughters) of the original owner and the heirs.

equity. *Common meaning:* ownership; the difference between the value of a property and the amount owed on it. *In law:* justice based on principles of fairness rather than statute and common law; remedies other than money damages.

execute. *Common meaning:* to carry out something; to put someone to death. *In law:* also, to sign a will or contract; to collect on a money judgment.

exemplary. *Common meaning:* serving as a good example to be emulated. *In law:* serving as a bad example to deter others from similar behavior <exemplary damages>.

expectant. *Common meaning:* pregnant. *In law:* contingent, said of an interest in property.

facial. *Common meaning:* of the face; a beauty treatment. *In law:* of a challenge to a statute on the basis that it is unconstitutional on its face (always unconstitutional); of an attack on a complaint as insufficient to state a claim; readily apparent.

fact. *Common meaning:* a true thing. *In law:* a thing that a jury or a judge (in a bench trial) has determined to be true, whether it really is or not <findings of fact>.

factor. *Common meaning:* a thing to be considered. *In law:* also, a commission merchant, a garnishee, or a discount buyer of accounts receivable.

fee. *Common meaning:* a charge for a service. *In law:* an inheritable and transferable interest in real property.

fixation. *Common meaning:* a preoccupation or obsession with something or someone. *In law:* the recording of a creator's work in tangible form, as is required by federal law for copyright protection.

foreign. *Common meaning:* of another country. *In law:* also, of another jurisdiction, especially another state <a judgment from a foreign court>.

fraud. *Common meaning:* loosely, anything false. *In law:* rigorously, a deception carried out deliberately and successfully to induce someone to do something to his or her own detriment.

frolic. *Common meaning:* merrymaking. *In law:* not a detour (see above), but an employee's major departure from business for personal reasons; the employer is not liable for an employee's torts on a frolic because it is outside the scope of employment.

garnish. *Common meaning:* something added to a plate of food to add color, ornamentation, or flavor. *In law:* to attach property being held by a third party (such as wages held by an employer), in order to pay the owner's debt (such as delinquent child support).

hearsay. *Common meaning:* loosely, a rumor. *In law:* rigorously, testimony about a statement, writing, or other assertion made outside court and offered into evidence to prove the truth of its content.

heir. *Common meaning:* loosely, anyone who inherits from an estate. *In law:* more precisely, someone who inherits by intestate succession rather than by will.

holding. *Common meaning:* of a court decision, the outcome. *In law:* of a court decision, the determination of a question of law necessary for the outcome, as distinct from a comment on a nonessential question of law (obiter dictum) or a finding of fact.

holograph. *Common meaning:* by error from "holography," a hologram or three-dimensional image. *In law:* a writing done entirely in the maker's handwriting, especially a will or deed.

homicide. *Common meaning:* a crime of murder or manslaughter. *In law:* not necessarily a crime, but any killing of one human being by another, including a lawful killing such as one done in self-defense.

ignore. *Common meaning:* to deliberately disregard. *In law:* of a grand jury, to decline to indict an accused person (return a no bill), especially on the basis that the charge is groundless or the evidence insufficient.

impeachment. *Common meaning:* a formal charge against a government official, especially a president or judge (but not, as many believe, the removal from office). *In law:* a challenge to the veracity of a witness or the reliability of documentary evidence.

impertinent. *Common meaning:* rude. *In law:* irrelevant, especially said of matter contained in a pleading that does not pertain to any issue material to the cause of action.

implication. *Common meaning:* an inference from one truth of what else must necessarily be true. *In law:* an involvement or connection, especially with a scheme of misconduct or crime.

impossibility. *Common meaning:* inability to exist at all. *In law:* the doctrine in contract law that excuses a party from meeting an obligation because a presupposed condition has failed for any of a variety of reasons, some well short of physical impossibility.

indorse. *Common meaning:* an alternative spelling of *endorse*; to support. *In law:* to sign on the back, especially the back of a check or other negotiable instrument.

infant. *Common meaning:* a baby. *In law:* as easily, a strapping 17-year-old fullback; a minor (under 18 in most jurisdictions), with the legal disability of infancy.

infection. *Common meaning:* contamination by disease. *In law:* contamination by crime or contraband <a cargo infected by any amount of smuggled drugs subjects the entire ship to seizure>.

information. *Common meaning:* knowledge. *In law:* a charging instrument filed by a prosecutor without the need of a grand-jury indictment, often used for misdemeanors but also used by many states for felonies.

initiative. *Common meaning:* readiness to lead or start an activity. *In law:* a procedure, available in some states, that allows voters to propose a law and force a vote on it by the legislature or by the electorate at large.

injury. *Common meaning:* a physical bodily trauma. *In law:* any violation of a legal right, including one that results in property damage or economic loss <the breach of contract was a civil injury redressable by money damages>.

innuendo. *Common meaning:* a suggestive comment, usually with a sexual or derogatory connotation. *In law:* a statement in an indictment more fully explaining the charge, or in a pleading of defamation explaining why the words said by the defendant were actionable.

integrated. *Common meaning:* not separated, especially by race or gender. *In law:* of a contract, containing the final agreements between parties and, if fully integrated, all the agreements <the court will not hear extrinsic evidence to challenge a fully integrated contract>.

interference. *Common meaning:* the meddling in or obstruction of something. *In law:* also, a patent-office proceeding to determine which of two or more applicants claiming the same invention is the first inventor.

interrogatory. *Common meaning:* a question. *In law:* more specifically, a set of written questions addressed to the opposing party in the discovery phase of a lawsuit <rules of procedure govern how many questions may be asked in an interrogatory>.

intervention. *Common meaning:* a stepping in to stop or settle a problem. *In law:* more specifically, the entering of a lawsuit by a third party, in order to protect that party's independent interests.

invest. *Common meaning:* to put money into something with an expectation of financial gain. *In law:* to confer a legal interest, right, or authority in someone <the will invests the spouse with sole title to the homestead>.

knowledge. *Common meaning:* actual awareness. *In law:* notice, whether perceived or not; sometimes a person will be deemed to have constructive knowledge regardless of subjective awareness, as when there is a public record that the person should have found.

lapse. *Common meaning:* a gap or termination. *In law:* also, the failure of a gift in a will because the beneficiary predeceased the maker of the will.

leakage. *Common meaning:* loss of a liquid from a faulty container. *In law:* the decline in value of a copyrighted work because of unauthorized copying <recording artists see leakage by Internet piracy as a major threat to their livelihood>.

legacy. *Common meaning:* the reputation one leaves behind; to a college or university, the child of a prominent graduate. *In law:* a gift in a will of personal property or, less frequently, money.

letters. *Common meaning:* written communications. *In law:* a document formally granting some authority or right <letters patent>.

lie. *Common meaning:* to recline; to tell a falsehood. *In law:* of a cause of action, to have merit in an area of law <a remedy will lie in tort for a customer injured because of a shopkeeper's negligence>.

limitations. *Common meaning:* restrictions or boundaries. *In law:* a period set by statute for a criminal offense or a cause of action, beyond which time any prosecution or lawsuit is barred <statute of limitations>.

malice. *Common meaning:* hatred, spite, ill will. *In law:* a term of art with different meanings in different areas of law, but generally meaning either intent to do harm or a reckless disregard of a known, high risk that harm would result.

mandate. *Common meaning:* a strong electoral victory. *In law:* an order from an appellate court to a lower court, directing it how to proceed with the case; a judicial command to a court officer to carry out a court order.

mayhem. *Common meaning:* rioting, bedlam, disorder, even rowdy merrymaking. *In law:* historically, the common-law felony of intentionally crippling someone or cutting off a limb so as to deny the king his services as a soldier; in modern times, maiming.

misadventure. *Common meaning:* an accident or misfortune. *In law:* the accidental killing of a person by someone acting lawfully and bearing no malicious intent.

moot. *Common meaning:* beside the point, so not worth debating. *In law:* unsettled, so worth debating as a hypothetical (archaic except in the term *moot court*); but also not debatable because another issue has already decided the outcome on other grounds <a moot point>.

notice. *Common meaning:* sensory awareness of something. *In law:* as easily, no awareness at all, but just a good reason why one should have become aware ("constructive notice") because, for example, a public record existed or because a reasonable person would have thought to ask.

notorious. *Common meaning:* infamous; widely known for some evil or misdeed. *In law:* of common knowledge, so that anyone with an adverse interest is deemed to have been on notice <open and notorious possession>.

option. *Common meaning:* a choice. *In law:* a contract to hold an offer open for a specified time.

paper. *Common meaning:* a document or report. *In law:* a negotiable instrument <bearer paper is payable to anyone in possession of it>.

partition. *Common meaning:* a room divider. *In law:* a dividing of two or more people's joint or common interest in a single property, either by splitting the land into tracts or by selling the property and splitting the proceeds.

perfect. *Common meaning:* to achieve something's final form. *In law:* to conform with a law by correctly finishing all steps necessary to secure a record, or to protect an interest.

perfection. *Common meaning:* the pinnacle of quality. *In law:* the validation of a security interest as against other creditors, usually by filing a financing statement or by taking possession of the collateral.

performance. *Common meaning:* an artistic presentation. *In law:* the carrying out of a contract obligation <a unilateral contract can be accepted only by the performance of the thing sought by the offeror>.

permissive. *Common meaning:* tolerant of behavior that others might object to. *In law:* permissible, especially of claims that may or may not be joined in a suit as the party wishes <permissive counterclaim>; wrongfully permitted <permissive waste>.

person. *Common meaning:* a human being. *In law:* a legal being, either a born human being or a legal entity such as a corporation.

personality. *Common meaning:* a person's unique demeanor, and especially a friendly disposition. *In law:* the status of being a person (born human, corporation, or other entity) as recognized by law.

pledge. *Common meaning:* a promise. *In law:* property put in a creditor's possession as security for a debt <pawn is the most common form of pledge security>.

positive. *Common meaning:* certain. *In law:* formally enacted or established, as opposed to customary or natural <positive law>; by an act, as opposed to by an omission <positive misprision>.

prefer. *Common meaning:* to favor one thing over another. *In law:* to bring a charge against a criminal defendant, or to present a case to a grand jury <prefer charges>.

preference. *Common meaning:* the tendency to favor one thing over another. *In law:* a transfer of money or property by an insolvent person or company to a creditor before filing for bankruptcy, to the detriment of other creditors.

prejudice. *Common meaning:* to evoke a bias, especially one based on emotions. *In law:* to put one at a legal disadvantage; to impair a legal right or a cause of action <disallowing this evidence will unfairly prejudice our case>.

prescription. *Common meaning:* an instructed course of action, especially a regimen of medicine. *In law:* a rule or set of rules; also, the gain or loss of title by long-term open and notorious possession or by prolonged nonuse <easement by prescription>.

presents. *Common meaning:* gifts. *In law:* (with *these*) this instrument; the term is part of the archaic and meaningless clause "know all men by these presents."

presumption. *Common meaning:* an assumption, especially based on some evidence. *In law:* procedurally, an inference based on some evidence; a legal presumption carries some weight by shifting the burden of producing evidence to the other party.

privilege. *Common meaning:* a benefit granted, as opposed to a right. *In law:* a right, (1) of immunity from forced testimony <attorney–client privilege>; (2) of immunity from tort liability <affirmative defense of privilege>; or (3) to a specially conferred exception to a duty <work-product privilege>.

privy. *Common meaning:* an outhouse. *In law:* a person with a legal interest in a transaction.

process. *Common meaning:* a way of doing something. *In law:* a writ or summons, especially to answer a petition or to appear in court <original process>.

profit. *Common meaning:* a net financial gain. *In law:* also, a nonpossessory interest in land, giving one the right to fish, cut timber, mine minerals, let animals graze, or in some other way remove things.

progeny. *Common meaning:* a person's descendants. *In law:* a line of court decisions stemming from and further developing a landmark holding <*New York Times v. Sullivan* and its progeny>.

prohibition. *Common meaning:* the banning of something, especially alcohol. *In law:* a writ from a higher court to a lower court ordering it to stop proceedings that exceed the lower court's jurisdiction.

publish. *Common meaning:* to put a writing or a musical composition on the market. *In law:* to declare a will to contain the maker's true intentions; to show the jury evidence during a trial; to make a defamatory statement to a third person.

puffing. *Common meaning:* blowing, panting. *In law:* hyping; in the law of false advertising, expressing an overblown opinion as contrasted with stating an unsubstantiated or misleading claim as a fact.

quiet. *Common meaning:* to silence. *In law:* to secure a title to property or another legal right by having potential challenges declared invalid <action to quiet title>.

quit. *Common meaning:* to resign. *In law:* to leave rented property <quit the premises>.

raise. *Common meaning:* to increase or to bring up. *In law:* also, to alter a check so that it purports to pay more than the maker intended <a raised check>.

real. *Common meaning:* actual, genuine. *In law:* of land and buildings; of the type of property that is fixed and immovable, in contrast with personal property (chattels) <real estate; real action>.

recall. *Common meaning:* to remember something, or a manufacturer's calling back of products to repair a defect. *In law:* a petition and election to remove someone from public office, or retraction of a court's judgment or mandate, usually to correct errors.

receiver. *Common meaning:* a telephone handset or a football player. *In law:* a neutral party assigned to take possession of assets that are being litigated or are involved in a bankruptcy proceeding.

recital. *Common meaning:* an artistic performance, especially by music or dance students; repetition of poetry or prose, especially to an audience. *In law:* a statement in a contract or deed, identifying the parties and detailing facts surrounding the transaction (once introduced by "whereas" and "therefore," but that usage is fading).

recover. *Common meaning:* to get over, as an illness; to get back, as a cost or a loss. *In law:* to win money damages in a lawsuit; to collect on a judgment.

rectify. *Common meaning:* to make right. *In law:* for a court: (1) to change ambiguous or misstated wording in a contract or deed in order to enforce the intent of the parties; or (2) to make minor textual changes in a statute to carry out its purpose.

reduction. *Common meaning:* the process of making something smaller. *In law:* as used in the patent-law phrase "reduction to practice," the refinement of an inventive concept to the point at which a prototype or sample has been or could be made.

reform. *Common meaning:* to change a system in order to get rid of corruption or to bring it up to date. *In law:* to change the wording of a writing such as a contract or deed, in order to make it enforceable or to carry out the intent of the makers.

regress. *Common meaning:* to backslide; to revert to a lesser state. *In law:* the reentering of a place, or the right to do so <an easement of ingress, egress, and regress>.

rehabilitation. *Common meaning:* therapy for a dependency, a physical handicap, or criminal tendencies. *In law:* restoration of a witness's credibility after it has been impeached by the other side; reorganization of a bankrupt's finances.

relief. *Common meaning:* solace or charity. *In law:* a remedy, especially an equitable remedy such as injunction or rescission.

remainder. *Common meaning:* what's left over. *In law:* what's left after a will's specific instructions are carried out; also, a third party's future interest in real property, an interest that will become possessory upon the natural termination of the intervening estate.

removal. *Common meaning:* eviction. *In law:* the transferring of a lawsuit from a state court to a federal court, either on good cause and the petition of a defendant or because the suit involves a violation of civil rights.

repose. *Common meaning:* restful serenity, a nap. *In law:* a permanent cutoff period for lawsuits over a certain matter <statute of repose>, or the doctrine that a final judgment, plus any appeal, should bar all further legal proceedings.

repugnant. *Common meaning:* repulsive. *In law:* inconsistent, contradictory, not reconcilable <a race-based classification repugnant to the Fourteenth Amendment>.

return. *Common meaning:* generally, a coming back. *In law:* specifically, the return of a process, writ, or other court document, along with the server's report of what was found or done <return of writ>; a report <tax return; election returns>.

reversion. *Common meaning:* a return to a previous state or behavior. *In law:* the automatic return of an interest in property to a grantor who has conveyed less than the entire interest the grantor owns <the owner of a fee simple who grants an estate for life retains a reversionary interest in the property>.

rider. *Common meaning:* one who rides something. *In law:* a supplemental writing attached to a proposed statute, an insurance policy, or some other document, adding further provisions to the main document.

ripeness. *Common meaning:* of a fruit or vegetable, the state of being fully matured and ready to pick. *In law:* of a dispute, the state of being developed to a point at which judicial intervention is warranted; the constitutional "case or controversy" doctrine of avoiding premature adjudication.

salting. *Common meaning:* seasoning. *In law:* a labor-union practice of getting a union member (the "salt") employed at a nonunion shop with the intention of organizing the workers and calling for a collective-bargaining election.

savor. *Common meaning:* to enjoy the taste or experience of something. *In law:* to take on the character of or to be closely associated with something <a death savoring of foul play; an interest in property savors of the realty>.

schedule. *Common meaning:* a timetable or itinerary. *In law:* an attachment to a document, itemizing things referred to in the main document <Schedule A is an inventory of business assets>.

seal. *Common meaning:* to close tightly. *In law:* a distinctive impression used to authenticate a document; at common law, a seal rendered contract obligations indisputable, but that distinction is gone today in most jurisdictions <contract under seal>.

seasonable. *Common meaning:* just right for the season. *In law:* timely; within the time specified in a contract or, if no time is specified, within a reasonable amount of time.

secrete. *Common meaning:* to discharge, as a gland produces a bodily fluid. *In law:* to conceal and keep secret, a term common in legal writing <the defendant secreted the documents to avoid their discovery>.

security. *Common meaning:* safety. *In law:* collateral for a loan; any interest or instrument relating to finances; a note, stock, bond, debenture, certificate of deposit, etc.

seduction. *Common meaning:* any person's nonviolent persuasion of another person to have sex. *In law:* at common law, a man's nonviolent persuasion of a previously chaste woman to have sex.

self-help. *Common meaning:* a genre of publishing centered on motivational and self-improvement tips. *In law:* a nonlegal remedy for a wrong; e.g., methods outlined in the UCC for merchants to deal with breaches of contract without going to court.

servant. *Common meaning:* a domestic employee; an employee with a high duty of loyalty and service <public servant>. *In law:* any employee <master–servant relationship>.

service. *Common meaning:* assistance; rite; repair. *In law:* the formal delivery to someone of a legal paper such as a pleading, a summons, or a writ <service of process>.

set aside. *Common meaning:* to put to one side; to earmark funds for some purpose. *In law:* to overturn a conviction or to vacate a judgment or court order <the appellate court set aside the damages judgment and remanded the case for relitigation on that issue>.

setback. *Common meaning:* a reversal of fortune. *In law:* a minimum distance that must be preserved between property lines and any building erected on the lot, as specified in a deed or a zoning ordinance.

several. *Common meaning:* a few. *In law:* referring to the liability of multiple tortfeasors, separate rather than joint; severable, so that each defendant is responsible for only a share of the judgment.

shrinkage. *Common meaning:* a laugh line in a *Seinfeld* episode. *In law:* loss of inventory that is due to things like pilferage, spoilage, and breakage.

sidebar. *Common meaning:* a supplemental and related article published along with a main article. *In law:* the side of a judge's bench where the judge and lawyers can talk but the jury can't hear; a conference held at that place.

signal. *Common meaning:* a sign. *In law:* in a legal citation, an introductory word or phrase that tells the reader how the citation relates to the statement in the text; common signals are *see, see also, but see, see generally, compare . . . with, cf., accord,* and *contra.*

signature. *Common meaning:* a person's handwritten name. *In law:* as easily, under the UCC, a logo on a letterhead or fax cover sheet, or any other mark used with the intention of authenticating a writing.

simple. *Common meaning:* easy. *In law:* of an estate, unconditionally inheritable and assignable <fee simple>; of a crime, not aggravated by use of a deadly weapon or other consideration <simple assault>; of a contract, not made under seal <simple contract>.

simultaneous. *Common meaning:* of two events, happening at the same time. *In law:* of two deaths, happening within 120 hours of each other, for the purpose of construing wills under the Uniform Simultaneous Death Act and the Uniform Probate Code.

specification. *Common meaning:* a detailed listing, as of materials, parts, steps, and the like. *In law:* the taking of title to property by innocently converting it to another form, such as wood into furniture or grapes into wine; in patent law, a detailed description of how an invention is made and used.

standing. *Common meaning:* status, rank. *In law:* the state of having enough of a stake in a controversy to support asking a court for a remedy; to have standing, a party must have suffered an actual injury related to the zone of interests that the statute sued under was intended to protect.

stay. *Common meaning:* to stop or remain. *In law:* more specifically, to suspend a legal proceeding or execution of an order, usually pending some further deliberation <stay of execution>.

strike. *Common meaning:* to hit; to stop work in a labor dispute. *In law:* to dismiss a potential juror; to expunge statements from a trial record <motion to strike the witness's last statement>.

style. *Common meaning:* fashion, flair, manner, rhetoric. *In law:* a case name <the complete style of the case is *Vanna White v. Samsung Electronics America, Inc.*>.

surcharge. *Common meaning:* an added tax, especially a steep one. *In law:* also, a second mortgage, a fiduciary's liability to a court for misconduct, and a number of other meanings of only historical significance.

surrogate. *Common meaning:* a stand-in. *In law:* a probate judge.

tail. *Common meaning:* a caudal appendage. *In law:* a limitation on the inheritability of an estate, specifying that only actual offspring or only specified offspring may inherit <fee tail>.

taint. *Common meaning:* to contaminate. *In law:* to corrupt <do large campaign contributions taint the electoral process?>.

taking. *Common meaning:* the acquisition of something. *In law:* the acquisition by the government of private property for a public purpose by condemnation and with compensation, or the property's drastic diminution in use or value because of a law or regulation.

toll. *Common meaning:* of a bell, to ring; a fee, especially to use a highway or make a phone call. *In law:* to suspend the running of a time period, such as under a statute of limitations; to take away a right, such as the right of entry.

traverse. *Common meaning:* to cross over or through a place, or to lie across something. *In law:* a detailed answer to an opposing party's pleading, denying the allegations it contains.

trespass. *Common meaning:* the entry onto someone else's property without permission. *In law:* also, historically and as used in the Bible, any wrongful act; and in the development of common law, any wrongful injury to a person or property, and the legal writ to remedy that injury.

trust. *Common meaning:* confidence and reliance, especially in someone. *In law:* an arrangement in equity whereby a settlor gives legal title to some property to a trustee, who uses the property for the good of one or more beneficiaries; also, a business combination seeking to monopolize a market.

umpire. *Common meaning:* an official in baseball and other sports. *In law:* in arbitration, a person assigned to decide how to resolve a dispute after arbitrators have failed to agree.

unclean hands. *Common meaning:* dirty hands. *In law:* a metaphorical defense in equity, established by showing that the plaintiff acted in bad faith and therefore does not deserve equity ("he who comes into equity must come with clean hands").

undertake. *Common meaning:* to take on, as a task. *In law:* to guarantee something <the manufacturer undertakes that the product is free of defect> or to guarantee that someone else will do something <the father will undertake the son's car loan>.

use. *Common meaning:* function, operation, consumption, utility. *In law:* before the Statute of Uses (1536), equitable ownership and the right to possession of land that another person holds legal title to, for the purpose of rendering the interest inheritable.

utter. *Common meaning:* to speak. *In law:* to pass or attempt to pass a forged check; to hold out that an instrument is genuine, especially when it is not <utter a forgery>.

variance. *Common meaning:* variation. *In law:* variation between a pleading and proof, or a criminal charge and evidence; official permission to use land in a way that would otherwise violate a zoning ordinance.

veracity. *Common meaning:* the personal quality of honesty and truthfulness. *In law:* truth or accuracy of a statement; some purists consider this usage substandard, but it is common in law.

verdict. *Common meaning:* loosely, the outcome of a trial. *In law:* rigorously, the finding of facts by the jury (or the judge in a bench trial), as distinguished from the final judgment or sentence.

vested interest. *Common meaning:* loosely, any personal interest. *In law:* rigorously, an interest—whether possessory or future—that is fixed in law and is not contingent on any other event or condition.

waste. *Common meaning:* something left over or unusable; devastation; garbage; excrement. *In law:* actual damage, change, or legal encumbrance to property, caused by a tenant to the harm of someone with a future interest in the property; a common-law action to remedy waste.

work. *Common meaning:* to labor; to operate. *In law:* for patent-law purposes, to fully develop and market an invention <work the invention>.

writing. *Common meaning:* words on paper. *In law:* for purposes of copyright, "any physical rendering of the fruits of creative intellectual aesthetic labor," including music, art, movies, even pantomime (*Goldstein v. Cal.*, 412 U.S. 546, 561 (1973)).

wrong. *Common meaning:* an evil; an injustice. *In law:* something that causes a physical injury or detriment to a legal right; a tort, or an act that makes the wrongdoer liable to the other party.

> "The major fault in modern prose generally is Stuffiness. . . . For most people . . . in most situations, in the writing of everyday serious expository prose, it is the Stuffy voice that gets in the way. The reason it gets in the way, I submit, is that the writer is scared. If this is an age of anxiety, one way we react to our anxiety is to withdraw into omniscient and multisyllabic detachment where nobody can get us."
>
> —*Walker Gibson*

§ 12
Troublesome Words

12.1 Jarring words are speed bumps on the road to comprehension. When your reader hits a term that is misspelled or not phrased correctly or somehow shocking to the sensibilities, your message becomes secondary for a moment. The reader is distracted, trying to figure out what's wrong here.

Worse, these distractions have a cumulative effect on the reader's opinion of the writer's competence and credibility. In this chapter are tips for preventing these distractions.

Usage Problems in Legal Writing

12.2 Use words correctly and precisely.

(a) *Correctness.* Although the notion of linguistic correctness may seem absolute—right or wrong—it is mutable. Words change over time: they take on new meanings and lose old meanings for any number of reasons. But this is usually a very gradual process. And so much the better when it is slow, because the language remains relatively stable. One generation can communicate with the next, and with many generations after that. What is "correct" (some prefer to say "appropriate") is a word choice that, in a given age, (1) is consistent with historical usage, especially that of the immediate past, and (2) preserves valuable distinctions that careful writers have cultivated over time. By meeting these standards, the legal writer achieves a greater degree of credibility with an educated readership.

(b) *Precision.* Often either of two words will suffice in a sentence, but the shades of meaning differ. There is, for example, a difference between saying that a doctrine is *old* and saying that it is *venerable*, between calling a treatise *compendious* and calling it *voluminous*; and between characterizing a person as *drunken* as opposed to merely *drunk* on a specific occasion. Careful writers make distinctions. They cultivate an awareness of words and their connotative differences. They would no more write *incidental to* when they mean *incident to* than they would try to drive a nail with the handle of a screwdriver.

(c) *Usage problems.* What follows is a fairly detailed list of terms that are sometimes misused in legal writing. Writers and editors need not memorize the list or the advice; they should, however, acquaint themselves with the words that often cause problems so that, when the need arises, they know to consult a usage guide such as this one.

a; an. *A* precedes a word that starts with a consonant sound; *an* precedes a word that starts with a vowel sound. Note that it's the sound and not necessarily the letter that counts <an unimportant exception to a universal rule>. The word *historical* and its variants cause missteps, but usage authorities generally agree that since the *h* is pronounced, the word takes an *a* <an hourlong talk at a historical society>. Likewise, an initialism (whose letters are sounded out) may be paired with a different article from the one used with a similar-looking acronym (which is pronounced as a word) <an HTML website for a HUD program>.

abandon; desert. For the most part, these words overlap. But when it's a plan or an enterprise that is being left behind, use *abandon*.

abjure; adjure. To *abjure* something is either to formally renounce it <the new leader abjured the palatial trappings of the old regime> or to refrain from it <both sides abjured violence>. To *adjure* someone to do something is to plead or to make the person swear to do it. It used to mean to order someone to do something under threat of a curse. We don't do curses today (not that kind, anyway), but this obsolete meaning has not died out entirely: the word is occasionally used to mean to require by law.

abolition; abolishment. Stick to *abolition*, which is the more natural and more common term.

abrasion. See CONTUSION.

abrogate; arrogate. To *abrogate* something (usually a law, treaty, or other agreement) is to abolish it <the invasion abrogated a nonaggression pact signed just weeks before>. To *arrogate* something (usually a power or right) is to commandeer it to oneself or assign it to another <the regents fired the dean and arrogated that office's financial responsibilities to the president>.

absolve of; absolve from. To *absolve* is to wipe away. But there's a fine distinction: we are *absolved of* our debts and other obligations, but *absolved from* our crimes and other transgressions.

abstruse. See OBTUSE.

accept. See EXCEPT.

acceptance; acceptation. *Acceptance* is broad enough to handle most common meanings of these terms. *Acceptation* is marginally better to denote widespread public use of a word or phrase <these words are used as jargon, not according to their ordinary acceptation>.

accepter; acceptor. *Accepter* is the common spelling. In law, we use *acceptor* for one who *accepts* (pays) a draft or *accepts* an offer (to parallel *offeror*).

access, ***vb.*** No firewall is secure enough to stop the spread of this bit of computerese (meaning "to gain access"). But use it in legal writing and you run the risk of facing a luddite judge who will bang out a judgment for your opponent on a Smith-Corona.

accessory. See PERPETRATOR.

accommodate; accommodable; accommodatable. Repeat over and over: two *m*'s. Make it a mantra until it's second nature. *Accomodate* [spell *accommodate*] is a red flag of sloppy writing to the literate reader, who will be hard-pressed to resist the urge to *sic* you in any responsive brief. The adjective *accommodable* (preferred over *accommodatable*) is gaining use in employment law.

accomplice. See PERPETRATOR.

accord; accordance. If you're *in accord* with someone, the two of you agree. If you perform your obligations under that agreement, you have acted *in accordance* (not *in accord*) with its terms.

accord and satisfaction. See COMPROMISE AND SETTLEMENT.

accounting; bookkeeping. *Accounting* is the management of financial affairs, especially of a company. It entails making judgments about such things as tax deductions, acquisitions, and stock offerings. *Bookkeeping* is the clerical maintenance of financial records.

accuse. See ALLEGE.

acknowledgment; verification. The difference between these two legal terms is what is sworn to. An *acknowledgment* attests only that the attached signature is genuine. A *verification*, on the other hand, is an acknowledged writing containing a further sworn statement that the contents of the writing are true.

acquiesce. To *acquiesce in* something means "I'll do it, but I don't have to like it." It is a passive acceptance rather than an affirmative endorsement. For example, if a court interprets a statute a certain way, and Congress does not amend the statute to effectively overturn the court's decision, Congress is said to have *acquiesced in* that interpretation. The phrase *acquiesce to* is not as traditional or idiomatic. *Acquiesce with* is always wrong.

acquittal; acquittance. A criminal defendant walks after an *acquittal*. A debtor is freed from an obligation with an *acquittance* (a written release).

acquitted of; acquitted from. Always the first—never the second.

acuity; acumen. Both words mean "sharpness" in a figurative sense, and both can also denote mental sharpness. But *acumen* applies only to mental sharpness <the nominee's legal acumen was never in question>, while *acuity* applies more often to the physical senses <visual acuity is a requirement for flight school>.

adapt. See ADOPT.

adequate; sufficient. Avoid using the qualitative *adequate* (good enough) to mean quantitatively *sufficient* (plenty or big enough). In contract law, a legal detriment or anything of economic value is *sufficient* consideration, but we compare the value of what each party brings to the table to decide whether the consideration is *adequate* (so that the bargain is fair). *Adequate enough* is a substandard redundancy.

adherence; adhesion. While *adherence* is usually figurative <adherence to a code of ethics>, *adhesion* is usually literal <adhesion of a window decal>. The exceptions in law are the contract of *adhesion* (a one-sided, take-it-or-leave-it contract) and a third-party nation's *adhesion* to some but not all of a treaty's terms.

adjure. See ABJURE.

administer; administrable. Because *administrator* and *administration* appear so much in legal usage, we sometimes trip over the simple verb *administer*. Don't backpedal from those noun forms to arrive at the silly variant *administrate*. And an estate that can be distributed by this process is *administrable*, not *administratable* or *administerable*.

administrator; executor. A person distributing a decedent's estate is an *administrator* if appointed by a court, or an *executor* if named in the will. The feminine forms (*administratrix* and *executrix*) are becoming obsolete, since *administrator* and *executor* are considered gender-neutral.

admission; admittance. *Admission* is usually permission to enter, whereas *admittance* is physical entry only. *Admittance* is often misused where *admission* is meant <she received her notice of *admittance* [read *admission*] into college>.

admission; confession. In law generally, an *admission* is any concession or stipulation. But in criminal law, reserve *confession* for an admission of guilt.

admittance. See ADMISSION.

admonition; admonishment. Both are correct; prefer the more common *admonition*.

adopt; adapt. You *adopt* something when you accept responsibility for it <adopt a child> <adopt a contract>. You *adapt* to a new situation <adapt to married life> or *adapt* something for a purpose different from that of the original <adapt an old farmhouse into a bed-and-breakfast>.

adopted; adoptive. The child is *adopted* (legally taken in as one of the family). The parents are not *adopted* by the child and should not be so labeled. They are the *adoptive* mother and father.

adverse; averse. *Adverse* (think *adversary*) describes something we face that blocks our way. In a lawsuit, that something is a person (the *adverse* party), but elsewhere it is more often a condition <the climbers faced adverse weather conditions>. *Averse* (think *aversion*) describes our negative reaction to something <the plaintiff was averse to any settlement offer>.

advert. See ALLUDE.

advise; advice. The first term is the verb, the second the noun. Trying to be formal (but sounding pompous), some writers use *advise* for *told*—when only information and no advice is communicated.

advocate. See BARRISTER.

affect; effect. These words are confused fairly often, but they are usually simple to straighten out: to *affect* something is to have an *effect* on it. If it's a verb meaning "to influence," use *affect*; if it's a noun meaning "result," use *effect*. Then watch for the exceptions. *Effect* as a verb meaning "to bring about" is common in legal writing <the *Brown* decision effected a profound change in society>. Less common are (1) *effect* as a noun meaning "possession" <personal effects>; (2) *affect* as a verb meaning "to put on airs" <affecting a British accent>; and (3) *affect* as a noun meaning "emotional response" (rare outside psychology). For more on *effect*, see EFFECT.

affirmance; affirmation. Reserve *affirmance* for an appellate-court ruling upholding a trial-court decision. Use *affirmation* for all other meanings. In law, *affirmation* is also the term for an oath without any reference to religion.

affirmative (or negative), in the. The construction *answered in the affirmative* (or *negative*) has been roundly criticized as pompous jargon. In formal legal writing, the alternatives are not much better. But in all other contexts, ask whether you really want to use such stilted language. Then say no.

afflict. See INFLICT.

age of capacity; age of consent; age of majority; age of reason. All these phrases have developed separate doctrinal meanings; be careful to use the right one. *Age of capacity* is the age at which one may take legal action, such as signing a contract, writing a will, or bringing a lawsuit. *Age of consent* is the age at which one can agree to marry or to have sexual relations. *Age of majority* is the age at which the law considers one an adult and entitled to legal rights (beyond those of the age of capacity), such as voting. *Age of reason* is the age at which one is considered to know right from wrong, and so may be sued in tort or charged with a crime.

aggravate; irritate; annoy. Misusing *aggravate* (to worsen a condition, but not really to irk a person) can really *irritate* (annoy) some readers. And if you've *irritated* them by that misuse in conversation, you will only *aggravate* the situation if you commit the same error in writing.

agreement; bargain; contract. *Agreement* is the broadest term, meaning an understanding between parties. *Bargain* is the further agreement to exchange promises (or a promise for a performance), regardless of consideration. With sufficient consideration (and other legal requirements), a *contract* is formed.

aide; aid. *Aide* is the helper; *aid* is the help.

alibi. See EXCUSE.

allege; accuse; contend. To *allege* something is to say that it's true before it has been proved, especially in court <the plaintiff alleges negligence on the part of the defendant>. Facts—not people—are alleged, so the common phrase "*alleged* robber" is not quite correct. *Allege* should not be used informally to mean "assert," "claim," "declare," "maintain," or the like. To *accuse* someone of something is to say that that person did it, and especially to bring formal charges <the accused slayer>. To *contend* something is to state a position <we contend that the witness is biased>.

allot. See A LOT.

allow. See PERMIT.

allude; advert; elude. To *allude* to something is to suggest it indirectly. To *advert* to it is to refer to it directly. To *elude* is to evade or escape. Be careful not to misuse *elude* for *allude*.

allusion; illusion. An *allusion* is an implied reference, especially an indirect evocation of a literary work. The near-homonym *illusion* is something that appears to be something that it is not, such as an optical *illusion*. See ILLUSION.

a lot; alot; allot. *A lot* is the correct term for "many" or "much." *Alot* appears a lot, but it's never correct. *Allot* is both an unrelated term meaning "to allocate" and an occasional misspelling of *a lot*.

alternative; alternate. *Alternative* is the more frequently used term, meaning one of several options (not necessarily one of two, as the word's Latin root suggests). An *alternate* is a substitute.

ambiguous; ambivalent. Communication that is unclear because it is open to more than one reasonable interpretation is *ambiguous*. A person who has mixed emotions about something is *ambivalent*.

amenable; amenity. To be *amenable* to process is to be subject to a court's jurisdiction <the foreign corporation was amenable to suit under the long-arm statute>. Loosely, then, to be *amenable* is to be subject to persuasion <the defendant may be amenable to a plea bargain>. *Amenity* has nothing to do with law, except maybe to denote one of the luxurious adornments in a conference room: it is a pleasant accommodation or a pleasant demeanor.

amend; amends; emend. To *amend* a document, law, or constitution is to correct or improve it, often by adding something new. To make *amends* is to correct a wrong done to someone. To *emend* text is to correct errors in it.

amenity. See AMENABLE.

amiable; amicable. Friendly people are *amiable.* A friendly relationship is *amicable.* The first is best used to describe people, the second dealings between people.

among. See BETWEEN.

amoral. See IMMORAL.

amount. See NUMBER.

amuse. See BEMUSE.

an. See A.

anecdote; anecdotal. These two terms regarding stories of real-life events carry different and somewhat contrary connotations. An *anecdote* is presumed to be true (and funny), while *anecdotal* evidence is usually considered unreliable because it has not been subjected to scientific scrutiny. Cf. ANTIDOTE.

angry. See MAD.

annoy. See AGGRAVATE.

antepenultimate. See ULTIMATE.

anticipate; expect. Although the use is widespread, careful legal writers should avoid using *anticipate* to mean *expect.* Restrict *anticipate* to its original sense, to forestall by action taken in advance of an occurrence <we don't anticipate [read *expect*] any problems with the trial (but trials are unpredictable, and a good lawyer prepares for the unexpected)>.

antidote; anecdote. Laughter is the best medicine? Not here. *Antidote,* a potion that neutralizes a poison, is sometimes misused where the writer meant *anecdote,* a funny and supposedly true story. One who has been poisoned is probably in no mood for jokes. See ANECDOTE.

antinomy; antimony. *Antinomy* is the word you're looking for to denote contradicting authority, such as inconsistent caselaw or one judge's reasoning that is at odds with another's. *Antimony* is a metallic element.

anxious; eager. *Anxious* connotes an element of fear (think *anxiety*), so it should not be used as a synonym for *eager.* An *anxiously* awaited phone call is one that you'd probably rather not answer, while an *eagerly* awaited call you'd pick up on the first ring.

appellate; appellant; appealer; appellor. A court of appeals is an *appellate* court, despite some references outside legal writing to *appellant* courts. *Appellant* is the correct term for one who appeals a decision: *appealer* never caught on, and *appellor* is an archaic British term that has nothing to do with modern practice.

appertain; pertain. Don't use *appertain* as just a fancy way to say *pertain.* To *pertain to* is to relate to <the clause pertains to assignment of risk>; this is the more common term. To *appertain to* is to belong to by right <the defendant's rights appertaining to the Fifth Amendment>.

apply; follow. Technically speaking, if a court is bound by precedent it will *apply* that law to the facts of the present case for a fairly mechanical outcome. If the court is not bound by the precedent but finds the reasoning persuasive, it may *follow* that precedent.

appraisal; appraisement. *Appraisal* is the general term for an objective assessment of value. In law, an *appraisement* is an appraisal of the value of a decedent's estate.

appraise; apprise; apprize. To *appraise* something is to estimate its value <the broker appraised the house at $150,000>. To *apprise* someone is to inform that person about something <please apprise me of the appraised value before putting the house on the market>. Writers occasionally misuse *appraise* when they mean *apprise*. To *apprize* something is to value it highly <the judge's apprized collection of colonial Spanish lawbooks>.

appraisement. See APPRAISAL.

apprise; apprize. See APPRAISE.

appropriate; expropriate. Both verbs mean "to take away" (but note that *appropriate* can also mean "to give to," as when a legislature appropriates funds for a project). Courts distinguish between the terms according to who's doing the taking: *appropriate* is the general term, but a government *expropriates* private land for public use by its power of eminent domain.

approve; endorse; approve of. To *approve* something is to give it formal acceptance <approve a budget>. To *endorse* something indicates more active support for it <the mayor endorsed the governor's reelection bid>. To *approve of* something is less concrete; it denotes a favorable opinion <most Americans approve of free trade>. Cf. ENDORSE.

apt; likely. In the best usage, things in general are *apt* to occur under certain circumstances <it's apt to be rainy in April>; whereas specific things are *likely* to occur under specific circumstances <it's likely to rain this afternoon>. *Apt* also means "appropriate" <an apt response>.

arbiter; arbitrator. *Arbiter* is the general term for someone who settles disputes, and especially someone authorized to do so, such as a judge. An *arbitrator* is someone who conducts an *arbitration*. (Use varies, though: in Scotland it is an *arbiter* who conducts *arbitration*.) The cliché is *final* or *ultimate arbiter* (not *arbitrator*).

arbitration. See MEDIATION.

arbitrator. See ARBITER.

arrogate. See ABROGATE.

as. See LIKE; SINCE.

assault; battery. Most laypeople—and modern penal codes—do not distinguish *assault* from *battery*. But in criminal law and tort law, an *assault* is a threat or an attempt to commit *battery* (a harmful or offensive touching), but only if the threat or attempt was perceived by and alarmed the other person.

assay; essay. To *assay* something is to analyze it. To *essay* something is to attempt it. The verbal use of *essay* is unduly formal, even obscure; so for clarity you should avoid it.

assembly; assemblage. Both words apply to a collection, especially of people. But *assembly* connotes organization and purpose and is more formal than *assemblage*. One might speak of the *assembly* of a model ship from an *assemblage* of parts, for example.

assent; consent. The first connotes a positive and voluntary agreement <assent to a proposal of marriage>, while the second is neutral in connotation and can apply even when the agreement is given reluctantly <consent to a strip search>.

assessment. See TAX.

assignment; assignation. What's the difference between being on *assignment* and being in an *assignation*? The first is a delegated mission, the second an illicit rendezvous. Actually, *assignation* could legitimately cover the other meanings of *assignment* (e.g., transfer of an interest), but you know your readers would snicker.

assumption; presumption. An *assumption* is an unverified belief that something is correct. You can *assume* all you like, but it won't have any legal effect. A *presumption*, on the other hand, carries weight in the courtroom: it raises an inference that must be rebutted by the opposing party.

assure; ensure; insure. You *assure* a person (always a person as the object) that something will be done. You make preparations to *ensure* that it will be done. You call your underwriter's agent to *insure* yourself against financial loss if it doesn't get done.

attachment. See SEQUESTRATION.

attain; obtain. To *attain* something is to accomplish it <the dieter attained his weight-loss goal>. To *obtain* something is to acquire it <the law-school graduate passed the bar exam and obtained her law license>.

attorney's fees. Use the singular by default, the plural (*attorneys' fees*) only if the fees will actually be split among multiple attorneys.

avenge; revenge. Motive is the message in this word choice. One *avenges* a wrong done to anyone by seeing that the wrongdoer pays. But *revenge* is not about high notions of justice; it's about settling a personal score. While the first term may have positive connotations, the second usually carries some negative ones.

averse. See ADVERSE.

avocation. See VOCATION.

avoid; void. Remember that *avoid* means something different to lawyers (to make *void*) and to laypeople (to evade). While its general meaning is perfectly proper in legal writing, the careful writer may prefer to *avoid* it (in the common sense) if its use can create confusion about which meaning was intended.

awhile; a while. The one-word form is correct as an adverb meaning "for a short period of time" <let's wait awhile>. But when it's part of a prepositional phrase, it's no longer an adverb: it's an article (*a*) plus a noun (*while*) <let's wait here for a while> <we'll go in a while>.

bail; bale. The first is the legal term for the security that gets someone released from jail. The second is a big bundle of hay, cotton, or the like.

bar; debar; disbar. To *bar* someone is to stop that person from doing something <the statute of limitations bars this suit>, or to keep the person out of someplace <trustees voted to bar the fraternity from campus for two years>. *Debar* is a fading legalism meaning "to prevent someone from doing or having something" <this compulsory precedent debars the court from dismissing our suit>. To *disbar* a lawyer is to revoke the license to practice <disbar for misconduct>.

bargain. See AGREEMENT.

barrister; advocate; solicitor. In the United Kingdom, there are two types of lawyers: *barristers* (called *advocates* in Scotland), who argue cases in superior court; and *solicitors*, who counsel clients, prepare legal documents, and make limited court appearances (especially in lower courts).

battery. See ASSAULT.

because. See SINCE.

because of. See DUE TO.

behalf. See ON BEHALF OF.

behest. See REQUEST.

belabor; labor. You will see *belabor* used to mean *labor* (to perform fatiguing work) more often than you will see it in its original meaning (to beat physically). Be aware, though, that some readers will object to the strictly incorrect phrase *belabor the point* (read *labor the point*).

bemean. See DEMEAN.

bemuse; amuse. These are not synonyms. One who is *bemused* is usually not at all *amused*, but rather confused or lost in thought.

benefactor; beneficiary. A *benefactor* is on the giving end of a gift, a *beneficiary* on the receiving end.

beneficent; benevolent. A person who is *beneficent* (disposed to doing kind deeds) performs acts that are *benevolent* (helpful, kind). *Beneficence* is the character trait; *benevolence* is the conduct.

beneficiary. See BENEFACTOR.

benevolent. See BENEFICENT.

bequest. See REQUEST; DEVISE.

beside; besides. A fairly common error is the use of *beside* (next to, compared to) to mean *besides* (except, also) <it will take something *beside* [read *besides*] money to get the plaintiff to settle>.

between; among. The old "rule" that *between* refers to two things and *among* to more than two is not quite right—never has been. The distinction is the relationship between or among the various things. If it's distinctly one-to-one, use *between* even if there are more than two in total <personal bonds between senators>. If it's collective, use *among* <consensus among senators>.

bi-; semi-. *Bi-* means "two" <bicycle> <bifocal> <bilateral>. *Semi-* means "somewhat" and, specifically, "half" <semicircle> <semifinals> <semisweet>. But the literal meanings have been abused in practice when used as periodic prefixes: *biannual* has come to be synonymous with *semiannual*, meaning "twice a year" (*biennial* means "every other year"), and *biweekly* newspapers publish twice a week. To avoid confusion, spell it out to your reader <the board meets every other week>.

billion; trillion; milliard. The names of large numbers can be ambiguous. In the U.S. a *billion* is a thousand million (9 zeros), but in most other countries a *billion* is traditionally a million million (12 zeros: what Americans call a *trillion*). The British term for what Americans call a *billion* is a *milliard*, but that word has almost disappeared.

black-letter; blackletter. The first term is a Gothic or Old English typeface <a book's cover with black-letter type>. The second term describes well-settled principles of law <blackletter law>. And even though *blackletter* for law derives directly from *black-letter* typeface, by convention it is losing its hyphen.

blackmail; graymail; greenmail; feemail. *Blackmail* is the usual word for illegal extortion; the other terms are spinoffs. The CIA coined *graymail* to describe the effort of a criminal defendant to avoid prosecution by threatening to disclose classified information on the witness stand. *Greenmail* is the buying of stock in a target corporation, threatening a hostile takeover, and then selling back the stock at an inflated price. *Feemail* is the unethical practice of extracting a legal fee by duress, threat, or intimidation.

blameworthy; culpable. In law, a simple and useful distinction has developed between these two terms, which were formerly synonymous. Today, we use *blameworthy* in civil disputes and *culpable* in criminal cases. An exception might arise in a claim for punitive damages: a writer might find *blameworthy* too weak to describe the defendant's conduct. Shun the ambiguous *inculpable*: it means "not guilty," but it can be misunderstood to mean "capable of being made guilty." Cf. GUILTY; NONCULPABLE.

blatant; flagrant. What is *blatant* is conspicuous <the videotape evidence exposed the defendant's alibi as a blatant lie>. What is *flagrant* is also conspicuous, but done with arrogant disdain as well <the mayor's junket to Tahiti was a flagrant waste of taxpayers' money>.

bombastic. Don't nibble at the word's bait: it has nothing to do with an explosive temper. Rather, a *bombastic* person is pompous in speech and manner, and unduly theatrical. It originally meant "stuffed with cotton padding" and still describes a stuffed shirt.

bona fide; real. In legal writing, *bona fide* is a term of art, its definition varying with the area of law and tweaked by caselaw and statutes <bona fide purchaser for value>. Outside legal writing, it just means "real" <a bona fide Grandma Moses> <a bona fide apology>. To avoid confusion, avoid its use in legal writing.

bona fides; good faith. *Bona fides* is an inferior way of saying *good faith*; writers should much prefer the latter phrase. If *bona fides* is used, however, keep in mind that despite its appearance and pronunciation [boh-nuh FIE-deez], it is singular <the defendant's bona fides is not an issue>.

bookkeeping. See ACCOUNTING.

born; borne. Of the two past participles of *bear*, *born* applies only to birth in a passive sense <born in the U.S.A.> <native-born citizen>. *Borne* applies in other senses: "carried" <canister borne by ship> <with that doctrine borne in mind> and "given birth to" <she has borne three children>.

breach; broach; breech. Lawyers should have no trouble handling *breach* in its contract-law sense, meaning "to break." *Broach* means "to tap into": literally to put a hole in something (such as a keg) to let the liquid out, and figuratively to open up a subject for discussion. So you could either *breach* a dam or *broach* it—the first of those choices being the more usual one. *Breech* is the back part of something, especially a gun or the buttocks.

bribery; extortion. If you offer something of value in exchange for corrupt conduct, it is *bribery*. If you demand something in exchange for corrupt favors, it is *extortion*. But if the person on the receiving end is a public official, acceptance under color of public office is *extortion*, even if the gift was unsolicited.

bring; take. If the movement is toward you, use *bring* <please bring me my glasses>; if it's toward someone or something else, use *take* <I need to take my dog to the vet>. Misusing *bring* and *brought* for *take* and *took* is surprisingly common.

broach. See BREACH.

building. See FACILITY.

burglarize. See ROB.

can; may. We all know that *can* denotes ability and *may* permission. Most of us blatantly misuse the terms in speaking, at least on occasion, but in writing we *can* do better. The meanings almost merge when the context is whether one *can* legally do something—that seems like a question of permission, but it's still about ability: can it be done without breaking a law?

cannon; canon. Sometimes writers mistakenly pull out the big gun (*cannon*) for one of *canon*'s senses, especially a body of doctrines <canon of ethics>.

canvas; canvass. *Canvas* is the heavy cloth, used in such activities as painting. To *canvass* is to solicit votes, to count votes, to examine votes, or to debate.

capitol; capital. You'll find the state *capitol* (the building where the legislature sits) in the *capital* city. With an *o*, the term always means a building for the legislature. In all other senses it's *capital*.

carat; karat; caret. The weight of a jewel is measured in *carats* <a 1-carat diamond>. The purity of gold is measured in *karats* <24-karat means pure gold> (but note that in British English it is also spelled *carat*). A *caret* is an insertion mark on a manuscript, usually marking an edit.

career; careen. A car that *careers* down the street travels at full speed. A sailboat that *careens* around a turn tips dangerously to one side. The use of *careen* to indicate high-speed and erratic movement is a corruption that may be too common to call error, but it should still be avoided in formal writing.

caret. See CARAT.

caselaw; case law; case-law. All three variants appear regularly, but *caselaw* is increasingly prevalent.

catalogue; catalog. Despite the increasing popularity of the shortened term, *catalogue* is still the preferred spelling.

cause célèbre; cause. At law, a *cause célèbre* is a trial or decision involving a famous person or a sensational event. Loosely, then, it refers to a notorious person or event. But it does not properly refer to a *cause* or movement.

cede; secede; concede. To *cede* something is to give it up. To *secede* is to formally withdraw from an organization. To *concede* something is to admit it, especially a fact or defeat.

censor; censer; sensor. A *censor* is someone who reviews writings and art and excises offensive or otherwise objectionable content. Writers sometimes have trouble with its spelling, and land instead on *censer* (an incense burner on a chain) or *sensor* (a mechanical detector).

censor; censure. To *censor* writings, art, and other works is to inspect them and excise objectionable (or merely embarrassing) content. To *censure* someone is to criticize or officially reprimand that person.

center on; center around; revolve around. Since the center is a single point, it is illogical to say that something *centers around* anything. Rather, it may *center on* it or *revolve around* it.

certainty; certitude. A person may know something to a *certainty* (especially if it can be objectively proved), or know it with *certitude* (especially if it's a matter of faith). The thing that is known is a *certainty*, but never a *certitude*.

cession; session. *Cession* is the act of ceding (giving up); *session* is the act of sitting (meeting formally).

character; reputation. What you really are, good and bad, is your *character*; what other people think you are, good and bad, is your *reputation*.

childish; childlike. These words carry opposite connotations: *childish* suggests a stubborn immaturity; *childlike* suggests innocence and ingenuousness.

cite; citation; site; sight. To *cite* a reference (never *cite to* a reference) is to relate its importance to the issue at hand and to identify its source <on this point, the brief cited *Palsgraf*>. In general use, the term also means to point out, either for good <cited for bravery> or for ill <cited for speeding>. The colloquial use of *cite* as a noun meaning *citation* is out of place in formal writing <one footnote alone contained 24 *cites* [read *citations*]>. *Cite* and *site* (place) are sometimes confused, as are *site* and *sight* (to see or the thing seen).

citizen; subject. The distinction is to whom you owe political allegiance: the nation collectively or a monarch. If it's the former, you're a *citizen*. If it's the latter, you're a *subject*.

citizenship; domicile; residence. *Citizenship* is one's status as a member of a nation, with the rights and privileges that this status carries with it. *Domicile* is where one lives with the intent to stay; it refers particularly to a state, county, and city. *Residence* is, broadly, where one's home is, or the building itself. One may have many *residences* but only one *domicile*. Note that the U.S. Constitution refers to *citizens* of the states, so for purposes of federal diversity jurisdiction, *citizenship* and *domicile* are the same.

claim preclusion. See COLLATERAL ESTOPPEL.

clean; cleanse. The first term is literal, the second figurative: you *clean* your hands and *cleanse* your soul.

cleanliness; cleanness. Fastidious people (and their surroundings) are noted by their *cleanliness*. When not referring to people, the correct word is *cleanness*.

cleanse. See CLEAN.

clearly; obviously. As sentence adverbs <Clearly, this is true>, these weasel words are often exaggerators. They may reassure the writer but not the reader. If something is clearly or obviously true, then demonstrate that fact to the reader without resorting to the conclusory use of these words.

cleave; cleft; clove; cloven; cleaved. *Cleave* is really two verbs with nearly opposite meanings. To *cleave* in one sense is to split in two <lightning can cleave a mighty

oak>; that word is inflected *cleft* (or *clove*), *cloven*. To *cleave* in the other sense is to stick together <wet hair cleaved to the forehead>; that word is inflected *cleaved*, *cleaved*.

clench; clinch. Both words mean to grasp or tighten, but *clench* is literal <clench fists>, while *clinch* is usually figurative <clinch victory>. Exceptions crop up in woodworking <clinch with a screw>, metalworking <clinch with rivets>, and boxing <tired and bloodied, he could only clinch his opponent and pray for the bell>.

climactic; climatic; climacteric. The adjective formed from *climax* (culmination) is *climactic*. The adjective formed from *climate* (prevailing weather) is *climatic*. *Climacteric* was once preferred over *climactic*, but its status today is anticlimactic.

clinch. See CLENCH.

closure; cloture. *Closure* is the act of closing something or the state of being closed; it is most commonly used today as vague psychobabble <seeking closure>. *Cloture* is a narrow term for the parliamentary procedure of forcing a cutoff of debate and a vote on a proposal.

clove; cloven. See CLEAVE.

coequal; equal. On rare occasions *co-* may add something that *equal* can't do alone. But the word probably would not exist today if it weren't for our "*coequal* branches of government."

cognoscenti. So spelled. The *cognoscenti* are the experts in a field, those in the *know*. *Cogniscenti* is one of many possible misspellings. It's an embarrassing word to misspell, since to do so leaves the writer out of the *cognoscenti* in the reader's mind. Prefer simpler terms such as *experts*. The singular form is *cognoscente*.

cohabit. An unmarried couple who live together *cohabit*. *Cohabitate* is a needless variant formed from the noun *cohabitation*.

cohort; cohorts. *Cohort* is a singular mass noun that strictly refers only to an uncountably large group <the candidate's cohort of followers>. But it has been misused for so long as a synonym for *colleague* <the candidate huddled with her closest cohorts> that this use is dominant today. Either way you use the term may confuse some readers and irritate others, so you should avoid it in formal writing.

coin a phrase (term; word). To *coin a phrase* is to use it for the first time, not to repeat an old cliché.

collaborate; corroborate. To *collaborate* is to cooperate with someone in an endeavor <to be competent to stand trial, an accused person must be able to collaborate in the defense>. To *corroborate* something is to confirm it <an eyewitness corroborated the defendant's statement>.

collateral estoppel; res judicata. These two forms of preclusion have long been confused. *Collateral estoppel* (issue preclusion) bars relitigation of a material issue that has been argued and ruled on before. *Res judicata* (claim preclusion) bars relitigation of an entire dispute after a final judgment has been entered.

collegial; collegiate. *Collegial* corresponds to *colleague* <a collegial environment for all the lawyers—associates and partners alike>; *collegiate* corresponds to *college* <collegiate athletics>.

colloquy; colloquium. A *colloquy* is a discussion, especially with a judge; the verb form is *collogue*. A *colloquium* is an academic seminar.

commendable; commendatory. If you donate to a worthy cause, that is *commendable* (worthy of praise). The recipient may respond by presenting you with a *commendatory* plaque (one that expresses praise).

common. See MUTUAL.

commonwealth; commonweal. A *commonwealth* is a state, nation, or group of nations in which the people have a say in their own governance. The *commonweal* is the public well-being. Cf. TERRITORY.

compare with; compare to. *Compare with* is the usual phrase, meaning to note similarities and differences <the purpose of the colloquium is to compare the compensatory mechanism of the common law with that of the civil law>. *Compare to,* however, means to emphasize similarities; it often appears in a metaphorical or poetic construction <shall I compare thee to a summer's day>.

compel; impel. To *compel* an action or decision means to force it, to leave the actor no alternative <the justices knew their decision would compel an end to the recount>. To *impel* an action or decision means to push the actor in that direction, especially by mental suasion <they should declare the causes that impel them to secede>.

compendious; voluminous. A *compendious* book is an abridgment. A *voluminous* output fills a large book or many volumes. *Compendious* is often misused to also mean "large," but in fact these words bear nearly opposite meanings.

competence; competency; competent. *Competence* is the general term for fitness or ability. *Competency* is the narrow legal term for fitness to stand trial or to give testimony, and for questions of sanity. For both words, the corresponding adjective is *competent.*

complacent; complaisant; compliant. A *complacent* person is comfortable and self-satisfied—even, by connotation, smug and foolhardy <the general warned budget-makers not to become complacent in peacetime>. A *complaisant* person is agreeable, often to the point of being a pushover <advisers worried that the President had been too complaisant at the summit>. A person who is *compliant* is obedient <the old-style CEO had expected a more compliant workforce>; a product or service that is *compliant* is in accordance with applicable regulations <the manufacturer replaced the out-of-spec goods with compliant ones>.

compliment; complement; supplement. *Compliment* (to praise, flatter, or bestow) is frequently misused for its look-alike, *complement* (to round out) <fine wine *compliments* [read *complements*] a fine meal>. To *supplement* something is to add to it, but without the nuance of completing. See COMPLIMENTARY.

complimentary; complementary; supplementary. A *complimentary* comment is a bit of praise; a *complimentary* ticket is free. A *complementary* accessory enhances an outfit. *Supplementary* income adds to a main source of support. See COMPLIMENT.

comprise; compose. The most frequent error in using these terms is signaled by the phrase *comprised of.* Strictly speaking, since *comprise* means "to include," the phrase makes no sense. John, Paul, George, and Ringo *composed* (*were comprised in*) the Beatles. The Beatles *comprised* (*were composed of*) John, Paul, George, and Ringo.

comprising. See INCLUDING.

compromise and settlement; accord and satisfaction. The first phrase can apply to the agreement to resolve any legal dispute. The second phrase is narrower, usually applying to contract law: the parties reach an *accord* (a substitute for the original contract obligation), and performance of the *accord* gives the formerly aggrieved party *satisfaction*.

compulsive; compulsory. The first term implies a psychological obsession <compulsive behavior>; the second means "mandatory" <compulsory-attendance laws>.

concede. See CEDE.

conclusory; conclusive. The appearance of *conclusory* in tens of thousands of legal opinions is *conclusive* proof that the word does in fact exist, despite its absence from many dictionaries. It describes a statement that puts forth a conclusion but not the reasoning behind it. *Conclusive* means "authoritative."

concurrence; concurrency. *Concurrence* in general denotes an agreement. In law it means a judge's agreement with the outcome of a decision, but for reasons different from the majority opinion. It also refers to that judge's separate written opinion. *Concurrency* means the simultaneous (*concurrent*) running of multiple criminal sentences (as contrasted with consecutive, cumulative, or "stacked" sentences).

concussion. See CONTUSION.

condemn; contemn. In legal senses, *condemn* means to pass judgment against <condemned to death>, to take property by eminent domain <the city condemned the lots for a runway-expansion project>, or to declare a building uninhabitable <the long-abandoned tenement building was condemned>. *Contemn* means to show contempt; in legal writing it is used in the context of contempt-of-court proceedings.

condemner; condemnor. The first is correct in the general sense of one who passes an adverse judgment. But when the government is taking property by eminent domain, it's the *condemnor*.

condole. See CONSOLE.

conferral; conferment. Both terms mean the same thing: the act of *conferring* or what is *conferred*. But *conferral* predominates in legal writing, *conferment* in popular writing.

confession. See ADMISSION.

confident; confidant; confidante. To be *confident* is to be assured and determined. A *confidant* is a friend you can trust with your secrets; the word is also spelled *confidante*, although that feminine variant is disappearing.

conformity; conformance. The first is standard English; the second is a needless variant seen too often in legal writing.

congruous; congruent. *Congruous* and *congruent* both describe a good fit, harmony, or conformity between two things. But *congruous* is best used with people and qualities; *congruent* best deals with physical forms and geometry. The negative form *incongruous* is more common than either of the other terms; it means "inconsistent, unexplainable."

connive; conspire. If you *connive* at something, you look the other way when you should object. It is passive in that sense, whereas if you *conspire* with someone you take an active role.

connote; denote. Words often *connote* more than their literal meanings *denote*. They pick up nuances that invite good or bad reactions. But remember that words alone carry *connotations*; acts do not <what does this protest *connote* [read *suggest*]?>.

consent. See ASSENT.

consequent; subsequent. Both words describe something that follows another event. But *consequent* further describes something that happens as a result of the first event <speeding and the consequent accident>. *Subsequent* merely denotes time, not causation <subsequent Congresses acquiesced in the Court's interpretation>.

conservator; curator. As legal terms, both refer to the guardian appointed by a court to care for an incompetent person. The first term predominates, but the second is used in some states.

consist of; consist in. The first term is used with physical things <the flag consists of 50 stars and 13 stripes>. The second is used with abstract things <the driver's negligence consisted in speeding and not paying attention>.

console; condole. To *console* someone is to comfort that person. To *condole* with someone is to express sympathy; it is more often seen in the noun form, *condolence*. *Condole* is intransitive, so while you may *console* a friend, you can't *condole* a friend.

consolidation. See JOINDER; MERGER.

conspire. See CONNIVE.

constructive; constructional. In legal usage, the first term applies to something that is imposed by law <constructive notice> <constructive trust>. The second refers to construing writings, such as wills or statutes <constructional canons>.

consul. See COUNSEL.

contagious; infectious. These terms are distinguished in medicine. A *contagious* disease is easily spread by personal contact <influenza is highly contagious>. An *infectious* disease is spread by germs and viruses in the environment, or from person to person only by certain types of contact <HIV is infectious but not spread by casual contact>.

contemn. See CONDEMN.

contemporary; contemporaneous. Both terms describe things that happen at the same time. But the first is used as an adjective or a noun, usually referring to people <Lord Coke and Shakespeare were contemporaries>. It can also mean "contemporary with us" (i.e., "modern") <contemporary fashions>. *Contemporaneous* is usually used with things and events <two theaters of war were raging contemporaneously>.

contemptuous; contemptible. If you feel contempt, you are *contemptuous* of some person or thing. If you are *contemptible*, you give others reason to feel contempt for you. Cf. CONTUMACIOUS.

contend. See ALLEGE.

contingent fee; contingency fee. The fee is *contingent* on success, not a charge for some *contingency*. The first phrase is better, but both are common.

continual; continuous. The first means "recurring," the second "uninterrupted." If you get *continual* calls from telemarketers, you may suffer a *continuous* headache.

continuance; continuation; continuity. To laypeople a *continuance* is going ahead with something now, but to a lawyer a *continuance* postpones a trial, so it means not going ahead till later. A *continuation* can be going forward without interruptions, or resuming after an interruption. *Continuity* is the absence of interruption.

continuous. See CONTINUAL.

contract. See AGREEMENT.

contravene; controvert. To *contravene* something is either (1) to conflict with or impair it <new fighting threatened to contravene peace efforts>, or (2) to violate it <this call contravened the gag order>. To *controvert* something is to speak against it or contradict it <our witness will controvert the plaintiff's version of what happened>.

contribution; indemnity. *Contribution* is a partial payment of a monetary award, made by one defendant to another. *Indemnity* is full payment under a legal duty, such as an insurance policy or a judgment.

contributory; contributive; contributorial; contributional. *Contributory* describes the contribution of money or physical things; *contributive* is an inferior way to say "conducive" <diligent outlining is *contributive* [read *conducive*] to success in law school>. *Contributorial* describes one or more contributors, and *contributional* describes one or more contributions.

controvert. See CONTRAVENE.

contumacious; contemptuous. The first is the legal term describing one who intentionally disobeys a court order and is therefore subject to punishment for *contempt* of court. The second is used for the same purpose, but less frequently. Outside legal usage, *contemptuous* dominates. See CONTEMPTUOUS.

contusion; abrasion; concussion. If you fall off your bicycle, you may get a *contusion* (bruise) or an *abrasion* (scrape or cut). But if you're wearing your helmet, you're not as likely to get a *concussion* (head injury from a hard hit).

convicted (of, for). A hapless defendant is *convicted of* a crime or *convicted for* a criminal act, but is not *convicted in* anything.

convince; persuade. We hope to *convince* a jury to view the facts our way (mental state), then to *persuade* them to return a favorable verdict (action). Watch the prepositions: one is *convinced of* or *convinced that*, but one is *persuaded to* do something.

copulate; fornicate. While both terms refer to the same act, they differ in their legal implications. The first can be used regardless of the marital status of the parties. The second refers only to an unmarried person having sexual intercourse with another; it is still a crime in some places.

copy. See REPLICA.

copyrighted. This is the correct adjective; *copywritten* is not a proper word.

corespondent; correspondent. The first term is always a legal term, meaning either (1) one of two or more *respondents* (appellees), or (2) an adulterous spouse's paramour joined in a divorce suit (in the days before no-fault divorce). The second term covers all usual meanings, as in news reporter, letter-writer, or business representative.

corporal; corporeal. *Corporal* describes something relating to the body <corporal punishment>. *Corporeal* describes *having* a physical body <corporeal manifestation>; it is sometimes misused for *corporal.*

corpse; corpus; corpus delicti; corpus juris. These are all terms for bodies of one sort or another. A *corpse* is a dead human body. A *corpus* is the body of assets held in a trust. *Corpus delicti* is literally "the body of the crime," the *actus reus* in modern law (not necessarily the dead body as popularly thought, but proof that a crime has been committed). Watch out for the humorous but distasteful misspelling, *corpus delecti. Corpus juris* is a body of law, the term used in the sixth century's Justinian Code and today's legal encyclopedia, *Corpus Juris Secundum.*

correctional; corrective. If there are problems in the *correctional* system (prisons), the legislature should take *corrective* (remedial) action.

correspondent. See CORESPONDENT.

corroborate. See COLLABORATE.

council. See COUNSEL.

counsel; counselor; council; councillor; consul. *Counsel*, as a noun, is an adviser (also *counselor*) or the advice itself. As a verb, it means "to give advice." A city *council* passes local ordinances; a person serving on a *council* is sometimes called a *councillor.* A foreign government's representative is a *consul.*

courtesy. See DOWER.

court-martial; courts-martial. The word is always hyphenated, never combined or separated into two words. Because *court* is the noun and *martial* the adjective, the plural form is *courts-martial.*

credible; creditable; credulous; incredulous. If you're an honest person, both you and what you say will be *credible* (believable). Honesty is a *creditable* (praiseworthy) trait. Those who will believe anything are *credulous* (gullible). And those who simply can't believe what they are hearing are *incredulous* (unbelieving).

crevice; crevasse. A *crevice* is a small crack, as in a plaster wall; a *crevasse* is a gaping chasm, as on a glacier.

criminal. See UNLAWFUL.

culpable. See BLAMEWORTHY; GUILTY.

curator. See CONSERVATOR.

currently. See PRESENTLY.

curtesy. See DOWER.

curtilage; messuage. The area immediately surrounding a house is its *curtilage*, a term that is sometimes misspelled *curtilege* (perhaps through the influence of *privilege*). The house, curtilage, and outbuildings together are the *messuage.*

curtsy. See DOWER.

custody; possession. The first term is applicable to people and things <a suspect in police custody>, the second to things only <take possession of a new car>. In a master–servant (or employer–employee) relationship, the servant has *custody* of the master's chattels, but not *possession.*

damage; damages; injury. The first is the harm <the accident caused damage worth $50,000>, the second the compensation for that harm <the jury awarded $50,000 in damages>. What seems like an obvious distinction—that property sustains *damage* but a person sustains an *injury*—does not hold up in legal usage: people are *damaged* and property *injured* all the time.

deadly; deathly. A poisonous snake is *deadly* (it can kill you). A sudden ghostly silence might seem *deathly* (deathlike).

death statute; survival statute. A *death statute* lets the family recover the economic benefit they would have received but for the death. A *survival statute* lets a tort action survive the decedent so that the decedent's estate may recover damages.

debar. See BAR.

deceive; defraud. To *deceive* me is to mislead me into believing something that is not true. To *defraud* me is to get me to act in reliance on that misconception so that I suffer some detriment.

decided. See DECISIVE.

decimate; destroy. To *decimate* something is to do great damage to it, but not to *destroy* it. From the Latin word for "one-tenth," it was a repressive tactic in which every tenth person in a rebellious village or a defeated army was put to death. It's an inappropriate word choice when applied to some different percentage <the tornado *decimated* [read *destroyed*] half the homes in the small town>.

decision; judgment; decree; opinion. Judges make and issue (but do not write) *decisions, judgments,* and *decrees.* The caselaw we read in law school is the judges' written *opinions.* In the past, a *judgment* came from a court of law, while a *decree* came from a court of equity, admiralty, probate, or divorce; but there is no longer any such distinction. Cf. VERDICT.

decisive; determinative; resolute; decided. A fact that compels a decision is said to be *decisive* or *determinative.* To lawyers, facts are *decisive;* but to others, this word more often describes people who are *resolute. Decisive* is frequently misused where *decided* (clearly identified) is intended <the Mets will start the Series with a *decisive* [read *decided*] advantage in pitching>.

declaim. See DISCLAIM.

decree. See DECISION.

deduce; induce; deduct; deduction; induction. We *deduce* an answer by applying general rules to specific facts. We *induce* an answer by collecting specific facts and looking for a general rule. *Deduct* (to subtract) is sometimes misused to mean *deduce,* perhaps because the noun form (*deduction*) is the same for both words. *Induction,* the noun form of *induce,* is much more common than the verb.

de facto; de jure. Something that is *de facto* is not authorized or mandated by law, but exists in fact <de facto government> <de facto segregation>. Something that is *de jure* is established by law <de jure custody rights>.

defamation; libel; slander. *Defamation* is the communication of a falsehood that damages the reputation of someone. If it is recorded, especially in writing, it is *libel;* if it is merely spoken and unrecorded, it is *slander.*

defective; deficient; deficiency; defect. A *defective* thing is faulty. A *deficient* number or amount is insufficient. *Deficient* may mean *defective* only in the sense that something is missing, not that the design is flawed. (When writing of due-process rights, for instance, if notice is *deficient* it is also said to be *defective*.) Watch out for the noun forms, too: don't use *deficiency* (inadequate in number or amount) to mean *defect* (fault).

defense; defence. See OFFENSE.

deficient; deficiency. See DEFECTIVE.

definite; definitive. A *definite* answer is clear and exact. A *definitive* answer is final, conclusive, and authoritative. Supreme Court decisions are *definitive* but sometimes not so clear. The error comes when a writer tries to elevate the mundane word *definite* <the jury was visibly irritated at the witness for refusing to give a *definitive* [read *definite*] answer>.

defraud. See DECEIVE.

de jure. See DE FACTO.

delegate. See RELEGATE.

deliberate; deliberative. A *deliberate* act may be intended and planned <a deliberate act of terrorism> or slow and methodical <the deliberate pace of the rulemaking process>. *Deliberative* relates to debate <the Senate is a deliberative body>; it is misused when substituted for *deliberate* <the race went to the more *deliberative* [read *deliberate*] tortoise>.

delimit; limit. To *delimit* something is to refine its meaning by finding its limits <courts struggled to delimit the newfound right to privacy>. The word is misused when substituted for *limit* to mean "restrict."

delusion. See ILLUSION.

demean; bemean. The meanings of these words have shifted over time. To *demean* oneself originally meant "to behave" (hence, *demeanor*), and to *bemean* someone was to debase or belittle that person. Today, *demean* means what *bemean* once did, and *bemean* has faded into obscurity.

demur; demure. To *demur* in law is to file a *demurrer*, admitting the facts as the plaintiff has pleaded them but denying that they state a cause of action. More generally, to *demur* is to object (make a *demurral*), especially on moral grounds. The adjective *demure* describes a coy or restrained person.

denote. See CONNOTE.

dependence; dependency. *Dependence* is reliance on someone or something. *Dependency* is a much narrower term, meaning a land ruled by but not annexed by another country.

dependency. See DEPENDENCE; TERRITORY.

deport; deportment; deportation. *Deport* may mean either to behave in a particular way or to expel from a country. In the first sense, the corresponding noun is *deportment*; in the second sense, *deportation*.

depository; depositary. At one time, a *depository* was a place (such as a bank) to deposit things, especially money; *depositary* was reserved for people. Then the

Uniform Commercial Code used *depositary* to refer to banks. Outside UCC contexts, the old distinction is still a good one.

deprecate; depreciate. To *deprecate* someone or something is to express disapproval. To *depreciate* something is to belittle it; if something *depreciates*, it loses value. The phrase should be *self-depreciating*, but *self-deprecating* is well established.

desert; dessert. *Just deserts* is a cliché that should be avoided. But if you do use it, don't sugarcoat it by picking the wrong word. A *dessert* is an after-dinner treat and nothing more. In law, to *desert* is to abandon a spouse, family, or military duties. Cf. ABANDON.

desirable; desirous. A *desirable* person or thing is alluring; seeing a desirable person or thing stirs *desirous* emotions in us.

despoliation; spoliation. *Despoliation* means "plunder and ruin," but so does *spoliation*. Be careful to avoid the misspellings caused by false association with *spoil*.

dessert. See DESERT.

destroy. See DECIMATE.

determinative. See DECISIVE.

detract; distract. Keep *detract* intransitive <grammatical errors detract from any brief's impact> and *distract* transitive <typos distract the reader's attention away from the message>.

device; devise. The *-c-* spelling is the noun <an ingenious device>. The *-s-* spelling is the verb <surely we can devise a way to settle this>.

devise; bequest; legacy. As the common-law terms developed regarding wills, a *devise* was a gift of real property, a *bequest* was a gift of personal property, and a *legacy* was a gift of money. The terms have shifted somewhat: modern usage includes money as a *bequest*, and U.S. statutes consider items of personal property to be *devises*.

diagnosis; prognosis; prognostication. The doctor gives you a *diagnosis* (what is wrong with you), and then discusses your *prognosis* (what course the disease will take; what your chances of recovery are). A *prognostication* is a forecast or prophecy. It usually connotes mysticism (except when used to mean a weather forecast), and it is not used to signify a medical prognosis.

dietitian; dietician. Although both spellings are acceptable, the first is preferred.

different from; different than. The first phrase is usually the better choice. The second can be smoother idiomatically when *than* substitutes for *from what* <after *New York Times v. Sullivan*, "malice" in defamation law meant something different than it did before>.

differ from; differ with. To *differ from* something is to deviate from it <your numbers differ from mine>. To *differ with* someone is to disagree with that person <I have to differ with you about those numbers>.

dilemma; Hobson's choice. If you face two bad options, you're in a *dilemma*. A *Hobson's choice*, strictly speaking, is a take-it-or-leave-it situation: no choice at all. But that literal meaning has been obscured in American usage, and today the phrase has come to mean, like *dilemma*, the choice between two evils.

disbar. See BAR.

disburse. See DISPERSE.

disc. See DISK.

disclaim; declaim. The word for disavowing a warranty is *disclaiming*. To *declaim* is to give a public speech <the Declaration was written to be declaimed in every town square>.

disclose; expose; divulge. All three words mean "to make (something) known." But *disclose* does not carry the connotations of scandal that *expose* does, nor the connotations of betrayal or confession that *divulge* does <disclose financial backing> <expose corruption> <divulge state secrets>. To *expose* something is also to place it in danger <expose to liability> <expose to the elements> or to reveal to view <the curtain rose, exposing an elaborate set> <the flasher was arrested for exposing himself in public>.

discomfort; discomfit. To feel *discomfort* is to feel uneasiness. To *discomfort* someone else is to make that person feel uneasy. Strictly speaking, to *discomfit* an enemy is to utterly destroy it or to dash its plans and leave it in a state of total confusion. But today about all that's left of that meaning is "to confuse." And since a confused person is usually uneasy as well, the distinction and the meaning have both become, well, confusing.

discrete; discreet. A *discrete* thing is distinct from others <the crime has five discrete elements>. To be *discreet* is to be either tactful <he discreetly declined> or circumspectly confidential <the reporter was discreet about the informant's identity>.

disinformation; misinformation. Both words denote incorrect information. But *disinformation* means *misinformation* that is deliberately created or spread for some purpose, usually as propaganda.

disingenuous. See INGENIOUS.

disinterested; uninterested. A *disinterested* person is objective in the sense of not having any legal or financial interest involved in the outcome of a dispute, nor any bias toward the parties or the facts. An *uninterested* person has no intellectual interest in the people or the controversy, and probably doesn't care how it is resolved. A judge must be *disinterested*, but should never be *uninterested*. The distinction is eroding in general usage, but it remains sharp in legal writing.

disk; disc. *Disk* is the correct spelling for most uses <computer disk> <a slipped disk in his back>. The exceptions are audio and video *discs*, *disc* brakes, and the parts of a plow that turn up the soil.

disorganized; unorganized. Something that is *disorganized* is usually chronically or inherently so <my desk is a disorganized mess>, or else thrown into disarray by events <the mayor's unexpected resignation left City Hall utterly disorganized>. *Unorganized* has no such negative connotations <the "blue flu" sick-out appeared to be spontaneous and unorganized>.

disperse; disburse. To *disperse* a crowd is to break it up; to *disperse* things is to distribute them. To *disburse* money is also to distribute it, but note that this word can be used only in connection with money.

disposal; disposition. The words share the same general meaning (the getting rid of), but the connotations are very different. *Disposal* connotes getting rid of unwanted things <garbage disposal>, while *disposition* connotes a planned distribution <disposition of the assets of an estate>.

distinctive; distinguishable; distinguished. Something that is *distinctive* is recognizable out of others of the same type <a distinctive birthmark>. *Distinguishable* is generally synonymous with *distinctive*, but in law it is the word used to argue why a rule in a precedential case should not apply to the facts in the present case <that case is distinguishable because no consent was involved>. Someone who is *distinguished* is held in high regard <a distinguished senior judge>.

distract. See DETRACT.

divorcé; divorcée. See FIANCÉ.

divulge. See DISCLOSE.

doctrinal; doctrinaire. *Doctrinal* is used to describe a *doctrine*; it is neutral in connotation. *Doctrinaire* describes a dogmatic person and connotes stubbornness and narrow-mindedness.

domicile. See CITIZENSHIP.

dominant; predominant; dominate; predominate. *Dominant* and *predominant* are adjectives <a dominant personality> <the predominant political party>. *Dominate* and *predominate* are verbs <dominate the game> <neither party predominates in the legislature>. Note that *predominate* does not take an object. One thing does not *predominate* another; rather, it *predominates* in its field. A common error is to use the verb forms as adjectives.

double jeopardy. See FORMER JEOPARDY.

doubtless; doubtlessly; no doubt; undoubtedly. *Doubtless* is already an adverb, so it is incorrect to tack on *-ly*. *No doubt* says the same thing as *doubtless*, only more strongly. And *undoubtedly* is an even stronger word.

dower; curtesy; dowry; curtsy; courtesy. *Dower* (the right of a widow to a life estate in a third of her husband's land) and *curtesy* (the right of a widower to a life estate in all his wife's land) live on in some forms in a few U.S. jurisdictions. *Dowry* is the collection of assets that a wife brings into a marriage. *Curtsy* (a woman's bow made by bending the knees) and *courtesy* (politeness) are common slips for *curtesy*.

dowry. See DOWER.

drowned; was drowned. The active voice suggests an accidental death; the passive voice suggests foul play.

drunk; drunken. If you are *drunk*, you are intoxicated. If you are a *drunken* sot, you are habitually drunk. The first term implies an instance of intoxication, the second a constant tendency toward intoxication. Also, people are *drunk*, but their behavior is *drunken* (with the idiomatic exception of *drunk driving*). Finally, remember that *drunk* is the past participle of *drink* <have you drunk any coffee this morning?>.

dual; duel. *Dual*, an adjective meaning "two," is often misspelled *duel*. *Duel* is the noun and verb dealing with the formal two-way combat, traditionally with pistols or swords.

due to; because of. Strictly speaking, *due* is a noun <give them their due> or an adjective <due process>. That is why purists sanction its use (1) after a *be*-verb, as a predicate adjective <the delay was due to bad weather>, and (2) to modify a noun <the delay due to bad weather upset the whole schedule>. Sticklers object to using *due to* as a preposition <*due to* [read *because of*] bad weather, the trial was delayed>. Others think their scorn is undue. In any event, when a preposition is needed, *because of* is a stronger and safer choice.

duplicate. See REPLICA.

each other; one another. *Each other* requires that there be only two actors <the two advocates clearly respected each other>. *One another* takes three or more <the states that had enacted the model law all honored one another's child-support judgments>.

eager. See ANXIOUS.

ease. See FACILITY.

economic; economical. See FINANCIAL.

effect; effectuate. In legal writing at least, these terms can be distinguished. To *effect* a result is to bring it about <effect a change in trade policy>. To *effectuate* something is to give effect to the purpose behind it <regulations designed to effectuate the enabling legislation> <a good executor tries to effectuate the testator's wishes as closely as possible>. For more on *effect*, see AFFECT.

e.g.; i.e. The first is the abbreviation (for *exempli gratia*) that you want when citing examples <top-tier law schools, e.g., Yale, Harvard, and Michigan>. The second (short for *id est*, "that is") is used where further explanation is due <the Framers insulated Article III judges from the political fray, i.e., they are appointed for life and not easily subject to removal>. But *i.e.* is often misused to mean "for example." Despite their appearance to the contrary in this entry, *e.g.* and *i.e.* should not be italicized. And they should each be followed by a comma.

elicit; illicit. To *elicit* a reaction is to draw it out of someone <the question was intended to elicit an angry response>. Writers occasionally misuse *illicit* (illegal) when they mean *elicit* <fighting words may *illicit* [read *elicit*] more than the speaker bargained for>. Cf. UNLAWFUL.

elude. See ALLUDE.

e-mail. When a plural form is called for. prefer *e-mail messages* over *e-mails*.

embarrass. See HARASS.

embassy; legation. An *embassy* is where you will find a foreign country's ambassador. A *legation* houses offices of other diplomatic agents such as envoys and ministers.

emend. See AMEND.

emigrant; emigrate; emigré. See IMMIGRANT.

eminent. See IMMINENT.

empathy; sympathy. We feel *empathy* when we are mentally able to put ourselves into a work of art or another person's situation and get a deeper understanding of it, as if it were happening to us. We feel *sympathy* when we are sad at someone else's sorrow.

endemic. See EPIDEMIC.

endnote. See FOOTNOTE.

endorse; indorse. *Endorse* is correct in every sense except one. To sign commercial paper is to *indorse* it, and the Uniform Commercial Code has effectively made that distinction inviolate. Also note that *indorse* means "to sign on the back," so the phrase *indorse on the back* is redundant. See APPROVE.

enervate; innervate. These terms have opposite meanings: to *enervate* is to sap of energy, while to *innervate* is to pump full of energy.

enforceable. See FORCIBLE.

enhance; improve. A quality (never a person) that is *enhanced* is expanded or raised. The word in general use has positive connotations <a dash of salt to enhance the flavor>, but not always so in law <an enhanced sentence> <the enhanced-injury doctrine>. If it is a person who is better than before, use *improve* <we go to college to improve ourselves>.

enjoin from; enjoin upon (to). Depending on whether the injunction is negative or positive in effect, the target is *enjoined from* doing something, or *enjoined upon* to take action. The first sense is prevalent in the United States.

enormity; enormousness. *Enormity* is often misused to denote *enormousness* (hugeness). In fact, *enormity* means "great evil, heinousness" <the enormity of the terrorists' attacks>.

ensure. See ASSURE.

enumerable; innumerable. These words sound alike, but they designate almost opposite qualities. An *enumerable* number can be counted <our options are few and enumerable>, but an *innumerable* number is impossible or impractical to count, usually because it is too large <death by innumerable paper cuts>.

enure. See INURE.

envelop; envelope. To *envelop* something is to surround it. An *envelope* is an item of stationery.

envious; enviable. One who envies another is *envious* of that person. What one envies in another person is some *enviable* trait or asset. Cf. JEALOUS.

epidemic; pandemic; endemic. An *epidemic* is a local outbreak of a disease (or by extension, of anything, usually something bad). A *pandemic* is the spread of a disease across a large area, such as throughout a country or worldwide. A disease that is *endemic* to an area or a population is continuously present there; indigenous plants and animals are also *endemic* to their native area, and a quality that is *endemic* in a person occurs naturally or habitually.

equal. See COEQUAL.

essay. See ASSAY.

estoppel. See WAIVE.

evoke; invoke. To *evoke* is to draw something out of others <evoke memories> <evoke bittersweet tears>. To *invoke* is to call upon something, especially for help <invoked the Fifth Amendment> <invoked martial law>. A common error is using *evoke* where *invoke* is needed <the judge *evoked* [read *invoked*] the name of Solomon in handing down the decision>.

exalt; exult. To *exalt* people or things is to lift them up (in esteem or rank) and honor them. To *exult* is to rejoice.

example. See EXEMPLAR.

ex ante; ex post. These two reader-unfriendly phrases describe how a matter is being examined, as from the beginning or in hindsight. An *ex ante* examination is made from the standpoint of someone who does not yet know how things will come out, so it is subjective. An *ex post* examination looks at all the circumstances as they developed, so it is objective. Prefer less confusing terms such as *prospective* (for *ex ante*) and *retrospective* (for *ex post*).

except; accept. To *except* something is to leave it out. To *accept* something is to take it in. *Except* and *excepted* are sometimes misused for their near-opposites, *accept* and *accepted.*

exceptional; exceptionable. Something *exceptional* is out of the ordinary, and usually superior <the lawyer won over the jury with an exceptional closing statement>. Something *exceptionable* is objectionable <the lawyer's exceptionable mention of insurance triggered an angry rebuke from the judge>. The second term is sometimes used incorrectly when the writer means *exceptional.*

ex-convict; ex-felon. A person released from prison is an *ex-convict* or, informally, an *ex-con*. But someone convicted of a felony remains a *felon* for life (or at least until pardoned), so *ex-felon* is incorrect.

excuse; justification; alibi. In criminal law, these terms are distinguished. We consider duress, for example, a valid *excuse* for most crimes (as if to say, "You did wrong, but it wasn't your fault"). We consider self-defense a legitimate *justification* (as if to say, "What you did wasn't wrong under the circumstances because it avoided a greater harm"). An *alibi* is not an *excuse* or a *justification*, and it is not just any defense. It is specifically a defense that the accused was somewhere else when the crime occurred.

executor. See ADMINISTRATOR; TRUSTEE.

executory; executorial. *Executory* describes something that will take full effect in the future <an executory interest in property>. *Executorial* describes an estate's *executor* or what the executor does <completed all executorial duties>.

executrix. See ADMINISTRATOR.

exemplar; example. An *exemplar* is a type of *example*. In law, it is a typical sample, as of handwriting, a signature, or a voice, that is used to identify the writer or speaker. In general use, it is an ideal example.

ex-felon. See EX-CONVICT.

expect. See ANTICIPATE.

explicit; implicit. What is *explicit* is detailed and obvious <the contract is explicit: time is of the essence>. What is *implicit* is suggested, assumed, or necessary to carry out the purpose <further powers necessary and proper to carry out the federal government's enumerated powers are implicit in the Constitution>.

expose. See DISCLOSE.

ex post. See EX ANTE.

ex post facto; post hoc. *Ex post facto* means "after the fact." *Post hoc* is short for *post hoc, ergo propter hoc* ("after this, therefore because of this"). It is often misused to mean "after the fact" <that testimony is just *a post hoc* [read *an ex post facto*] rationalization>.

expropriate. See APPROPRIATE.

extension; renewal. These terms are distinguished in law: after a contract or lease expires, the parties may continue their relationship by an *extension* (under the same agreement) or by a *renewal* (under a new, often identical agreement).

extortion. See BRIBERY.

exult. See EXALT.

facility; ease; building. Properly, *facility* is the *ease* with which something can be done <a double axel performed with facility> or the physical things that make something easier or possible <recreational facilities>. But the word has been so overused for *building* as to become meaningless <school *facilities* [read *buildings*]>; avoid that sense in formal writing.

fact; factual. Ambiguities can arise because to most people these terms refer to the truth <the fact is that any Supreme Court nominee will be grilled in the confirmation hearings> <a factual account of the campaign>. But in law they more often refer to events that the parties disagree about and that can probably never be known with certainty <the facts of the case are in dispute> <just because a jury made a factual determination doesn't make your lie true>.

farther; further. The best way to handle these terms is to use the first literally <from here it's farther to Paris than to London> and the second figuratively <the justices did not overturn the doctrine, but they refused to extend it any further>.

faze; phase. The term meaning "to fluster" is *faze*. But it is common to see the term *phase* used instead, especially in the negative <escape *unphased* [read *unfazed*]>.

feemail. See BLACKMAIL.

feign; feint. To *feign* something is to fake it <the driver feigned ignorance of the speed limit>. In boxing and fencing, to *feint* is to *feign* an attack in order to mislead the opponent <the challenger feigned a right jab, then stunned the champ with a left uppercut>.

fewer; less. Use *fewer* when referring to numbers <the First Monday demonstrations drew fewer protesters this year>; use *less* when referring to volume, amount, or degree <the senior judge has less influence these days>. It is redundant to say "a fewer number" because the sense of number is included in the meaning of *fewer*. Make it "a smaller number" or simply "fewer."

fiancé; fiancée; divorcé; divorcée. Concern over gender-neutrality has not reached these French loanwords for a man (one *e*) and a woman (two *e*'s) before and after marriage.

fictional; fictitious. *Fictional* is generally neutral in connotation, referring to such things as literary novels and judicial constructions <a fictional story based on real characters> <that fictional person called "reasonable">. *Fictitious* connotes a sham, something either fraudulent or nonexistent <the rancher purported to collateralize the loan with a fictitious herd of cattle> <the teen's fictitious driver's license was nothing but trouble>.

figuratively. See LITERALLY.

financial; economic; economical. When writing about a company's or household's money, use *financial* <the Nasdaq collapse brought financial ruin to many dot-com companies>. When writing about managing resources (including money) on a large scale, regional or nationwide, use *economic* <rising energy prices often signal an economic downturn>. Reserve *economical* to mean "thrifty."

finding; holding. Strictly speaking, a court makes *findings* on questions of fact and *holdings* on questions of law.

flagrant. See BLATANT.

flair; flare. A *flair* is a knack <a flair for words> or stylishness <the ballet was performed with flair>. A *flare* is a sudden flame-up or a bright fire used to provide light <the flares from burning oil wells marked Saddam's final blow against Kuwait>.

flammable; inflammable; nonflammable. *Flammable* has become the accepted term meaning "capable of burning," beating out the synonym *inflammable*. *Inflammable* can be ambiguous, since the intensive *in-* prefix can be mistaken to mean "not." And this is a word that we don't want people to confuse. The term for "not capable of burning" is *nonflammable*.

flare. See FLAIR.

flaunt; flout. To *flaunt* something is to show it off <if you've got it, flaunt it>. To *flout* something (esp. a law or an order) is to disregard it with contempt <the ousted dictator openly flouted the arrest warrant until the new regime arrested him>. *Flaunt* is often misused as a substitute for *flout*, perhaps because it sounds similar and also suggests "taunt."

flounder; founder. To *flounder* is to flail about or struggle wildly (think *flounder = fish out of water*), not to fail. The word for the latter meaning is *founder*.

flout. See FLAUNT.

follow. See APPLY.

footnote; endnote. If they are at the bottom of the page, they are *footnotes*. If they are collected at the end, they are *endnotes*.

forbear; forebear. To *forbear* is to refrain from doing some act <in the settlement the plaintiff agreed to forbear any future claims>. A *forebear* is an ancestor <the tribe's oral traditions perpetuated the stories of their forebears' wanderings>. Each term is often misused for the other.

forcible; forceable; enforceable; forceful. *Forcible* is standard only where the force is physical <DEA agents forcibly entered the warehouse>. Note the spelling with an *i*: *forceable* is obsolete. But *enforceable* is standard <the court held that the contract was fully enforceable>. *Forceful* is correct for literal or figurative force <a forceful reaction to the protesters' rock-throwing> <a forceful appeal for unity>.

forebear. See FORBEAR.

forego. See FORGO.

foreword; preface. The introduction to a book is a *foreword* only if it is written by someone other than the book's author. If the author wrote it, it's a *preface*. And although it does appear in a forward position in the book, it is always an error to call it a *forward* (read *foreword*).

forgo; forego. To *forgo* something is to do without it <let's forgo the chitchat>; to *forgo* a legal right is to waive it <the defendant agreed to forgo a jury trial>. To *forego* something is to go before it <in light of the foregoing discussion, this court should grant summary judgment>. The misuse of *forego* for *forgo* is lamentably widespread.

formality; formalism; formalistic. *Formality* is strict adherence to rules, manners, or customs. *Formalism* is also adherence to rules, but with the emphasis on procedural minutiae regardless of substance and fairness. Both *formalism* and its adjective form, *formalistic*, are usually pejorative terms.

formally; formerly. To do something *formally* is to do it either according to proper custom <formally attired> or in accordance with procedural requirements <a formally executed will>. Writers occasionally misuse *formally* when they mean *formerly* (previously).

former; latter. These terms refer only to the first and second of two things in a set. They are misused when they refer to the first three things in a series of nine, for example.

former jeopardy; double jeopardy. *Former jeopardy* means prosecution by the same government for a crime that one has previously been convicted or acquitted of. *Double jeopardy* includes *former jeopardy*, but also describes a situation in which a defendant has been convicted of multiple counts, one of which is a lesser-included offense of another (as for robbery and assault).

formerly. See FORMALLY.

fornicate. See COPULATE.

fortunate; fortuitous; gratuitous. Something *fortunate* is lucky <you were fortunate to win the door prize>. Something *fortuitous* happens by chance, but it may be either good or bad luck <a fortuitous turn of events made me late for my interview>. *Gratuitous* means "free" <beverage is gratuitous with any meal> or "unnecessary" <the movie had too much gratuitous nudity>, but it is occasionally confused with *fortuitous*.

fortunately. See HOPEFULLY.

founder. See FLOUNDER.

from whence. See WHENCE.

fulsome. What is *fulsome* is overdone to the point of being disgusting; it especially applies to cloying flattery. Yet when the word appears, it is most often misused (with unintended irony) in the phrase *fulsome praise*.

funeral; funereal; funerary. *Funeral* is a noun and also an adjective <funeral procession>. *Funereal* describes a funeral-like mood <a funereal gloom fell on the campaign headquarters>. *Funerary* describes things that are used in a burial <the funerary canopy>.

further. See FARTHER.

gantlet; gauntlet; gamut. You run the *gantlet* and throw down the *gauntlet*. The first is a punishment in which a person runs a path between two rows of tormentors. The second is a glove, thrown down as a challenge to a duel and picked up as an acceptance of the challenge. *Run the gauntlet* is a common misstep. *Run the gamut* means "to have a full range" <the buffet ran the gamut from soup to nuts>.

garnishment. See SEQUESTRATION.

gauntlet. See GANTLET.

gender. See SEX.

generative; generational. *Generative* describes the creation of offspring. It is misused when discussing *generations*, as when counting *generational* steps to determine next of kin.

genericness; genericism. *Genericness* is the accepted noun form of *generic*, as used in trademark law. *Genericism* appears infrequently.

gibe; jibe; jive. A *gibe* is an angry taunt <gibes from the dissatisfied audience>; but today it is also a good-natured teasing <gibes among poker buddies>. The word is also a verb <to gibe one's opponents>. To *jibe* with something is to agree with it <these numbers jibe with our budget projection>. To *jive* is to deceive by fast talking, to taunt, or to dance the jitterbug. *Jive* is sometimes misused for *jibe*.

glance; glimpse. By idiom, these words for "a quick look" go with different verbs and prepositions. One takes (or gives) a *glance at* something, but gets a *glimpse of* it.

good faith. See BONA FIDES.

gorilla. See GUERRILLA.

gourmet; gourmand. These are similar words for a lover of food and drink, but they have wildly different connotations. A *gourmet* is a sophisticated connoisseur, while a *gourmand* is a glutton.

gratuitous. See FORTUNATE.

graymail. See BLACKMAIL.

greenmail. See BLACKMAIL.

grievous. Often misspelled *grievious*.

grisly; grizzly; grizzled. *Grisly* describes something bloody or horrifying. *Grizzly* describes a bear or gray hair; in the latter sense it is synonymous with the more common *grizzled*.

guarantee; warranty; guaranty. *Guarantee* looks to the future, as assurance that something will or will not be done. *Warranty* looks to the present and past, by accepting legal responsibility that things are as they were represented. *Guaranty* is mostly used as a noun, and is interchangeable with *guarantee*.

guarantor. See SURETY.

guerrilla; guerilla; gorilla. A *guerrilla* is an irregular soldier engaged in surprise attacks and sabotage. This spelling is preferred over *guerilla*. A *gorilla* is a big ape and a big laugh when misused to mean *guerrilla*.

guilty; culpable. A jury (or the judge) decides whether the accused is *guilty* or *not guilty*. But that finding doesn't change how *culpable* (blameworthy) the accused truly is. Although the first term occasionally arises in civil suits <guilty of misrepresentation>, it is usually (and better) restricted to criminal contexts. Cf. BLAMEWORTHY; INNOCENT.

habitable; inhabitable; uninhabitable. The first two terms are synonyms. Modern usage prefers *habitable* as the term for "fit to be occupied." As *inhabitable* has declined in use, it has become ambiguous (i.e., seen as a negative form) and ought to be avoided. The antonym is *uninhabitable*.

hairbrained. See HAREBRAINED.

hale into court; haul into court. These two phrases are correctly used to indicate a compelled appearance. *Hale into court* is the original phrase. *Haul into court*, which creates a mental picture of being physically dragged into the courtroom, is more evocative. *Hail into court* is a common error.

hallucination. See ILLUSION.

hand up an indictment; hand down a decision; hand down a verdict; return a verdict. A grand jury *hands up* (never *down*) an indictment, presenting criminal charges to the court. A judge *hands down a decision*. A petit jury *hands down a verdict* or, more properly, *returns a verdict*.

hanged; hung. *Hanged* is the correct past tense for the capital punishment. *Hung* (often misused to mean *hanged*) is the correct past tense for all other meanings.

harass; embarrass. These terms *embarrass* those who misspell them (is it one *-r-* or two?). Think of it this way: *harass* has one *-r-* but two pronunciations (accent either syllable).

harebrained. This is the correct term for "reckless"; *hairbrained* is a common error.

haul into court. See HALE INTO COURT.

havoc. See WREAK HAVOC.

healthy; healthful. In the best usage, what is *healthy* is itself in good health; the word should refer only to living things. What is *healthful* promotes good health <a healthful diet keeps you healthy>. Today the words are often used interchangeably.

hesitancy; hesitation; hesitance. Someone who *hesitates* has the quality of *hesitancy* (reluctance), while the act itself is *hesitation* (pause). *Hesitance* is an inferior variant of *hesitation*.

hijack. This is the correct spelling (not *highjack*). Robbers may *hijack* vehicles and their loads, but not people; people taken by force are *kidnapped*.

historic; historical. *Historic* refers to someone or something that significantly changed *history* <the historic D-Day invasion>. *Historical* means "of history" <a historical society> or "occurring in the past" <the clerk's records were full of historical details about the town's early families>. Since both words start with a consonant sound, they take the article *a* rather than *an*.

hoard; horde. A *hoard* is a hidden supply, especially of something valuable or scarce. A *horde* was originally a wandering tribe of barbarians, and today by extension it is a mob or an army.

Hobson's choice. See DILEMMA.

hodgepodge. See HOTCHPOT.

hoi polloi; hoity-toity. The *hoi polloi* is the masses. Perhaps because of *hoity-toity* (pretentious, and by extension a mocking pejorative to describe the upper crust), *hoi polloi* is sometimes misused to refer to high society.

holding. See FINDING.

home in; hone in. *Home in* is the correct phrase for getting nearer and nearer the target <the carrier pigeon circled overhead, homing in on its cage>. The erroneous substitution of *hone in* is a recent development.

homicide. See MURDER.

hone in. See HOME IN.

hopefully; fortunately. Use of *hopefully* to mean "it is hoped" (rather than "in a hopeful manner") is widespread, even in legal writing. It is defensible as a sentence adverb similar to *fortunately* and *certainly* <fortunately, the jury agreed with us [which doesn't mean that the jury agreed in a fortunate manner]>. But *hopefully* used this way has been condemned for so long that writers use it at their peril. Its use is a distraction—and careful writers avoid distractions.

horde. See HOARD.

hotchpot; hotchpotch; hodgepodge. *Hotchpot* is the original term, derived from a meal in which all the ingredients are shaken together. By extension it applied to an estate whose assets were consolidated and then distributed. In U.S. community-property states, *hotchpot* also means property belonging to the community. *Hotchpot* is still the preferred term in legal writing, but in ordinary use the term evolved into *hotchpotch* and then to today's dominant form, *hodgepodge*.

hung. See HANGED.

hypothesize; hypothecate. To *hypothesize* is to form a hypothesis about something. In admiralty and in civil-law jurisdictions, to *hypothecate* is to pledge something without taking either title or possession. *Hypothecate* should not be used to mean *hypothesize*.

ideal. See IDYLLIC.

idyllic; ideal. An *idyllic* place may be very nice, but it's not *ideal* (as some writers mistakenly believe). Rather, it may be rustic, charming, and picturesque <an idyllic alpine village>, or simple and stress-free <an idyllic childhood>. The word derives from *idyll*, a short poem, often with a pastoral theme.

i.e. See E.G.

if and only if; only if. *If and only if* can be expressed more concisely and forcefully by cutting it in half: use *only if*.

ignorant; stupid. Even the smartest person is *ignorant* (unaware) of some things. And a person who is *stupid* (of low intelligence) is not *ignorant* of all things.

illegal. See UNLAWFUL.

illegal alien; undocumented worker. *Illegal alien* is the usual phrase for one who has entered the country illegally. *Undocumented worker* is a politically correct euphemism. *Illegal* should not be considered pejorative in the phrase because (1) it is true (unauthorized entry did violate the law), and (2) *illegal* is not synonymous with *criminal*, so it is not a severe aspersion.

illegible; unreadable. *Illegible* describes handwriting or printing that is not clear enough to be read <it was the victim's handwriting, but the words were illegible>. *Unreadable* refers to content that is so poorly written as to be almost impossible to understand <the judge dreaded the thought of opening another unreadable brief>.

illicit. See ELICIT; UNLAWFUL.

illusion; delusion; hallucination. An *illusion* is a deceptive appearance <the company's "profits" turned out to be the illusion of a creative accountant>. A *delusion* is an illusion with added elements of danger, self-deception, and prolonged influence <delusions of grandeur>. *Delusion* refers to an erroneous mental belief, whereas *hallucination* is an erroneous sensory perception <the drug induced colorful hallucinations>. Cf. ALLUSION.

immanent. See IMMINENT.

immigrant; emigrant; immigrate; emigrate; emigré. A person who leaves one country to live in a second is an *immigrant* in the second and an *emigrant* in the first; the person has *immigrated to* the new country and *emigrated from* the old. An *emigré* is one who flees a country (or is expelled) for political reasons.

imminent; eminent; immanent. *Imminent* means more than just "near" or "probable"; it means "very close at hand and almost certain to happen" <imminent bodily harm>. *Eminent* means "distinguished" <the eminent justice> or "highest" <eminent domain>. *Immanent,* which is sometimes confounded with *imminent,* means "spiritually pervading the material world."

immoral; amoral; unmoral. An *immoral* person is affirmatively evil. An *amoral* person is indifferent to concerns of morality. An *unmoral* being (such as an animal) is incapable of having moral values.

immunity; impunity. *Immunity* is the exemption from some responsibility or liability <the senator could not be sued for the defamatory floor speech because the Speech or Debate Clause conferred immunity>. *Impunity,* a narrower term, means freedom from punishment for one's acts <enjoying diplomatic immunity, some embassy employees are flouting our traffic laws with impunity>.

impair. See IMPUGN.

impartable; impartible. Something *impartable* is capable of being made known or given (i.e., *imparted*). Something *impartible* is incapable of being divided into parts; the word is common in describing an estate.

impassable; impassible. See PASSABLE.

impeachment; removal from office. *Impeachment* is a charge of official wrongdoing, not a conviction. *Removal from office* is the penalty upon conviction.

impecunious. See PECUNIARY.

impel. See COMPEL.

impertinent. In common usage an *impertinent* person or remark is sassy and rude, especially to a superior. But in law, *impertinent* retains its original sense of "not pertinent" or "irrelevant to the issue at hand."

impinge; infringe. These similar terms, commonly used interchangeably, have different connotations. To *impinge* is to touch, bump up against, or strike; to *infringe* is to trespass onto, damage, or weaken. The intransitive *impinge* requires an *on* or *upon* phrase <impinge on your time>. *Infringe* is best used as a transitive verb <infringe patent rights>, but it can also be intransitive <infringe on the neighbor's right to quiet enjoyment>.

implicit. See EXPLICIT; IMPLIEDLY.

implicitly. See IMPLIEDLY.

implied. See IMPLIEDLY.

implied contract; quasi-contract. At one time these terms were distinct: an *implied contract* was one "implied in fact" by the parties' actions, and a *quasi-contract* was (as it still is) one "implied in law" as a remedy for unjust enrichment. Today, the former phrase is used for both, making it confusing when it is used for either. It's best avoided altogether.

impliedly; implicitly; implied; implicit. *Impliedly* is an awkward substitute for *implicitly.* It's also something of a legalism, since most nonlawyers don't know what it means. *Implied,* on the other hand, is a more straightforward term than *implicit.* Lawyers do love their implications.

imply; infer. The writer *implies* a subtle meaning without explicitly stating it. The reader *infers* that subtle meaning by "reading between the lines." These two terms are confused less in legal writing than elsewhere, but missteps still occur.

impotence. See STERILITY.

improve. See ENHANCE.

impugn; impair; impute. To *impugn* something is to raise doubts about it <don't impugn your opponent's integrity>. To *impair* something is to weaken it <don't impair the investigation>. To *impute* something is to attribute it to someone or something <don't impute blame without proof>. *Impugn* is sometimes misused where the writer meant *impair* or *impute.*

impunity. See IMMUNITY.

impute. See IMPUGN.

inaugural; inauguration. The swearing-in ceremony for the President or a governor is the *inauguration.* Things pertaining to the inauguration are *inaugural* <inaugural ball> <inaugural gown>. The *inaugural address* is often shortened to the noun *inaugural.*

in behalf of. See ON BEHALF OF.

incidentally. This word means "pertaining to something other than the current main topic." It is sometimes misspelled *incidently.*

incident to; incidental to. If one thing is *incident to* another, both things are part of an inseparable whole <a deposition incident to the lawsuit>. If one thing is *incidental to* another, the two things are only loosely associated <a trade agreement incidental to the arms-control summit>.

including; namely; comprising. When laying out a list, introduce it with the term *including* only if the list is not exhaustive. Otherwise, use *namely* or *comprising,* both of which signal an exhaustive list. It is a maxim of judicial construction that *including* signals a nonexclusive list. But if your writing may be the subject of litigation, you should be explicit and use a phrase such as *including but not limited to* or *consisting only of.*

incompetence; incompetency; incompetent. *Incompetence* is the general term for a lack of fitness or ability. In law, *incompetency* is the narrow term for unfitness to stand trial or to give testimony, and for questioning sanity. In both senses, the corresponding adjective is *incompetent.*

incredulous. See CREDIBLE.

inculcate; indoctrinate. The choice of words depends on the subject and object: you *inculcate* values into people, but you *indoctrinate* people with values. You don't *inculcate* people with values.

inculpable. See NONCULPABLE.

indemnity. See CONTRIBUTION.

indictment; information; presentment. These are all charging instruments. An *indictment* is a formal charge, usually of a felony, handed up by a grand jury after an investigation or presentation of evidence by the prosecutor. It is required in the federal system and in most states for serious charges, typically those punishable by a year or more in prison. An *information* is a charging instrument that is sworn by the prosecutor and requires no grand-jury action. An *information* is used for less serious offenses, and in some jurisdictions, such as California, for felonies as well. Historically, a *presentment* was a charge handed up by a grand jury on its own initiative. While the procedure is no longer used, the term lives on as part of the Due Process Clause of the Fifth Amendment.

indispensable; necessary; proper. Of parties joined in a lawsuit, an *indispensable* party is someone without whom the matter cannot be fairly tried, and whose absence requires that the suit be dismissed. A *necessary* party is someone who should be joined, but whose absence does not render the matter untriable. A *proper* party is someone who may be joined if the plaintiff chooses to do so.

individuals. See PERSONS.

indoctrinate. See INCULCATE.

indorse. See ENDORSE.

induce. See DEDUCE.

induction. See DEDUCE.

inequity; iniquity. Both beg for justice to be done, but *inequity* typically refers to civil justice and *iniquity* to criminal justice. *Inequity* is unfairness <the court conceded that the harsh bright-line rule would sometimes result in inequity>, while *iniquity* is evil <the defendant never showed regret over the fruits of his iniquity>.

inexpert; nonexpert. To be *inexpert* at something is to be unskilled at it <the teen's inexpert driving kept his parents jumpy>. *Nonexpert* says nothing about skill; it merely designates a witness who is not an expert witness <a nonexpert witness may give opinion testimony about matters of common knowledge>.

infamous; infamy. See NOTORIOUS.

infant; infancy; minor; minority; nonage. To most people, a child ceases to be an *infant* at an early age, but in law *infancy* continues until the age of majority, usually 18. To avoid confusion, it is better to use the terms *minor* and *minority*. *Nonage* is a rarer term for legal infancy.

infected; infested. To be *infected* is to be contaminated, especially with disease but by extension with moral corruption. To be *infested* is to be overrun with vermin. Metaphorically, then, a bad neighborhood is *infected by* crime and *infested with* criminals. And any amount of contraband on a ship *infects* the whole vessel and subjects it to seizure.

infectious. See CONTAGIOUS.

infer. See IMPLY.

infested. See INFECTED.

inflammable. See FLAMMABLE.

inflict; afflict. You *inflict* (impose) bad things *on* people <this bill inflicts more burden on the taxpayer>. You can also *afflict* (torment) people *with* bad things <the dilatory defense lawyer afflicts adversaries with walls of discovery requests>. But *afflict* is most often used without the prepositional phrase <corruption afflicts even the noblest organization>. And as an adjective, *afflicted* can take the preposition *with* or *by* <afflicted with disease> <afflicted by an enemy>.

information. See INDICTMENT.

infringe. See IMPINGE.

ingenious; ingenuous; disingenuous. An *ingenious* person or idea is very clever <an ingenious invention>. An *ingenuous* person is naive and childlike <the witness seemed ingenuous, incapable of fabrication>. *Ingenuous* is more often seen in its opposite, *disingenuous,* meaning "falsely appearing to be open and honest" <the tipster stood to gain from our investment, so we worried that he was being disingenuous>.

inhabitable. See HABITABLE.

inherent. See INNATE.

iniquity. See INEQUITY.

injury. See DAMAGE.

innate; inherent. *Innate* (inborn) qualities and aptitudes are with you from birth <an innate gift for mathematics>. Nonliving things have *inherent* qualities and properties instead <the inherent malleability of gold>.

innervate. See ENERVATE.

innocent; guilty; not guilty; nolo contendere. *Innocent* is not an option for either a plea or a verdict. A defendant may plead *guilty, not guilty,* or *nolo contendere* (no contest). Verdicts are *guilty* or *not guilty.* In press accounts the term *innocent* is used to prevent the possible error of omitting *not* from the verdict when reporting an acquittal. Cf. GUILTY.

innumerable. See ENUMERABLE.

inquiry. See QUERY.

insidious; invidious. These two types of unpleasantries differ in style. What is *insidious* is underhanded, sneaky, hidden, working slowly, or waiting to spring a trap <the "grassroots" movement turned out to be a well-planned, insidious power grab>. What is *invidious* is based on creating or spreading ill will <invidious racial discrimination>.

insoluble; insolvable. See SOLUBLE.

instantly; instantaneously; instanter. If something happens *instantly,* it happens immediately <the driver was killed instantly>. If it happens *instantaneously,* it happens in an imperceptible span of time <when the driver turned the ignition key, the bomb went off instantaneously>. *Instanter* is a pompous Latinism for *instantly;* it should be banned from your vocabulary instanter.

insure. See ASSURE.

insurgence; insurgents; insurgency. An *insurgence* is an uprising. *Insurgents* are the people rising up. *Insurgency* is the state of or tendency to revolt.

insurrection; revolt; rebellion; revolution. An *insurrection* is a public uprising against the government. If the insurrection seeks to overthrow the government, it is a *revolt.* If the revolt is widespread, it becomes a *rebellion.* And if an uprising succeeds in overthrowing the government, it is a *revolution.*

intense; intensive. *Intense* is the preferred term in most legal contexts, where *intensive* adds nothing new <when race is involved, state action receives more intense scrutiny from the courts>.

intensely. See INTENTLY.

intent; intention; motive. *Intent* is the mental state of resolving to do something (especially, in law, to commit a crime). *Intention* is often used in place of *intent;* it has no connotations regarding crime, but it sometimes carries a sexual connotation <bad intentions>. *Motive* is the reason for doing something.

intentional. See VOLUNTARY.

intently; intensely. Both adverbs describe a high degree of intensity. But acting *intently* shows intense concentration. One might act *intensely* with no concentration at all, as in a fit of rage.

interment; internment. *Interment* is a burial. *Internment* is confinement, especially of aliens during wartime.

internecine. The term originally described a war of extermination, and later a war in which both sides suffer great slaughter. Today it means "mutually destructive; deadly to both parties." It is often misused to describe any internal controversy.

internment. See INTERMENT.

interpretative; interpretive. *Interpretative* is the traditional form. Although *interpretive* is becoming more accepted, careful writers should avoid it.

inure; enure. *Inure* is the standard spelling, *enure* a variant. The ordinary meaning is "to become accustomed to a bad situation" <the POW became inured to the squalid conditions>. In legal use, it means "to take effect," usually to benefit someone <the bond's maturity will inure to the bondholder's benefit>.

inveigh; inveigle. To *inveigh* against something is to rant on about it <protesters inveighed against globalization>. To *inveigle* is to beguile or cajole someone into doing something <the salesman inveigled the customer into taking a test drive>.

invidious. See INSIDIOUS.

invoke. See EVOKE.

irregardless. See REGARDLESS.

irrespective. See REGARDLESS.

irritate. See AGGRAVATE.

issue preclusion. See COLLATERAL ESTOPPEL.

its; it's. This basic spelling rule is still a common error: *its* is the possessive form of *it* <each court has its local rules>; *it's* is a contraction of *it is* <it's foolhardy to ignore local rules>. When you see the apostrophe, think "*it is*" to make sure that *it's* the right form.

jealous; envious; zealous. *Jealous* properly applies only in romantic relationships <a jealous suitor>. *Envious* applies to resentment over another person's good fortune <envious of the new partner's success>. A *zealous* person is ardent <a zealous young convert>; it is occasionally confounded with *jealous*, perhaps because a lover can be either or both. Cf. ENVIOUS.

jibe; jive. See GIBE.

joinder; consolidation. *Joinder* is the act of bringing additional parties into a lawsuit. *Consolidation* is the act of combining multiple lawsuits into a single suit. Cf. MERGER.

joint tenancy; tenancy in common. A *joint tenancy* is a property interest held by multiple owners with identical interests and rights of survivorship. A *tenancy in common* is an interest held by multiple owners with undivided (and not necessarily equal) shares and no rights of survivorship.

judgment; judgement. *Judgment* is the preferred spelling in American English and in British legal writing. *Judgement* is standard in British general writing. Cf. DECISION; VERDICT.

judicial; judicious. *Judicial* has several meanings relating to courts <judicial restraint>, courtrooms <judicial sequestration>, decrees <judicial order>, and the law in general <judicial privilege>. But *judicious* touches the law only by analogy: it means "discreet; prudent; well thought out."

justification. See EXCUSE.

karat. See CARAT.

knowledge; notice. *Knowledge* is awareness of a fact or condition. In law, *notice* does not require actual knowledge. It can be constructive knowledge: notice imputed to a person who had reason to know of a fact or condition (for instance, because it was a public record). *Constructive knowledge* means *notice*, but *notice* is the better term.

labor. See BELABOR.

laches. See WAIVE.

latent. See PATENT.

latter. See FORMER.

laudable; laudatory. Good deeds are *laudable*, i.e., they deserve praise. If someone praises them, those comments are *laudatory*, i.e., they express praise.

lay. See LIE.

leach. See LEECH.

lead; led. The past tense of *lead* (as in "to guide") is *led*. But there is a tendency to spell it *lead*, perhaps because the metal *lead* is pronounced *led*, and the past-tense *read* rhymes with *led*.

lease; let. Both are correct verbs for the renting out of property. *Let* is not slang or substandard; in fact, its use goes back 300 years earlier than *lease*. Only the lessor *lets* the property, but either party may be said to *lease* it.

led. See LEAD.

leech; leach. *Leech* is a noun: the blood-sucking worm or the houseguest who won't go away. *Leach* is a verb: to percolate water in order to remove solids.

legacy. See DEVISE.

legation. See EMBASSY.

lend. See LOAN.

less. See FEWER.

lessor; lessee. *Lessor* and *lessee* are the correct terms—not *leasor* and *leasee.*

let. See LEASE.

levee; levy. *Levee* is the spelling of the word for (commonly) a riverbank and (rarely) a state reception. *Levy* is the spelling of the noun and verb for laying and collecting taxes, drafting soldiers and sailors, and seizing property to satisfy a judgment.

libel. See DEFAMATION.

lie; lay. You *lay* down your book and *lie* down on the bed. Last night you *laid* down your book and *lay* down on the bed. Every night this week you *have laid* down your book and *have lain* down on the bed. Same with *lie low* (present) – *lay low* (past) – *lain low* (past participle).

life-and-death; life-or-death. While it may be counterintuitive for an "either–or" phrase, *life-and-death* is the standard idiom <a life-and-death struggle>.

like; as. *Like* is a preposition, not a conjunction. It can precede a noun <in like Flynn> <it looks like a winner>. If what follows is a clause (with a verb), use *as* <steady as she goes> <she talks as if she means it>.

likely. See APT.

limit. See DELIMIT.

literally; figuratively. Something *literally* means exactly what the words say it means (think *literature*). *Literally* is used illiterately when employed as an intensifier <the defendant was *literally sweating bullets* [read *was sweating bullets*] as the verdict was read>. In the example, the defendant was *figuratively* (metaphorically) sweating bullets, although you would never write it that way—just omit *literally* in such a phrase.

litigable; litigatable. *Litigable* is the correct term for an issue suitable for trial.

litigator. See TRIAL LAWYER.

loadstar. See LODESTAR.

loan; lend. In best usage, *loan* is a noun and *lend* is a verb. But when what is being *lent* is money, *loan* as a verb is acceptable.

loathe; loath; loth. To *loathe* is to detest <the plaintiff loathed the defendant>. To be *loath* to do something is to be reluctant <the lawyer was loath to let the hotheaded witness testify>; *loth* is a rare variant form. The usual error is to use the verb *loathe* where the adjective *loath* was intended.

locus; situs. Both refer to a place where an event happened or where property is located. But *locus* is more specific, referring, for instance, to the piece of property itself <the locus passed to the decedent's son>. *Situs,* on the other hand, refers to the jurisdiction where the event happened or the property is located <the law of the situs governs foreign property belonging to the estate>.

lodestar. The guiding star (usually Polaris)—and by extension a guide for setting fees and damages—is so spelled. Avoid *loadstar.*

loose; loosen; lose. To *loose* something is to free it completely <the guards loosed the dogs at the first sign of a break>, while to *loosen* something is to partially unbind it <after supper Dad loosened his belt>. Writers sometimes misspell *lose* as *loose* <Dad should *loose* [read *lose*] some weight>.

loth. See LOATHE.

luxurious; luxuriant. What is *luxurious* is elegant and indulgent <luxurious accommodations>. What is *luxuriant* is fast-growing and abundant <a luxuriant flower garden>.

mad; angry. The use of *mad* to mean "angry" dates back to at least 1300, but there was a movement in the early 20th century to limit its definition to "insane." Since it carries a negative connotation, its use in that sense is limited. It's a perfectly proper term for *angry*, but since it's been stigmatized it should probably be avoided in formal writing.

maelstrom. This term denotes a whirlpool and, by extension, a turbulent situation. It is often misspelled *maelstorm*.

majority; plurality. A *majority* is more than half—50% plus one or more <a bare majority at 51%>. A *plurality* is less than a majority but still the highest percentage among three or more figures <a plurality of 42% in a three-way race>. Of legal precedents, a *majority* opinion (one in which most of the judges join) is stronger than a *plurality* opinion (in which one or more swing votes determine the outcome, but for different reasons).

make do. The phrase meaning "to get by with what you have" is *make do*. The error of writing *make due* is common.

malfeasance; misfeasance; nonfeasance. *Malfeasance* is wrongful or illegal conduct, especially by someone in office. *Misfeasance* is either (1) conduct that, while not itself illegal, is done in a wrongful manner, or (2) a trespass or transgression. *Nonfeasance* is the failure to act when one has a duty to do so.

malice aforethought. See WILLFULNESS.

malodorous. See ODIOUS.

maltreatment. See MISTREATMENT.

mandate. See VERDICT.

manslaughter. See MURDER.

mantle; mantel. A *mantle* is a cloak or other loose-fitting cover. A *mantel* is an enclosure for a fireplace. Legal writers often figuratively cloak things with *mantles* <protected by the mantle of prosecutorial immunity>, but occasionally slip and use the wrong homonym.

marriage; wedding. *Marriage* is the wedded state, a legal relationship. A *wedding* is the ceremony at which two people are married.

marshal; Marshall. *Marshal* is always spelled with one *-l-* unless it is a name.

masterful; masterly. Careful writers use *masterful* to describe domination, as of a master over a servant <the swaggering governor was a masterful presence in the statehouse>. The right term to describe artistic or professional mastery is *masterly* <a masterly performance by the young virtuoso>.

may. See CAN.

mean; median. The *mean* is the statistical average of a set of numbers <the mean of the set 1, 2, 999 is 501>. The *median* is the middle number in an ordered set <the median of the set 1, 2, 999 is 2>.

meantime; meanwhile. In common use, *meantime* most often appears in the phrase *in the meantime,* although the term can also stand alone. *Meanwhile* should always stand alone.

medal. See METTLE.

meddle. See METTLE.

media; medium; mediums. *Media* is plural and should take a plural verb <the news media are going to be all over this story>. But it has been used as a mass noun with a singular verb for so long that the usage is now considered standard <the media is overplaying this story>. A single type of mass-media outlet is still called a *medium* <the medium of television became popular after World War II>. *Mediums* is the plural only when referring to clairvoyants <two mediums attended the séance>.

median. See MEAN.

mediation; arbitration. These are the two standard forms of alternative dispute resolution. *Mediation* is nonbinding negotiation through a neutral third party in an attempt to reach a settlement. *Arbitration* is the submission of the parties' cases to one or more neutral third parties, who hand down a decision that is usually binding on the parties.

medium; mediums. See MEDIA.

meet out. See METE OUT.

memoranda; memorandums. Although both plural forms are correct, *memoranda* is far more common. *Memoranda* is sometimes misused as if it were singular.

meretricious; meritorious. *Meretricious* derives from the Latin word for "prostitute"; it means "alluring by deception." *Meritorious* generally means "praiseworthy," but in law it describes a claim or defense that has legal merit and a chance to succeed. Obviously, the writer who inappropriately describes a client's claim as *meretricious* does so at great peril: the judge may decide that the claim is unmeritorious.

merger; consolidation. When two companies combine by *merger,* the company that absorbs the other retains its corporate identity and structure. When two companies *consolidate,* they form a new corporate identity and structure and shed their previous ones. Cf. JOINDER.

meritorious. See MERETRICIOUS.

mesalliance; misalliance. *Mesalliance* is a marriage between people of different social positions. *Misalliance* is an incompatible marriage. By definition, a *misalliance* can't be a happy marriage, but a *mesalliance* may be.

messuage. See CURTILAGE.

metal. See METTLE.

mete out. This is the correct spelling of the phrase meaning "to allot" (as praise, pay, or punishment). *Meet out* is an error seen most frequently in the past tense <the commissioner *meeted out* [read *meted out*] fines to players on both teams>.

mettle; meddle; medal; metal. The first two, especially, can be tricky. *Mettle* is courage or inner strength <your first trial will test your mettle>; to *meddle* is to interfere <don't meddle in my business>. A *medal* is an award, often made out of *metal*.

militate. See MITIGATE.

millennium. So spelled. The roots are *mille* (thousand) and *annus* (year), so the word needs both *l*'s and both *n*'s.

milliard. See BILLION.

minimize; minify; minimalize. To *minimize* something is to hold it to a minimum. To *minify* something is to depreciate it or to hold out that it is smaller than it really is. *Minimalize* is not a word and should not be used where *minimize* is intended.

minor; minority. See INFANT.

minuscule. So spelled. The root of *minuscule* (very small) is *minus*, not *mini-*. *Minuscule* is among the most common misspellings in legal writing.

minutia; minutiae. *Minutia* is the singular, *minutiae* the plural of this word, which means "a petty detail." Writers often tend to treat the first as plural, and sometimes mistake the second as singular.

misalliance. See MESALLIANCE.

mischievous. Often misspelled *mischievious*.

misfeasance. See MALFEASANCE.

misinformation. See DISINFORMATION.

misprision. In law, *misprision* most often refers to the concealment of certain crimes by a nonparticipant <misprision of felony>. In common use it most often means "mistake" <a misprision of language>. The word is often misspelled *misprison*.

misquote; misquotation. See QUOTE.

mistreatment; maltreatment. *Mistreatment* is the general term for "abuse." It may be anything from neglect to physical abuse. *Maltreatment* involves rough physical treatment.

mitigate; militate. To *mitigate* something is to make it less severe or forceful <to mitigate the harshness of the bright-line rule, courts soon began carving out exceptions>. To *militate* is to influence strongly <the persuasive force of the foreign court's reasoning on the issue militated in favor of following suit>. Something can *militate for* or *against* (though not *toward*), but cannot *mitigate for* or *against.*

momentarily. See PRESENTLY.

motive. See INTENT.

murder; manslaughter; homicide. One who unlawfully kills another person with malice aforethought commits *murder.* If the killing was not malicious, it was *manslaughter. Homicide* is the general term for any killing of another person. *Homicide* does not denote a crime: the carrying out of a death sentence is a homicide.

mutual; common. What is *mutual* is reciprocal <the partners' mutual respect>. What is *common* is shared <the parents' common love for their child>. Two people may have a *common* friend, but not strictly speaking a *mutual* friend. The use of *mutual* invites redundancies: agreement and cooperation, for example, are by definition *mutual*. In law, a *mutual mistake* should more properly be called a *common mistake*, but the phrase is carved in judicial stone and unlikely to change.

namely. See INCLUDING.

naturalist; naturist. A *naturalist* is one who studies nature, such as a biologist, or one who paints or writes about nature and the outdoors. A *naturist* is a nudist.

naught; nought. Of these alternative spellings for the word meaning "nothing," *naught* is usually used in the general sense and *nought* is reserved for the mathematical zero.

nauseous; nauseated. To be *nauseous* is to cause nausea <the nauseous clams>. To be *nauseated* is to feel nausea <he felt nauseated after eating the clams>. The use of *nauseous* to mean *nauseated* may happen too often for it to be called incorrect, but careful writers will still use the right term. One easy solution is to avoid *nauseous* altogether and to use either *nauseating* or *nauseated* instead.

necessary. See INDISPENSABLE.

negative, in the. See AFFIRMATIVE, IN THE.

no doubt. See DOUBTLESS.

noisome; noisy. *Noisome* is etymologically related to *annoyance*, not *noise*. Something *noisome* is smelly, harmful, or offensive <a noisome swamp>—it offends the nose, not the ears.

nolo contendere. See INNOCENT.

nonage. See INFANT.

nonculpable; inculpable. The meaning of *nonculpable* is clear: "not blamable." But the meaning of *inculpable* is not: it could mean either "not blamable" or "able to be blamed." Because of the ambiguity, writers should avoid *inculpable* (which, in fact, traditionally means "blameless"). Cf. BLAMEWORTHY.

nonexpert. See INEXPERT.

nonfeasance. See MALFEASANCE.

nonflammable. See FLAMMABLE.

not guilty. See INNOCENT.

notice. See KNOWLEDGE.

notorious; notoriety; infamous; infamy. All four terms can carry negative connotations of a bad reputation. But *notorious* and *notoriety* may also be neutral; *infamous* and *infamy* always reek of evildoing.

nought. See NAUGHT.

number; amount. If you can count them, you have a *number* of them <she handles a large number of civil-rights cases>. Otherwise, you measure the *amount* <a large amount of her time is spent on civil-rights cases>.

observation; observance. An *observation* is a perception of something, or a pertinent comment based on observation and analysis. An *observance* is the adherence to a law or custom.

obtain. See ATTAIN.

obtuse; abstruse. Anything *obtuse* is dull or blunt. Anything *abstruse* is hidden or hard to discover. So the first can describe a dull-witted person, and the second an esoteric idea.

obviously. See CLEARLY.

odious; odorous; malodorous; odoriferous; odiferous. *Odious* (hateful) and *odorous* (smelly) are sometimes confounded. Of the variants of *odorous*, *malodorous* is quite bad-smelling and *odoriferous* is good-smelling. *Odiferous* is a mistaken variant of *odoriferous*.

offense; defense; offence; defence. *Offense* and *defense* are the American English spellings. *Offence* and *defence* are the British English spellings; they sometimes appear in older American texts.

officious; official. An *officious* person is pushy and meddlesome. An officer may or may not be *officious* but is by definition *official*.

old. See VENERABLE.

on; upon. The simple preposition *on* is almost always better than its dressed-up sibling *upon*. Avoid using *upon* just to affect a tone of formality. It is useful, however, to introduce a causal or temporal event <the banker called police immediately upon discovering the embezzlement> <please respond upon receipt>.

on behalf of; in behalf of. To act or speak *on behalf of* someone is to act as that person's representative <counsel entered a not-guilty plea on behalf of the defendant>. To act or speak *in behalf of* someone or something is to do so in its praise or defense <five students spoke in behalf of the suspended professor>.

one another. See EACH OTHER.

only if. See IF AND ONLY IF.

operable; operational; operative. Something *operable* is capable of being operated <the old tractor was still operable>. Something *operational* is able to function <the collector hoped to have the computer network operational by tax season>. Something *operative* is either in effect <the new ordinance was not yet operative> or most relevant <the penal code, not the highway code, had the operative definition>.

ophthalmologist; oculist; optometrist; optician. An *ophthalmologist* and an *oculist* are medical doctors specializing in the treatment of eyes. An *optometrist* is a licensed practitioner who conducts sight exams and writes prescriptions for eyeglasses. An *optician* is a person who makes eyeglasses.

opinion. See DECISION.

oppress; repress. To *oppress* a people is to subjugate them through persecution and other inhumane treatment. To *repress* a people is to control or subordinate them. *Oppress* is the stronger term.

oral. See VERBAL; PAROL.

oration. See PERORATION.

ordinance; ordnance. An *ordinance* is a law of narrower scope than a statute, especially a municipal regulation <a zoning ordinance>. *Ordnance* is artillery, ammunition, and other military weaponry <resupply ordnance to advance troops>.

orient; orientate. To find east is to know all directions, so to *orient* yourself is to get your bearings <the judge read the statement of facts to get oriented to the parties

and the controversy>. *Orientate* adds an extra-syllable irritant but adds no meaning to the word.

overrule; overturn; reverse; set aside; vacate. A judge may *overrule* an objection, and an appellate court may *overrule* a precedent. The court may also *overturn* the precedent, in whole or in part. *Overturning* may also be a gradual process of eroding an old doctrine. The last three terms usually apply to what an appellate court does to a trial court's decision: to *reverse* it is to change the outcome, but to *set* it *aside* or *vacate* it is to erase the judgment so that no one wins and the parties go back to the trial court.

overturn. See OVERRULE.

pallet; palette; palate. A *pallet* is a makeshift bed or a short crate that items are stacked on for shipping and storing. A *palette* is an artist's board for mixing colors. A *palate* is the roof of the mouth and, by extension, the sense of taste.

palming off. See PASSING OFF.

pandemic. See EPIDEMIC.

parameter; perimeter; periphery. A *parameter* (usually plural) is a number or variable in a mathematical equation, and by extension a factor in any consideration <narrow your web search by using more specific parameters>. Outside math and science, it is jargon to be avoided. *Perimeter* is the outer boundary of a space <perimeter fence>. *Periphery* is also the outer boundary, but whereas *perimeter* is a clear line, *periphery* can be of uncertain reach <the periphery of the town>.

parol; oral; parole. In law, *parol* is often used to mean *oral.* But in contracts, *parol* evidence can also be a writing other than the contract itself. It is sometimes spelled *parole,* but that should be discouraged to avoid confusion with the conditional release of prison inmates.

parricide; patricide. Both mean the murder of one's father (or the person who commits such a murder). But *parricide* is more general: it applies to the murder of any close relative, and also to the murder of a ruler.

partake in; partake of. To *partake in* (and sometimes *of*) is to take part in <partake in a public forum>. To *partake of* is to get a share of <partake of the cake and ice cream> or to suggest a certain attribute <a crime that partakes of racism>.

parties. See PERSONS.

partly; partially. If the parts are physical or the measure is of an extent, use *partly* <a partly finished building>. If speaking of a quality or the measure is of degree, use *partially* <partially recovered from an illness>. If either word works in the context, choose *partly* as less ambiguous: *partially* also means "showing favoritism" <the shares were partially divided among the children [incompletely divided, or unfairly divided?]>.

passable; impassable; passible; impassible. *Passable* and *impassable* refer to whether something can be passed <the coalition's work made the legislation passable> <the blizzard made the road impassable>. *Passible* (rare) and *impassible* refer to whether someone can feel pain or emotions <a passible God has human qualities> <an impassible old codger>. The *-ible* terms are common misspellings where the *-able* terms are meant.

passed. See PAST.

passible. See PASSABLE.

passing off; palming off; pawning off. The first two phrases mean "selling goods or services under circumstances where the buyer is misled about the source." *Passing off* is standard in law, but both phrases are common in lay usage. *Pawning off* is a fairly common error.

past; passed. When writing of time, it is surprisingly easy to misuse *passed* when *past* is the right word—after all, the *past* has *passed* <reminiscing about years *passed* [read *past*]>. At other times, it is the *passing* itself that is referred to, so *passed* is the right choice <days passed in quiet reverie>.

pastime. So spelled. It is a compound of *pass* (not *past*) and *time*.

patent; latent; patent. A *patent* thing is open and obvious <that's a patent lie>. A *latent* thing is hidden <discover a latent talent>. Both terms are pronounced with a long *a*. The noun *patent*, with a short *a*, is a limited-term monopoly granted to an inventor.

patricide. See PARRICIDE.

pawning off. See PASSING OFF.

peaceful; peaceable. To be *peaceful* is to be serene or not involved in armed conflict; to be *peaceable* is to be disinclined toward war or confrontation.

peak; peek; pique. A *peak* is a mountaintop, a *peek* is a surreptitious look, and a *pique* is a fit of resentment. *Pique* is also a verb meaning "to arouse" or "to annoy." *Peak* and *peek* are sometimes switched in pure blunder. And *peak* also sometimes appears where the writer meant *pique* <the First Amendment argument *peaked* [read *piqued*] the judge's interest>.

pecuniary; pecunious; impecunious. *Pecuniary* means "concerning or consisting of money" <the schedule listed the plaintiff's pecuniary damages>. *Pecunious* means "wealthy" <a pecunious financier>. *Impecunious* means "poor" <a judgment against an impecunious defendant is worthless>.

peddle; pedal; soft-pedal. To *peddle* something is to sell it. To *pedal* is to pump with the foot, as in riding a bicycle or operating the *pedals* on a piano. One of those piano pedals muffles the sound, so by extension to *soft-pedal* something is to tone down the intensity. In this sense the phrase is sometimes misspelled *soft-peddle*.

peek. See PEAK.

pejorative. This word, meaning "disparaging," is so spelled—not *perjorative*.

penal; punitive; penological. *Penal* relates to punishment <a penal institution>. *Punitive* means "intended to punish" <punitive damages>. *Penological* relates to the study of punishment and rehabilitation <penological research>. *Penological* is misused when applied as a five-syllable substitute for *penal*.

pendant; pendent. A *pendant* is a piece of jewelry. *Pendent* is an adjective meaning "suspended"; in law it refers to an associated but subordinate state claim allowed in a federal suit <pendent jurisdiction>.

penological. See PENAL.

penultimate. See ULTIMATE.

people. See PERSONS.

percent; per cent; %. The one-word spelling is better, but the symbol is best.

perimeter. See PARAMETER.

periphery. See PARAMETER.

permit; allow. While these are used synonymously, there is a connotative nuance. To *permit* something is to give it some form of approval <overruling the objection, the judge permitted the question>. To *allow* it to happen connotes no approval, just the lack of opposition <hearing no objection, the judge allowed the question>.

peroration; oration. The conclusion of a speech is the *peroration*, and in best usage the term is restricted to that meaning. Some writers misuse the word to denote a rousing *oration* (speech) or writing.

perpetrator; accomplice; principal; accessory. Participants in a crime are sorted out by two schemes: (1) *perpetrator* and *accomplices*, and (2) *principals* and *accessories*. In the first scheme, the *perpetrator* carries out the crime, while *accomplices* aid in its preparation and execution. In the second scheme, the *principals* carry out the crime. *Accessories* are not present at the scene but help prepare (*accessories before the fact*) or help elude arrest (*accessories after the fact*). In most jurisdictions, an *accessory after the fact* is not considered an *accomplice* but is guilty of obstructing justice.

perquisite; prerequisite. A *perquisite* is a job benefit; the term is often shortened to *perk*. A *prerequisite* is a condition that must be met in order to qualify for something.

per se. In general usage, *per se* can mean "as such" <there is no "bond exchange" per se> or "by itself" <segregation per se is less of a problem today than underfinancing>. At law it carries this latter meaning, describing a legal status that exists without the need of additional evidence <the doctrine of negligence per se requires no proof of fault>. If the phrase modifies a noun, it almost always follows the noun. With other parts of speech it may precede the word it modifies.

persecute; prosecute. To *persecute* a people (especially a religious minority) is to oppress them. To *prosecute* is to press criminal charges against someone or to pursue a patent application.

persevere. So spelled—not *perservere*.

persons; people; individuals; parties. The choice between the words *persons* and *people* is best made by ear. The traditional advice is that *persons* usually refers to small numbers of identified people, but *people* is more natural in most contexts. *Persons* sounds stuffy, as does *individuals*. *Parties* should be restricted to its legal sense, referring to separate sides in a dispute.

perspicuous; perspicacious. Clear and lucid reasoning is *perspicuous*. The person whose acute discernment and shrewdness led to the perspicuous reasoning is *perspicacious* (wise).

persuade. See CONVINCE.

pertain. See APPERTAIN.

phase. See FAZE.

picaresque; picturesque. A *picaresque* story tells the adventures of a rogue. A *picturesque* scene is one that would make a nice picture. And *picturesque* language paints a vivid picture.

pique. See PEAK.

pitiful; pitiless; pitiable. To be *pitiful* was originally to be full of pity, but in modern usage to be *pitiful* is to be detestable. To be *pitiless* is to show no compassion, and to be *pitiable* is to deserve the pity of others.

playwright. So spelled—not *playwrite.*

pleaded; pled; plead. A century of pleas to use the correct past tense (*pleaded*) has had little effect: *pled* is acceptable in American legal usage. Still, *pleaded* is dominant and best used in legal writing. The variant past-tense *plead* is objectionable because it looks like a present-tense verb (like *read* or *lead*).

plurality. See MAJORITY.

populace; populous. The *populace* is the population. *Populous* is an adjective describing a heavily populated area.

pore. The verb meaning "to read carefully" is *pore* (over), but in writing it is frequently misspelled *pour.*

possession. See CUSTODY.

post hoc. See EX POST FACTO.

practical; practicable. What is *practical* is either (1) realistic, not just theoretical <the new formbook made a practical difference for litigators>, or (2) advantageous <it wasn't practical to pay so much more for little added benefit>. The noun form is *practicality.* What is *practicable* is feasible <the budget increase made the hiring of another clerk practicable>. The noun is *practicability.*

precede; proceed; preceed. *Precede* and *proceed* are switched surprisingly often. To *precede* is to go before <her husband preceded her in death>, while to *proceed* is to go ahead <you may proceed, counselor>. *Precede* is sometimes misspelled *preceed.*

precedent; precedence. A *precedent* is a previous event that may guide our way through a present, similar event. At law, it is a judicial decision that is binding or persuasive on an issue at hand. The plural, *precedents,* is a homonym (at least in American English) of *precedence,* meaning "priority." The two words are sometimes confounded.

precipitate; precipitous. Actions and demands are *precipitate* (sudden; with unrestrained speed; rash) <a simple phone call might have prevented the precipitate filing of this lawsuit>. Steep slopes are *precipitous;* any use of this term with an action should convey the metaphor of a fall <the Internet rumor caused the company's stock to go into a precipitous decline>.

predominant; predominate. See DOMINANT.

preface. See FOREWORD.

premise; premises. The first word is a proposition from which a conclusion is drawn <a faulty premise leads to an unreliable conclusion>. The second, always plural, is the space inside the boundaries of a piece of property <leave the premises at once>.

prerequisite. See PERQUISITE.

prescribe; proscribe. To *prescribe* something is to order or direct it, especially a rule or treatment <the legislature prescribed a policy favoring mediation over litigation>. To *proscribe* something is to ban it <the new statute proscribes open containers of alcohol in the passenger compartment>.

presently; currently; momentarily. *Presently* may mean "immediately" or "soon," and in modern usage it has come to mean "now"; careful writers choose a more precise term. *Currently* means "now" and causes no problems. But *momentarily* is another ambiguous term, strictly meaning "lasting for a moment" but loosely meaning "in a moment."

presentment. See INDICTMENT.

prestigious. See PRODIGIOUS.

presumption. See ASSUMPTION.

presumptive; presumptuous. *Presumptive* is the term to use when writing of a legal *presumption* <the senior party to an interference is the presumptive first inventor>. *Presumptuous* means "arrogant and pushy" <the presumptuous summer clerk was blowing any chance for a job offer>.

preventive; preventative. Although *preventative* is common, *preventive* is the better term.

prideful. See PROUD.

principal. See PERPETRATOR.

principal; principle. *Principal* is usually the adjective meaning "main"; *principle* is the noun meaning "tenet." But *principal* is a noun when it stands for a main person <the high school principal> or primary funds <principal and interest>.

probity; probative. *Probity* is integrity and honesty <the judicial nominee had a solid reputation for probity>. Something *probative* either (1) tends to prove something <the autopsy photos were disallowed because their prejudicial nature far outweighed their probative value> or (2) explores new territory <the lawyer slipped a few probative questions into the interrogatories>.

problem. See QUANDARY.

proceed. See PRECEDE.

prodigious; prestigious. Something *prodigious* is exceptional in size or extent <preparation for the trial required a prodigious effort from everyone>. Something *prestigious* is esteemed <selected for the prestigious Order of the Coif>.

profit. See PROPHESY.

prognosis; prognostication. See DIAGNOSIS.

promulgate; propagate. To *promulgate* is to announce or declare, especially a law or rule <regulations promulgated by agencies are first published in the Federal Register>. Writers sometimes slip up by using *propagate* (to reproduce or disseminate) instead.

proper. See INDISPENSABLE.

prophesy; prophecy; prophet; profit. To *prophesy* is to predict <critics prophesy disaster>. *Prophecy* is the prediction <but their last prophecy proved wrong>. *Prophet* is the one predicting <there will always be a prophet of doom>. *Profit* is a net financial gain <as long as there's a profit to be made in scaring people>.

proscribe. See PRESCRIBE.

prosecute. See PERSECUTE.

prostrate; prostate. To *prostrate* yourself is to lie facedown on the ground; it denotes total surrender or exhaustion. The *prostate* is the gland at the base of a male's bladder; it is a common error to refer to the *prostrate* (read *prostate*) gland.

protrude; protuberance. At first glance these words with similar looks and meanings appear to have the same root. But they don't. To *protrude* is to stick out; a *protuberance* bulges out. Sometimes writers want to put the second *r* of *protrude* after the *t* in *protuberance*.

proud; prideful. Both mean "with pride," but *prideful* connotes arrogance to a moral fault.

proved; proven. *Proved* is the past participle of the verb *prove*, except in the catchphrase *innocent until proven guilty* and the Scots verdict of *not proven*. In other contexts, use *proved* <no motive has yet been proved>. *Proven* is an adjective <the defendant's presence was a proven fact>.

punitive. See PENAL.

purposely; purposefully. Something done *purposely* is done with intent, on purpose <the defendant purposely ran the red light>. Something done *purposefully* is done with a definite purpose in mind <the stalker purposefully collected information about the model>.

quandary; problem. A *quandary* is a confused mental state <the low settlement offer left the plaintiff in a quandary>. The term is misused when referring to the puzzle or problem itself <the clash of precedents presents a problem [not a quandary] for the court>.

quasi-contract. See IMPLIED CONTRACT.

query; inquiry. A *query* is one question, not an investigation. An *inquiry* may be a single query or a course of questioning, such as an investigation.

quote; quotation; misquote; misquotation. Traditionally, *quote* is a verb, *quotation* a noun. But the casual use of *quote* as a noun appears often, even in otherwise formal writing. The analogous points apply to *misquote* and *misquotation*.

rack. See WRACK.

rare. See SCARCE.

ratiocination; rationalization. *Ratiocination* is the process of reasoning. *Rationalization* is the process of making something rational, but more often the term denotes false reasoning, used after the fact to explain away or justify something that otherwise does not make sense.

real. See BONA FIDE.

rebellion. See INSURRECTION.

rebut; refute. To *rebut* something is to offer evidence or arguments to counter it. To *refute* something is to disprove it beyond doubt. The words are not interchangeable: to *rebut* an argument is to try to *refute* it. Perhaps because the *t* is doubled in *rebuttal* and other forms, *rebut* is occasionally misspelled *rebutt*.

recension. See REPUDIATION.

reciprocity; reciprocation. *Reciprocity*, the more common word, is the mutual respect by two entities of each other's interests or policies <the states' reciprocity

statutes allow an attorney from either state to participate in lawsuits in the other state>. *Reciprocation* is an act done in reciprocity <since the other party did not object to our minor motion, in reciprocation we will not object to theirs>.

recital; recitation. In a contract or deed, a *recital* is an introductory statement of who the parties are, some background of the transaction, and what the document purports to accomplish. In a pleading it is an allegation. In general it is a statement of facts. *Recitation* is an act of reciting, not the recital itself; it connotes a public statement before an audience.

recklessly. See WANTONLY.

recover back. See RELATE BACK.

re-create; recreative; recreate; recreational. The hyphen makes quite a difference. To *re-create* something is to create it again; its adjective form is *recreative* (no hyphen). To *recreate* is to enjoy a leisure activity; its adjective form is *recreational.*

recur; reoccur. If something *recurs*, it happens again repeatedly with some regularity <a recurring nightmare>. Something that *reoccurs*, on the other hand, merely happens a second time; there is no connotation of its continued repetition <if this problem ever reoccurs, call me at once>.

recuse; recusal; recusation; recusement; recusancy. To *recuse* oneself is to remove oneself as a judge or juror, usually because of a conflict of interests. *Recusal* is the corresponding noun, although *recusation* is standard in civil-law jurisdictions and is sometimes used elsewhere. *Recusement* is rarer but also appears. *Recusancy* is an unrelated word that means "refusal to submit to authority."

reek; wreak. To *reek* is to stink (or, as a noun, a bad odor). To *wreak* is to inflict something bad on someone. Cf. WREAK HAVOC.

referable. So spelled—not *referrable.*

referendum. Both *referendums* and *referenda* are acceptable plurals. Use of the first is increasing.

referral; reference. Both correspond to *refer* (to someone or something), but *referral* has acquired the special meaning of sending a client to a specialist or passing a client's information to a third person.

re-form; reform; reformation. The hyphen affects meaning. To *re-form* is to form again; the noun is *reformation.* To *reform* is to change law, policy, or procedures for the better, and especially to make them fairer; its noun is *reform.*

refractory; refractive. Something *refractory* is hard to manage, as an unruly child or a stubborn disease. Something *refractive* bends light rays; the term is restricted to the field of optics.

refrain; restrain. You *refrain* from doing something yourself, whereas other people *restrain* you.

refute. See REBUT.

regardless. This is the correct form. Use of the nonword *irregardless* —probably a confounding of *regardless* and *irrespective*—is a badge of illiteracy.

register; registrar. In reference to one who keeps records, a *register* is usually a public official <register of wills>, while a *registrar* usually works for an educational institution <transcripts are available in the registrar's office>.

regrettable; regretful. Unfortunate incidents are *regrettable* (worthy of regret); the people who are sorry about their role in those incidents are *regretful* (feeling regret).

rein; reign. A *rein* is a bridle strap, used to control a horse. By extension it is the means of controlling other things <the Senate usually gives a new President free rein to pick a cabinet>. *Reign* is the rule of a sovereign <England flourished during Elizabeth I's reign>. Perhaps because of the connotation of control, people sometimes write *reign in* when they mean *rein in*.

relate back; recover back. Although *re-* verbs are usually incorrect when used with *back*, these phrases are not redundant. *Relate back* refers to the doctrine of *relation back* <the amendment relates back to the date of the original pleading>. And common law distinguishes *recover*, meaning "to collect" <recover damages>, from *recover back*, meaning "secure return of" <the plaintiff sought to recover back the loan collateral>.

relater; relator. A *relater* is a narrator. A *relator* is a party seeking mandamus or quo warranto to force a public official to perform a legal duty.

relegate; delegate. To *relegate* someone originally meant to send them into exile; the essence of the word is to send something away. Today we may *relegate* someone to a lesser assignment <the DA relegated Pat to misdemeanors> or *relegate* a matter to some other authority to make or enforce a decision <the board relegated the grievance to a subpanel>. To *delegate* also means to send away, but with the authority to act as one's agent or representative <the senior partner delegated Robin to negotiate the merger>.

relevance; relevancy. Prefer the first.

relic; relict. A *relic* is something that survives from the past <relics from a Phoenician shipwreck>. *Relict* is an obscure, legalistic, and much inferior term for a widowed spouse.

relief. See REMEDY.

reluctant. See RETICENT.

remedial; remediable. *Remedial* describes a corrective measure <remedial English> and, in law, a legal remedy <the remedial device of a resultant trust>. *Remediable* describes something that can be remedied <the storm damage was severe but remediable>.

remedy; relief; remediation; remediate. Historically, a *remedy* was what one sought from a court of law <a legal remedy> and *relief* was what one sought in a court of equity <equitable relief>. *Remediation* is the process of remedying <environmental remediation>. *Remediate*, a back-formation from *remediation*, is used in the context of environmental cleanups.

remit; remission; remittance. *Remit* has several meanings in the sense of "to transfer something" or "to ease up." The noun for all senses but one is *remission*—when it is money that is sent, the funds are a *remittance*.

removal from office. See IMPEACHMENT.

renewal. See EXTENSION.

reoccur. See RECUR.

repellent; repulsive; repugnant. Something *repellent* wards off or drives away (people, insects, etc.). Something *repulsive* has the same effect, but only because it is truly disgusting. To most people, *repugnant* means the same thing as *repulsive* (disgusting). To lawyers it retains its original meaning of "contradictory." So when we write that a proffered interpretation of a will is *repugnant* to the testator's intent, we can do so without holding our noses.

repetitive; repetitious. To describe something that happens again and again, *repetitive* is usually neutral in connotation (although "repetitive stress syndrome" may change this), while *repetitious* often connotes that the repetition is tiresome.

replica; copy; duplicate; reproduction. In best usage, a *replica* is a precisely detailed copy. Originally, the term denoted a copy made by the original artist, but that sense is lost in American English. It has come to denote a model, especially on a smaller scale <a replica of the Empire State Building>. A *duplicate* is an exact copy. A *reproduction* is a close copy, and especially one made after the original is no longer available.

repress. See OPPRESS.

reprise; reprisal. A *reprise* is a repetition, as of an artistic performance or, in law, an annual payment from an estate or manor. A *reprisal* is a hostile act taken in retaliation for a previous wrong.

reproduction. See REPLICA.

republication; revival. In the law of wills, *republication* is the repetition of execution formalities for a previously revoked will, thereby making it valid again. *Revival* is the restoration of a revoked will by revoking the superseding will. In most jurisdictions revoking a will that revoked a previous will does not *revive* the previous will, but *republication* always does.

repudiation; rescission; recension. In contract law, *repudiation* is behavior or words indicating a party's clear intent not to perform future obligations. *Rescission* is a party's cancellation of a contract for good reason, such as the other party's material breach. *Rescission* is also a vacating, as of a statute. The word is misspelled many ways (*recision*, *recission*, *rescision*). *Recension* is the revision of a writing.

repugnant. See REPELLENT.

repulsive. See REPELLENT.

reputation. See CHARACTER.

request; behest; bequest. If people ask you to do something, you act at their *request*. If you promise them you'll do it, or if they order you to do it, you act at their *behest*. *Bequest*, which some confuse with *behest*, is a gift in a will and nothing else.

rescission. See REPUDIATION.

residence. See CITIZENSHIP.

residue; residuary; residual. *Residue* is that which is left behind; in law it is that part of an estate or trust left over after all other distributions have been made. *Residuary* is the best adjective to use in this legal sense, although *residual* is used as well. In nonlegal usage, *residual* is universal.

res judicata. See COLLATERAL ESTOPPEL.

resolute. See DECISIVE.

restive; restful. *Restive* (restless) is almost the opposite of *restful*, which describes a peaceful condition. *Restive* can also mean "stubborn."

restrain. See REFRAIN.

retainer; retainage. A *retainer* is what a client pays a lawyer to take a case, or the client's authorization to act as legal representative. *Retainage* is money withheld by a property owner from a contractor's payment pending completion of the work and release of all liens.

reticent; reluctant. *Reticent* is often misused to mean *reluctant* (unwilling to act). But its real meaning is much narrower: it means reluctant to speak, unable to speak freely, or just naturally quiet.

retract. See REVOKE.

return a verdict. See HAND UP AN INDICTMENT.

revenge. See AVENGE.

reverse. See OVERRULE.

reverse; reversal; revert; reversion. To *reverse* is to turn around; its noun form is *reversal* <a reversal of fortune>. To *revert* is to go back to a previous condition; its noun is *reversion* <reversion of a contingent estate>.

revival. See REPUBLICATION.

revoke; retract. Both mean "to take back," but in contract law one *revokes* an offer and *retracts* an anticipatory repudiation.

revolt. See INSURRECTION.

revolution. See INSURRECTION.

revolve around. See CENTER ON.

rob; steal; burglarize. A criminal *robs* you (takes your goods from your person with real or threatened bodily harm), *steals* your goods (from anywhere, whether you're around or not), and *burglarizes* your house or car (breaks in with the intent to commit a felony, usually *stealing*).

roll; role. *Roll* (in its meaning as "roster") and *role* (in its meaning as "a part in a play," literally and metaphorically) are commonly confused <the firm's *role* [read *roll*] of clients was impressive> <even though he played only a bit *roll* [read *role*] in the bank robbery, it was his third felony>.

sacrilegious. The functional opposite of *religious* does not believe in orthodox spelling; the correct term is *sacrilegious*, which corresponds to the noun *sacrilege*. *Sacreligious* is a fairly common misspelling.

salvager; salvor. The common term for one who rescues property from a shipwreck is *salvager*. But in admiralty law it is *salvor*.

sanction. This word can bear opposite meanings, both as a noun and as a verb. It can mean *penalty* (or to *penalize*) <the bar association's sanctions for commingling a client's funds range from suspension to disbarment>, or it can mean *approval* (or to approve) <the charity sanctioned the fundraising event>.

scarce; rare. Both adjectives describe something that is hard to come by. But a common object may be *scarce* at times <vine-ripened tomatoes are scarce in winter>, whereas in best usage a *rare* item is always in short supply, and usually of high cost and quality <collecting rare stamps>.

seasonal; seasonable. What is *seasonal* relates either to the seasons <a seasonal display of spring fashions> or to something that happens in a particular season <the seasonal nature of the sugaring>. What is *seasonable* is either timely <a seasonable appeal> or (more often in the negative) in the right season <seasonably warm for August>.

secede. See CEDE.

sedition; treason. *Sedition* denotes plotting to incite action against the government. *Treason* denotes actual acts taken against the government.

semi-. See BI-.

sensor. See CENSOR.

sensuous; sensual. *Sensuous* (related to or stimulating any of the five senses) has no indecent overtones. *Sensual* (pleasing to the five senses, and especially relating to sexual gratification) does. The terms are often confounded.

sequestration; attachment; garnishment. *Sequestration* is the court-ordered seizure of property at issue in a lawsuit. *Attachment* is court-ordered seizure of property as security for the payment of a judgment. *Garnishment* is a proceeding in which a judgment creditor seeks to have property owned by the judgment debtor, but in the possession of a third party, turned over to the creditor.

servicemark. See TRADEMARK.

session. See CESSION.

set aside. See OVERRULE.

sewer; sewage; sewerage. A *sewer* is a pipe carrying wastewater. *Sewage* is what the sewer carries. *Sewerage* is the sewer system or the act of removing sewage.

sex; gender. Although these terms are often used as synonyms, there is a trend in academic circles to restrict *sex* to the biological differences between man and woman, and use *gender* to refer to psychological and sociological dispositions.

shares. See STOCK.

sheer; shear. *Sheer* is the spelling for the adjective describing a steep cliff or a transparent fabric, or the verb meaning "to swerve" or "to change direction." *Shear* is the verb for cutting (especially, fleecing a sheep) and (in the plural form) the noun for scissors or some other cutting instrument.

sight. See CITE.

since; because; as. *Since* can mean "because" or "from that time on." Its meaning is occasionally ambiguous: if "the father hasn't made support payments since he was denied visitation," was the denial his motive or just the time the payments stopped? *As* can also carry two similar meanings, "because" or "during that time." In the first sense, *as* is weaker than *because* or *since*. *Because* is typically the best pick, both for strength and for always being unambiguous. But sometimes *since* is just the word to express causation more mildly <since I've got you on the phone anyway . . .>.

site. See CITE.

situs. See LOCUS.

slander. See DEFAMATION.

social; sociable; societal. *Social* relates to living among other people <social skills>. *Sociable* means "friendly; interactive with other people" <a sociable guest>. *Societal* deals with society itself <societal breakdown>.

soft-pedal. See PEDDLE.

solicitor. See BARRISTER.

soluble; insoluble; solvable; insolvable. *Soluble* and *insoluble* can apply to physical solutions <the material must be soluble in water> and mental solutions <most mathematicians today believe that the old conundrum is insoluble>. But *solvable* and *insolvable* can apply only to mental solutions <without the missing clues, the crossword puzzle was insolvable>. *Insolvable* is the preferred negative form, not *unsolvable*.

sometime; some time. *Sometime* means "at some time," but just when is uncertain <the break-in occurred sometime last night>. *Some time* means "for some time," but the duration is uncertain <the new rules will take some time getting used to>.

species; specie. *Species*, meaning a specific type of plant, animal, or other general category of living thing, is both singular and plural, so it is erroneous to write of one *specie* in this sense. *Specie* is coined money. It takes a plural form only when writing of the coins of more than one country.

specious. See SPURIOUS.

spiritual; spirituous. Something *spiritual* relates to the spirit world or is concerned with religious things. Something *spirituous* contains alcoholic spirits.

spoliation. See DESPOLIATION.

spurious; specious. Both words mean "false." But *spurious* best describes people and things that are superficially attractive but ultimately fake <a spurious autograph>, while *specious* applies to reasoning <a specious argument>.

stationary; stationery. What is *stationary* is standing still. *Stationery* is writing paper and related supplies (think *stationer*).

staunch; stanch. A *staunch* supporter is loyal and zealous. To *stanch* a flow is to stop it, especially to stop bleeding.

steal. See ROB.

sterility; impotence. *Sterility* is the inability to conceive or sire offspring. *Impotence* is a male's inability to perform sexually.

stock; shares. *Stock* is the proportional part of a corporation's capital or principal fund owned by one who buys *shares*. While *stock* is a mass noun <some stock>, *shares* is a count noun <20 shares of IBM>.

strait; straight; straitjacket; straitlaced. A *strait* is a tight spot, literally a narrow passage between two large bodies of water <Strait of Hormuz> and figuratively a precarious situation <in dire straits>. *Straight* means "linear" and, by extension, "upright." It is *strait* and not *straight* that forms words implying tight constraint, such as *straitjacket* and *straitlaced*.

strategy; tactics. *Strategy* is the long-range plan for winning something, especially a military campaign <Nixon's Southern strategy>. *Tactics* are short-term maneuvers for winning individual battles <strong-arm tactics>.

stupid. See IGNORANT.

subject. See CITIZEN.

subsequent. See CONSEQUENT.

sufferance; suffrance; suffrage. *Sufferance* is the correct spelling, *suffrance* a common error. *Suffrage* is the right to vote; its spelling may influence some to misspell *sufferance.*

sufficient. See ADEQUATE.

sui generis; sui juris. If something is *sui generis*, it is in a class by itself, unlike others <if databases can't be copyrighted, perhaps we need to devise some form of sui generis protection>. A person who is *sui juris* is of legal age and capacity or has full civil rights <all parties to the suit being sui juris>. As with other Latinisms, each phrase should be avoided whenever a suitable English substitute would work.

sumptuous; sumptuary. What is *sumptuous* is extravagant and expensive. What is *sumptuary* is meant to regulate someone's extravagant and expensive purchases, and also to curb bad habits.

supersede; supersession. *Supersede* (to take the place of) may be the most misspelled word in legal writing: it appears as *supercede* in almost a thousand federal-court opinions. It derives from the Latin *sedeo* (sit), not *cedo* (yield). *Supersession* is the noun.

supplement. See COMPLIMENT.

supplementary. See COMPLIMENTARY.

surety; guarantor. Both pledge to accept responsibility for another person's debt, but a *surety* takes primary responsibility on an equal level with the principal, whereas a *guarantor* takes secondary responsibility and becomes liable only if the principal defaults.

surplus; surplusage. *Surplus* is anything left over—an excess. In law, *surplusage* is text that adds no additional meaning and serves no purpose in the document. In all other senses, *surplusage* is a poor variant of *surplus.*

survival statute. See DEATH STATUTE.

suspicious; suspect. *Suspicious* can describe someone who arouses suspicion <a suspicious loiterer> or someone who suspects <the officer became suspicious>. As an adjective, *suspect* means "untrustworthy" <with no chain-of-custody foundation, the blood-sample evidence was suspect>. As a verb, *suspect* connotes a more fully formed belief than does the noun *suspicion* <I suspect that you are hiding something from me>. As a noun, *suspect* denotes the person under suspicion <police arrested a suspect in the robbery>.

sympathy. See EMPATHY.

systematic; systemic. What is *systematic* is either done as part of a formal system <Jim Crow laws were systematic racism> or methodical <a systematic review of the literature>. An affliction that is *systemic* is not isolated but affects multiple organs.

tactics. See STRATEGY.

take. See BRING.

talisman; talismanic; talesman. A *talisman* is a charm believed to have magic powers. The term is used as a pejorative by judges to suggest that a doctrine being relied on is not above scrutiny. The plural is *talismans*, not *talismen*. The adjective form is *talismanic*. *Talesman* is a rare term for a person available to replace a dismissed juror.

tantalizing; titillating. What is *tantalizing* is alluring but always just beyond our grasp. What is *titillating* tickles us.

taut; taught. *Taut* means "tight," as a tightrope, a stressful emotion, or discipline. *Taught* (the past tense of *teach*) is sometimes misused in its place <the bodybuilder's *taught* [read *taut*] abs>.

tax; assessment. A *tax* is a levy on the general population to raise funds that will be spent for the benefit of an entire community <a tax to support highway construction>. An *assessment* is a special levy just on those who will benefit from the expenditure of those funds <an assessment to pay for curbs and sidewalks in one neighborhood>.

tax evasion; tax avoidance. *Tax evasion* is escaping payment of taxes by illegal means, such as hiding income or claiming fictitious dependents. *Tax avoidance* is escaping payment of taxes by legal means, such as buying tax-exempt securities or investing in a tax-deferred pension plan.

tenancy in common. See JOINT TENANCY.

territory; dependency; commonwealth. U.S. *territories* and *dependencies* are part of the United States but not a part of any single state; *territories* (e.g., Guam) have their own legislatures, while *dependencies* (e.g., the Philippines, formerly) are governed by U.S. law. A *commonwealth* (e.g., Puerto Rico) is an autonomous nation voluntarily affiliated with the United States. Cf. COMMONWEALTH.

testamentary; testimonial. *Testamentary* refers to wills, *testimonial* to oral evidence. It is surprising how often *testamentary* is erroneously used for *testimonial* in judicial opinions, perhaps because the context is often "documentary and *testamentary* [read *testimonial*] evidence."

that; which; who. *That* introduces a restrictive clause, one that can't be left out without changing the meaning of the sentence <all businesses that violate antitrust laws should be shut down [not all businesses, just some]>. *Which* introduces a nonrestrictive clause, one set off by commas and whose omission would not change the meaning <the statute, which was signed yesterday, will take effect on September 1>. *Who* can be restrictive or nonrestrictive; it follows the same rules <the candidate who spoke at the school won the election> <you, who disagreed with me, voted for the loser>. Cf. WHO.

their. See THERE.

there; their; they're. Basic but still misused homophones: *there* is the direction <over there> or place <where there is life>, *their* is the possessive of *they* <all their worldly belongings>, and *they're* is the contraction of *they are* <they're on the way>.

therefore; therefor. *Therefore* is the common term for "consequently" <the plaintiff did not appear; the suit was therefore dismissed>. *Therefor* is used in legal writing to mean “for that” or “for it” <I bought a car, paying $22,000 therefor>—but it’s clunky and easily avoided by better wording.

they’re. See THERE.

third party; third-party. As a noun, use two words <the third party in the suit>; but hyphenate the phrase when used as an adjective <a third-party defendant> or an informal verb <the defendant third-partied two other companies>.

threshold; withhold. Although *threshold* does not derive from “hold,” it is often misspelled as if it did <across the *threshhold* [read *threshold*]>. *Withhold* does contain the word “hold,” hence the double-*h*. *Withhold* is sometimes used incorrectly to mean “deny” <as punishment, she was *withheld* [read *denied*] phone privileges>.

thus; thusly. *Thus* is already an adverb; it does not need the *-ly* ending.

timber; timbre. *Timber* is the correct spelling for all meanings except the musical term meaning “tonal quality” (*timbre*).

titillating. See TANTALIZING.

tolerance; toleration. *Tolerance* is the attribute of being tolerant; *toleration* is an act of tolerance.

torpid. See TURBID.

tortious; tortuous; torturous. *Tortious* refers to acts that give rise to actions in tort <tortious battery>. *Tortuous* means “full of twists and turns” <a tortuous mountainside road>. *Torturous* means “involving torture” <a torturous interrogation>.

toward; towards. There is no distinction between these two words. *Toward* is universally preferred in the U.S.; *towards* is preferred in the U.K.

toxology; toxicology. *Toxology* is the study of archery; *toxicology* is the study of poisons.

trademark; tradename; servicemark; trade dress. A *trademark* is a name, phrase, logo, or other graphic element that identifies a company’s goods or services. It is always one word. By custom, a *tradename* identifies the company itself, although in law it is not distinguished from a trademark. A *servicemark* is a trademark on services. *Tradename* and *servicemark* both appear frequently as two words, but the one-word forms are increasingly dominant. *Trade dress*, the overall appearance of a product or business, may also be protected by trademark laws.

treason. See SEDITION.

treble; triple. As verbs, these terms are usually interchangeable. As adjectives, they are distinguished. What is *treble* is three times as much as something else <treble damages>; what is *triple* is composed of three parts <triple play>.

trial lawyer; litigator. An attorney who takes part in a trial, on either side, is a *trial lawyer* and a *litigator*. But increasingly, the term *trial lawyer* denotes plaintiff’s attorneys who specialize in suits for personal injuries, medical malpractice, and other torts. An earlier distinction was a connotation that *trial lawyers* enjoyed the front-line advocacy of trials, while *litigators* preferred behind-the-scenes discovery and pleadings.

trillion. See BILLION.

triple. See TREBLE.

triumphal; triumphant. *Triumphal* describes a thing associated with a triumph <the conquerors erected a triumphal arch at the city's gate>. *Triumphant* describes how the victors feel after a triumph <triumphant shouts of joy>.

trustee; trusty; executor. A *trustee* is a fiduciary designated to hold legal title over trust property and to use it for the good of one or more beneficiaries. A *trusty* is a trusted prisoner who is given special privileges and may perform some tasks for prison guards. An *executor* is one who collects the property of an estate and distributes it according to the wishes of the testator. Nonlawyers sometimes call this person a *trustee.*

turbid; turgid; torpid. What is *turbid* is unclear: literally, dark with stirred-up mud or smoke <turbid waters>; figuratively, confused <the statute seemed to be deliberately turbid>. What is *turgid* is literally swollen <a river turgid from heavy rains> and figuratively pompous <a turgid but empty speech>. What is *torpid* is literally numb <a torpid bear in hibernation> and figuratively sluggish <the mind torpid in old age>.

ultimate; penultimate; antepenultimate. Counting backward from the end, *ultimate* means the last, *penultimate* means next-to-last, and *antepenultimate* means the one before the next-to-last.

undocumented worker. See ILLEGAL ALIEN.

undoubtedly. See DOUBTLESS.

unequivocal. So spelled. *Unequivocable* is not a legitimate word, but it is used quite often nonetheless.

unexceptional; unexceptionable. An *unexceptional* thing is ordinary. An *unexceptionable* thing is inoffensive or, in law, not cause for an objection.

unfazed. See FAZE.

uninhabitable. See HABITABLE.

uninterested. See DISINTERESTED.

unique; unusual. Strictly speaking, *unique* is an absolute term meaning "one of a kind." In common usage it can't take an intensive modifier <*very unique* [read *unique*]>. Using *unique* loosely to mean *unusual* is not normally acceptable in formal writing. But in contract law, the term is used in a less-than-absolute sense when addressing the adequacy of money damages in a prayer for specific performance.

unlawful; illegal; illicit; criminal. These appear in order of increasing stigma. An *unlawful* act is one not approved by law, but not necessarily against the law, either. It could be a civil wrong, or an offense that no one would consider particularly blameworthy, such as overparking. An *illegal* act is a violation of law, but even this term can apply to civil offenses. *Illicit* carries a strong connotation of immorality, and *criminal* denotes punishable wrongdoing. Cf. ELICIT.

unmoral. See IMMORAL.

unoccupied. See VACANT.

unorganized. See DISORGANIZED.

unphased. See FAZE.

unreadable. See ILLEGIBLE.

unusual. See UNIQUE.

unwritten. See VERBAL.

upon. See ON.

use; usage; utilization; utilize. Always *use* the simple term unless there's a reason not to. *Usage* is a separate term altogether, meaning "a custom or practice." *Utilization* and *utilize* connote using something to its best advantage; the words are appropriate only when that meaning applies.

v.; vs. In case citations, "versus" is abbreviated *v.* <*Bush v. Gore*>. In all other contexts, including the style of a case in a court paper, use *vs.*

vacant; unoccupied. For insurance purposes, a building is *vacant* if it has nothing in it, and *unoccupied* if no one lives there.

vacate. See OVERRULE.

variance; variation. In law, *variance* refers to a difference between what was pleaded or charged and what is proved at trial. It also refers to a permit to use land in a way that would otherwise violate zoning laws. The phrase *at variance* also means "in disagreement" <the holding was at variance with the rule in most circuits>. A *variation* is any departure from the norm or the past; this general term should not be used where the specific meaning of *variance* is needed.

venal; venial. *Venal* describes a person (or, rarely, a thing) who is for sale— corrupt and disposed to accepting bribes <a venal code enforcer>. *Venial* means "minor" and "forgivable" <a venial sin>. But while the adjectives are almost opposite in effect (very corrupt vs. slightly corrupt), they look and sound close and are often confused for each other.

venerable; old. *Venerable* should not be used to mean merely *old.* It describes one who is worthy of great respect and reverence.

venial. See VENAL.

veracity; voracity. *Veracity* is the human character of truthfulness <the rabbi had a wide reputation for veracity>. It is sometimes used loosely as an equivalent of *accuracy* <challenge the veracity of the witness's statement>, but this use should be avoided. And the mistake of using *voracity* (gluttony) in error is a frightening prospect.

verbal; oral; unwritten. *Verbal* means "of words"; *oral* means "spoken." In the best usage, *verbal* should not be used in place of *oral* to mean "unwritten" <*verbal contract* [read *unwritten contract*]>, since writing and speech both comprise words. But it's a common slip-up that legal writers seem especially prone to.

verbiage. This best means "wordiness," a stylistic fault. It is less often used with neutral connotations to mean *wording* <the actual *verbiage* [read *wording* or *text*] of the contract>. But since it has always had connotations of bad writing, this use is often confusing and should be avoided.

verdict; judgment; decision; mandate. A *verdict* is handed down by a jury (or a judge, in a bench trial), then the trial judge issues a *judgment.* The losing party may appeal the *judgment* (not the *verdict*). An appellate court reaches a *decision* and issues its *judgment.* If more action is required of the trial court, the appellate court will issue a *mandate* instructing the lower court what to do. Cf. DECISION.

verification. See ACKNOWLEDGMENT.

vilify. So spelled. *Villify* is a common error.

vocation; avocation. The first is what you do for a living; the second is what you do for relaxation. Your *vocation* is your career; your *avocation* is your hobby.

void; voidable. In law, a *void* contract (or marriage) is not a contract at all and never was. A *voidable* contract is a contract until a party with justification declares it void. Cf. AVOID.

voluminous. See COMPENDIOUS.

voluntary; intentional. An act can't be inculpatory unless it was *voluntary* (done consciously), so one can't be held accountable for acts done while sleepwalking, for example. But whether the actor consciously intended a wrongful consequence of a *voluntary* act—whether the outcome was *intentional*—goes to the degree of culpability. The first term looks at the nature of the act itself, the second at the motive behind the act.

voracity. See VERACITY.

vs. See V.

waive; waiver; laches; estoppel; wave; waver. To *waive* a right is to give it up. A *waiver* must be voluntary, so the word is misused when substituted for *laches* (the equitable doctrine that unreasonable delay can bar relief) or *estoppel* (the equitable doctrine that bars a party from contradicting a previous stance). *Waive* is sometimes misused for the common verb *wave*. Also, *waiver* is sometimes used where *waver* (to vacillate) is intended.

wangle. See WRANGLE.

wantonly; recklessly. In criminal law, a person acting *wantonly* acts with malice (intent), while a person acting *recklessly* does not.

warranty. See GUARANTEE.

wave; waver. See WAIVE.

wedding. See MARRIAGE.

whence; from whence. *Whence* means "from where" or "from which," so *from whence* is considered redundant <go back *from whence* [read *whence*] you came>. Even so, it has been used that way for five centuries, by the likes of Shakespeare and Dickens. *Whence* sounds stilted anyway and should be avoided.

whether; whether or not. *Whether* does not usually need *or not* because that sense is included in the word itself <the issue is *whether or not* [read *whether*] the statute applies to resident aliens>. The one exception occurs when the phrase means "regardless of whether" <the bill's supporters have the votes to override a veto, so it will become law whether or not the President signs it>.

which. See THAT.

while away; wile away. Both of these synonymous phrases for leisurely passing time are accepted and have long been used. But the second was originally a corruption of the first, which is preferred.

who; whom. *Who* is the subject, *whom* the object. If the sentence is so complex that it is hard to tell whether the term is subjective or objective, you should probably rework the sentence. Cf. THAT.

who's; whose. Pronoun contractions and possessives can require a second look to be sure the writer picked the right form. But as with *it's* and *its*, the apostrophe always marks the contraction. *Who's* is the word for *who is*, *whose* the possessive for *of whom*.

whosever; whoever's. The strictly correct possessive form is *whosever*; it should be used in formal writing. The more common *whoever's* (also a contraction for *whoever is*) is standard in casual use.

wile away. See WHILE AWAY.

willful; wilful; willfull. The first is the American spelling. The second is British. The third is always wrong.

willfulness; malice aforethought. An act done *willfully* is done voluntarily, intentionally, and with the specific intent of accomplishing the outcome. *Willfulness* is an element of a number of crimes, while *malice aforethought* is an element only of murder. The latter does not imply *malice* in the everyday sense of hatred or ill will, but rather means the specific intent to kill, to inflict serious bodily harm, or to commit a dangerous felony, or the total disregard for human life ("depraved heart").

withhold. See THRESHOLD.

workers' compensation; workmen's compensation. The phrases are always plural (not *worker's* or *workman's*). The gender-neutral first phrase has become standard.

worst comes to worst; worse comes to worst. The second phrase may be more logical, but the first phrase is idiomatic. And since idiom beats logic in language every time, use *worst comes to worst.*

wrack; rack. To *wrack* is to wreck completely; a *wrack* is a shipwreck. To *rack* is to torture by stretching on a *rack*. When something completely falls apart, it "goes to *wrack* and ruin." When you search your memory for an answer, you *rack* (stretch) your brain.

wrangle; wangle. *Wrangle* (to argue heatedly) is sometimes mistaken for *wangle* (to get by scheming or to succeed despite obstacles) <he tried to *wrangle* [read *wangle*] an invitation to the Inaugural Ball>.

wreak. See REEK.

wreak havoc. The past tense of this phrase is *wreaked havoc*, not *wrought havoc* (a common error). Aggravating circumstances may also *play havoc*, *work havoc*, or *create havoc*. Cf. REEK.

wreath; wreathe. *Wreath* is the noun for an ornamental circle made of plants. *Wreathe* is the verb meaning "to encircle."

wrong; wrongful. What is *wrong* may be either incorrect <the wrong trousers> or evil <stealing is wrong>. What is *wrongful* may be either without legal right <a wrongful beneficiary> or else illegal or immoral <a wrongful assault>.

your; you're. Basic but still misused homophones: *your* is the possessive <it's your right>; *you're* is the contraction for *you are* <you're right about that>.

zealous. See JEALOUS.

Idiomatic Prepositions

12.3 Use the correct preposition for the meaning you intend.

(a) *Idiomatic phrasing.* Legal idiom, no less than English idiom generally, consists of characteristic ways of saying things. Among the trickiest of these are prepositional constructions. For example, the legal stylist knows that a party may be either *estopped from* doing something or *estopped to* do something, but is never *estopped in* or *for* doing it. This type of knowledge comes very gradually, through wide reading of legal texts.

(b) *List of prepositional pairings.* Some wordings cause even the most experienced writers to pause. For example, should it be *conform to* or *conform with*? As it happens, they're both perfectly proper. This illustrates, though, that careful writers often need assurance on a tentative choice of a preposition. What follows is a listing of the prepositional pairings that legal writers most commonly pause over. In the list, angle brackets contain the word or type of word that goes with a certain preposition; *inf.* indicates that the word goes with an infinitive (and, in some instances, a specific infinitive); and ~ stands in for the word itself where it commonly follows a preposition.

abandoned, *adj.* by <a spouse>; to <foreclosure>; for <another plan>.

abetted, *vb.* in <a crime>; by <an accomplice>.

abide, *vb.* by <an agreement; a law>; with <a person; a condition>.

abscond, *vb.* with <a stolen item>; from <a place>.

absolve, *vb.* of <a debt; an obligation>; from <guilt>.

abstain, *vb.* from <voting>.

abstention, *n.* from <voting>; in <a vote>.

abstract, *n.* of <title>; from <a writing>; in ~.

abuse, *n.* of <discretion; power>; heap ~ on <a person>; hurl ~ at <a person>; take ~ from <a person>.

abut, *vb.* on, upon, *or* against <a property>.

accede, *vb.* to <a demand>.

acceleration, *n.* of <payment>.

acceptance, *n.* of <a settlement>; by <the recipient>; from <a donor; a colleague>; toward <a colleague>; on *or* upon ~.

accessory, *n.* to <a crime>; before *or* after <the fact>.

accomplice, *n.* to <a crime>; of <a coconspirator>; in <crime>.

accord, *n.* over *or* about <an issue>; with, between, *or* among <another party>; in ~.

accord, *vb.* with <a policy>.

account, *vb.* to <a person>; for <an action; a person>.

accusation, *n.* of <a charge>; by <an accuser>; against <an accused>; about <an offense>.

accuse, *vb.* of <a charge>.

accused, *adj.* of *or* with <a charge>; by <an accuser>.

acquiesce, *vb.* in <an action; a policy>.

acquit, *vb.* of *or* on <a charge>; from <an obligation>; [oneself] by <redemption>.

acquitted, *adj.* of *or* on <a charge>; by <a judge or jury; redemption>.

act, *n.* of <a legislature; God; aggression>; against <an opponent>.

act, *vb.* on <a proposal>; toward *or* with <another>; to <*inf.*>; against <an opponent>; as <a role>; like <a role model>; for <another person>.

adherence, *n.* to <a rule>; in ~.

adhesion, *n.* to <a surface>; contract of ~.

adjourn, *vb.* for <an interval; a purpose>; to <a place>.

administration, *n.* of <an enterprise; an estate>.

admissible, *adj.* in <court>; into *or* as <evidence>; for <a limited purpose>; against <a party>; over <an objection>; of <another explanation>.

admission, *n.* of *or* about <a fact>; by *or* from <the admitting person>; to <another person>; against <one's interests>; to *or* into <a place>.

admit, *vb.* to <doing something>; into *or* to <a place; a group>; to <a person>; of <a state or condition [e.g., failure]>.

adoption, *n.* of <a child; a contract; a cause>; by <the one adopting>; up for ~.

adversary, *n.* of <an opponent>.

adverse, *adj.* to <a situation; an interest>.

advert, *vb.* to <a reference>.

advise, *vb.* about *or* on <an issue>; against <a decision; an act>; of <a right; a situation>; in <a lawsuit>; to <*inf.*>.

advisement, *n.* about *or* of <a development>; under ~.

affirmation, *n.* of <truth>; by *or* from <the affirming person>; in ~.

agent, *n.* of *or* for <a principal>; in <a transaction>.

aggravated, *adj.* by <an intensifying factor>.

aid, *vb.* for <a need>; against <an enemy>; in *or* with <an undertaking>.

alibi, *n.* for <the time a crime was committed>.

alienation, *n.* from <a person; a group; society>; of <a relationship; property>.

allegation, *n.* of <a charge>; by <an accuser>; against <an accused>; about *or* over <a fact>.

ambiguity, *n.* about <a fact>; of <a communication>.

ambivalent, *adj.* toward *or* about <a person; a situation>.

analogous, *adj.* to *or* with <another thing>.

annotation, *n.* of <a writing; an issue of law>; by <the author>; about <the subject>.

annulment, *n.* of <a marriage>.

answer, *vb.* for <a misdeed>; to <a person wronged; an authority>; by <an atonement; a punishment>.

appeal, *n.* to <a higher court; a person>; of *or* by <the appellant>; from <the judgment>; for <a change in the judgment>; before <the higher court>; on ~.

appeal, *vb.* to <a higher court; a person>; from <the judgment>; for <a change in the judgment>.

appearance, *n.* of *or* by <a party in court>; for <a client>; through <a lawyer>; in <a jurisdiction>; before <a court>.

apprise, *vb.* of <information>.

arbitrate, *vb.* between <parties>; in <a dispute>.

arraignment, *n.* of <an accused>; on *or* for <an offense>; by *or* before <a magistrate>; in <a courtroom>.

arrest, *n.* of <an accused>; for <an offense>, by <an officer>.

assault, *n.* on *or* of <a victim>; for <a motive>; by <an attacker>; with <a weapon>.

assignment, *n.* of <an interest>; by *or* from <an assignor>; to <an office; a task>; on ~.

assimilate, *vb.* into *or* with <a community>.

assumption, *n.* about <a fact>; of <a risk; a role>; by *or* of <the assumer>.

asylum, *n.* in <a place>; from *or* against <oppression>; grant ~ to <a person>; for <a refugee>; seek ~ from <a nation>.

attachment, *n.* to <a document; an interest>; of *or* on <property>; by <a court; a sheriff>; for, to, *or* toward <satisfying a judgment>.

attempt, *n.* at <an act>; by <the actor>; on <a person's life>; to <*inf.*>.

attest, *vb.* to <the truth>.

attorney, *n.* at <law>; in <fact>; of <record>; for <a client>; power of ~; with *or* of <a firm>.

authenticate, *vb.* as <genuine>.

authentication, *n.* of <genuineness>; as <genuine>; by *or* from <a warrantor of genuineness>.

authority, *n.* over, in, *or* for <a domain>; of <an officer>; from <a delegator>; to <*inf.*>; on ~ of <a grant of power>; person of ~; in ~; on good ~; an ~ on <a subject>.

averse, *adj.* to <a thing; a situation>.

award, *n.* to <an honoree>; of <an honor>; for <an accomplishment>; by *or* from <an honorer>.

badge, *n.* of <a state, condition, or position [e.g., slavery, honor]>.

bail, *n.* post ~ for <a person>; release on ~.

bail, *vb.* out of <jail; a plane>; out <water from a leaking boat>.

bailee, *n.* of <property>.

ban, *n.* on <a thing; an activity>.

ban, *vb.* from <a place>.

banish, *vb.* to *or* from <a place>.

bar, *n.* to <an action>; of <a material [e.g., gold, chocolate]; a state or nation [e.g., the state bar of Arizona]; an area of law [e.g., the public-law bar]>; case at ~.

bar, *vb.* from <a place>.

bargain, *n.* with *or* between <people>; from <a seller>; on <a thing>.

bargain, *vb.* with <people>; for <a price; an agreement>; over <a thing>.

barratry, *n.* of <a person>.

barter, *vb.* for <a thing>; with <a person>.

battery, *n.* of <a person>.

bearer, *n.* of <a thing>.

behalf, *n.* on ~ of <a client; a principal>; in ~ of <a person or cause the actor supports>.

beneficiary, *n.* of <a gift>.

benefit, *n.* of *or* from <an advantage>; for *or* to <a person>.

benefit, *vb.* from *or* by <an advantage>.

bequest, *n.* from <a benefactor>; to <a beneficiary>; of <a gift>; of ~ to; to [*or* for] the ~ of.

bias, *n.* against, toward, *or* for <a person; a class of people>; on *or* about <an issue>; of <a person>.

bill, *n.* of <rights, lading, etc.>; for <goods; services>; from <a creditor>.

bill, *vb.* for <goods; services>; to <a debtor>.

binding, *adj.* on <a person>.

boilerplate, *n.* of *or* in <a contract>.

bona fides, *n.* of <a person; a claim>.

bond, *n.* for <a thing ensured>; of <a relationship>; with, between, *or* among <people>.

boycott, *n.* of *or* on <an enterprise>; by <patrons>.

boycott, *vb.* for <a reason>; by <a tactic>.

breach, *n.* of <a duty>; in ~.

bribe, *vb.* to <*inf.*>; into <doing something>; by *or* with <an inducement>.

bribery, *n.* of <a person>.

broker, *n.* for <a principal>; of <goods; services>.

burden, *n.* of <proof, persuasion, production, etc.>; on *or* to <a person>; to <*inf.*>.

burden, *vb.* with *or* by <a load>.

burglary, *n.* of *or* at <a place>; by <a perpetrator>.

bylaw, *n.* of <an organization>.

cajole, *vb.* into <doing something>; by <a means>.

camera, *n.* [*judge's chambers*] in ~.

capacity, *n.* of <a room; a container>; for <learning>; to <*inf.*>; at full ~; fill to ~; as *or* of <a position>.

capital, *n.* of <a place>.

capitulate, *vb.* to <an adversary>; on <an issue>.

care, *n.* of <a caregiver; a dependent>; for <a dependent>; against <a danger>; in <an action>.

care, *vb.* for <a dependent>; about <something; someone>.

case, *n.* of <a person; a thing; a legal action>; about *or* over <a situation>; against <a person>; in <chief>; make a ~ for *or* against.

cause, *n.* of <action; a result>; for <a reaction>; for ~.

cause, *vb.* by *or* with <an action; a thing>; to <*inf.*>.

cease, *vb.* to <*inf.*>; from <an action>.

cede, *vb.* to <another person>.

censure, *vb.* for *or* over <an act>; as <a criminal, perjurer, etc.>.

chain, *n.* of <command, custody, etc.>.

challenge, *n.* of <a difficulty; a dispute>; for <a prize>; by <a contest>; from <a contestant>; about *or* over <an issue>; to <*inf.*>.

change, *n.* of <venue, heart, etc.>; for <money; the better/worse>; by <a cause>; from <an old form>; into <a new form>; in <form>.

character, *n.* of <a quality>.

characterize, *vb.* as <one of two or more possible types>.

characterized, *adj.* by <a quality>.

charge, *n.* of <an accusation>; for <goods; services>; on, to, *or* against <an account>; at *or* against <a person or thing>; in [*or* take] ~ of; judge's ~ to the jury.

charge, *vb.* with <an accusation>; for <goods; services>; on *or* to <an account>; to <*inf.*>; with <a responsibility>; at <a person; a thing>; into *or* out of <a place>.

citation, *n.* of *or* from <a reference>; for *or* against <an assertion>; for <a distinction; a petty offense>; by <a superior; a police officer>.

civil, *adj.* toward <a person>.

claim, *n.* of <an allegation; a person>; for *or* against <a person; a disputed thing>; on *or* to <a thing>; by *or* from <a claimant>.

claim, *vb.* for <a person>; to <*inf.*>.

claimant, *n.* to <property>; in <an action>.

clerk, *n.* of, at, *or* in <an institution>.

clerk, *vb.* for *or* at <a judge; a court; a law firm>.

closing, *n.* of <a thing; a case>; on <property>.

cloud, *n.* on <a title; a patent>; of <a complicating quality>; over <a troubled person>; under a ~.

coalesce, *vb.* into <a whole; a union>; around <a common concern>.

coalition, *n.* of, between, *or* among <partners>; with <another partner>; for <a purpose>.

code, *n.* of <conduct, statutes, etc.>; for <an encryption>; in ~.

codicil, *n.* to <a will>; of *or* by <a testator>.

coerce, *vb.* into <doing something>.

coercion, *n.* of, by, *or* from <other people>; to <*inf.*>; under ~.

coincident, *adj.* with <another event>.

coincidental, *adj.* to <another event>.

collaborate, *vb.* with <another person>; in, on, *or* over <an enterprise>.

collateral, *n.* for *or* on <a loan>; as *or* for ~.

collateral, *adj.* to <the main proceeding; the main issue>.

colloquy, *n.* with *or* between <two people [esp., a judge and a criminal defendant]>.

collude, *vb.* to <*inf.* [esp., defraud]>; with, between, *or* among <someone to defraud a third person>; in <a scheme to defraud>; against <the victim of a fraud>.

collusion, *n.* to <*inf.* [esp., defraud]>; by, with, between, *or* among <someone to defraud a third person>; in <a scheme to defraud>; against <the victim of a fraud>; in ~.

comity, *n.* of, between, *or* among <cooperating entities>; to <a foreign court's proceedings>.

commitment, *n.* to <an enterprise; an institution>; of <a participant; an institutionalized person>; for <a purpose; a term>; by <a participant; a person instigating an institutionalization>; against <one's will>; in <an institution>; to <*inf.*>.

compare, *vb.* with <something else [an objective comparison]>; to <something else [a metaphorical exaltation]>.

compensate, *vb.* for <a loss>; by <an atonement>.

competence, *n.* of <a person [to do something]>; in *or* with <a skill>.

competency, *n.* to <*inf.* [esp., stand trial]>.

compliance, *n.* with <an order; a law; a policy>; of, from, *or* by <people>; by <a means>; in ~ with.

complicity, *n.* in <a crime>; of <a participant in a crime>.

comply, *vb.* with <an order; a law; a policy>; by <a means>.

conclusion, *n.* of <law; a proceeding or event>; by <the person reasoning or proceeding>; about <a question>; of <an event>; to <*inf.*>; in ~.

conclusive, *adj.* of <a decision>.

concur, *vb.* with <another person>; in <a decision>.

concurrence, *n.* of *or* by <a person in agreement>; in, on, to, with, *or* about <a judicial opinion>; with the ~ of; in ~ with.

concurrent, *adj.* with <a contemporaneous event; an additional penal sentence>.

condemn, *vb.* to <a punishment>; for <a public use>; as <a criminal, traitor, etc.>.

condition, *n.* of <a state or quality>; for <a reciprocal promise>; on ~ <that>.

condition, *vb.* on <a requirement>; to *or* for <an undertaking; a changed situation>; to <*inf.*>.

conflict, *n.* of <interest, laws, authority, etc.>; over *or* about <an issue>; with, between, *or* among <adversaries>; in ~ with.

conform, *vb.* to <social expectations>; with <specifications>.

connive, *vb.* with <another person>; at <wrongdoing>; to <*inf.*>.

consecutive, *adj.* to <another event; an additional penal sentence>.

conservator, *n.* of, for, *or* to <a minor; an incompetent person; a failed business>.

consider, *vb.* for <a position>; as <one aspect of a person>.

consideration, *n.* of *or* for <a contract obligation; a mitigating circumstance>; by *or* from <a person>; to <an offer; a suggestion>; on further ~; take into ~; in ~ of; out of ~ for.

consignment, *n.* of <goods>; to <a seller>; for <an owner>; on ~.

consistent, *adj.* with <another consideration>.

conspiracy, *n.* to <*inf.*>; of *or* by <participants>; against <a target>.

conspire, *vb.* to <*inf.*>; with <one or more other people>; against <another person>.

constrain, *vb.* from <doing something>.

construe, *vb.* as <a characterization; an interpretation>.

contempt, *n.* of <authority [esp., a court or Congress]>; for *or* toward <a person; a thing>; by *or* from <a person>; in ~; beneath ~.

contingent, *n.* of <supporters; people>; from, to, *or* in <a place>.

contingent, *adj.* on *or* upon <a condition>.

continuance, *n.* of <a trial>.

contract, *n.* to <*inf.*>; of <nature of contract>; for <terms of contract>; with <the other party>; under ~.

contribution, *n.* to <an enterprise; a fund>; for <a purpose>; by *or* from <a contributor>; toward <a fundraising goal>.

conveyance, *n.* of <property to a new owner>; by *or* from <the previous owner>; to <the new owner>.

convict, *vb.* of *or* for <a crime>.

conviction, *n.* of *or* for <a crime>.

copyright, *n.* of, in, on, *or* for <a work>; under ~.

corpus, *n.* of <a trust>.

counsel, *n.* of *or* from <an adviser>; for <a purpose>; to <*inf.*>; of ~.

counsel, *vb.* to <*inf.*>; about <an issue>.

course, *n.* of <dealing, conduct, etc.>; for <a destination>; through <a subject, field, etc.>; in *or* on <an academic subject>; on *or* off ~; as a matter of ~; in the ~ of; of ~.

covenant, *n.* to <*inf.*>; of <warranty, etc.>; by, with, *or* from <a promisor>; between <two people>.

credit, *n.* of *or* to <a person>; for *or* against <an amount>; by *or* from <a creditor>; on ~.

credit, *vb.* to <an account>; with *or* for <an accomplishment>.

crime, *n.* of <offense, passion, omission, etc.>; against <persons, property, humanity, etc.>.

custody, *n.* of *or* over <a dependent; property>; [take *or* award ~] from *or* to <a person>; [in the ~] of <a custodian>; [in ~] under <legal authority>; [in ~] for <a charge; a conviction>; [in ~] at <a jail, prison, etc.>; into ~; in ~.

damages, *n.* of <an amount>; for <an injury>; from <a tortfeasor>; to <a person>; in <a judgment>; sue for ~.

deal, *vb.* in <goods>; with <customers>; about *or* over <terms of a sale>; from <a deck of cards>; to <card players>.

debt, *n.* of <a person; an amount>; to <a creditor>; [impose a ~] on <a person>; in [*or* out of] ~; go into ~.

deceive, *vb.* into <doing something>.

decide, *vb.* to <*inf.*>; for *or* against <a party>; against <doing something>; between *or* among <alternatives>; on <a selection>; about <an issue>.

decision, *n.* of, from, *or* by <a person>; about *or* on <an issue>; in <a case>; for *or* against <a party>.

declaration, *n.* of <a status [e.g., default, intent]>; of, by, *or* from <a person>; to <*inf.*>.

deed, *n.* to *or* for <property>; in <a person's name>; of <trust, etc.>.

deed, *vb.* to <a person>.

defamation, *n.* of <character, etc.>.

default, *n.* of <an obligation>; in ~; by ~.

default, *vb.* on <a loan>.

defect, *n.* of <quality; legal status [form; parties; substance]>; in <a product>.

defect, *vb.* from <one side>; to <the other side>.

defend, *vb.* against *or* from <a charge>; by <a strategy>; [~ oneself] to <an authority>.

defendant, *n.* in <a lawsuit; a prosecution>.

defense, *n.* in <a lawsuit; a prosecution>; of <a defendant; a cause>; against *or* to <a charge>; in ~ of <a person>.

defer, *vb.* to <a person>; in <an option>.

deference, *n.* to <a person; a situation>.

defiance, *n.* of <authority>; toward <a person; an institution>.

deficiency, *n.* of <an amount>; in <an account; a policy>.

defraud, *vb.* into <doing something>; of <a thing; an amount>.

degree, *n.* of <a quality>; in <a field of study>; [awarded a ~] by <an institution>; [earn a ~] from <an institution>; to some ~.

deliberate, *vb.* over, on, *or* about <a decision>.

delinquent, *adj.* in <payment>.

delivery, *n.* of <a thing>; to <a person>; for <a purpose>; at <a place; a time>; by <the deliverer>; from <the sender>; in ~ of <a thing>; on *or* upon ~.

demand, *n.* on *or* to <a person>; by *or* from <the demander>; of *or* for <a thing; an action>; against <an estate; a corpus>; on ~; in ~.

demur, *vb.* at *or* to <an objectionable suggestion>.

denial, *n.* of <a charge; a request>; by <an accused; a provider>; to <a questioner; a customer>; in ~.

deplete, *vb.* of <all contents>.

deposition, *n.* in *or* for <a lawsuit>; of *or* from <a witness>; by <the deposer>.

descent, *n.* from <a parent>; of <a progeny>; pass by ~ to *or* from.

despoil, *vb.* of <a possession>.

destitute, *adj.* of <resources; hope>.

detract, *vb.* from <the whole; a more important aspect>.

detriment, *n.* to <a person; an enterprise>; to one's ~.

detrimental, *adj.* to <an interest [esp., a legal or financial interest]>.

devise, *n.* of <property>; to <a beneficiary>; from *or* by <a testator>; in <a will>; through <a will; an estate>; <pass> by ~.

devolve, *vb.* upon <a successor; an appointee>; into <a worsened condition>; to <a successor>.

dictum, *n.* in *or* from <a judicial opinion>; of *or* by <a judge; a judicial opinion>; about <the content>; in ~.

differ, *vb.* from <something else>; on, about, *or* over <an opinion>; with <another person>.

digest, *n.* of <cases>.

digress, *vb.* from <the main subject>.

diligent, *adj.* in *or* about <a responsibility>.

disability, *n.* of <a person; a legal incapacity>; to <perform a life function; take a legal action>.

disabuse, *vb.* of <an idea; an opinion>.

discharge, *n.* of <an obligation or position; a lawsuit; a gun>; from <a debt; an obligation or position; a hospital>; by <a creditor; a judge; one in authority>; for <a reason>; in ~ of <an obligation>.

disclaimer, *n.* of <a legal right or duty; a warranty>; by <a manufacturer, seller, service provider, or other party to a contract>; in <a contract; a notice>.

discovery, *n.* of <information>; by <a party>; from <a witness>; under <rules of procedure; a court order>.

discretion, *n.* to <*inf.*>; of, with, *or* over <a decision-maker>; of, by, toward, *or* from <a confidant>.

discriminate, *vb.* against <a class of people>; by <a means>; between *or* among <two or more things>; <one thing> from <another>.

discriminating, *adj.* in, about, *or* with <taste, fashion, etc.>.

discrimination, *n.* against <a class of people>; of *or* by <one who discriminates against a class of people>.

discriminatory, *adj.* toward <a class of people>.

disfavor, *n.* of <a person>; <earn> ~ by <doing something>; in ~ with.

dismissal, *n.* [*lawsuit*] of <a lawsuit>; with *or* without <prejudice>; for <a reason [e.g., want of prosecution, cause]>; by <a judge>; from <prosecution>.

dismissal, *n.* [*employment*] of <an employee>; for <cause>; by <an employer>; from <employment>.

dispense, *vb.* with <a thing>; to <people>.

dispose, *vb.* of <a thing>; for <a person>; by <a means>.

disposed, *adj.* toward <a person>; to <*inf.*>.

disposition, *n.* of <property [esp., in an estate]; character>; toward <a person>.

dispossessed, *adj.* of <a thing>.

dissent, *n.* from <a dominant opinion; a policy>; in <a case>; by <a judge; a protester>; over, against, with, *or* toward <a policy>.

dissociate, *vb.* from <a person; an organization>.

dissuade, *vb.* from <doing something>.

dissuaded, *adj.* by <a person; a reason>.

distinct, *adj.* from <something else>.

distinction, *n.* between <two things>; of <an accomplishment>; <serve> with ~; <person> of ~.

distinguish, *vb.* between *or* among <two or more things>; <one thing> from <another>; by <a difference>.

distinguishable, *adj.* from <something else>; by <a difference>.

distinguished, *adj.* for *or* by <an accomplishment>.

distribution, *n.* of <property [esp., by intestacy]; money [esp., net earnings to shareholders]>; to, between, *or* among <heirs; people [esp., shareholders]>; by <an estate's administrator; a funding organization; a corporation>; for <a purpose>.

diverge, *vb.* from <a central point; a main path>.

diversity, *n.* of <a thing [e.g., interests, opinions, citizenship]>.

divert, *vb.* from <one place>; to <another place>; for <a purpose>.

divest, *vb.* of <an asset>; by <a means>.

divorce, *n.* from <a former spouse>; of <a person>; over <a situation>.

docket, *n.* of <a court>; on the ~.

docket, *vb.* for <a trial or hearing date>.

documentation, *n.* of <an event; a fact>; for <a claim; an allegation>; by <a means>; from <a source>.

dominion, *n.* over <a possession>; of <a realm>.

draft, *n.* on <a bank>; for <an amount; a person>; of <a writing>; from <a maker; a writer>.

due, *adj.* to <a reason; a creditor>; for <a change>; on, by, *or* before <a time>, from <a debtor>; to <*inf.*>; come ~.

duress, *n.* of <a threat>; from <a person>; under ~.

duty, *n.* to <*inf.*>; to *or* toward <a person>; of <care>; on <an import>; on [*or* off] ~; in the line of ~.

easement, *n.* on, in, through, across, *or* over <property>; by <type [e.g., necessity, estoppel]>; for <a purpose [e.g., ingress–egress]>; from <a grantor; a predecessor in interest>; to <a grantee; a successor in interest>.

ejectment, *n.* of <an occupant; an owner>; from <property>; by <the person ejecting the occupant>; for <a reason>.

elicit, *vb.* from <a person>.

embargo, *n.* on <a product; a nation; a news story>; by <the one imposing the embargo>; against <another nation>; lift an ~ from <another nation>; under ~.

embezzle, *vb.* from <an employer; a client>.

embezzlement, *n.* of <an employer's money or property>; by <the embezzler; the means of embezzlement>; from <the embezzler's employer>.

emigrate, *vb.* from <an old home country>; to <a new home country>.

employment, *n.* of <an employee>; by <an employer>; for <a position; a term>; at <will>; under <contract>; to <*inf.*>.

encroach, *vb.* upon *or* on <another's property or rights>.

encumber, *vb.* with <a burden>; by <a debt>.

encumbrance, *n.* on <a title>.

endorsement, *n.* of <a candidate; a product>; by <a person>; for <an office>. Cf. INDORSEMENT.

endow, *vb.* with <an asset; an advantage; a talent>.

endowment, *n.* of *or* for <an institution; a field>.

enjoin, *vb.* from <an action>; to <*inf.*>; upon *or* on <a person to *inf.*>.

entice, *vb.* into <doing something>; with *or* by <an inducement> to <*inf.*>.

entitled, *adj.* to <a thing>; to <*inf.*>.

entrapment, *n.* of <a person>; by <police; a means>; into <a crime>; by ~.

entrust, *vb.* to <a person>; with <a thing>.

equal, *adj.* to <a thing; a person; a task>; in <size; number; ability>; of <a person>.

equality, *n.* between *or* among <people>; in <a field>.

equate, *vb.* with *or* to <another thing>.

equity, *n.* of *or* through <a remedy>; for <an injustice>; from <a court>; toward <a person>; in <a situation>; in <property>; in ~.

escheat, *vb.* to <the state>.

escrow, *n.* for <a purpose; a person>; of <an account>; by <a depositor; a depositary>; in ~.

estate, *n.* of <a deceased>; at <will>; for <years>; in <reversion>; on <limitation>; by <curtesy>.

estopped, *adj.* from *or* to <an assertion; an action>; by <one's own contradictory assertion or action; contract>; on <legal principle>; under <a statute; a contract>.

estranged, *adj.* from <a former companion [esp., a spouse]>.

estrangement, *n.* from <a former companion [esp., a spouse]>; between <two people>; over <a situation>.

eviction, *n.* of <an occupier of property>; from <occupied property>; by <the owner>; for <a reason>.

evidence, *n.* of <an alleged fact>; for *or* against <a side in a trial>; by *or* from <a provider; a witness>; in <a trial>; plant ~ on; <piece, shred, scintilla, etc.> of ~; in ~; into ~.

examination, *n.* of <a person; a situation>; about <a situation>; by <an examiner; a lawyer>; on *or* in <an academic subject>; on closer ~.

exception, *n.* to <a rule; a ruling>; for <a person>.

exchange, *vb.* of <things>; for <another thing>; with <another person>; by <a person>.

exclusion, *n.* of <evidence; income>; for <a reason>; by <a judge; the tax code>; from <evidence; taxation>.

exculpate, *vb.* from <an accusation>.

excuse, *n.* for <an action>; of <a reason>; by *or* from <an accused>; to <*inf.*>.

execution, *n.* of <a person; a will; a contract; a court order; a money judgment>; for <a capital crime; enforcement of a judgment>; by <a person>.

executioner, *n.* of <a condemned person>.

executor, *n.* of <a deceased person's estate>.

exemplar, *n.* of <a person's handwriting, voice, or other identifying characteristic>.

exempt, *adj.* from <an obligation>.

exhaustion, *n.* of <options>; from <an effort>; state of ~; to ~.

exhibit, *n.* of *or* in <evidence>; for <viewing>; by <a party>; on ~.

exonerate, *vb.* from <an accusation>.

expert, *n.* in *or* on <a field>; at <a skill>; with <the tools of a skill>.

explicit, *adj.* about <a meaning; an intention>.

expostulate, *vb.* about, upon, *or* on <a topic>; with <another person>.

exposure, *n.* to <the elements; the public>; of *or* about <a scandal>; by <a person>; in <the media>; die of ~.

expound, *vb.* on *or* upon <a weighty subject>; to <a person>.

expropriate, *vb.* from <a property owner>; for <a public use>.

expungement, *n.* of *or* from <a record>; by <a court>.

extortion, *n.* from <a person>; of <a thing of value; an act; a public official>; by <a person; a public official>; to <*inf.*>; by ~.

extradition, *n.* of <a suspect>; to *or* from <another state or nation>; in <a prosecution>; by <the foreign jurisdiction>.

extraneous, *adj.* to <the thing itself>.

extrapolate, *vb.* from <known data>; to <*inf.* [esp., make an assumption about an unknown thing]>.

extricate, *vb.* from <a situation>; by <a means>.

extrinsic, *adj.* to <the thing itself>.

eyewitness, *n.* to <an event>.

faithless, *adj.* to *or* toward <a person [esp., an employer]>.

familiar, *adj.* to <a person>; with <a fact; a person>.

fastidious, *adj.* about <details; a personal habit>.

feasible, *adj.* to <*inf.*>.

fee, *n.* for <a service>; of <an amount>; from <the charger>; to <do something>.

fiat, *n.* to <*inf.*>; from <a court; an executive>; by ~.

fiduciary, *n.* of <a client, trust beneficiary, shareholders, etc.>.

finder, *n.* of <fact>.

fine, *n.* for <an offense>; on <a person>; of <an amount>; by *or* from <a magistrate>.

fixture, *n.* of <property>; in <a place>.

foreclosure, *n.* of *or* on <mortgaged property>; by <a lender; a governmental entity>.

forfeiture, *n.* of <assets>.

forgery, *n.* of <a check; a signature; a work of art>; by <a forger>.

franchise, *n.* of <a business>; to <*inf.*>.

fraud, *n.* on <a person; the community; a court, agency, etc.>; in <the inducement; the factum>; by <the actor>.

freedom, *n.* of <speech, religion, etc.>; from <oppression, censorship, etc.>; to <*inf.*>; grant ~ to <a person>; secure ~ for <a people>; gain ~ from <a tyrant>.

frustration, *n.* of <purpose>; over *or* toward <a situation>; in ~.

fundamental, *n.* to <a higher-order right or principle>; [*pl.*] of <a discipline>; for <advancement>.

furlough, *n.* to <*inf.*>; on ~.

garnishment, *n.* of <wages; assets>; for <a debt; execution of a judgment>; by <a court>.

generalize, *vb.* about <a conclusion>; from <observations>.

generous, *adj.* with <money, help, advice, etc.>; in <doing something>; to *or* toward <a person>; that was ~ of <a person> to <*inf.*>.

germane, *adj.* to <an issue>.

gibe, *n.* at <a person>; about <an incident; a person>; [pl.] of <others>; for <a reason>.

glean, *vb.* from <an experience>.

gloat, *vb.* over <a success>.

goad, *vb.* into <doing something>; to <*inf.*>.

grant, *n.* of <a right; money>; for <a purpose>; to <a person>; by *or* from <a grantor>; to <*inf.*>.

grapple, *vb.* with <an issue>; for <an object>; to, onto, *or* with <a larger object, for safety>.

grievance, *n.* against <a person>; about <a situation>; of <an aggrieved person>.

grieve, *vb.* for, after, *or* over <a lost loved one>; with <another person>; at <a loss>.

gross, *n.* a ~ of <things>; easement in ~.

grounds, *n.* for <taking action>; to <*inf.*>; on [what] ~.

grouse, *vb.* about <a situation>.

guarantee (guaranty), *n.* of *or* about <security>; against <defects>; for <performance of an obligation>; by *or* from <the guarantor>; to <the person being assured>.

guard, *vb.* against <something happening>; from <attack>; stand ~ for <a protected person>; stand ~ over <a protected thing>.

guardian, *n.* of <a dependent>; for <a purpose>.

guest, *n.* of <a host>; in *or* at <a place>; on <the premises>.

guilt, *n.* for <a crime>; by <association>.

guilty, *adj.* of <a crime>; feel ~ for *or* about <doing something>.

habit, *n.* of <doing something>; by ~; in [*or* out of] the ~ of; force of ~.

haggle, *vb.* over *or* about <a thing; an issue; a price>; with <a person>.

hail, *vb.* from <a place>; as <a champion, a great thinker, etc.>.

hale, *vb.* into *or* to <a place [esp., court]>; before <a person [esp., a judge]>.

haul, *vb.* into *or* to <a place [esp., court]>; before <a person [esp., a judge]>; to, from, around, across, etc. <a place>; between <two places>; at, on, *or* upon <a rope; reins>; on, upon, *or* to <the wind [naut.]>.

hazardous, *adj.* to <health; well-being>; to <*inf.*>.

hearing, *n.* on, for, *or* about <a purpose>; by <a court; a regulatory agency>; in <a case>; ripe for ~; at ~.

heat, *n.* of <passion>.

hedge, *vb.* against <a possible loss>.

hegemony, *n.* of <one nation; one power>; over <other nations [esp., in a region]; other powers [esp., in a field]>.

heir, *n.* to <an estate>; of <a deceased person>.

hesitant, *adj.* about <doing something>; to <*inf.*>.

hesitate, *vb.* over, about, *or* in <taking action>; for <a period of time>; to <*inf.*>.

hinder, *vb.* in <doing something>; from <accomplishing something>; for <a reason>; by <a means>.

hindrance, *n.* to *or* of <a person; an enterprise>; from <an adversary; an adverse condition>; without ~.

holder, *n.* in <due course>; for <value>; of <commercial paper>.

holding, *n.* of *or* by <a court>; on <a question of law>; in <a case>.

holdover, *n.* from <a lease>.

hostile, *adj.* to *or* toward <a person; a group; a nation>; about *or* over <a situation>.

hypothesize, *vb.* about <a posited situation>.

identify, *vb.* as <a particular person>; to <a person [esp., police]>; with <another person>; by <a distinctive characteristic>.

immaterial, *adj.* to <an issue>.

immigrate, *vb.* from <that country>; into *or* to <this country>.

immunity, *n.* from *or* to <liability; a sanction; a disease>; of <a person; a cause of immunity>; by <authority granting immunity>; on *or* in <a lawsuit>; under <a law; a doctrine>; grant ~ to <a person>; grant of ~ for <a person; liability>.

immunization, *n.* against <disease>.

impeachment, *n.* of <an official; a witness>; on *or* for <a charge>; by <a legislature; a questioner>.

impel, *vb.* to *or* into <action>; to <*inf.* [esp., take action]>.

impelled, *adj.* by <a force; an obligation>; to *or* into <action>; to <*inf.* [esp., take action]>.

impinge, *vb.* on, upon, against, *or* at <a thing; a person; a right>.

implicated, *adj.* in <a crime; an enterprise>; with <others involved>.

implicit, *adj.* in <another idea>.

implied, *adj.* in <law>; by <a suggestion>.

import, *vb.* from <another country>; to <this country>.

impose, *vb.* on *or* upon <a person>; for <a favor>; to <*inf.*>.

improvement, *n.* of *or* to <a thing>; on *or* upon <property>; in <a condition; an area>; by <a means>; over, on, *or* upon <a previous condition>.

impulse, *n.* to <*inf.*>; on ~.

impute, *vb.* to <a person>.

inadmissible, *adj.* into, to, *or* as <evidence>; for <a purpose>.

inaugurate, *vb.* as <an official>.

incapacity, *n.* to <*inf.* [perform; take legal action]>; of <a person>.

incident, *adj.* to <an event>.

incite, *vb.* to <action>; to <*inf.*>.

incompetence, *n.* at *or* in <a field; a skill>; of <a person>; to <*inf.*>.

incompetency, *n.* of <a person>; to <*inf.* [esp., stand trial; testify]>.

inconsistent, *adj.* with <another statement, activity, etc.>.

incorporation, *n.* of *or* by <a company>; for <a purpose>; into <another thing>; articles of ~.

inculcate, *vb.* in, on, *or* into <a person>.

incumbent, *adj.* on or upon <a person>; to <*inf.*>.

indecency, *n.* of <a person>; toward <another person>.

indemnify, *vb.* from *or* against <loss; liability>; for <damages>; under <a contract; a judgment>; in <a lawsuit>.

indemnity, *n.* from *or* against <loss; liability>; under <a contract; a judgment>; seek ~ from <an insurer>.

independent, *n.* of *or* from <another person; one reason>.

indicative, *adj.* of <a conclusion>.

indictment, *n.* on *or* for <a crime>; in <a prosecution>; of <an accused>; by <a grand jury>; under ~.

indigenous, *adj.* to <a place>.

indignant, *adj.* toward *or* to <a person>; about, at, *or* over <a situation>.

indistinguishable, *adj.* from <something else>.

indorsement, *n.* of <a negotiable instrument>. Cf. ENDORSEMENT.

inducement, *n.* to <a person>; to <*inf.*>.

inequality, *n.* between <two groups of people; two things>.

infer, *vb.* from <a statement>.

influence, *n.* of, by, *or* from <a person>; on *or* over <another person>; for <good or evil>; about, in, on, *or* against <a decision>; to <*inf.*>; under the ~.

inform, *vb.* on *or* against <a person>; to <another person [esp., the police]>; of *or* about <information>.

infringement, *n.* of, on, *or* upon <a right>; by <a person>; under <a law; a doctrine>.

inheritance, *n.* of <property; money>; by <an heir>; from <a deceased person>; pass by ~.

inhibit, *vb.* from <doing something>.

injunction, *n.* against *or* on <a person>; to <*inf.* [do something]>; of <an action>; from <a court>; under ~.

injury, *n.* to *or* of <a person>; by *or* from <a person; a means>; in <an incident>; inflict ~ on <a person>.

innocent, *adj.* of <a charge>.

innuendo, *n.* about <a person; an allegation>.

inquest, *n.* into <a crime; a death; a situation>; by <an authority>.

inquire, *vb.* about *or* into <a matter>; after <a person>; of <the person being asked>.

inquisitive, *adj.* about <a matter>.

insinuate, *vb.* into <a situation>; to <a person>.

instill, *vb.* in *or* into <a person>.

insulate, *vb.* from *or* against <an adverse condition>.

insurance, *n.* against <loss; liability>; from <an insurer>; on <property>; for <an enterprise>.

intent, *n.* to <*inf.*>; of <a person; doing something>; with ~ to <*inf.*>.

intercede, *vb.* for <a person>; with <another person>; in <a dispute>.

interest, *n.* of <a person; a principle>; on <an investment>; for <an investment; an investor>; from <a depositary>; at <a rate>; in <an enterprise; an activity>; in <a person's> ~ [to <*inf.*>]; of ~ to <a person>.

interference, *n.* in *or* with <an activity; a relationship>; of, by, *or* from <a person>.

interpleader, *n.* petition in ~.

interrogatory, *n.* to <a party>; from <an adversary>; about <an issue>.

intervention, *n.* in *or* into <a lawsuit; a dispute>; of, by, *or* from <an intervenor>; for <a purpose>; against <an action>; to <*inf.*>.

intimidate, *vb.* into <doing something>.

intolerance, *n.* against *or* toward <a group of people; a religious or political group>; to <a medication; a food>.

intolerant, *adj.* of *or* toward <a group of people; a religious or political group>.

intrude, *vb.* into <a place>; on or upon <a right or privilege>.

inure, *vb.* to <a person's benefit>.

invasion, *n.* of <an interest [e.g., privacy]; a country>; by <a person; an invading country>; for <a purpose>; from <a place>; against <a country>; under ~.

inveigh, *vb.* against <an enemy; a doctrine>.

inveigle, *vb.* into <doing something>; out of <a possession>; into, in, out of, away from, etc. <a place>; by <guile>.

invest, *vb.* in <a security; a venture>; with <authority; a covering>.

investigation, *n.* into, of, *or* about <a situation>; of <a person; a situation>; by <an investigator>; on closer ~; under ~.

irreconcilable, *adj.* with <a contradictory thing>.

irrelevant, *adj.* to <an issue>.

issue, *n.* of *or* about <a question>; at *or* in ~; take ~ with.

jibe, *vb.* with <another person's opinion; another set of facts>.

joinder, *n.* of <another party; another claim; remedies>; in <pleading>; to <*inf.* [esp., defeat jurisdiction]>.

judgment, *n.* of *or* from <a court>; for <the winning party>; against <the losing party>; on *or* in <a case>; about <an issue>; concur in a ~; dissent from a ~; sit in ~; in <a person's> ~.

jurisdiction, *n.* over <a person; a subject matter>; of <a court; an agency>; to <*inf.* [e.g., review a judgment, adjudicate a claim, impose a penalty]>; on *or* over <a place [e.g., an Indian reservation]>; under <a statute; Article III>; under <a court's; an agency's> ~; confer ~ upon *or* on <a court; an agency>; outside [*or* within] <a court's> ~.

jury, *n.* of <peers, 12, 6, etc.>; in <a trial>; trial by ~.

justice, *n.* of <the peace>; for <a wrong>; by <a means>; to <a person>; bring to ~.

justification, *n.* for <an action>; with *or* without ~.

justified, *adj.* in <doing something>; by <mitigating circumstances>.

kidnapping, *n.* of <a victim>; for <a reason [esp., ransom]>; by <a perpetrator>; from <a place>.

landlord, *n.* of <a rental property>.

lapse, *n.* in *or* of <e.g., time, subscription, judgment, concentration>; time ~ between <two events>; mental ~ by <a person>.

lapse, *vb.* into <e.g., unconsciousness, a coma, a bad habit>; will ~ on.

larceny, *n.* of <a thing>; by <a perpetrator; a means>; over *or* under <an amount>.

law, *n.* of <a legal area; a jurisdiction>; in <a jurisdiction>; by ~; under the ~ of <a jurisdiction>; within the ~; against the ~; above the ~; get around the ~; attorney at ~.

lawsuit, *n.* over <a dispute>; by <one party>; against <the other party>; in <a jurisdiction>.

lawyer, *n.* for <a client>; with, at, *or* of <a firm>; in <a lawsuit>.

lease, *n.* of *or* on <property>; as *or* for <a purpose>; by <the tenant>; from <the landlord>; under ~.

leave, *n.* of <absence; the court>; by <a court>; on ~.

leave, *vb.* for *or* from <a place>; by <a means>; with *or* without <a thing; a person>; at, before, after, *or* during <a time; an event>.

legacy, *n.* of <a person; an accomplishment or notable quality>; from <a deceased person>; to *or* for <a beneficiary>.

lenient, *adj.* toward, on, *or* with <a person [esp., a criminal defendant]>; in <setting punishment>.

letter(s), *n.* of <e.g., administration, intent, credit>; from <the sender>; to <a person>; about <a subject>; in a ~; by ~.

levy, *n.* on <a taxpayer; a thing that is taxed>; of <property>; to <*inf.* [e.g., fund a project]>; for <a purpose>.

liability, *n.* for <a tort>; of <a tortfeasor>; to <another person>.

liaison, *n.* between <two people or groups>; from <one group>; to <another group>; with <a paramour>.

libel, *n.* of *or* against <a person>; by <the defamer>; in <a publication>.

license, *n.* of <intellectual property>; from <the owner of an intellectual-property right>; by <the licensee>; for <a use; a royalty>; through <a clearinghouse>; to <a person>; to <*inf.*>.

lien, *n.* on *or* against <property>.

liquidated, *adj.* by <agreement; litigation>.

liquidation, *n.* of <assets>; by <the owner; a bankruptcy trustee>; in ~.

litigation, *n.* of *or* over <a dispute>; by <the parties>; against <a defendant>; to <*inf.*>; in ~.

loan, *n.* of <a thing; money>; for <a purpose>; from <a lender>; to *or* by <a borrower>; on ~.

loss, *n.* of <bargain; consortium>; by <a person>; to <a person; a situation>; at a ~; for a ~.

magistrate, *n.* of, for, *or* in <a jurisdiction>.

maintenance, *n.* of <a thing; a person; a lawsuit>; on <a thing>; for <a purpose>; by *or* from <a person>.

majority, *n.* of <people; things>; for *or* against <a proposal; an opinion>; in <a group; an assembly>; in the ~; age of ~.

maker, *n.* of <a promissory note>.

malice, *n.* toward <a person; a group of people>; act with [*or* without] ~.

mandamus, *n.* to <*inf.* [e.g., vacate, rescind, review]>; of, from, *or* by <a court>; writ of ~.

master, *n.* of <a servant; an art>; at <an art>; over *or* in <a domain>.

material, *n.* to <an issue>.

mediation, *n.* of, over, *or* about <a dispute>; by *or* through <a neutral third party>; between <parties>; to <*inf.* [e.g., reach a settlement]>; in ~.

memorandum, *n.* of <law; content; a person; a date>; from, by, *or* to <a person>; about *or* on <content>.

merger, *n.* of, by, *or* between <companies>; with <another company>.

merits, *n.* of <a case>; on the ~.

militate, *vb.* against *or* in favor of <severity>.

misrepresentation, *n.* of *or* about <a fact>; by *or* to <a person>; in <a dealing>; by *or* through ~.

mistake, *n.* of <fact; law>; by <a person>; about <a fact>; in <doing something>; it was a ~ to <*inf.*>; by ~.

mistaken, *adj.* about *or* in <a fact; a belief>; for <another person>; by <a person>.

mitigation, *n.* of <damages; culpability>; by <an action; a person>.

monopoly, *n.* of, on, over, *or* in <a market; an industry>; by <a company; a means>.

mortgage, *n.* on <a property>; for <a property; an amount>; to, from, *or* with <a lending institution>.

motion, *n.* for <a court order [e.g., to quash an indictment, for a new trial]>; in <limine>, to <*inf.* [e.g., strike, suppress, transfer venue]>.

motive, *n.* for *or* behind <an action>; of <an actor>; to <*inf.*>; in <taking action>.

mulct, *vb.* of <money, a possession>.

muniment, *n.* of <title>.

murder, *n.* of <a person>; for *or* over <a motive>; by <a perpetrator; a means>; with <a weapon>; in *or* on <a place>.

necessity, *n.* of <life; an activity>; for <an activity>; of ~.

neglectful, *adj.* of *or* toward <a person; a condition>.

negligence, *n.* of *or* by <a person>; for <an injury>; in *or* about <conduct>; with <an instrumentality>; toward <another person>.

negotiable, *adj.* for <money>; by <a bearer; a payee>.

nonsuit, *n.* of <a claim; a defendant>; by <a plaintiff; a judge>; for <a reason>.

notice, *n.* of <a legal action; a condition>; to <an adverse party>; by *or* from <a person; a court>; on ~.

novation, *n.* of <a contract>; by <a new party>; in <a new agreement>.

nuisance, *n.* of, in, *or* over <a situation>; for *or* to <a person>; by <a person creating the nuisance>.

oath, *n.* of <office; allegiance>; by <a person taking an oath>; from <a person administering an oath>; administer an ~ to <a person>; to <*inf.*>; under ~; by ~; on ~.

objection, *n.* to <an act; a question; admission of evidence>; of, by, *or* from <the objector>; against, about, *or* over <a subject>; without ~; despite ~; over ~.

objective, *adj.* about <a perception; an opinion>.

obligation, *n.* to <a person>; to <*inf.*>; under [no] ~.

obstruction, *n.* of <justice; an investigation; an enterprise>; to <a flow; a process>.

obtrude, *vb.* upon *or* on <a person>; ~ <oneself> into <an affair>.

offense, *n.* of <a crime>; by <a perpetrator>; against <a victim>; take ~ at <an act; a comment>.

offer, *n.* to <*inf.*>; of <a deal; assistance>; for *or* on <a thing; a service>; from, by, *or* to <a person>.

officer, *n.* of <the court; the law; an organization>.

omission, *n.* of <an act; a fact>; by <a person>; from <a record>; <crime; act; sin> of ~.

operation, *n.* of <law; an enterprise>; by <a person>.

opinion, *n.* from, of, *or* by <a judge>; in <a case>; about *or* of <a situation>.

option, *n.* of <choices>; on <a thing for sale>; to <*inf.*>; on ~.

order, *n.* of <a court>; for <a thing>; by *or* from <a person>; to <*inf.*>; on ~; in ~ to <*inf.*>.

ordinance, *n.* of <a municipality>.

panel, *n.* of <people [e.g., jurors, judges, experts]>; on <a subject>.

pardon, *n.* of <an accused or convicted person>; by *or* from <a chief executive>; for <a crime>; grant a ~ to <a person>.

parity, *n.* with, between, *or* among <another person; another nation>; of *or* in <things; status>; [of currency and stocks] at, above, *or* below ~.

parole, *n.* of <a prisoner>; by *or* from <a parole board>; grant ~ to <a person>; on ~.

partner, *n.* of <another partner; a firm>; in <an enterprise>.

partnership, *n.* of, by, between, *or* among <all the partners>; with <another partner>; for <a purpose>; in <an enterprise>; by <estoppel>; under <a statute>; to <*inf.*>; in ~ with <other partners>.

party, *n.* in <a lawsuit>; to <a lawsuit; an enterprise; a conversation>.

patent, *n.* on *or* for <an invention>; from <the patent office>.

patented, *adj.* by *or* to <an inventor>.

payment, *n.* of <a debt; a cost>; to <a creditor; a seller>; by *or* from <a debtor; a buyer>; on *or* against <an account>; for <a thing>; into <a savings plan>; in ~ of [*or* for].

penalty, *n.* of <a punishment>; for <an offense>; from <a court; an adjudicator>; on *or* to <an offender>; under <a statute or regulation>.

performance, *n.* [*art*] of <a work of performing art>; by <an artist>; for *or* before <an audience>; in <a venue>; as <a role>.

performance, *n.* [*contract*] of <an obligation>; by *or* from <a promisor>; for <a promisee>; in ~ of <an obligation>.

perjury, *n.* of *or* by <a witness>; in *or* during <testimony>; on <the witness stand>.

perpetuity, *n.* in ~.

petition, *n.* for <legal action [e.g., bankruptcy, removal, review]>; of, by, *or* from <a petitioner>; to <a court>; to <*inf.* [e.g., change name]>; in <bankruptcy; admiralty>.

plaintiff, *n.* in *or* of <a lawsuit>.

plea, *n.* of <guilty; not guilty; nolo contendere; a defendant; type of plea [e.g., privilege, release]>; to <a charge; type of plea [e.g., the jurisdiction, the writ]>; in <a prosecution; type of plea [e.g., abatement, equity]>; for <court action [e.g., leniency]>.

plead, *vb.* to <a charge; an adversary's pleading>; for <a remedy>; in <response to a pleading>.

pleading, *n.* of <a party; a defendant>; for <a remedy>; by *or* from <a defendant>; in <a lawsuit; a prosecution>; to <a court>.

pledge, *n.* of <security; a promise>; for <a debt>; to <a creditor>; from *or* by <a surety>; against <default>; to <*inf.* [esp., perform]>.

plurality, *n.* of <people; things>; for *or* against <a proposal; an opinion>; in <a group; an assembly>; in the ~.

point, *n.* of <law; fact; procedure [e.g., error]>; about <an issue>; to <*inf.*>; on ~.

possession, *n.* of <property>; by <a person>; take ~ from <a previous possessor>; charged with ~; in ~ of.

power, *n.* of <an authority [e.g., attorney, the press]>; for <a purpose [e.g., good or evil]>; from <a source>; over <an underling>; under <legal authority>; to <*inf.*>; in ~; by the ~ vested in me.

prayer, *n.* for <relief>; to <a court; a deity>.

precedence, *n.* over <something else>; of <a criterion for ordering>.

precedent, *n.* of <a case>; for <a decision>; from <a case; a jurisdiction>.

precedent, *adj.* to <an event>.

preclude, *vb.* from <doing something>; by <a means>.

precursor, *n.* of *or* to <something else>.

predicated, *adj.* on *or* upon <a ground>.

predispose, *vb.* to <a type of action; a quality>; to <*inf.*>.

predominance, *n.* of *or* by <a person; an idea>; over <someone else; something else>; in <a field>.

preeminence, *n.* of <a person>; over *or* in <a field>.

preemption, *n.* of *or* from <a legal action>; by <a legal doctrine>; under <legal authority>.

preference, *n.* for <one choice>; to <a person>; in ~ to <another choice or person>.

preferred, *adj.* over <an alternative>; by <a person>; in <a situation>.

prejudice, *n.* against, toward, *or* to <a class of people>; with [*or* without] ~.

prejudicial, *adj.* to <one side of a dispute>.

preliminary, *adj.* to <an event>.

premeditation, *n.* with ~.

premises, *n.* of <an occupant>; for <a use>; on [*or* off] the ~.

premium, *n.* on <a charge>; at a ~.

preoccupation, *n.* with <a thing; a quality; a person>.

preparatory, *adj.* to <an event>.

preponderance, *n.* of <evidence>.

prerequisite, *n.* to *or* for <a more advanced thing>.

prescription, *n.* for <a medicine; an outcome>; of <a person>; by ~.

presumption, *n.* of <a fact [e.g., innocence, undue influence]>.

pretext, *n.* for <another action>; to <*inf.*>; on, under, *or* at any ~.

prevail, *vb.* against *or* over <a person [in a contest]>; on *or* upon <a person [to do something]>.

principal, *n.* of <an institution [e.g., a school]; an agent; an investment>.

principle, *n.* of <a belief system; a science>; with *or* in <a person>; against <an unethical act>; on ~; in ~.

priority, *n.* over <another person; another thing>; in <a field>; as <a status>.

privilege, *n.* of <a legal advantage [e.g., immunity]; good fortune [e.g., meeting an esteemed person]>; to <*inf.*>.

privity, *n.* of <a legal relationship [e.g., contract]>; with <another person>; between <two people>; in ~.

probate, *n.* of <a will; an estate>; in <a court>; to [*or* into] ~; at ~.

probation, *n.* of <a jail or prison term>; in <a sentence>; for <a conviction; a convicted person>; by *or* from <a judge>; on ~.

probative, *n.* of <the truth or falsity of an assertion>.

procedure, *n.* for <doing something [esp., conducting a lawsuit]>.

proceed, *vb.* against <a person [esp., in a lawsuit]>; to *or* from <a place>; with <an activity>; by <a means>.

proceeding, *n.* of *or* in <a tribunal; an assembly>; against <an accused>; for <a purpose>; to <*inf.*>.

proceeds, *n.* from <an event>.

proclivity, *n.* for, to, *or* toward <a quality; an activity>; to <*inf.*>.

procure, *vb.* for <a person>; by <a means>; at *or* in <a place>; from <another person>.

proffer, *n.* of <a thing [esp., evidence]>; to <a court; a person>; by, of, *or* from <the offeror>; against <the other party>.

proficient, *adj.* at *or* in <an activity>.

progress, *n.* in <an undertaking>; against <an adversary>; toward <a goal>; by <a means>; in ~.

prohibit, *vb.* from <doing something>; by <a means>; under <an authority>.

prohibition, *n.* on *or* against <doing something>; of *or* against <a thing>.

promise, *n.* to <*inf.*>; of <a performance; the promisor>; by *or* from <the promisor>; to <the promisee>.

proof, *n.* of *or* about <a fact>; by <a means; a person>; from <a person>; in <a trial; a proceeding>; burden of ~.

propensity, *n.* for, to, toward, *or* of <an activity; a quality>; to <*inf.*>.

propinquity, *n.* to <a place>; of <blood [closeness of relationship]>.

prosecution, *n.* of <a criminal case; a patent application; an enterprise>; for <a charge>; by <a prosecutor>; against <a defendant>; in <a case>; under <a penal statute>.

protection, *n.* of <a person; a thing>; against *or* from <a threat>; by <a means>; under ~.

protective, *adj.* of *or* toward <a person>.

provoke, *vb.* into <doing something>; to <*inf.*>.

proximate, *adj.* to <a nearby thing>.

proxy, *n.* for <another person>; to <*inf.* [do something on someone else's behalf>; by ~.

punish, *vb.* for <an offense>; as <an offender>; by <a means>.

punishable, *adj.* by <a means>.

punishment, *n.* of *or* to <an offender>; for <an offense>; by *or* of <a means>; from <a court; an authority>.

purport, *adj.* to <*inf.* [esp., be something]>.

qualified, *adj.* for <a task; a position>; as <a position>; by <a condition>; to <*inf.* [do something]>.

rancor, *n.* of <a person>; toward *or* against <another person>; over <a situation>; with *or* without ~.

ratification, *n.* of <a compact [esp., a contract, a charter, a constitutional amendment, or the like]>; by *or* from <the parties to the compact>.

reasonable, *adj.* for <a person in some position>; about <a situation>; to <*inf.* [esp., act in a certain way]>; under *or* in <the circumstances>.

rebuttal, *n.* of *or* to <an assertion; a presumption>; by, of, *or* from <an adversary>; in <an exchange>; on ~; in ~.

receipt, *n.* of <a thing>; for <a payment>; by <the receiver>; from <the payee>; in ~ of <a thing>; on [*or* upon] ~.

receiver, *n.* of *or* for <a thing [esp., the subject matter of litigation]>; under <legal authority>.

reciprocate, *vb.* for <an act>; with *or* by <another act>.

reciprocity, *n.* between <two people; two organizations; two governments>; for <an act>; from <another person, organization, or state>.

recital, *n.* of <facts [esp., preliminary expository clauses in a contract or deed]>; in <a contract or deed>.

recklessness, *n.* of *or* by <a person>; in *or* about <an act>; toward <another person>.

reconcile, *vb.* with <another person>; to <a situation>.

record, *n.* of <a proceeding>; for <an appeal>; from <a prior proceeding>; on [*or* off] the ~; for the ~; of ~.

recourse, *n.* to <a court; a remedy; an alternative>; for <a person; a dispute>; against <an injustice; a person>; for <a person>; in <a situation>; under <a statute; a doctrine>; without ~.

recusal, *n.* of *or* by <an adjudicator>; from <a proceeding>.

redemption, *n.* of <commercial paper [e.g., stock, bond, coupon]; an oppressed people>; by <a company; a liberator>; from <oppression>; in <forgiveness; restitution>.

reformation, *n.* of <a contract>; by <a court>; to <*inf.* [e.g., carry out the intent of the parties]>.

regard, *vb.* as <stature>; with <emotion [esp., contempt>.

rehabilitation, *n.* of <a criminal; a drug or alcohol abuser; a witness; a bankrupt's financial affairs>; by *or* through <a means>.

release, *n.* from <an obligation; custody>; of <a person; a thing>; by *or* from <a person granting release>; into <custody of another person>; under <legal authority>; upon <habeas corpus>; deed of ~.

relegate, *vb.* to <a lesser position; another decision-maker>.

relevant, *n.* to <an issue>.

reliance, *n.* on <another person's promise>; of *or* by <a person>; in ~ on.

relief, *n.* for <an inequity; a party>; of <type of equitable remedy>; by *or* from <a court>; under <legal authority>; from <a bad situation>; to <a person>.

remainder, *n.* of <an estate; an amount>; to *or* in <a remainderman>.

remand, *vb.* to <a lower court>; from *or* by <an appellate court>; for <further proceedings>; with <instructions>; of *or* in <an appeal>; on ~.

remedy, *n.* for <an injury; infringement of a legal right>; of <type of remedy>.

removal, *n.* of <a thing; a state-court lawsuit>; to <a place; a federal court>; from <a place; a state court>.

renege, *vb.* on <a promise>.

renowned, *adj.* as <a master in some field>; for <an accomplishment>; by <the public>.

renunciation, *n.* of <a right; a criminal undertaking>; by *or* from <a person>; for <a purpose>.

repatriate, *vb.* from <a country of exile or immigration>; to <a former home country>.

replete, *adj.* with <things; a quality>.

reply, *n.* to <an accusation; a communication; a person>; by *or* with <an answer>; from <a person>; through <an intermediary>; in ~ to.

representation, *n.* of <a client; a thing; a condition>; as <attorney>; in *or* for <a legal problem>; before <a tribunal; an agency>; to *or* by <a person>.

reprove, *vb.* for <a fault>.

repudiation, *n.* of <a contract; a debt; a relationship>; by *or* from <a person>; over <a situation>.

reputation, *n.* as <one of a particular character>; for <deeds; character>; by ~; stake one's ~ on.

rescission, *n.* of <a contract>; by <a party>; for <a good reason>.

respite, *n.* from <a bad situation>; without ~.

restitution, *n.* for <damage; injury>; of <an amount>; from *or* by <a person>; to <an injured person>; in <a sentence>.

restraint, *n.* of <a thing [e.g., trade]>; on <a right [e.g., alienation]>; by *or* from <a person>; toward <another person>; in <conduct>.

reversion, *n.* to <a grantor; a prior state>; of <an estate; a thing>; from <an intermediate estateholder>.

revocation, *n.* of <an act; a power; a trust>; by <the revoker>.

right, *n.* of <legal benefit [e.g., privacy, survivorship, way]>; under <a source of legal right>; of ~; by all ~ [*pl.*].

robbery, *n.* of <a person>; by <a perpetrator>.

royalty, *n.* for <a license>; to <the owner of an intellectual-property right>; from <a licensee>.

rule, *n.* of <type of rule [e.g., law, reason, capture]; a sovereign>; in <source of rule [e.g., Shelley's Case]; a territory>; against <a practice [e.g., perpetuities, accumulations]>; for <doing something [e.g., distributing an intestate estate]>; by <a sovereign>; over <a dominion>.

rulemaking, *n.* by *or* of <a regulatory agency>; in <an area of jurisdiction>.

ruling, *n.* of, by, *or* from <a court; a regulatory agency>; for <a winning party>; against <a losing party>; in <a case>; on *or* about <an issue>.

sale, *n.* of <a good; a service>; for <a price>; by <the seller>; to <the buyer>; through <an intermediary>; on <a discounted item>; on ~; for ~.

sanction, *n.* [*endorsement*] of, from, *or* by <an authorizing agency>; for <an approved act or event>; to *or* on <an approved action or event; a person responsible for an approved act or event>.

sanction, *n.* [*penalty*] [*usu. pl.*] against, on, *or* upon <a hostile nation>; by, of, *or* from <a court or disciplinary agency>; for <a condemned act>; under <a law; a rule>; under ~.

satisfaction, *n.* of <a debt; a promise; a promisee>; for <a debt; a promise>; by *or* from <an alternative performance; a promisor>; at *or* in <a performance>; with, over, *or* about <a situation>; give ~ to <a creditor; a promisee>; to one's ~; in ~ of <a promise>.

schism, *n.* between <two people; two factions>; over <an issue>.

scintilla, *n.* of <evidence>.

scope, *n.* of <employment; authority>.

scrutiny, *n.* of <an argument>; by <a court>; under ~.

search, *n.* of <a place; a person>; by <a person [esp., a police officer]>; for <a thing [esp., evidence, contraband]; a wanted person; a lost person or thing>; in, inside, at, *or* through <a place; a container>; with *or* without <a warrant>; in ~ of.

secured, *adj.* by *or* with <a surety; collateral; physical protection>; for <a person>; from *or* against <loss; damage>.

segregate, *vb.* from <one group from another>; into <separate groups>; for <a purpose>.

seised, *adj.* of <property>.

seisin, *n.* in <deed; fact; law>; covenant of ~; livery of ~.

seizure, *n.* of <a thing; a person>; by <a person [esp., a police officer]>; for <evidence; arrest>; at, from, *or* in <a place; a container>; with *or* without <a warrant>.

sentence, *n.* of <a punishment>; by *or* from <a judge; a jury>; for <an offense>; to <a convicted person>; in <a prosecution>; under <a statute>.

sequestration, *n.* of <a jury; property or funds in legal dispute; property owed to an enemy nation>; by <a court; a government>; for <security pending the outcome of a dispute>; from <outside influence>; in *or* inside <a place>.

setoff, *n.* for, of, *or* against <a counterclaim; a credit>; by <a party; the amount owed by the other party>; under <a statute; a doctrine>; right to a ~.

settlement, *n.* of, on, *or* in <a dispute; a lawsuit; an estate>; by, between, *or* among <the parties>; for <a sum of money; a performance; an acceptable distribution>; with *or* from <the adverse party>.

settlor, *n.* of <a trust>.

share, *n.* of *or* in <the whole>.

share, *vb.* in <the whole>; with, among, *or* between <others>.

shelter, *vb.* from *or* against <a threat>; by *or* with <a means>.

shield, *vb.* against *or* from <a danger>; by *or* with <a means>.

situs, *n.* of <property; an event>; law [*or* court] of the ~.

skeptical, *adj.* of *or* about <something>.

slander, *n.* of <title>; by <a defamer>; about, toward, *or* against <a person>.

smuggle, *vb.* into *or* out of <a place>; past, through, *or* by <customs>; across <a border>.

solicitation, *n.* of <a thing; a potential customer or client; someone to commit a crime; prostitution>; from *or* by <a person>; to <*inf.* [esp., donate something or do something]>.

speculate, *vb.* about *or* on <a possibility>; in *or* on <an investment>.

speculation, *n.* in <goods; a commodity; land; an investment>; over *or* about <an outcome; a mystery>; by, of, *or* from <a person>; on ~.

spoliation, *n.* of <evidence; goods in transit>.

standard, *n.* of <care; proof; living>; for <a decision>; in, for, *or* throughout <an industry>.

standing, *n.* to <*inf.* [esp., bring suit]>; in <a community>; with <another person>.

state, *n.* of <condition [e.g., mind, shock, disrepair]>.

statement, *n.* of <facts; financial affairs>; to *or* for <an intended audience>; by *or* from <the speaker>; on *or* about <a subject>; against <a person; an issue; interests>; through <a spokesperson>.

statute, *n.* of <type of statute [e.g., frauds, limitations, wills]>; by ~; under ~.

stay, *n.* of *or* in <type of stay [e.g., execution, trial]>; by *or* from <a court; an executive>.

stipulation, *n.* by *or* from <a party>; of *or* on <a fact>; by ~.

stock, *n.* in *or* of <a corporation>; take ~ in *or* of.

subjective, *adj.* about <a perception; an opinion>.

sublease, *n.* of <a rental property>; from *or* by <a tenant>; to <a third party>; for <a term; a purpose>; under ~.

subpoena, *n.* of <a person; a document>; for <a trial; a hearing; discovery>; by *or* from <a party; a court>; to <*inf.* [esp., appear in court]>; under ~; serve a ~ on <a person>.

subpoena, *vb.* as <a witness>; to <*inf.* [esp., appear in court]>; for <a trial; a hearing; discovery>.

subservient, *adj.* to <another person; a thing>.

subsidy, *n.* for <a purpose; a project>; to <a person; an organization>; of <an amount>; from *or* through <a funding organization; the government>.

succession, *n.* of <people; events>; to <a position; a legal right>; from <a seller; an assignor; a testator>; by ~; in ~.

summons, *n.* to <a person>; to <*inf.* [esp., testify]>; from *or* by <a court>; in <a trial; a hearing>; with <notice>; under ~; serve a ~ on <a person>.

suppression, *n.* of <evidence>.

surcharge, *n.* on <an item>; of <an amount>; for <a purpose>.

surety, *n.* for <the obligation [esp., debt] of another person>.

taint, *n.* of <a negative quality; an illegal activity>.

taint, *vb.* with *or* by <a negative quality; an illegal activity>.

tainted, *adj.* with *or* by <a negative quality; an illegal activity>.

taking, *n.* of <property; game>; for the ~.

tangential, *adj.* to <a main topic>.

tantamount, *adj.* to <a crime; another type of thing>.

tariff, *n.* on <an import; an export>; of <a rate>.

tax, *n.* on *or* against <a person; a thing; a transaction>; for <a purpose>; from <a taxpayer>; to <a government>; of <a rate>.

teem, *vb.* with <things>.

tenancy, *n.* for <a term>; by <the entireties>; in <common>; from <period to period>; at <sufferance; will>.

tendency, *adj.* to <*inf.* [do something]>; toward <a quality; a type of action>.

tender, *n.* of <money; performance of an obligation>; by <a debtor; a promisor>; for <an offer; a bid>; in <cash; check; other means of payment>.

testament, *n.* of <a person [by a will]>; to <a meaning>.

testation, *n.* of <property [by disposition according to a will]>.

testify, *vb.* about *or* on <a subject>; for *or* against <a party>; to <an assertion>; under <oath>; in <a trial>; before <a judge; a jury>.

testimonial, *n.* to <success against obstacles>; of <an endorser>.

testimony, *n.* of, by, *or* from <a witness>; for *or* against <a party>; on *or* about <a subject matter>; in, during, *or* before <a trial; discovery>.

theft, *n.* of <a thing>; by <a thief>; from <a victim>; over *or* under <an amount>.

threaten, *vb.* to <inf.>; with <harm>; by <a means>.

thwart, *vb.* in <an attempt>; by <a means>.

title, *n.* to <property>; of <a writing; a record>; <abstract; chain; muniment> of ~.

tort, *n.* of <type of tort [e.g., battery, negligence]>; an action in ~.

trademark, *n.* of *or* on <a product>.

tradename, *n.* of <a company>.

traffic, *vb.* in <contraband [esp., drugs]>.

trample, *vb.* on <rights>.

transcript, *n.* of <a trial>.

transfer, *n.* of <venue; funds>; from *or* to <a place; an account>.

transform, *vb.* from <one form>; into *or* to <another form>.

transgress, *vb.* against <a person; a limit>.

transmute, *vb.* into <another form>.

treatise, *n.* on, about, *or* in <a subject>; of *or* from <an author>.

trespass, *vb.* on *or* onto <property of another>; against <another person>.

trial, *n.* of <an accused; a lawsuit>; for <a charge>; in <a lawsuit>; on <the merits>; to <the bench>; by <jury; one's peers>; before <a judge>; over <an issue; a dispute>; on ~; at ~; ready for ~; go to ~; bring to ~.

trust, *n.* [*a legal entity*] for <a beneficiary>; of *or* by <a settlor>; hold in ~.

trust, *n.* [*confidence*] of *or* by <a person>; in *or* toward <another person>; about <a matter>; to <*inf.*>.

trust, *vb.* in <a belief>; with <a thing; information>; to <a person>; ~ someone to <*inf.*>.

trustee, *n.* of <a trust; a school; a beneficiary>; for <a settlor>; over <the corpus of a trust>.

unanimous, *adj.* in <agreement; opposition>.

unbecoming, *adj.* in, to, *or* of <a person in some position>.

unbiased, *adj.* toward <a person; a class of people>; about <a subject>.

unburden, *vb.* of <a liability; a secret>.

unconcerned, *adj.* over, about, *or* at <an event>; with <doing something>.

uncooperative, *adj.* toward *or* with <a person>; in <a process>; about <doing something>.

unequal, *adj.* to <something else>; in <amount; number; a quality>.

unequaled, *adj.* at <a skill>; in <a field>; by <any other>.

unfair, *adj.* to, with, *or* toward <a person>; about <a subject>; in <dealings>.

unfaithful, *adj.* to <a person; a cause>; in <a responsibility>; by <a means>.

unfit, *adj.* to <*inf.* [fill a role]>; as <a person in some capacity>; for <a position>.

union, *n.* of <people [esp., workers], factions, or nations; things>; for <a purpose>; by <a uniting principle or entity>; against <an enemy>; with <another person, faction, or nation>.

unique, *adj.* in <a field; itself>; to <a place; a class>.

unity, *n.* of <requirements for a joint tenancy [e.g., interest, possession, time, title]>.

unjustified, *adj.* in <doing something>.

unleash, *vb.* on *or* against <an adversary>.

unprepared, *adj.* for <an occurrence>; to <*inf.*>.

unqualified, *adj.* for <a position>; to <*inf.*>.

unreasonable, *adj.* of <a person>; to <*inf.*>; in <doing something>.

usage, *n.* of <trade; custom>; in <a field; a population>.

use, *n.* of <a thing>; by <a person>; for <a purpose>; against <an adversary>; with <another thing>; as <a means>; in <an undertaking>; in ~; of ~ to.

vacillate, *vb.* between <positions>; in *or* on <a decision>; from <one thing>; to <another thing>; with <changing influences>.

variance, *n.* with <a pleading; a charging instrument>; from <a zoning restriction>; at ~ with.

vengeance, *n.* on <an enemy>; for <an injustice>; with a ~.

verdict, *n.* of <outcome [e.g., guilty, not guilty]>; for *or* against <an accused; a party>; by *or* of <a jury; a judge>; in <a case>.

verification, *n.* of <a fact>; from *or* by <a confirmer>.

vest, *vb.* in <a person>; with <authority>.

veto, *n.* of <a bill>; by <a chief executive>; for *or* over <an issue>.

void, *adj.* of <legal effect>; for <a legal infirmity>; by <reason of a legal doctrine; court order>; as <a matter of law>.

voidable, *n.* by <one party>; for <a legal doctrine>.

vouch, *vb.* for <a person; a fact>.

waiver, *n.* of <a legal right>; by *or* from <a person>.

ward, *n.* [*a minor*] of <a guardian; the state>.

ward, *n.* [*a political subdivision*] of *or* in <a municipality>.

warrant, *n.* for <a search; an arrest>; to <*inf.* [esp., search a place; seize a thing or a person]>; in <an investigation>; of <arrest>; with *or* without ~; swear out a ~ against <a person>; serve a ~ on <a person>.

warranty, *n.* of <a covenant [e.g., title, habitability]>; of, by, *or* from <a seller>; to <a buyer>; for *or* on <a product>; against <a defect>; under ~; in ~.

weigh, *vb.* against <an argument; a person; a standard>; on <one's mind>; in <for a flight or a fight>; in *or* out <for a contest>; out <a measure for use or sale>.

weight, *n.* of <the evidence>.

wheedle, *vb.* into <doing something>; <information> from *or* out of <a person>; into, out of, away from, etc. <a place>.

withdraw, *vb.* from <a position; a community; an account>; to <another position; seclusion>.

witness, *n.* to <an incident>; for *or* against <a party>; in <a lawsuit>; on <the stand>; bear ~ to.

wrangle, *vb.* with <a person; a question>; over *or* about <a dispute>.

wrest, *vb.* from <a person>.

writ, *n.* of <type of writ [e.g., certiorari, error, habeas corpus, mandamus]>.

yield, *vb.* to <a person; an order>.

zone, *n.* of <type of zone [e.g., privacy, danger]>.

zoning, *n.* of <property>; for *or* against <a land use>; by <a municipality>.

Offensive Language

12.4 Avoid needlessly offending readers with your word choice.

(a) *Characteristics.* Avoid references to irrelevant personal characteristics such as sex, race, ethnicity, disability, age, religion, sexual orientation, or social standing. When a characteristic is relevant to the facts, law, issues, or analysis, refer to it as neutrally as the circumstances allow.

(b) *Professional conduct.* Rules governing professional conduct often include admonitions against bias and prejudice. For example, Rule 8.4(d) of the Model Rules of Professional Conduct states: "It is professional misconduct for a lawyer to . . . engage in conduct that is prejudicial to the administration of justice." Comment 3 of this rule states: "A lawyer who, in the course of representing a client, knowingly manifests by words or conduct, bias or prejudice based upon race, sex, religion, national origin, disability, age, sexual orientation or socioeconomic status, violates paragraph (d) when such actions are prejudicial to the administration of justice." State rules contain similar provisions.

(c) *Ineffective advocacy.* Comments that betray a writer's conscious or unconscious biases or ignorance may cause readers to lose respect for the writer, diminish the writing's persuasiveness, and evoke a response opposite to that intended. Avoid direct quotations that use offensive or outdated terms. Paraphrase the meaning in plain English. If the quoted writer's prose is too distinctive to paraphrase, consider editing slightly by inserting a neutral term or descriptive phrase in brackets in place of the antiquated language. Also, an insult, no matter how wittily or subtly expressed, will detract from your point. Courts may use internal sanctions, such as issuing fines and striking pleadings. Disciplinary actions and suits for libel or slander are also possible. For example, in *In re Vincenti*, 704 A.2d 927, 929–34, 938–44 (N.J. 1998), an attorney was disbarred to end a long history of abusive, intimidating, and contemptuous behavior. And in *Hoeffer v. Florida*, 696 So. 2d 1265, 1265–66 (Fla. Dist. Ct. App. 1997), an attorney was held in contempt of court for using profane language and threats against the opposing counsel.

(d) *Unwarranted distinctions.* Referring to a personal characteristic, such as sex, race, or disability, may suggest that the distinction is important. Such a reference may imply that the person's situation is unusual or unexpected. It may sound limiting or patronizing. For instance, the statement *Ruth Bader Ginsburg is perhaps the greatest woman judge of all time* implies that she is a great judge "for a woman," but maybe not so good if compared to male judges. If the writer did not mean to limit the scope of the comparison, *woman* should be deleted or the whole sentence recast. Another example: writing *Barbara Jordan was an outstanding black representative* suggests that she stands out only among black representatives as a group, and also that it is unusual for a black person to hold high office. But when writing *Barbara Jordan was the first black woman to represent a southern state since Reconstruction*, the function of the racial reference is clearer. Also, a reference may imply that the characteristic has some bearing on a legal issue or credibility. For example, a needless reference to a criminal defendant's race may suggest that race is somehow related to and predictive of behavior. And a pointless mention of a witness's physical disability (e.g., blindness) may invoke a reader's biases (e.g., a presumption of diminished mental capacity).

(e) *Person first.* Whenever reasonable, a characteristic's label should be used as an adjective, whether applied to a person or a thing, instead of a noun. In other words, instead of referring to *a Jew, a black, a gay*, or *a deaf-mute*, emphasize the person by writing *a Jewish child, a black woman, a gay man, a deaf and mute person.*

(f) *Equivalence.* When writing about more than one group, use equivalent labels whenever possible. Distinctively labeling only one group implies that it is to be regarded as superior or inferior to the other, or that one group is normal and the other is not. Instead of *blacks and Asian-Americans*, write *African-Americans and Asian-Americans.* Some labels, although equivalent, are not commonly used and could make your prose sound awkward. People of European descent are usually labeled *white.* Many find *European-American* stuffy, and *Anglo* (commonly heard in the Southwest) inaccurate. If a specific label is not applicable, then use the common label, even if it is not equivalent (e.g., *whites and Chinese-Americans*). Sometimes there is no reasonably equivalent label. For instance, one is or is not a disabled person; only one distinguishing label exists. Do not invent a label just to achieve balance.

(g) *Slang.* Slang can diminish the authority of your writing and destroy any sense of objectivity. Slang terms may have additional connotations that expand or restrict their meanings. For instance, the slang terms *straight* and *gay* may denote two types of sexual orientation, so the words appear to be correlated. But *gay* (and *lesbian*) also applies to cultural, political, and social contexts, not just sexuality. And *straight* carries connotations of morality, righteousness, or rigidity, and may have a positive or negative implication, depending on the context. The casual use of inflammatory terms, such as referring to the police as "gestapo" or an objectionable law in terms of "genocide," is for shock entertainers, not professional writers. The tactic is bound to backfire. The writer seeks to inflate an issue by linking it to a historic enormity or injustice. The irritated reader may discount the issue to less than its true size.

(h) *Jargon.* Using outdated and offensive jargon shows poor research and a lack of knowledge. No responsible writer should misuse another field's current technical language. For example, until the 1970s, some popular medical terminology, such as *mongolism* and *Siamese twins,* had racial and ethnic roots. These terms have been replaced with more accurate and ethnically-neutral equivalents (i.e., *Down's syndrome*; *conjoined twins*). Similarly, until the 1960s, shipping and engineering jargon commonly included a highly offensive racial slur (*see, e.g., N.C. v. Hamilton,* 141 S.E.2d 506, 508 (N.C. 1965); *MV Belgrano v. Oetker,* 189 F. Supp. 103, 105 (D. Or. 1960) (referring to some undefined portion of a winch)). The terms have long since been replaced with neutral phrases.

(i) *Euphemisms.* Although they are meant to avoid unpleasantness, euphemisms tend to be very broad, vague, and sometimes inaccurate. A euphemism such as *mobility-impaired* might be useful if referring to an entire class of people who share a broadly defined characteristic (i.e., difficulty walking). But it is meaningless when applied to an individual. Few disabilities are absolute; rather, they come in many degrees. An impairment may be relatively slight (e.g., walks with a cane) or substantial (e.g., uses a wheelchair). Not all euphemisms should be avoided. At times, a direct or explicit term might divert the reader's attention from the issue; a softer substitute is desirable then. For instance, the terms *bastard* and *illegitimate child* historically attach to an innocent person. *Nonmarital child* and *child out of wedlock* convey the same meaning without offense.

(j) *False friends.* Some legitimate words are similar in appearance (and sometimes sound) to slurs. If you think a word or phrase might be questionable, consult a dictionary. There is almost always a neutral substitute that serves exactly the same function. Just a few words that have created problems are *niggardly* (having an ancient and obscure derivation, and meaning *stingy*), *yellow* (when used in a negative sense, e.g., *coward*), *welsh* (meaning *to break a promise* or *to avoid payment,* and unrelated to the Welsh people), *blackguard* (meaning *rascal* and unrelated to skin color), and *chicanery* (meaning *trickery,* apparently of French origin and dating to 1609, whereas *Chicano* is thought to have come from the Mexican-Spanish *mexicano* and did not appear until 1947). Of course, if a word is the best choice for a particular writing, use it. It is not reasonable to purge your vocabulary of every good word that might be misperceived, especially if it lacks an equivalent or if rephrasing results in an awkward and stilted sentence.

(k) *Labels.* People are sensitive about how they're described, so try to use the term that is currently preferred by the affected individual or group. Labels change. For example, by the mid-1980s, *disabled* had been widely adopted to describe people with disabilities, replacing *handicapped.* By the mid-1990s, *disabled* seemed insensitive and the common label became *challenged.* But by 2001, *disabled* was widely acceptable again and *challenged* was discarded as a "politically correct" euphemism. The racial designation preferred by African-Americans evolved through the twentieth century from *colored* <National Association for the Advancement of Colored People> to *Negro* <United Negro College Fund> to *black* <National Black Law Students Association> to the current preference. The preference of American Indians shifted to *Native American* and back again. In some instances, labels may have subtly different denotations (e.g., *Eskimo, Inuit, Tlingit*), or more than one acceptable label may be in use simultaneously (e.g., *black, African-American*), or a label may be accepted or preferred in one geographic area but not another (e.g., *Hispanic, Latino/Latina, Chicano/Chicana*). Be aware of what's current—and appropriate.

(l) *Suitability.* Some labels are acceptable for a thing but not a person. For example, one can say that a rug is Oriental (a rug of particular style and manufacture) or mention an Asiatic bear (a species of bear), but Asian-American people consider it offensive to say that a person is Oriental or Asiatic instead of Asian.

(m) *Capitalization.* Labels for race, ethnicity, and religion are capitalized in some circumstances.

- Labels drawn from geographic origins are always capitalized and hyphenated (e.g., *African-American, Asian-American, Mexican-American, Swedish-American*).

- Labels naming an ethnic origin are usually capitalized (e.g., *Berber, Celtic, Hispanic, Inuit, Tutsi*).

- Labels based on color (e.g., *black, white, brown*) are rarely capitalized unless placed at the beginning of a sentence or included in a title (e.g., *Black Law Students Association*).

- Labels naming a religious faith and its members are always capitalized (e.g., *Buddhism* and *Buddhists*). When used as an adjective, a religious name is capitalized if it retains its religious basis (e.g., *Protestant work ethic*; *Shinto temple*). Several words, such as *catholic, protestant,* and *methodist*, are similar or identical to religious names but have nonreligious meanings; these are never capitalized unless they are part of a title or at the beginning of a sentence.

(n) *Gender-neutral language.* Masculine pronouns (e.g., *he, him*) should be avoided unless you're writing only about men. Below are eight techniques for gender-inclusive writing.

- *Plural antecedents.* Use a plural noun instead of a singular noun. This allows you to use plural pronouns.

  Not this: *A lawyer* must affirm that *he* has truthfully advised *his* client.

  But this: *Lawyers* must affirm that *they* have truthfully advised *their* clients.

- *Recasting.* Rephrase the sentence to eliminate the need for personal pronouns.

  Not this: If *a man or woman* dies without a will, *his or her* property will be disposed of under the laws of intestate succession.

  But this: If *a person* dies without a will, *the decedent's* property will be disposed of under the laws of intestate succession.

- *Rewriting.* Rewrite the sentence.

  Not this: Either the angry father or the mother will have to change *her* attitude before the custody hearing starts.

  But this: The father and the mother are both angry; at least *one of them* must calm down before the custody hearing starts.

- *Articles.* Use an article instead of a pronoun.

  Not this: An accused person must actively waive *his* right to speak to *his* lawyer.

  But this: An accused person must actively waive *the* right to speak to *a* lawyer.

- *Indefinite pronoun.* Rephrase the sentence and use an indefinite pronoun, preferably without a personal pronoun.

  Not this: Every defendant without an attorney can ask the court to appoint one for *him*.

  But this: Every defendant *who* needs an attorney can ask the court to appoint one.

- *Repeated noun.* Repeat the noun, but only if you can keep repetition to a minimum.

  Not this: If a creditor has in *his* possession some property belonging to the debtor, *he* may be entitled to retain possession until *she* repays the debt.

  But this: If a creditor has possession of some property belonging to the debtor, *the creditor* may be entitled to retain possession until *the debtor* repays the debt. (If you have to repeat the noun more than twice, it may be better to recast the sentence.)

- *Imperative mood.* Use the imperative mood to eliminate the need for explicit pronouns.

Not this: Before the trial of a case, a lawyer shall not communicate with anyone *he* knows to be a member of the venire.

But this: *Lawyers* must not communicate with known veniremembers before the trial begins. (The pronoun *you* is understood.)

- *"He or she."* Use the phrase *he or she* sparingly. And do not use it at all if you must repeat the pronouns in the immediate context. Rephrase the sentence instead.

  Not this: Each plaintiff must file *his* suit separately, or else *he* will not be allowed to complain about the disparate treatment *he* has suffered.

  But this: If a plaintiff does not file an individual suit, the court will not hear *his or her* claim of disparate treatment.

(o) *Titles.* When possible, avoid using gender-specific terms, such as titles that have increasingly archaic feminine suffixes (such as *-ess*, *-ette*, or *-ix*) or that use *man* as a suffix or prefix. Many words have ready substitutes.

Instead of this:	**Try this:**
administratrix	administrator
anchorman	anchor
aviatrix	aviator
businessman	businessperson; executive; entrepreneur
cameraman	camera operator; photographer
chairman	chair
congressman	representative
craftsman	craftworker; crafter; artisan
draftsman	drafter
executrix	executor
fireman	firefighter
foreman	supervisor; manager
foreman of the jury	presiding juror
housewife	homemaker
layman	nonlawyer; layperson
maid	housekeeper
mailman	mail carrier; letter carrier
mankind	humanity; humankind
manpower	workforce; staff; human resources
newsman	reporter
ombudsman	ombuds
policeman	police officer
postman	mail carrier; postal worker
prosecutrix	prosecutor
repairman	repairer
salesman	sales clerk; salesperson
spokesman	representative
testatrix	testator
tribesman	tribe member
venireman	veniremember
watchman	guard; security officer
workman	worker

(p) *Gender-specific language.* When writing about something that concerns a matter related to only one gender (e.g., women's rights; men's health) or referring to an institution that is inherently single-sex (e.g., a convent or sorority), use sex-specific language. In this circumstance, trying to write in gender-neutral language is likely to produce peculiar or even absurd prose (e.g., "A person who suffers bodily injury during his or her pregnancy is entitled to damages.").

(q) *Age references.* Consider how specific an adjective of age is—or is not—before using it. It's better to specify age without qualification (e.g., *Mr. Ali is 72 years old*), by using modifiers sparingly and cautiously (e.g., *an older teenager*), or by substituting a different adjective (e.g., *an inexperienced bank teller*). Describing someone as *young* is not necessarily complimentary: depending on the context, it may describe an infant or a 30-year-old, or it may connote immaturity or vigor. Consider: *The young lawyer prepared the appellate brief.* If this sentence appeared in a negative passage, perhaps about how an appeal was mishandled, *young* may take on the sense of *inexperienced* or *incompetent*, and may subtly shift blame onto the brief-writer's shoulders. Likewise, something *old* may be either useless or venerable. And the adjective is imprecise because it broadly refers to something from the past, either the recent past <do you still have that old newspaper, the one dated yesterday?> or the distant past <that old book belonged to Henry VIII>. Applied to people, *old* suggests at least a degree of physical infirmity and age-related restrictions, especially weakness and senility. Because the connotations of *old* may be inaccurate, many people prefer the less restrictive label *senior citizen* to *old person*. The phrase *senior citizen* is not of recent coinage (it's been around since 1938). It's not a euphemism for *old* because its denotation is not restricted to age but encompasses political and social contexts as well. The term is usually applied to a person who has attained or is close to attaining retirement age, but has not necessarily retired.

(r) *Sexual orientation.* When writing about a person's sexual orientation, avoid using adjectives that connote choice (e.g., *avowed*). And avoid using adjectives that imply a disclosure against the person's will or an element of shame, unease, or guilt (e.g., *acknowledged*, *admitted*, and *confessed*).

(s) *Religious references.* Unless the subject or issue is one that plainly intertwines law and religion (e.g., freedom of religion), a legal writer who uses religious imagery, quotations, parables, and analogies will always sound biased to a reader whose spiritual background is dissimilar. And a reader who is unfamiliar with the sources of the writer's religious allusions will miss the writer's point. Or a reader might perceive an attempt to evoke unwarranted sympathy, or to sanctify a person or thing, or to unfairly legitimize an argument with theology rather than law.

§ 13
Editing and Proofreading

13.1 Review your work closely and systematically to improve the style.

(a) *Two readings necessary—three desirable.* No matter how good an editor you become, you will never do your best work until your second or third read-through and mark-up. If you mark during your first read-through—and it is always good to have pen in hand to make the most obvious corrections—you will almost inevitably be engaged in low-level editing. Only after you have read through the entire piece, and understand something about the whole, will you be able to make your best edits. They will be more searching, more detailed, and more substantive. They will look beyond the immediate word or the immediate sentence.

(b) *Worsening the piece.* Immature or inexperienced self-editors often say that their first draft is the best, and that every time they edit, their prose gets worse. An editor can indeed worsen a piece of writing, as by unintelligently applying unintelligent "rules." (One example of this is changing every sentence-starting *But* to *However*.) But this is like saying that a beginning golfer gets worse after a lesson (often true): the solution is not to stop taking lessons, but to keep on so that one reaches a higher level of proficiency.

13.2 Habitually ask yourself the six Orwellian questions.

(a) *The six Orwellian questions.* In one of the most famous essays ever written, "Politics and the English Language," George Orwell wrote that a scrupulous writer, while writing each sentence, asks these crucial questions:

(1) What am I trying to say?

(2) What words will express it?

(3) What image or idiom will make it clearer?

(4) Is this image fresh enough to have an effect?

(5) Could I put it more shortly?

(6) Have I said anything that is avoidably ugly?

(b) *Applicability to editing.* The Orwellian questions apply as much to self-editors and (with a change to the third person in #1, #5, and #6) to editors as they do to writers. In fact, they might apply with even greater force to second and third drafts, since one of the goals of the first draft is simply to get words down freely on paper. If posing these questions stifles the writer unduly—if they bring on writer's block—then they are best posed while revising.

13.3 Tighten the style by ridding the draft of verbosity.

(a) *Tightening generally.* Verbosity is like dust: each time you write, it reappears. It may be just a few extra words here, a few there. But the cumulative effect dulls the prose, which becomes a little heavier and slower and (typically) less clear. The comments that follow explain several good techniques to tighten writing. Although these techniques may seem simple, you will acquire them only with diligent effort.

(b) *Minimizing the passive voice.* Look for passive-voice constructions that you can make active (see 10.27, 10.43(c)). Instead of *The documents were then signed by Jillson*, try *Jillson then signed the documents.* Besides yielding a more engaging sentence, a passive-to-active edit usually saves two words: the auxiliary verb and the preposition *by.*

(c) *Uncovering buried verbs.* Search for abstract nouns that hide actions (see 10.43(a)). These are sometimes called "buried verbs" or "nominalizations." For example, you can often turn *-ion* words back into verbs; instead of *is in violation of,* try *violates.* Other suffixes that signal buried verbs include *-ment* (instead of *make an investment*, try *invest*), *-ance* (instead of *provide assistance*, try *assist*), and *-ity* (instead of *in conformity with*, try *conforming to*).

(d) *Trimming prepositional phrases.* Cut down on prepositions, especially *of*-phrases (see 10.43). Instead of writing *at the time of the execution of the documents by Jillson* (*execution* here being a fancy equivalent of *signing*), try *when Jillson signed the documents.* You will frequently find ways of turning a prepositional phrase into a single word (instead of *after a while*, try *later*), or even eliminating it altogether without sacrificing anything.

(e) *Replacing wordy phrases.* Edit down the typical multiword phrases that displace more straightforward words (see 11.2(c)). Instead of *a number of,* write *many* or *several*; instead of *prior to the time when*, write *before*; instead of *until such time as*, write *until.* Edits such as these become mental habits; ultimately they become second nature.

13.4 Sharpen the writing by reducing abstractions.

(a) *Sharpening generally.* Vagueness can result from uncertainty (all you know is that it was a *motor vehicle*), from the mental haze of abstract thought (you know that it was an *SUV*, but you have come to prefer generic words such as *motor vehicle*), or from a worm in the brain that makes one yearn for official-sounding prose (so that you prefer to say that *the pedestrian sustained injuries consequent to a motor-vehicle collision*). To sharpen prose is to combat vagueness. If you can say that it was an *SUV* or *car* or *tractor-trailer* or *pickup truck* or *motorcycle*, then do. If you can give the pedestrian and the driver names, then do. If you can give a down-to-earth description, you'll be writing better: *Peter Grobowski, driving his SUV, hit Jill Bartson from behind as she was crossing the street.* Or: *As Jill Bartson crossed the street, Peter Grabowski rounded the corner in his SUV and struck her down from behind.* Do your homework and get your facts right, but make your writing as concrete as you reasonably can. Try to convey a mental image of what you describe. Even if you have tried to do this in the first draft, read later drafts with an eye to sharpening the image.

(b) *Nouns and verbs.* It is often said that writers should rely on nouns and verbs to carry the message, shunning adjectives and adverbs. As the examples above show, that is good advice. But it goes too far: adjectives and adverbs can add spice to any writing. What is bad writing—and especially bad legal writing—is to just declare, for example, that your adversary's conduct was "unconscionable" rather than telling the facts that make it so. It is this sort of conclusory use of descriptive words that writers must watch for.

13.5 Try a phased approach in editing, making several passes through the document: begin with large, structural edits; then make basic sentence-level edits; then look for subtler sentence-level edits; finally, polish the piece for clarity.

(a) *Systematic approach.* When editing, you can work at any of various levels. You might reorganize the whole document. You might improve the flow from paragraph to paragraph. You might correct word choices (as when the first draft misuses *principal* for *principle*, or *lead* for *led*) and misspellings. You might correct punctuation. You might shorten your average sentence length. You might ensure that your headings will be useful to readers who want to skim the document. Or you might double-check the citations to make them perfectly consistent and fully accurate. But you will never be able to do all these things at once. For maximal effect, each type of edit will probably require a separate sweep through the document. So systematize your editing into several steps: try concentrating on so-called "macro" edits before "micro" edits. Focus on overall structure and flow before making nitpicky refinements in individual sentences. In the comments that follow are four suggested stages of editing.

(b) *Stage one: macro edits.* Check to see whether (1) the central point emerges quickly and clearly; (2) the logic is both explicit and sound; (3) every strong counterargument has been rebutted; (4) the arguments fit together and flow one into the next; and (5) the tone is relaxed but forceful.

(c) *Stage two: basic micro edits.* Check to see whether you can edit (1) legalisms; (2) *be*-verbs that have bolder replacements; (3) passive voice where active voice would be better; (4) prepositional phrases that prop up wordy constructions; and (5) any obvious faults in word choice, grammar, or punctuation.

(d) *Stage three: advanced micro edits.* Challenge yourself to cut each sentence by 25%. Collapse sentences into clauses, clauses into phrases, and phrases into single words. When you can, replace long words with shorter ones, and fancy words with simpler ones. If you find a *which* that has neither a preposition nor a punctuation mark before it, change it to a *that*; if the result does not make sense, recast the sentence.

(e) *Stage four: polishing.* Read through again, asking yourself whether you can clarify the point with an example or an analogy. Be sure that in every passage, you have been clear about who is doing what to whom. Try to be objective about whether the ideas flow smoothly, and whether a sense of momentum will carry the reader through. Ensure that you have quoted only as much as necessary; that you have woven every block quotation into your narrative, rather than dumping it on the page and hoping that it will do your work for you; and that you have supplied each block quotation with an informative lead-in before the colon.

13.6 Learn and use the standard proofreaders' marks.

(a) *The necessity of editing on paper.* Although it is possible to accomplish a great deal on the computer screen, the time inevitably comes when you will need to edit a printout. This is especially so in team editing, when several people mark up a draft and then the various edits are collated into a single document. But it is also true of a document edited by a single person. When you hold the paper, as opposed to reading copy on a computer screen, you will see further opportunities for improvement.

(b) *The value of standard marks.* Proofreaders' marks are a kind of visual jargon: they are shorthand ways of telling typists and compositors what changes to make on a manuscript page. It is important for everyone to speak the same language—to know how to mark deletions, insertions, and corrections, how to designate punctuation marks, and how to correct a misspelling. Everyone should know that a circled "stet" (with accompanying dots below the altered text) means that the original should stand without the errant edits, that bracket-like marks indicate how type should be aligned on the page, and that different types of underlining show that the designated type should be changed to italics or boldface. Otherwise, misunderstandings mean wasted time, and as lawyers know, time is money. So it is well worth the small investment of time for everyone in a law office to become familiar with proofreaders' marks.

(c) *List of proofreaders' marks.* For a complete set of proofreaders' marks, see the table inside the back cover.

> "If you know something you can state it clearly. If you have not mastered the thought you are not yet in a position to pass it on to others, although sketching a rough draft for your own further analysis often proves useful."
>
> —*George J. Miller*

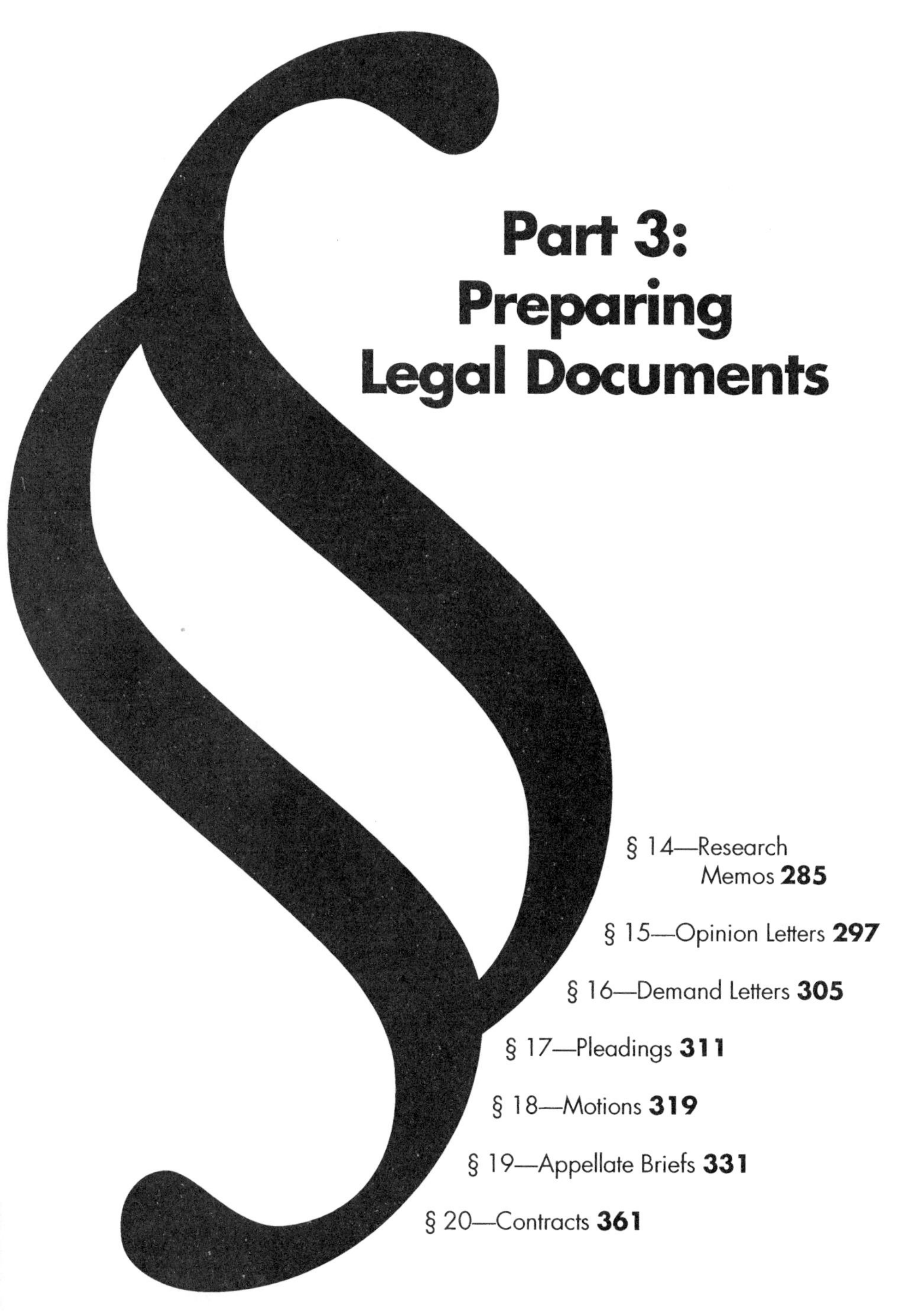

Part 3: Preparing Legal Documents

§ 14
Research Memos

14.1 Understand the main goals of a research memo.

(a) *Generally.* The primary purpose of a research memo is to analyze a legal problem—usually a particular client's legal problem—by summarizing the relevant facts, stating the applicable law, and applying the law to the facts in a way that will be readily understood. It memorializes how the law stands on one or more particular points on the date of the memo's completion. A memo must be primarily practical, not theoretical. Its purpose is predicting what a court will do in fact when presented with the issue in question. The memo is not a law-review article, balancing policy questions and weighing them first on the one hand, then on the other. It should be a blunt, practical analysis of what will happen in the courts, based on the facts presented and the current state of the law. Although the memo may deal with novel or creative arguments, it must assess them candidly. If no court has ever reached those arguments, then the memo must say so and focus on what the courts have done.

(b) *Audience.* There may be many intended readers of a research memo: the assigning attorney, the client, other lawyers involved in the case, and future readers within the organization who may someday deal with a related problem. In writing a research memo, always look beyond the immediate reader (such as the assigning attorney) and assume that other readers may need to understand the analysis. The purpose and gist of the memo should be clear at a glance.

(c) *Format.* The most important part of the memo is the front-page summary, which allows busy readers to understand quickly what your memo concerns. The summary may also remind an assigning attorney which of many assignments the memo pertains to. The first page should have an issue statement comprehensible to almost any reader (not necessarily someone familiar with your case), an answer to that question, and a reason for the answer. For this purpose, the headings "Question Presented," "Brief Answer," and "Discussion" (or "Support") are useful. If there are several issues, then the summary should contain the issues, the answers, and the reasons—all presented in an orderly way. Keep the brief answer with the question it refers to: that is, instead of questions 1, 2, and 3, followed by answers 1, 2, and 3, put question 1 and its answer, question 2 and its answer, and question 3 and its answer. When you summarize your main findings on the first page, the rest of the memo will probably fall neatly into place.

14.2 Think about the specific goals of your research memo.

(a) *Needs of the assigning attorney.* Find out what the purpose of the assignment is: the assigning attorney may be preparing for an opinion letter, a pleading, a motion, or some other document. Find out all you reasonably can about the facts of the case; if you don't, the research will be less useful. Once you know the purpose of the memo and the facts, you will be in a position to conduct research and report your findings with a reliable degree of precision.

(b) *Needs of the client.* Although many memos have only internal purposes, assigning attorneys often share them with the client. So report your research in a focused way, and double-check your work for any errors—especially factual errors that might skew the analysis. Be sure to tie your analysis to the client's particular problem and identify the important facts.

14.3 Avoid the common faults of research memos.

(a) *Not summarizing up front.* Some memo-writers avoid summarizing their main points on the first page for fear that readers might not read any further. Giving in to this fear, the writer might spread the conclusions throughout the middle of the memo or put them at the end (thinking, erroneously in this circumstance, that the "conclusion" must come at the end). The result wastes readers' time (inducing the question "Why are you telling me this?") and makes the memo less useful in future research on related points. Although the IRAC (issue–rule–application–conclusion) model may have some justification in law-school examinations, it is positively harmful if used as a way of organizing research memos.

(b) *Parroting an ill-phrased question.* Do not assume that a great deal of thought has gone into the phrasing of the question or questions that have been put to you. Two issues may be embedded in one. Or the question may have been put in a way that only an insider in the case would understand. Your job, as the writer of the memo, is to phrase the question in a way that will make the issue in the memo most easily understood. Even in the view of most senior lawyers who pause to consider the point, you shouldn't simply parrot the question as originally posed when you can improve on it. And rephrasing it will help you understand it. The assigning attorney relies on you to improve and sharpen the question based on your tailored research.

(c) *Surface issues.* A superficial statement of the issue ("Whether Micrologistics is estopped by the 1995 consent decree?") will be useful at most to a few readers for a short while. This almost inevitably results from the one-sentence *whether*-issue so common in "insider" memos. A more delicately structured issue, with separate sentences that contain the crucial facts in chronological order, will be more transparent to all types of readers ("In 2001, Micrologistics Corp. and Spamster Co. signed a consent decree in which Micrologistics admitted the validity and infringement of three Spamster patents. In 2002, Micrologistics significantly changed its product designs but faces another infringement claim from Spamster under the same patents. Given the 2001 consent decree, can Micrologistics challenge the validity of the Spamster patents in the current lawsuit?"). Keep each issue to no more than 75 words, and present the factual premises within it. Then give the brief answer immediately afterward.

(d) *Undue waffling in the answer.* Sometimes the brief answer must be "probably" or "it depends." When that is so, you must explain what your answer depends on. Weigh in with your best judgment on the issue ("X is likely because . . . . But A, B, and C are possible because . . . ."). Never hedge with vague reservations. Give your best answer with solid reasons, and to the extent that you must hedge, say why the answer is not clear-cut.

(e) *Beginning with lengthy facts.* To put a statement of facts at the fore is to begin in the middle. It is one way of refusing to summarize the issues at the outset. Although professors write law-school exams this way—with an intricate statement of facts followed by a series of brief questions—this is not a sound strategy in writing for one's colleagues. The issues and answers should come before a detailed statement of facts; and the crucial facts for each issue should be set out in the statement of the issue itself. It is true, of course, that you may want to *write* the detailed facts first to make certain you have mastered them, but you will end up placing them after the summary.

(f) *Omitting headings.* Even in a one-page memo, a few headings will serve as important guideposts. In a longer memo, they become obligatory. They will help the reader see the logical development and direction of the analysis as it draws toward a conclusion.

14.4 Study effective research memos.

(a) *Where to find them.* Outside a law office, well-written research memos are hard to come by, even in legal-writing books. But an excellent example of a research memo is reproduced in Bryan Garner's *Legal Writing in Plain English* 165–72 (Univ. of Chicago Press, 2001).

(b) *Two examples.* These samples are both internal memoranda. The first discusses a single legal question that is well settled. The second is more complex; the law is less clear.

> "When it comes to plain talk, lawyers are the worst. Most speak and write as if they live in a repository for dead bodies."
>
> —*Gerry Spence*

Memorandum

TO: PARTNER

FROM: ASSOCIATE

RE: Irwin & Nancy Brown, #01-523-5: Calculating Days in Real-Estate Option

DATE: 28 November 2001

Question Presented

Our clients the Browns contracted to buy a piece of residential property in Dallas. Under § 7(D)(1) of the earnest-money contract, the Browns paid a $250 option fee for "the unrestricted option to terminate the contract for 7 days after the effective date." The contract became effective on Saturday, November 17, so that seven days later was another Saturday, with Thanksgiving intervening. In the absence of any contractual definition of "day," how are the days calculated?

Brief Answer

For contract purposes, a day is a calendar day. Intervening Sundays and legal holidays are usually treated as calendar days. So the calculation begins with the first day after the effective date and ends on the seventh calendar day. Counting November 18 as the first day, the seventh and final day for exercising the option was Saturday, November 24.

Discussion

No statute defines "day" for contract purposes. But Texas common law provides that a day is a calendar day, unless otherwise defined by the parties.[1] A day begins at midnight and ends at the following midnight.[2] When the instrument provides that time is to be computed from or after a certain day or date, then the designated day is excluded, and the last day of the period is included.[3] Because the language of the clause quoted above provides for the period to begin

---

1 *Long v. Wichita Falls*, 176 S.W.2d 936, 938 (Tex. 1944); *City of Amarillo v. York*, 167 S.W.2d 787, 790 (Tex. Civ. App.—Amarillo 1943); *Dallas County v. Reynolds*, 199 S.W.2d 702, 703 (Tex. Civ. App.—Dallas 1918).

2 *York*, 167 S.W.2d at 790; *Reynolds*, 199 S.W.2d at 703.

3 *Home Ins. Co., N.Y. v. Rose*, 255 S.W.2d 861, 862 (Tex. 1953).

"after the effective date," November 17 is not included as a calendar day.[4] If the last day for a contract's performance falls on a Sunday or legal holiday, that day is not counted.[5] But there is no authority holding that an intervening Sunday or legal holiday is not counted as a calendar day unless the contracting parties so specify.[6]

There is no Texas law expressly on point. But there are two cases concerning option contracts for real estate and time of performance. The contractual periods in both cases overlapped with intervening Sundays and legal holidays.

In *Gaut v. Dunlap*,[7] the parties executed a contract for a real-estate sale. The agreement provided for the delivery of an abstract of title "within 10 days from the 18th day of December, 1915." The parties did not define "day." Citing the general rule that the contract's date of execution is excluded, the court held that the 10-day period began on December 19 and lasted through December 28.[8] The court took no notice of the fact that both a Sunday and a legal holiday (Christmas) had fallen between December 18 and 28. Both days were treated as ordinary calendar days and included in the 10-day period.

Similarly, in *Wilbanks v. Selby*,[9] the real-estate sale contract stipulated a 60-day period for exercising the option. The contract was executed on May 17. It contained no definition of "day." Wilbanks included the date of execution in his calculation of the 60-day period. But the court declared that the date of the contract must be excluded when calculating the last day for performance, and decided the period had ended on July 16, exactly 60 calendar days after May 17.[10] At least eight Sundays and three holidays, Memorial Day, Flag Day, and Independence Day, fell within the 60-day period. The court must have regarded the holidays and Sundays as ordinary calendar days and included them in calculating the option period.

One case, *Minor v. McDonald*, suggests that Sundays (and presumably holidays) are not counted as days and are excluded from the period when there is inadequate time to act.[11] But the

---

[4] *Id.*

[5] *Ley v. Patton*, 81 S.W.2d 1087, 1090 (Tex. Civ. App.—Beaumont 1935) (Sunday); *Glover v. Glover*, 416 S.W.2d 500, 502 (Tex. Civ. App.—Eastland 1967) (legal holiday).

[6] *See Home Ins. Co., N.Y.*, 255 S.W.2d at 862 (suggesting that parties can expressly choose to override common-law rule and include or exclude certain days from consideration).

[7] 188 S.W. 1020, 1021 (Tex. Civ. App.—Amarillo 1916).

[8] *Id.* at 1021–22.

[9] 227 S.W. 371 (Tex. Civ. App.—Amarillo 1921).

[10] *Id.* at 373.

[11] 140 S.W. 401, 402 (Tex. 1911).

period in question was 20 days, and the case's holding rested on statutory law, not a contract. *Minor* has been cited to support other statutory subject matter,[12] but it has never been applied to a common-law situation. The period in *Gaut* was shorter (10 days), but the case was decided five years after *Minor*, and the *Gaut* court apparently found that the intervening Sunday and legal holiday had no effect on the parties' ability to act. So the court counted the days as ordinary calendar days. A court today would be unlikely to apply *Minor* in the contractual situation here presented.

Conclusion

The precedents here cited strongly suggest that (1) a "day" means a calendar day and (2) the seven-day option period was not extended by the intervening Sunday or Thanksgiving holiday. The period began on Sunday, November 18, and expired as of midnight, Saturday, November 24.

---

[12] *Fidelity & Casualty Co. of N.Y. v. Millican,* 115 S.W.2d 464, 465–66 (Tex. Civ. App.—San Antonio 1938).

MEMORANDUM

To: Harold H. Jillofson

From: Katherine G. Pilchen

Date: April 2, 2002

Re: Rillerton Group Insurance Litigation, File No. 02-5949-234;
Insurer's possible communications with Rillerton's former employees.

Summary of Issues and Answers

1. **Ex parte communication with former employees.** Our client Rillerton, Inc. has sued its former insurance carrier for bad-faith denial of coverage. Rillerton is concerned that the insurer might attempt to contact Rillerton's former employees in their pretrial investigation. Are ex parte communications between a litigant and the former employees of its adversary permitted under Maryland law?

   Short Answer: Maryland law probably allows ex parte communication between a litigant and a former employee of its corporate adversary, unless the former employee is represented by counsel in the litigation. The out-of-state and federal courts that have considered the question allow ex parte contact. And the Committee on Ethics of the Maryland State Bar Association has concluded that such communications are generally permissible.

2. **Rules governing ex parte communications.** If such communications are allowed, what rules govern the communications?

   Short Answer: Professional Conduct Rules 4.3 and 4.4 protect Rillerton's unrepresented former employees. An opponent's attorney must make certain disclosures to the person contacted, including the client's identity and the attorney's role in the litigation. Also, the lawyer cannot induce a breach of the attorney–client privilege by asking about what a former employee said to corporate counsel. But the attorney may ask about the facts underlying the communication.

1

Discussion

1. Permissibility of ex parte communications

This question is undecided in Maryland. But a Maryland court would most likely follow the court decisions and bar-association opinions and comments that uniformly permit ex parte communications between an opposing party's attorney and the former employees of a corporate adversary.

A. Ethical Limitations Under Rule 4.2

In Maryland, Rule of Professional Conduct 4.2 (Rule 4.2) now controls an attorney's ability to contact parties and affiliated persons, such as employees, who are represented by lawyers. Historically, Maryland's bar association has advised us that under Rule 4.2 and its predecessor,[1] an attorney's ex parte contact with a corporate party's former employee is permissible as long as the former employee is not represented by counsel.[2]

Maryland's Rule 4.2, which has never been judicially interpreted, is patterned on Rule 4.2 of the ABA Model Rules of Professional Conduct (the Model Rule). The Model Rule is designed to govern an attorney's right to contact an opposing party. Its plain language does not prohibit ex parte contact with a corporate party's former employees, managerial or otherwise.[3] The comment explains that the rule applies to anyone known to be represented regarding the litigation, not just to those named as parties.[4] Paragraph 4 of the comment explains the limits of an attorney's ex parte communications with a corporate party's current agents and employees. In a formal opinion, the ABA refused to extend the Model Rule's interpretation to cover former employees because such a liberal interpretation would unduly restrain discovery.[5] Maryland courts regard the ABA's opinions on its Model Rules as highly persuasive authority.[6]

---

[1] Md. Code Prof. Resp. DR 7-104(A)(1) (1985). *See* Md. R. Prof. Conduct 4.2 cmt. (2001) (comparing rule and code).

[2] Md. State Bar Ass'n Op. 86-13 (1986); Md. State Bar Ass'n Comm. on Ethics Op. 90-29 (1990).

[3] ABA Comm. on Ethics & Prof. Resp. Formal Op. 91-359, at 3 (1991).

[4] ABA Comm. on Ethics & Prof. Resp. Formal Op. 95-396, at 9 (1995).

[5] ABA Formal Op. 91-359, at 3, 5; *see also* ABA Model R. Prof. Conduct 4.2 cmt. (1985).

[6] *Brown & Sturm v. Frederick Road L.P.*, 137 Md. App. 150, 180 (2001).

2

Many courts have addressed the Model Rule and its applicability to former corporate employees. The majority have held that the Model Rule applies only when there is an ongoing agency or employment relationship, and hence attorneys may contact a corporate party's former employees.[7] A few courts have held that an attorney may not contact a corporate party's former employee if the information obtained from that person could result in liability to the former employer, e.g., by respondeat superior; all but one of these cases predate the ABA's opinion refusing to extend the coverage of the Model Rule.[8] Only a few courts interpreted the Model Rule as forbidding any ex parte contact with former employees; all those cases have been vacated or superseded.[9]

The federal district court in Maryland has considered the permissibility of ex parte communication with former employees and decided that Maryland law allows contact only with former employees who have not been extensively exposed to confidential information.[10] At that time, Maryland's Rule 4.2 was nearly identical to the Model Rule.[11] Although the court discussed and analyzed Rule 4.2, the court applied proposed section 162 of the preliminary draft of the Restatement (Third) of the Law Governing Lawyers, which would impose a no-contact rule with regard to "a person whom the lawyer knows to have been extensively exposed to relevant trade secrets, confidential client information, or similar confidential information of another party interested in the matter."[12] The court cites no Maryland law in support of its decision and no other court has adopted the proposed section.

---

7 *See, e.g., Cram v. Lamson & Sessions Co.*, 148 F.R.D. 259, 262 (S.D. Iowa 1993); *In re Domestic Air Transp. Antitrust Litig.*, 141 F.R.D. 556, 561 (N.D. Ga. 1992); *Shearson Lehman Bros., Inc. v. Wasatch Bank*, 139 F.R.D. 412, 418 (D. Utah 1991).

8 *See Valassis v. Samelson*, 143 F.R.D. 118, 123 (E.D. Mich. 1992); *PPG Indus., Inc. v. BASF Corp.*, 134 F.R.D. 118, 121 (W.D. Pa. 1990); *Chancellor v. Boeing Co.*, 678 F. Supp. 250, 253 (D. Kan. 1988); *Amarin Plastics, Inc. v. Md. Cup Corp.*, 116 F.R.D. 36, 39–41 (D. Mass. 1987).

9 *See Curley v. Cumberland Farms, Inc.*, 134 F.R.D. 77, 86 (D.N.J. 1991) (noting vacation and withdrawa of opinions in the Ninth Circuit and a New York federal district court); *Public Serv. Elec. & Gas Co. Assoc. Elec. & Gas Ins. Servs., Ltd.*, 745 F. Supp. 1037, 1039 (D.N.J. 1990), *superseded by Klier v. Sordon Skanska Constr. Co.*, 766 A.2d 761, 769 (N.J. 2000); *see also Andrews v. Goodyear Tire & Rubber Co.*, 191 F.R.D. 59, 69–73 (D.N.J. 2000).

10 *Camden v. Maryland*, 910 F. Supp. 1115, 1122 (D. Md. 1996).

11 *Compare* ABA Model R. Prof. Conduct 4.2 (1986) (using word *person*) *with* Md. R. Prof. Conduct 4.2 (1987) (substituting *party* for *person*).

12 *Camden*, 910 F. Supp. at 1121 (quoting Restatement (Third) of the Law Governing Lawyers § 162 (Prelim. Draft No. 10, 1994)).

3

In 2001, Maryland's Rules of Professional Conduct were amended. The first sentence of Rule 4.2(a) is substantively identical to that of the Model Rule.[13] It clearly prohibits ex parte contact with individuals who are represented by counsel. The rule's new comment states that the "no contact" provision extends to a corporate party's "(1) *current* officers, directors, and managing agents and (2) *current* agents or employees who supervise, direct, or regularly communicate with the organization's lawyers concerning the matter or whose acts or omissions in the matter may bind the organization for civil or criminal liability."[14] Additionally, an attorney must not contact a "*current* agent or employee of the organization" if that person is in either of the two categories mentioned above.[15] The emphatic repetition of "current" strongly points to an intention to make the rule inapplicable to former employees. The comment also expressly refers to Rule 4.4(b) as covering communications with former employees.

B. Application to Rillerton's Former Employees

If a former employee is not represented by counsel in this litigation, a Maryland court will probably allow the insurer's attorney to make ex parte contact. The ABA's comments that unrepresented former employees are not included in the scope of Rule 4.2 are persuasive authority. The majority of courts have found no basis for limiting contact with former employees under Rule 4.2. And the comment to Maryland's version of Rule 4.2 makes it clear that Rule 4.2 is intended to cover only current employees. The court would probably not be persuaded by the reasoning of the courts that have found limitations in Rule 4.2, because those limits are not explicit in Rule 4.2 and may be covered by other rules and privileges.

---

13 *Compare* Md. R. Prof. Conduct 4.2(a) (2001) *with* ABA Model R. Prof. Conduct 4.2 (1985).

14 Md. R. Prof. Conduct 4.2 cmt. (2001) (emphasis added).

15 *Id.* (emphasis added).

4

2. Rules Governing Ex Parte Communication Between a Party and the Former Employees of an Opposing Party

If Rule 4.2 does not limit ex parte communications with Rillerton's former employees, then Rules 4.3 and 4.4, as well as the evidentiary rules of attorney–client privilege and work-product privilege, may still impose some restraints.

A. Rule 4.3

Rule 4.3, which covers communications with an unrepresented person, has never been construed by Maryland courts, but the language of the rule and the comment are plain. Maryland's rule and comment are identical to ABA Model Rule 4.3. Only one court has interpreted Model Rule 4.3, but the court held that the Model Rule and local rules based on it apply to contacts with former employees.[16] An opposing attorney cannot properly contact any former Rillerton employee unless the attorney identifies the client, reveals that the client is an adverse party to Rillerton, and explains the nature of the lawyer's role in the litigation.[17] This restrains an attorney from taking advantage of a person who has not retained a lawyer.

B. Rule 4.4

The ABA comment to Model Rule 4.4 prohibits an attorney from asking a former employee to disclose privileged information.[18] Maryland expressly incorporates this prohibitory language into Rule 4.4 itself.[19] Hence, an opposing party's lawyer must be careful not to induce the former employee to violate the attorney–client privilege when asking questions that may relate to communications between the former employee and the former employer's counsel.[20] The Maryland rule's comment expressly restricts a lawyer from *knowingly* inducing a waiver of privilege:

> Third persons may possess information that is confidential to another person under an evidentiary privilege or under a law providing specific confidentiality protection . . . . [P]resent or former organizational employees

---

[16] *DuBois v. Gradco Sys., Inc.*, 136 F.R.D. 341, 347 (D. Conn. 1991).

[17] ABA Formal Op. 91-359, at 5.

[18] ABA Model R. Prof. Conduct 4.4 cmt. (1986); *see* ABA Formal Op. 91-359, at 5.

[19] Md. R. Prof. Conduct 4.4(b) (2001).

[20] *Id.*; *see* ABA Formal Op. 91-359, at 5.

5

or agents may have information that is protected as a privileged attorney–client communication or as work product. A lawyer may not knowingly seek to obtain confidential information from a person who has no authority to waive the privilege.[21]

C. Attorney–Client Privilege

Attorney–client privilege is recognized as a rule of evidence in Maryland.[22] This privilege restricts ex parte communications to some extent, especially when coupled with Rule 4.4. The attorney–client rule is not an absolute protection since it protects only communications with an attorney, not the facts underlying those confidential communications. So an opponent's counsel may still ask about those facts.[23]

Conclusion

Unless a former Rillerton employee is represented by a lawyer, a court will probably allow ex parte communications with the employee by the insurer's attorney. The contact is limited only by the ethical rules that protect unrepresented people and the privilege protecting confidential communications.

Perhaps we should talk with Rillerton's general counsel about interviewing whichever former employees the company is most concerned about. Either in-house counsel or we could do this. But the practical problems here relate as much to maintaining good relations with former employees as they do to what the Maryland court might end up doing.

---

[21] Md. R. Prof. Conduct 4.4 cmt. (2001).

[22] *Blair v. Maryland*, 747 A.2d 702, 720 (Md. 2000) (attorney–client privilege).

[23] *Upjohn Co. v. United States*, 449 U.S. 383, 395 (1981).

6

§ 15
Opinion Letters

15.1 Understand the main goals of an opinion letter.

(a) *Purpose.* The phrase "opinion letter" denotes a broad category encompassing many types of letters that have different formats and purposes. There are usury opinions in loan transactions, title opinions in real-estate transactions, and closing opinions in securities offerings. Perhaps "opinion letter" would suggest to most lawyers an opinion of law, consisting of written advice provided to a client, who may choose how to act after considering the advice. That is the sense in which the phrase is used here. An opinion letter must not lull the client into a false sense of security. Relying on the letter should put the client in the best legal posture against any future dispute. But this reliance cannot guarantee that the client will stay out of court, and it cannot guarantee that the client will prevail in any resulting litigation. Another party can sue no matter how good an opinion letter is, and no matter how carefully the client has relied on it. Although relying on the letter should insulate the client against litigation as effectively as possible, the letter does not mean that the client will never need a court's help in getting someone else to comply with the law. And the letter does not provide a defense to someone else's lawsuit.

(b) *Format.* An opinion letter should open much as a research memo does, with a summary of the issue and your conclusion. Typically, this summary is less formal than that of a research memo; that is, it need not have a "Question Presented" and "Brief Answer" so labeled. The opening should set forth every assumption on which the opinion is based, the basic facts (woven into the issue), and the conclusion (with a brief statement of its basis). Then, after the summary, a full statement of facts may appear. Some opinions do not require a lengthy fact section; others, such as those concerning possible patent infringement or insurance coverage, do require one. After the summary, the body explains what legal principles apply, where they derive from, and how they apply to the facts. The conclusion then restates the main findings, preferably in a slightly different form (do not simply repeat the summary).

(c) *Answering the question.* Clients who seek opinions want to know what their rights and liabilities are and what the possible legal consequences are in a given situation. Avoid meandering before giving an answer. Although legal analysis of the client's situation is essential, an opinion letter should not resemble a treatise or law-review article. Focus on the specific facts presented and the particular legal issue to which they give rise, with a full assessment of the controlling legal principles. State your conclusions and advice as clearly as possible. Avoid giving a broad answer that could be applied to a different question or to the same question but with significantly different facts. Use plain English. If you use legal terms that the client may not know, explain them.

(d) *Alternatives.* No one likes receiving bad news. If there are alternative means by which the client's goal can be achieved or measures that can be taken to minimize or avoid harm, point them out. If you can't avoid a negative conclusion, at least avoid harsh statements such as "claims similar to those in your case have been flatly rejected by all courts." Find a softer way to express a disappointing conclusion (e.g., "all the cases on facts similar to this one have been unsuccessful"). But make certain that your conclusion cannot be read equivocally. If something is illegal, say so.

(e) *Limitations.* An opinion letter does not create legal rights, and your conclusion and advice are necessarily limited by the facts, the law, and the jurisdiction as they stand when the letter is prepared. Make sure that your letter sets them out. A specific opinion letter may have additional limitations. If the law is not entirely clear—and that is typically the situation when an opinion is sought—you will need to include a statement like this one: "It is impossible to predict with certainty what a court would hold. But given the facts as presented to me, I believe that a court in this state would . . . ." Or: "In a lawsuit, these questions would ultimately be decided by a fact-finder (perhaps a jury), and a fact-finder can be hazardous." Be explicit about every assumption that you make in rendering the opinion.

(f) *Who may issue the opinion.* Many law firms have strict guidelines on legal opinions. Some firms have an opinions committee. Typically, only a partner of the firm may issue an opinion, and often even the partner must have the approval of a member of the opinions committee. An opinion is typically rendered in the name of the firm, not in the name of an individual partner, and the firm name is signed at the end by an authorized partner. Be sure to find out what guidelines, if any, govern the issuance of opinions in the organization where you work.

15.2 Think about the specific goals of your opinion letter.

(a) *Particular client with particular needs.* Make sure that you understand the whole business context of the question. A client may not be sure what he or she really needs to ask. Work with the client to learn everything you can about the problem, and help the client see it from a lawyer's perspective. Doing this will help you focus your research and develop a satisfactory answer. And your allowing the client to participate in this way should make the client more confident in you and strengthen client relations.

(b) *Written vs. oral opinion.* You may conclude that a client's practices or intended acts violate the law, and you can't recommend a legal alternative. If a written opinion is potentially discoverable, you may decide to deliver the opinion orally—at least initially, allowing the client to respond to bad facts. (Retain in your file a detailed record of the conversation, your conclusion, and the basis for your conclusion.) If a client is unsophisticated and may have difficulty understanding a written opinion, you may want to make an oral presentation in addition to the written opinion. The two versions—oral and written—should be substantively identical. A written opinion should be marked with a legend stating that it is subject to the attorney–client privilege or the work-product doctrine, or both, as appropriate.

(c) *Legal effects.* Although an opinion letter does not create legal rights, it usually contains a statement of what a particular person's legal position is. A client who relies on the opinion may be liable for mistakes it contains. And although an opinion is not a guarantee, the drafting attorney may be subject to a malpractice lawsuit or disciplinary action if the attorney has been negligent (a question often decided with keen hindsight).

15.3 Avoid the common faults of opinion letters.

(a) *Failing to answer the question.* An opinion letter is ineffective if it does not both pose a clear issue and answer it. Not every issue has a firm yes-or-no answer, but an unambiguous conclusion should be stated with only specific and necessary qualifications or reservations.

Ex.: You have informed me that your horse occasionally roams onto the farm-to-market road next to your pasture. And because of increasing traffic on the road, you have asked me whether you have a legal duty to prevent your horse from doing this.

I conclude that you do not owe motorists a statutory or common-law duty to do so. The Texas legislature has not passed any law requiring a fence around a horse pasture, and there is no applicable city ordinance. The Texas Supreme Court has said that Texas does not follow the English common-law rule mandating fences to control livestock. The Court has also said that Texas is "traditionally a free-range state where cattle may roam unrestrained."

Reaching an unnecessarily tentative conclusion, hedged with general reservations and qualifications, won't give the client an answer that he or she can understand or any confidence in your advice.

(b) *Trying to use a formula.* Although there are common formats for opinion letters, there is no such thing as a "form" or "fill-in-the-blank" opinion. It might be possible to update an old one, but be extremely cautious—you must be sure that (1) a dissimilar fact does not change the applicable law, and (2) the law is still good. You may also have to adjust the old letter's tone to suit your own and your relationship with the client.

(c) *Leaping to a conclusion.* Answers must be supported by precedent and reasoning. But a broad or general discussion of the law isn't necessary or desirable; just explain how and why, on the law as it stands, the facts and their specific legal effects lead to your conclusion. You can adjust the depth and detail of your analysis, but remember that the client must understand how and why you reached the conclusion, as well as any inherent limitations.

15.4 Study effective opinion letters.

(a) *Review good examples.* Samples are hard to find outside a law office. Many legal-writing texts and books on practical legal drafting describe opinion letters but do not fully illustrate them. Ask senior colleagues for samples of their opinion letters written for different types of clients, especially for questions in the same area of law. Compare how much depth and detail is provided in the analysis, and the tone used.

(b) *Drafting guidance.* Perhaps the most important document for opinion-givers to examine is the American Bar Association's *Legal Opinion Project,* published at 47 Bus. Law. 168 (1991). Also valuable is the *Report of the Legal Opinions Committee Regarding Legal Opinions in Business Transactions,* 29 Bull. of Bus. Law Section, State Bar of Texas (Nos. 2 & 3, June–Sept. 1992); this report has been supplemented in 31 Bull. of Bus. Law Section, State Bar of Texas (No. 4, Dec. 1994) (regarding usury) and in 37 Tex. J. Bus. Law 1 (2001) (regarding business transactions generally). Two other recommended guides are *Drafting Legal Opinion Letters* (M. John Sterba ed., 2d ed. 1999) and Mary Barnard Ray & Barbara J. Cox, *Beyond the Basics* 357–72 (1991).

(c) *An example.* The example that follows was issued by a major California firm for a client who was dissatisfied with another law firm's services and was considering a malpractice lawsuit.

> "If . . . we are to be governed by written instructions and regulations the time has come when we, as a public, should demand that they be written in the best and the simplest English."
>
> —*B. Ifor Evans*

Belton, Forbes, Renshaw & Mitford

Attorneys at Law

666 Los Robles Avenue, Suite 1500
Pasadena, California 91101

Telephone (213) 212-8888
Fax (213) 212-7777

22 March 2002

Mr. Forsythe H. Howard
Biltmore Credit Corporation
850 E. Colorado Blvd., Suite 1000
Pasadena, CA 91101

Re: Evaluation of Weingarten & Pierce's
Representation of Biltmore Credit Corporation

Dear Mr. Howard:

You have asked Belton, Forbes, Renshaw & Mitford to review the performance of your prior counsel, Weingarten & Pierce ("W&P"), and its representation of Biltmore Credit Corporation concerning title issues in connection with Lot 2 of the Montrobles Tract, San Marino, Los Angeles County, California (commonly known as "Parcel 3"), and the actions of USMore Title Company.

Specifically, you have asked whether any of W&P's advice fell below the standard of care expected of legal professionals and, if so, whether Biltmore can now sue W&P for legal malpractice. In brief, we conclude that (1) at least some of W&P's advice fell below the level of skill and diligence that other members of the legal profession possess and would use in a similar situation, but (2) an action based in malpractice would probably fail because Biltmore will have great difficulty proving that it has incurred actual damages.

Of course, in discussing the actions and the advice of W&P, we have the benefit of examining the actions of W&P in hindsight. We have attempted to form our opinion on W&P's actions and advice without making unfair use of the perspective of hindsight. Moreover, a more detailed knowledge of the totality of the communications between the individuals at W&P and those at Biltmore might change the facts and assumptions on which this letter is based.

Although in many respects W&P did not provide the advice that we believe would have been appropriate to the situation, most of the matters on which we differ with W&P are those where competent lawyers could disagree.

Yet in one particular area, we believe that W&P failed to exercise the level of skill and diligence that other members of the legal profession possess and would use in a similar situation. Specifically, we believe that W&P's advice to Biltmore at the time of the settlement agreement between Biltmore and USMore Title was deficient. This conclusion is based on our understanding that W&P failed to discuss with Biltmore the potential scope of the release that Biltmore was to sign and failed to take the necessary steps to identify other claims that might have existed against USMore Title — claims that appear to have been released under the language of the agreement.

Based on information provided to us, we understand that when Biltmore acquired the Montrobles Tract through foreclosure, the property description attached to the deed of trust included only five of the six parcels of land at issue. Despite this, the title insurance issued by USMore Title erroneously insured the deed of trust's lien as a first-priority lien against all six parcels. This error gave rise to a claim by Biltmore against USMore Title, and the parties settled. During the settlement negotiations, Biltmore was represented by W&P. The settlement agreement contained a release that arguably released all claims, including future claims, that Biltmore had or may have against USMore Title.

Biltmore has informed us that when the settlement and release were being negotiated, W&P did not inform anyone at Biltmore about the possible scope of claims that it was potentially relinquishing under the language of the release. In other words, Biltmore did not understand the release's effect in possibly surrendering more claims against USMore Title than the claim at issue here. We believe that W&P should have discussed with Biltmore the possible scope of claims that Biltmore may have against USMore Title and the effect of the release on those potential claims. This failure, if it occurred, falls below the minimum standard of care required of attorneys.

In settling its case against USMore Title, Biltmore relied on additional information concerning Parcel 3 provided by USMore Title that proved erroneous. Specifically, USMore Title stated that the title search had been completed but failed to inform Biltmore that judgment liens had been recorded against the prior owners of the property. This misinformation has given rise to a potential claim by Biltmore against USMore Title. But in light of the language of the release contained in the settlement agreement, it is possible that Biltmore has no further legal recourse against USMore Title.

Further, before recommending that Biltmore sign the settlement agreement and release, W&P apparently failed to investigate the additional information provided by USMore Title, and failed to inform Biltmore that it had not investigated that

Letter to Forsythe H. Howard of
Biltmore Credit Corporation
22 March 2002
Page 2

information. We believe that, at a minimum, W&P should have informed Biltmore that it was relying solely on the information provided by USMore Title. In light of USMore Title's previous errors, we conclude that W&P should have independently verified the information provided by USMore Title. This failure, if it occurred, falls below the minimum standard of care required of attorneys.

Based on the information we have received, we find fault with the actions and advice of W&P in not fully advising Biltmore as a releasing party. But as explained more fully below, we do not believe that W&P's actions give rise to a claim for legal malpractice, since it is uncertain that all the elements for a malpractice claim can be shown.

A legal-malpractice claim arises if (1) the attorney has a duty to the client to use at least the level of skill and diligence that other members of the legal profession possess and use; (2) the attorney fails to use the appropriate level of skill and diligence in connection with the client's work; (3) this failure proximately causes injury to the client; and (4) the client suffers actual loss or damage as a result of the attorney's failure to act appropriately. *Nichols v. Keller*, 15 Cal. App. 4th 1672, 1682 (1993).

One of the primary duties of an attorney to the client is to advise the client of his or her rights. The standard of care owed by an attorney to his client "may be breached where the attorney fails to fully inform a client about his or her rights and the alternatives available under the circumstances." *Considine Co. v. Shadle, Hunt & Hagar*, 187 Cal. App. 3d 760, 765 (1986). *See also Ishmael v. Millington*, 241 Cal. App. 2d 520 (1966) (the attorney's failure to advise his client, failure to investigate matters of importance to his client, and failure to disclose pertinent information to his client could constitute legal malpractice). Indeed, "[n]ot only should an attorney furnish advice when requested, but he or she should also volunteer opinions when necessary to further the client's objectives." *Nichols*, 15 Cal. App. 4th at 1683–84. The attorney especially has an obligation to provide advice concerning matters "that may result in adverse consequences if not considered." *Nichols*, 15 Cal. App. 4th at 1684.

As discussed above, we believe that W&P had a duty to explain to Biltmore the fact that the release could be construed as releasing *all* future claims against USMore Title, whether or not those claims had arisen. The failure of W&P to advise Biltmore of the potential effect of the release could arguably give rise to a claim against W&P for legal malpractice.

But to maintain a malpractice claim, the alleged malpractice must have caused the client to suffer actual damages: "The mere breach of a professional duty, causing only

Letter to Forsythe H. Howard of
Biltmore Credit Corporation
22 March 2002
Page 3

nominal damages, speculative harm or the threat of future harm — not yet realized — does not suffice to create a cause of action" for the attorney's negligence or legal malpractice. *Albino v. Starr*, 112 Cal. App. 3d 158, 176 (1980). If any one of the four elements of a malpractice claim is absent, the claim will fail. *Nichols*, 15 Cal. App. 4th at 1682.

Biltmore has informed us that it is not certain whether Biltmore would have settled if it had been informed by W&P that, by signing the release, Biltmore would be releasing all future claims against USMore Title. The facts show that Biltmore potentially has a claim against USMore Title. But even if Biltmore had not signed the release, the chance of recovery from USMore would be speculative at best. If no damages were suffered by Biltmore, any claim for legal malpractice would be likely to fail.

In conclusion, we do not believe that the advice given by or the actions taken by W&P give rise to a claim by Biltmore against W&P for legal malpractice. Although W&P failed to advise Biltmore of the potential effect of the release on any future claims that Biltmore may wish to bring against USMore Title, it is uncertain whether Biltmore has suffered any damages as a result of W&P's actions. This uncertainty of actual damages would make a claim for legal malpractice difficult to prove.

Please contact us if you have any questions about the matters here discussed, or any other issues.

Very truly yours,

Belton, Forbes, Renshaw & Mitford

Letter to Forsythe H. Howard of
Biltmore Credit Corporation
22 March 2002
Page 4

§ 16
Demand Letters

16.1 Understand the main goals of a demand letter.

(a) *Gauging the reader.* A demand letter may serve various purposes. Typically, it should attempt to goad the adversary to capitulate—to do whatever is demanded. To this end, it should be reasonable and realistic, but it should probably convey the threat of litigation and its attendant costs and headaches if the adversary is not reasonable and realistic in turn. As a writer, you must get inside the recipient's head to understand what type of approach will succeed.

(b) *Meeting statutory requirements.* Sometimes, a demand letter gets sent only to comply with a statutory prerequisite for filing suit. The demanding party may hope to recover double or even treble damages; to do this, the demander may have to attach the letter to the initial pleading (usually either a complaint or a petition). In this situation, there may be no real possibility of resolving the dispute before legal proceedings begin. But the demanding party must send a letter that adequately alleges harm, requests a remedy, and allows a period for a resolution.

16.2 Think about the specific goals of your demand letter.

(a) *Strategy.* You must talk with your client specifically about what you hope to accomplish with the demand letter. Although you may hope to resolve the matter without filing suit, do not lead your client to expect such a favorable (and relatively inexpensive) outcome. (For that matter, never project an unduly optimistic attitude about what you might accomplish.) Work with the client to develop a clear understanding of what it would take to resolve the dispute satisfactorily short of litigation: returning property, paying money, acknowledging a right, or whatever it might be. Your demand should amount to something less than what you would ask for in court—so that the adversary will have an incentive to settle early.

(b) *Specificity and tone.* One legitimate purpose of a demand letter is to intimidate. Be sure that the recipient understands (1) your client's point of view, (2) what your client wants, (3) the deadline for complying (e.g., "by 4 p.m. (CST) on Wednesday, March 24"), and (4) that you have taken account of the recipient's essential position and found it either wholly or partly meritless. (You seek satisfaction only to the extent that the adversary's position lacks merit.) The tone should be a firm statement of position and intention; it should not be that of a bully.

(c) *Allowing an independent assessment.* Include enough information for the adversary to understand the claim. The letter must include enough facts (and have documents attached) so that the adversary may make an independent assessment of your position.

(d) *Collection letters.* Consumer-debt collection letters need to be especially clear and crisp. A collection letter must give all the warnings and include all the information required by federal and state law. Be sure to research the current state of the law. *See, e.g.*, Fair Debt Collection Practices Act § 809(a), 15 USCA § 1692g(a).

(e) *Deciding on the recipient.* If you are writing to a company or association, make sure you know who should receive the demand. If your client has been dealing unsuccessfully with a midlevel manager, you may decide that your letter should be directed to someone more senior—perhaps the owner or the president, or perhaps instead the general counsel (if there is one). You may want to have your client call the company to find out the name of a person with the authority to handle your demand. Get the full name (with the correct spelling) and title. There are two other possibilities. You can send the letter addressed simply to the corporation itself, at its corporate headquarters, where the mailroom should route the letter to the appropriate decision-maker. Or, if you really want to get the recipient's attention and signal your seriousness, you can send the letter to the corporate agent for service of process, whose address most states require to be filed with the secretary of state or other governmental department in charge of licensing corporations. If there is an insurer or a superior affiliate company, consider sending the letter—or at least a copy—to someone in a position of responsibility there.

(f) *Sending the letter.* Be sure that the letter reaches its intended recipient by sending an original by registered or certified mail (whichever is customary within your jurisdiction) and a copy by regular U.S. mail. If you are writing to an individual and you know both a home address and a work address, you may decide to send copies by both methods to both addresses (four letters in all). Your seriousness will not be lightly questioned. Do not, however, send copies to lots of people on your side or theirs.

16.3 Avoid the common faults of demand letters.

(a) *Typical shortcomings.* Demand letters often fail on several counts. They may be downright unintelligible to the lay recipient. They may be filled with hyperbole and therefore needlessly inflammatory, achieving just the opposite of the desired result. They may state the facts incorrectly. (Before writing, you must get reliable information from your client, preferably using documents to establish names and dates.) They may misstate the law. They may be vague about how the client wants to resolve the matter without litigation. They may get bogged down in minutiae. Avoid all these common pitfalls, any one of which might lead the recipient to question your seriousness or even your competence. After a few cases, your reputation for such excess diminishes the impact of any future demands.

(b) *Two caveats.* First, never seek civil restitution by threatening criminal punishment. This is unethical and often illegal. The Model Code of Professional Responsibility prohibits a lawyer from threatening to present "criminal charges solely to obtain an advantage in a civil matter." DR 7–105(A). Second, never, never, never send a demand letter to someone who you know has retained a lawyer in the matter. If the adversary has a lawyer, the demand must go to the lawyer—not to the adversary. If you don't know whether the recipient is represented by a lawyer, you might include this statement as a postscript: "I am writing to you without knowing whether you are represented by an attorney in this matter. If you are, then please let me know and I will communicate through your attorney."

16.4 Study effective demand letters.

(a) *Collect good examples.* Ask senior colleagues to share some model demand letters with you. If you're allowed to, photocopy the ones that strike you as particularly persuasive. Develop a file of good demands. Most jurisdictions have some characteristic variations here and there. In Georgia, for example, demands typically end with the sentence, "Govern yourself accordingly." Whether you make these types of phrases habitual in your own demands is for your supervisor (if you have one) to decide in the short run and for you to decide in the long run. But before you can decide, you must know what good demand letters look like. What you're looking for is a hard-to-achieve balance: pithy treatment yet with adequate detail; a threatening tone yet with a sensible suggestion for resolving the dispute; formal distance yet with the sense that a forceful, persistent human being (not an automaton) has written the letter. The successful demand letter requires adequate preparation, a fair amount of self-assurance, and a command of tone.

(b) *Two examples.* In example 1 below, a lawyer has written to a publisher in a borderline situation: an academic author appears to have misappropriated the title of another academic's work, with the false implication that the new work is a continuation of the old. Nothing has been published yet, and the letter seeks to ensure that no real misappropriation will take place. In example 2 below, the wrong is more clear-cut, and the demand is considerably more forceful.

> "Simple English is no one's mother tongue. It has to be worked for."
>
> —*Jacques Barzun*

David X. Sterling

Attorney at Law

Callinghast Plaza, 6040 Sherry Lane
Suite 1400
Dallas, Texas 75225

Telephone (214) 212-8888
Fax (214) 212-7777

5 December 2001

Ms. Phyllis Torping
Editor, Marginalia Publishing Inc.
717 Avenue of the Americas
New York, NY 10028

Re: Daniel Martin Schimmelman Copyright Protection
By Certified and Regular Mail

Dear Ms. Torping:

I represent Professor Daniel Martin Schimmelman, with whom you have corresponded about Bertrand Katt's annotated bibliography of articles on the English Renaissance. As you know, Professor Schimmelman's work, *The English Renaissance (1475–1525): An Annotated Bibliography* (published in 1985), is an important work of scholarship that has become the standard in the field. Now Mr. Katt has tried to appropriate this title by calling his book *The English Renaissance (1525–1575): An Annotated Bibliography.*

Before we even get into the law, you should concede that this matter has been handled very poorly. Mr. Katt didn't bother to check with the author of the seminal work he sought to update. Marginalia apparently did the same back in 1996. At the very least, these are serious breaches of academic courtesy.

More than that, though, Professor Schimmelman has been legally harmed. First, the fact that Mr. Katt and Marginalia have made it possible for *Books in Print* to record that Mr. Katt's book already exists seriously limits the marketable possibilities for Professor Schimmelman's own updating of his work. Second, this misrepresentation in the marketplace — apparently an attempt to forestall competition—suggests to reasonable observers that Mr. Katt's book is somehow an "official" updating of Professor Schimmelman's work. Third, it suggests that Professor Schimmelman himself isn't engaged in that work or perhaps is no longer capable of doing the work. And all this is seriously exacerbated by the fact that Mr. Katt has used the same title in *Books in Print*—regardless of what you now intend to call the book.

Given the harm to Professor Schimmelman's reputation, your actionable conduct could easily lead to a substantial award of damages, possibly including an assignment of all profits from the sale of Mr. Katt's book, a published apology, and attorney's fees. I therefore request that you immediately:

- Ensure that Mr. Katt's book in no way infringes my client's rights.
- Ensure that, if you do publish a noninfringing work, you include a full acknowledgment of Professor Schimmelman's seminal work dealing with 1475–1525, which was the germ of Mr. Katt's idea.
- Send two copies to Professor Schimmelman and two to me so that we can evaluate for ourselves whether any infringement has occurred.
- Take immediate corrective action with *Books in Print* and any other source that may have disseminated your misrepresentations about the existence and title of Mr. Katt's work.

These are reasonable demands. If I do not hear from you by December 19, my client will assess what legal recourse he should take against Marginalia and Mr. Katt.

Very truly yours,

David X. Sterling

Copy to Mr. Bertrand Katt (by certified and regular mail)

Potsdam, Herald & Schiffering

Attorneys at Law

419 Crystal Avenue, Suite 500
Detroit, MI 48801

Telephone (517) 212-8888
Fax (517) 212-7777

Bertrand R. Frankelshouse
Partner

7 January 2002

Francis B. Bolling, M.D.
Medical Associates of Dearborn
32345 Dearborn Parkway, #745
Dearborn, Michigan 48954

Re: Account #5214-1829-93
By Hand Delivery, Certified Mail, and Regular Mail

Dear Dr. Bolling:

Our firm represents the Michigan Commercial Bank, N.A., where you have several accounts. I write to demand immediate repayment of the $350,000 erroneously posted to your savings account.

On November 15, 2001, through clerical error at the Bank, a deposit of $350,000 was credited to your account 5214-1829-93. At the time, you had a little more than $12,000 in that account. Two weeks later, the Bank mailed out account statements, and then on December 4, you withdrew $362,519 and closed the account.

The Bank discovered the error in mid-December 2001 and has tried repeatedly to work with you to correct it. Specifically, Vice President Laura S. Diller spoke with you on the morning of December 17, asking for only the return of $350,000, without interest. You told her that you intend to keep the money—to which you have no legal entitlement.

Unless you deliver cash or a cashier's check (payable to the Bank) for $350,000 to my office by 3:00 p.m. on Friday, January 10, 2002, we will promptly institute legal proceedings against you, seeking damages significantly in excess of $350,000, together with interest, attorney's fees, and punitive damages.

Very truly yours,

Bertrand R. Frankelshouse

§ 17
Pleadings

17.1 Understand the main goals of a pleading.

(a) *What a pleading is.* A pleading is a formal document in which a party to a lawsuit sets out or responds to allegations, claims, denials, or defenses. In federal civil practice, the only pleadings are a complaint, an answer, a reply to a counterclaim, an answer to a cross-claim, a third-party complaint, and a third-party answer. Fed. R. Civ. P. 7(a). In other jurisdictions, the names may vary to include declarations, demurrers, general denials, replications, rejoinders, surrejoinders, rebutters, surrebutters, and the like. Unfortunately, the term "pleading" is sometimes misused to cover papers that are definitely not pleadings. Among these are process (a summons to appear in court, at a deposition, etc.), motions (an application for a court order), and discovery requests and responses (even when written)—none of which are properly classified as pleadings.

(b) *Complaints generally.* A complaint initiates a lawsuit, describes the harm suffered by the plaintiff, identifies the party responsible, and requests a remedy. Know the requirements of the courts in which you file a complaint. In some jurisdictions, the plaintiff alleges only the facts necessary to support the claim. In others, the plaintiff must give the opposing party adequate notice of a claim's nature, concisely state the grounds on which each claim is based, and request relief; the elements of the claim need not be established by statements of fact or law.

(c) *Complaints in federal court.* Under the Federal Rules of Civil Procedure (and many states with similar rules), the plaintiff's claim may be dismissed if it fails to state a claim on which relief may be granted. *See* Fed. R. Civ. P. 12(b)(6). This generally requires that the complaint state facts that, if proved, would entitle the plaintiff to some relief. And certain "special matters"—such as capacity, fraud, conditions precedent, and admiralty and maritime claims—have additional pleading requirements. *See* Fed. R. Civ. P. 9. For example, despite the general notice-pleading requirements of the Federal Rules, allegations of fraud or mistake must be "stated with particularity." Fed. R. Civ. P. 9(b).

(d) *Answers.* The defendant must admit or deny each of the plaintiff's allegations, and may also raise defenses. Except for special forms, such as affirmative defenses or objections to jurisdiction, defenses can usually be stated in general terms. In some jurisdictions, it is possible to file an answer that simply denies all the plaintiff's claims categorically (in an answer called a "general denial" or a "general demurrer"). Affirmative defenses and compulsory counterclaims must be raised in the answer; otherwise, they are lost.

(e) *Focus the dispute.* The pleadings should alert the court to the nature of the dispute, state the facts that give rise to the issues, and frame the issues to be tried.

17.2 Think about the specific goals of your pleading.

(a) *Protect your client's interests.* Filing pleadings can help preserve trial strategy, aid discovery, and stop the running of a statute of limitations. They may even help your client avoid going to trial.

(b) *Essential and additional claims.* In state-court actions, always assert the claims that are most important to the client in the initial pleading. Additional claims can usually be added later, after the advantages and disadvantages of litigating them have been considered. In federal-court actions, there are limited times to amend pleadings as a matter of course, after which amendments may be made only by leave of court (which is freely but not automatically granted) or by written consent of the adverse party.

(c) *Answer.* Brief, precise responses to the plaintiff's claims may narrow the issues for trial to only those that are disputed. If the plaintiff's allegations are general or ambiguous, repeated denials may broaden the issues that will be tried but may also shield against discovery and make the plaintiff's case appear weak. A longer response that recites supporting facts may promote settlement discussions, but it could also aid the plaintiff's preparation for trial. To avoid inadvertently failing to meet some alleged fact, an answer may deny each and every allegation contained in the complaint, except as admitted, qualified, or otherwise responded to.

(d) *Available defenses.* Present any specific or affirmative defenses that can or should be made against a claim; these usually must be pleaded immediately, or else they are waived. A general defense or denial alone may be inadequate because it does not encompass a specific or affirmative defense. Assert all available defenses in your answer. Some courts will not allow additional defenses later, particularly special or affirmative defenses. These are waived if not pleaded in the answer. But be careful not to assert a defense for which you have no good-faith support. The rules of the federal courts and many state courts treat such excess as sanctionable (see Fed. R. Civ. P. 11).

17.3 Avoid the common faults of pleadings.

(a) *Violating pleading rules.* Most jurisdictions have explicit rules for both the form and the substance of pleadings. Plead as the rules require, as by timely asserting all specific and affirmative defenses, pleading facts that show how venue is proper, or stating that the court has subject-matter jurisdiction over the claims and personal jurisdiction over the parties.

(b) *Overpleading.* Pleading too elaborately may backfire: what you plead, you must prove. Your opponent may argue that a failure of proof on some trivially or unnecessarily pleaded fact undermines your whole position.

(c) *Omissions in complaints.* Include every piece of essential information. The essential elements for a complaint are usually (1) a succinct statement of the grounds for the court's jurisdiction, (2) a succinct statement of the claim showing that the party is entitled to relief, and (3) a request for relief. The most common failing of complaints is not alleging facts necessary to state a claim. A necessary element may have been overlooked, or the drafter may have omitted facts that establish an element because the facts are undisputed. As a result, the incompletely alleged claim may be dismissed because no relief can be granted. Another common failing is to neglect asking for relief. Some jurisdictions do not allow requests for specific dollar amounts, but general relief—such as a demand for damages—must still be requested.

(d) *Omissions in answers.* The most common mistake that lawyers make in drafting an answer is failing to respond to every fact set out in the complaint. If the answer doesn't expressly deny a fact or allege a lack of knowledge about a fact, the fact is admitted. A second common error is failing to assert an affirmative defense or to raise a compulsory counterclaim in the answer. In most jurisdictions, defenses are waived if not asserted in the answer. The same is true of compulsory counterclaims. Moreover, an amended answer cannot undo an admission (even by omission) in the answer.

(e) *Amendments.* Reread your pleading after you have filed it. Most jurisdictions allow pleadings to be amended for a certain period without the need of court permission.

(f) *Reliance on boilerplate forms.* Consulting forms may be a good start. But whether the forms are commercial or in-house, they are only general guides. The facts will always be different. Laws change; so do courts' pleading requirements. And older pleadings are typically written in stuffy legalese. Draft pleadings in plain English, and tailor them to the facts of your case, the specific claim, the current state of the law, and the local rules.

(g) *Verbosity.* Pleadings should be written concisely and with particularity. Judges don't want to read lengthy arguments in pleadings and may strike nonconforming pleadings, sometimes with prejudice. For examples of abuses and sanctions, see *McHenry v. Renne*, 84 F.3d 1172, 1176 (9th Cir. 1996) (rejecting a "novelized form" complaint); *Gordon v. Green*, 602 F.2d 743, 744–45, 745 nn. 6, 7 (5th Cir. 1979) (refusing to struggle with pleadings totaling 4,000 pages and filling volumes).

17.4 Study effective pleadings.

(a) *Model forms.* Standardized forms are most helpful as formatting templates but should never be used as fill-in-the-blank pleadings. In other words, do not follow an illustrative form mindlessly; make certain that the form is fully tailored to your facts. The appendix to the Federal Rules of Civil Procedure contains many samples of different types of model pleadings for federal court. These are also available in Charles Alan Wright, Arthur R. Miller & Mary Kay Kane, *Federal Practice and Procedure* vol. 12A, app. D (2001). Another excellent resource is Michol O'Connor's *Federal Trial Forms* (updated annually). Most states also have formbooks illustrating acceptable pleadings for their courts. Before you begin to draft, check the local court rules to see precisely what requirements apply.

(b) *Drafting guidance.* Three recommended guides for drafting pleadings are Irwin Alterman, *Plain and Accurate Style in Court Papers* (1987); Mary Barnard Ray & Barbara J. Cox, *Beyond the Basics* 255–77 (1991); and Celia C. Elwell & Robert Barr Smith, *Practical Legal Writing for Legal Assistants* 308–75 (1996).

(c) *Two examples.* Example 1 below is a notice pleading seeking recovery of a debt and avoidance of a fraudulent conveyance of the debtor's property. The statement of jurisdiction and the facts are terse yet clearly outline the basis of the dispute. Example 2 is an answer to the complaint that complies with the requirements of Federal Rule of Civil Procedure 12(b).

> "There are sloppy dressers—and also sloppy speakers and writers. They clothe their thoughts in loose language. Their sentences are untidy. Their words don't button right. On the other side, those who make a fetish of grammar overdo a good thing and spoil it."
>
> —*Edward N. Teall*

Earl Jowitt Bouvier	§	United States District Court
	§	for the Northern District
Plaintiff,	§	of Illinois
	§	
vs.	§	
	§	
Webster Tomlinson and	§	
Burrill Stroud, Inc.,	§	
a Colorado Corporation,	§	
	§	
Defendants.	§	Civil Action No. 02-C-2247

Complaint on Claim for Debt and to Set Aside Fraudulent Conveyance Under Rule 18(b)

1. Earl Jowitt Bouvier is a citizen of the State of Illinois. Webster Tomlinson is a citizen of the State of New Mexico. Burrill Stroud, Inc. is a corporation incorporated under the laws of Colorado and has its principal place of business in Colorado. The amount in controversy, exclusive of interest and costs, is more than the minimum specified by 28 U.S.C.A. § 1332.

2. On April 21, 1996, Tomlinson executed a promissory note for $158,000 with interest thereon at the rate of 8% per year, payable to Bouvier on April 21, 1998.

3. Tomlinson did not make the promised payment on April 21, 1998.

4. Bouvier demanded payment from Tomlinson on at least five dates between April 21 and October 15, 1998.

5. Tomlinson has not paid any part of the $158,000 or the accrued interest.

6. On or about October 15, 1998, Tomlinson conveyed all his property, real and personal, to Burrill Stroud, Inc.

7. There was no legitimate purpose for Tomlinson's conveyance to Burrill Stroud, Inc.

8. Tomlinson's sole purpose for making the conveyance was to defraud Bouvier and to impede Bouvier's efforts to collect Tomlinson's debt.

Bouvier asks the Court to:

- enter judgment against Webster Tomlinson for $158,000 plus interest;
- declare Tomlinson's conveyance to Burrill Stroud, Inc. void and impose a judgment lien on the conveyed property; and
- order Tomlinson to pay Bouvier's costs.

Respectfully submitted,

____

Lawrence M. Humsberger
Illinois State Bar #57249310
Humsberger, Shiffen & Albers
315 W. Randolph St., Suite 3200
Chicago, IL 60606
(312) 476-8888

Earl Jowitt Bouvier	§	United States District Court
	§	for the Northern District
Plaintiff,	§	of Illinois
	§	
vs.	§	
	§	
Webster Tomlinson and	§	
Burrill Stroud, Inc.,	§	
a Colorado Corporation,	§	
	§	
Defendants.	§	Civil Action No. 02-C-2247

Webster Tomlinson's Answer to Bouvier's Complaint

First Defense

1. The complaint fails to state a claim against Webster Tomlinson on which relief can be granted.

Second Defense

2. If Tomlinson owes Earl Jowitt Bouvier any money, Tomlinson owes the debt jointly with Jacob Chadman Wharton.

3. Wharton is alive, is a citizen of Nebraska, and is subject to the jurisdiction of this Court as to both service of process and venue.

4. Wharton is not a party to this suit, but can be made a party without depriving this Court of jurisdiction.

Third Defense

5. The statute of limitations requires that suits to collect a debt be filed within four years of the date when the debt became payable.

6. Bouvier alleges that the debt became payable on April 21, 1998.

7. Bouvier filed this suit on August 6, 2002.

Fourth Defense

8. Tomlinson admits the allegations in paragraphs 1 and 2 of the complaint, alleges a lack of knowledge or information sufficient to admit or deny the allegation in paragraph 4, and denies each remaining allegation contained in the complaint.

Respectfully submitted,

____

Matthew S. Avant
Illinois State Bar #47748320
Avant & Carlisle
25 S. Wacker Dr.
Chicago, IL 60606
(312) 594-6666

I certify that on September 16, 2002, I served a copy of this answer by regular U.S. mail, postage prepaid, on Lawrence M. Humsberger, Humsberger, Shiffen & Albers, 315 W. Randolph St., Suite 3200, Chicago, IL 60606.

____

Matthew S. Avant

§ 18
Motions

18.1 Understand the main goals of a motion.

(a) *Purpose.* A motion is simply a request. If your client needs something from the court, move for it. You will be asking the judge to enter an order—for example, to compel discovery, to quash an indictment, to suppress evidence, to continue a trial date, to grant a summary judgment, or to change the venue.

(b) *Strategic advantages.* A motion may preserve your client's procedural rights (as with a motion requesting submission of a particular question to the jury) or substantive rights (as with a motion for a preliminary injunction). It may also serve to inform the court about an issue and advance your legal theory. For instance, a motion to strike irrelevant portions of the complaint may direct the court's attention to the real issues and reduce the number of issues for trial. Unmeritorious claims and defenses may be disposed of by a motion for summary judgment on those issues. Because most judges manage extensive dockets, the strategic use of motions may help educate the judge gradually about the merits of your case—or the lack of merit in your opponent's case.

18.2 Think about the specific goals of your motion.

(a) *Goals.* What advantage do you seek? While planning your litigation strategy, consider what types of motions may help you. For instance, if the opponent's physical or mental condition is an issue, you may need to move for an examination that could produce valuable evidence. A successful motion (to certify or decertify a class, for example, in a class action) may prove so advantageous that your opponent will settle out of court.

(b) *Proposed order.* In most jurisdictions, an advocate is required to submit what is called a "proposed order" or "form of order" with the motion. This is simply a draft of the order that the advocate would like entered, with blanks for the date and the judge's signature. Even if the jurisdiction in which you file the motion does not require a proposed order, prepare one: it will focus your mind on the precise relief that you are requesting, and it will let the court know how to rule in your favor. Do not write an order that "grants the motion"; rather, the order must be specific (e.g., "the trial is continued until March 2, 2004" or "the expert designation of Garrett Hobart is struck").

(c) *Cross-motions.* It may become necessary, by motion, to counter an adverse party's previous motion. For example, your opponent may file a motion to compel discovery; you might file an objection to the motion combined with your own motion for a protective order. Not every motion that an opponent files needs an equal and opposite motion. As in everything else, use judgment and discretion.

18.3 Avoid the common faults of motions.

(a) *Violating rules.* Federal and state courts have rules controlling both the substantive and the procedural aspects of motion practice. In some jurisdictions, the motion is separate from the memorandum in support of it, but in others the two documents are combined; learn the rules governing the courts in which you work. Rules also control vital details such as time limits for filing various types of motions and their supporting documents, as well as for any prehearing conferences. Some motions must be prefaced by a formal "notice of motion"—that is, a document stating that the motion is attached and setting out the date and time when the motion will be heard or submitted. The court may have a meet-and-confer requirement; if so, the movant's counsel must attach a certificate attesting that the attorneys for both sides have conferred about the subject of the motion, that they have been unable to come to an agreement, and that the movant's counsel now seeks the court's involvement. Some courts require an explicit request for oral argument if a party desires it. And most courts have length limits on motions and supporting memoranda. A violation of court rules may result in the denial of a motion or possibly sanctions.

(b) *Not getting to the point.* A good motion should clearly state the point for decision on the first page (as the first part of the text). Do not recite case history until you have asked for what you want. The burden of most courts grows year by year, and judges have only limited time to consider motions. So regardless of the jurisdiction, include a preliminary statement in which you synopsize the issue, say how you think it should be resolved, and briefly explain why. Leave less important details for the main body. You should try to win a motion in the first page and a half.

(c) *Overreliance on forms.* Although some courts have fill-in-the-blank motions for routine matters, many cut-and-paste forms are time-wasters. If you do not take the time to redraft the form to fit the particular facts of your case, you may inadvertently leave in irrelevant material. Besides wasting the court's time, a sloppy motion suggests that the writer is sloppy in other ways as well (in analyzing legal problems, in preserving clients' rights, and so on).

(d) *Failing to cite authority.* No order may issue without legal authority. Apart from preliminary procedural motions that are purely discretionary (asking the judge, for example, to let a party change lawyers), a motion must include the authority by which the judge can legally order the specific relief you are asking for. You may cite a statute or a case (or both), but you cannot just assume that the judge will know the grounds for your motion. Cite the authority, or else your motion may never even get a hearing on the merits.

(e) *Incorrect or frivolous contents.* Failing to double-check facts and authority is a common blunder. An erroneous citation reflects poorly on the writer's competence and wastes the court's time. The court won't look favorably on future motions from a writer who loses credibility in this way (and possibly faces sanctions). Filing pointless or repetitious motions may also be considered harassment.

(f) *Churning.* An attorney who files many motions with little success may lead the court to decide that the real purpose is delay and harassment. The client may begin to suspect that the lawyer is simply padding the bill. The court may even levy sanctions.

(g) *Educating your adversary.* Motions frequently educate the other side without any advantage. For example, a motion to dismiss for inadequate pleading often results in a court's allowing the defect to be cured. Likewise, a motion for summary judgment often sets out for the other side precisely what facts must be proved. Think hard before making a motion. Is it likely to be granted? Or will you simply be helping your opponent do whatever is necessary to have the motion denied? If the latter, you will also lose a ground for appeal.

18.4 Study effective motions.

(a) *Models.* Some excellent models appear in the appendix to the Federal Rules of Civil Procedure and in Michol O'Connor's *Federal Trial Forms* (updated annually). These forms exemplify clarity and simplicity. For a good before-and-after example, the "before" version being typically slow and legalistic and the "after" version being much more succinct and powerful, see Bryan A. Garner, *The Winning Brief* 393–411 (1999).

(b) *Guidance.* Good discussions of motion-drafting appear in Mary Barnard Ray & Barbara J. Cox, *Beyond the Basics* 278–99 (1991), and in Celia C. Elwell & Robert Barr Smith, *Practical Legal Writing for Legal Assistants* 379–402 (1996). A detailed checklist for drafting motions appears in Barbara Child, *Drafting Legal Documents* 80–82 (2d ed. 1992).

(c) *An example.* Unlike many motions, the sample omits the deadwood at the beginning and capsulizes the main reasons why the court should grant summary judgment. The supporting memorandum goes into greater depth with a statement of the precise issue, followed by a more detailed argument based on the undisputed facts and the law.

In the Court of Common Pleas
Franklin County, Ohio

JOYCE WARREN,	§	Case No. 01CVC-04-1588
	§	
Plaintiff,	§	
	§	
and	§	
	§	
AMERICAN AMARANTHUS INSURANCE COMPANY,	§	
	§	
	§	
Intervenor,	§	Judge Williams
	§	
v.	§	
	§	
JAY FINDLAY,	§	
	§	
Defendant.	§	

American Amaranthus Insurance Company's
Motion for Summary Judgment

In accordance with Rule 56 of the Ohio Rules of Civil Procedure, American Amaranthus respectfully moves the Court for summary judgment on the claims contained in its complaint for declaratory judgment. Although Mr. Findlay's insurance policy with American Amaranthus excludes coverage for his intentional acts, all the allegations against Mr. Findlay are for intentional acts. After 18 months of litigation, there are no genuine issues of any material fact relating to this point. American Amaranthus is therefore entitled to judgment as a matter of law.

Respectfully submitted,

____

Barbara L. Hull
State Bar No. 444444444
Marina H. Johnston
State Bar No. 555555555
HULL, BRIM & JOHNSTON
500 Park Place Ave.
Suite 1900
Cleveland, Ohio 44114
(216) 566-7777

ATTORNEYS FOR AMERICAN AMARANTHUS INSURANCE COMPANY

American Amaranthus Insurance Company's
Memorandum in Support of Its
Motion for Summary Judgment

1. Preliminary Statement

In deciding this motion, the Court is presented with a single issue:

> Jay Findlay's homeowner's insurance policy with American Amaranthus specifically excludes coverage for Findlay's intentional acts. Last spring, while the policy was in effect, Mr. Findlay hosted Joyce Warren at his house, where she claims that he physically abused her and attempted to kill her. She has now sued. Must American Amaranthus defend Findlay against these claims of assault and attempted murder?

Although Ms. Warren has now amended her complaint to allege that Findlay "negligently and recklessly assaulted her," this count fails to state a claim under Ohio law and should not influence the Court's decision on the critical issue posed above.

2. Background

On April 20, 2001, Joyce Warren filed suit against Jay Findlay, claiming that he had "knowingly, intentionally, and maliciously assaulted" her at his house earlier that month. (Complaint ¶ 2.) Specifically, she alleges that he injured her left eye and left cheekbone, that he cut and bruised her mouth, and that she suffered bruises and scrapes on her neck, arms, and chest. (*Id.*) She also alleges that Findlay "knowingly, intentionally, and maliciously" attempted to murder her. (*Id.* ¶ 4.) Five months later, she amended her complaint by adding a count alleging that he "negligently and recklessly assaulted her." (*Id.* ¶ 5.)

American Amaranthus moved to intervene in the case on October 26, 2001, in order to obtain this Court's determination of whether the insurer should be required to defend Findlay against Warren's claims. As fully explained below, American Amaranthus is entitled to a declaratory judgment stating that because of the terms of Findlay's insurance policy and because of the allegations contained in Warren's complaint (as amended), American Amaranthus has no duty to defend against Warren's claims.

3. Law and Argument

Two procedural points arise at the outset. The first is the standard for granting summary judgment. The Ohio Supreme Court favors summary judgment when a party fails to establish the existence of an element essential to that party's case.[1] In responding, a nonmoving party must demonstrate that there is a genuine issue of material fact.[2] This is just such a case. The second point is that American Amaranthus has properly sought declaratory relief. The Ohio Supreme Court has held that an insurer is entitled to intervene in a lawsuit brought against its insured so that it may raise questions about its potential liability.[3] This is precisely the question that American Amaranthus now raises.

---

[1] *See, e.g., Nelson v. Takoka*, 82 Ohio App. 3d 101, 107 (1992); *McKay v. Cutlip*, 80 Ohio App. 3d 487, 492 (1992).

[2] *McKay*, 80 Ohio App. 3d at 492.

[3] *Howell v. Richardson*, 45 Ohio St. 3d 365, 367 (1989) (relying on Ohio Revised Code ch. 2721); *Preferred Risk Ins. Co. v. Gill*, 30 Ohio St. 3d 108, 112 (1989) (same).

Although an insurer's duty to defend may arise even when a claim is false or fraudulent,[4] the specific policy at issue here explicitly states that this is so only "if the allegations, if true, would be covered." (Ins. Pol. ¶ 2.) All that matters is the language of the complaint—not an assessment of the insured's underlying acts or the results of those acts.[5] As the Supreme Court noted in *Gill*: "[T]he insurer has no duty to defend or indemnify its insured where the insurer demonstrates in good faith in the declaratory-judgment action that the act of the insured was intentional and therefore outside the policy coverage."[6] Hence the insurer need not defend against claims that would not be covered even if they were true.

Warren has made no allegations that, if true, would cause American Amaranthus to be liable. Although she has alleged various bodily injuries, the insurer would have liability only if these resulted from an "accident." (Ins. Pol., Defs. §, at 2.) There are only three counts in Warren's complaint, and none of them alleges the kind of unintentional circumstance or carelessness that would fit any accepted meaning of the word *accident*.[7]

---

[4] *Gill*, 30 Ohio St. 3d at 114.

[5] *Id.*

[6] *Id.* at 114–15.

[7] *See Black's Law Dictionary* 15 (Bryan A. Garner ed., 7th ed. 1999) (defining *accident* as "[a]n unintended and unforeseen injurious occurrence" and quoting insurance treatises); *Webster's New World Dictionary* 8 (3d coll. ed. 1994) (defining *accident* as either "an unforeseen event that occurs without anyone's fault or negligence" or "a happening that is not expected, foreseen, or intended").

In count one ("Civil Assault"), Warren alleges that Findlay "*knowingly, intentionally, and maliciously* assaulted the Plaintiff, causing injuries to her left eye and left cheekbone; lacerations and contusions to her mouth and face; and bruises and scrapes on her neck, arms, and chest." (Amended Complaint ¶ 2 (emphasis added).) She never alleges that these bodily injuries resulted from an accident. Yet the tort of civil assault centers on actions intended to cause harm—not on accidental actions.[8] For this reason, Findlay is not entitled to a defense on the first count.

In count two ("Murder"), Warren alleges that Findlay "knowingly, intentionally, and maliciously attempted to murder the Plaintiff, thereby causing the injuries described in Count One." (Amended Complaint ¶ 4.) Yet there can be no argument that this allegation is entirely inconsistent with the idea of an "accident." Hence Findlay is not entitled to a defense on the second count.

In count three ("Negligent and Reckless Assault"), Warren alleges that Findlay "negligently and recklessly assaulted" her. (Amended Complaint ¶ 5.) This count fails not only to state a claim that would be covered under Findlay's insurance, but also to state a claim under Ohio law. There is no cause of action for "negligent and reckless assault." Under Ohio law, a claim for assault (tortious or criminal) requires intent.[9] And an intentional act of the type here alleged is inconsistent with an "accident."

---

[8] *See Smith v. John Deere Co.*, 83 Ohio App. 3d 398, 406 (1993) ("An essential element of the tort of assault is that the actor knew with substantial certainty that his or her act would bring about harmful or offensive contact.").

[9] *See De Lisa v. Scott*, 47 Ohio App. 503, 510 (1934); *Williams v. Pressman*, 113 N.E.2d 395 (Ohio Ct. App. 1953); *Jones v. Wittenberg Univ.*, 534 F.2d 1203 (6th Cir. 1976).

Warren's placing the words "negligently and recklessly" before the word "assault" does not make the assault an "accident" under the meaning of the insurance policy. The amended complaint is a transparent attempt to bring Findlay's alleged acts within insurance coverage, but Warren's position is not supported by precedent, and "negligent and reckless assault" remains an oxymoron in Ohio law. So Findlay is not entitled to a defense on this count.

4. Conclusion

American Amaranthus should prevail in its declaratory-judgment action because Warren's allegations of assault, attempted murder, and "negligent" assault are not covered by Findlay's policy. Regardless of whether any of the claims might be true, they are not covered because they allege intentional acts that could not possibly be "accidents." American Amaranthus should not be required to defend Findlay because (a) its duty to defend arises solely from the allegations of the complaint, and (b) Warren has failed to allege an "accident" covered under the policy. American Amaranthus asks this Court to grant judgment as a matter of law.

Respectfully submitted,

____

Barbara L. Hull
State Bar No. 444444444
Marina H. Johnston
State Bar No. 555555555
HULL, BRIM & JOHNSTON
500 Park Place Ave.
Suite 1900
Cleveland, Ohio 44114
(216) 566-7777

ATTORNEYS FOR AMERICAN AMARANTHUS INSURANCE COMPANY

CERTIFICATE OF SERVICE

I certify that on January 15, 2002, I served a copy of this motion by regular U.S. mail, postage prepaid, on the following counsel of record:

Keith Fargo
297 South High St., Suite 2700
Columbus, Ohio 43215

Melanie H. Trew
444 Walnut Street, Suite 1580
Cincinnati, Ohio 45202

____

Barbara L. Hull

§ 19
Appellate Briefs

19.1 Understand the main goals of a brief.

(a) *Persuading judges.* The purpose of an appellate brief is to persuade an impartial reader—an extremely busy reader—to decide a dispute in your client's favor by holding that a lower tribunal's judgment or decision is or is not erroneous. To do this, you must efficiently convey your points, preferably by summing up their essence in a short preliminary statement at the very outset of the brief. By reading the first page and a half, the judge should have a good sense of what will follow in the remaining pages. The up-front summary is crucial to your persuasiveness.

(b) *Tone.* Your tone should be calm, forthright, and unflinching. It should not be heated, accusatory, defensive, or hyperbolic. You'll persuade by forcefully stating—but never overstating—the legal and factual support for your position. Ideally, you should set all this out in an interesting, engaging way.

(c) *State the pertinent facts.* Even if the only question before the court is one of law, a brief-writer must acquaint the court with the relevant facts. Never force a judge's clerk to dig through the record. Clearly, fully, and succinctly tell the court what the facts are before arguing about what the law is and how it applies to the facts. Although you must never misstate the facts, part of the advocate's art is to present the facts in the light most favorable to your client. After reading your fact section—even before getting to the legal discussion—the judge's reaction should be, "This side wins."

(d) *Identify the standard of review and governing law.* In at least one section of the brief, cite the appropriate standard of review for the issues on appeal: de novo, clearly erroneous, abuse of discretion, etc. *See* Fed. R. App. P. 28(a)(9)(B). On the merits, cite the applicable statutory or decisional law and explain why it is persuasive. Avoid merely stating general legal principles without tying them to specific facts. Instead of "A motion to dismiss lies where the complaint fails to set forth facts constituting a claim upon which relief can be granted," you should write: "Doe's complaint did not state a claim for slander because it never denied the truth of Roe's statement."

19.2 Think about the specific goals of your brief.

(a) *Appellant (seeking reversal).* The appellant's chief goal is to persuade the court that the lower court misinterpreted or misapplied controlling law. Sometimes, you must ask the court to devise or adopt a favorable principle that was unavailable to the lower court. This usually entails persuading the court that it would be legally sound to adopt a legal principle applied to factually similar cases in other jurisdictions. Occasionally, a case's facts may require a novel proposition of law to achieve justice. If such a proposition is supported solely by logic rather than precedent, the writer should explain why no citations are given. If the writer analogizes from other areas of the law, supporting citations should be included.

(b) *Appellee (seeking affirmance).* An appellee seeks to persuade the appellate court to uphold the lower court's decisions of law. You'll need to defend what the lower court has done. Sometimes, however, an appellee who is not satisfied with the relief granted below may seek to increase it as a result of an error affecting the relief. Or the appellee may seek to have counterclaims restored and tried (if dismissed) or retried. This is usually done in a cross-appeal, for which a slightly different set of briefing rules may apply; the appellee becomes a cross-appellant, and part of the appellee's brief functions as an appellant's brief.

(c) *Protect your client's interests.* Open with your strongest argument. Drop implausible or weak points: they will detract from your good ones. If you cannot achieve a complete victory, focus on achieving a partial victory, especially on the points of vital importance to the client (e.g., a client may be more concerned with having a right to privacy recognized than preserving an award of damages).

(d) *Enhance your reputation.* Make a good impression on your judicial readers. Advance your client's case while also being respectful to your opponent, fair in stating the facts and the law, and ethical in every particular. Be meticulous in following the court's briefing rules. Even details such as the color of the brief cover are important. Proofread your brief for misspellings, grammatical lapses, and other distractions. The attention you pay to details reflects your degree of care and professionalism.

> "I am the last one to suppose that a piece about the law could be made to read like a juicy sex novel or a detective story, but I cannot see why it has to resemble a cross between a nineteenth century sermon and a treatise on higher mathematics."
>
> —*Fred Rodell*

19.3 Avoid the common faults of briefs.

(a) *Omitting the standard of review.* An appellate court typically reviews judgments and decisions for errors. Whereas a trial court weighs evidence, assesses credibility, and finds facts, an appellate court determines only whether the trial court's factual findings were in error. In the federal system, a circuit court of appeals may reverse a factual finding made during a bench trial if it is clearly erroneous, but may reverse a jury's factual finding only if no reasonable juror could have so found. So the initial question on an appellate judge's mind is, What is the proper standard of review for each issue on appeal? Given this frame of mind, the brief-writer must focus on the standard and build it into the arguments for reversal or affirmance—never attempting to retry the case. Remember: appellate courts do not sit to decide cases. They sit to make sure that other courts have done so fairly, and they review cases with specific legal standards in mind.

(b) *Ignoring statutes and rules.* Some brief-writers either research their briefs inadequately or choose to ignore applicable statutes and rules. Either one is a gross lapse. Statutes affecting appellate briefs and the appellate court's briefing rules prescribe limitations on filings, such as time periods, as well as the form and substance of briefs. If a writer violates a rule, the court may refuse to accept the brief.

(c) *Using a shotgun approach.* Almost all judges dislike briefs that present every possible issue (meritorious or not), detail every fact (relevant or not), and argue points without making a concentrated analysis, establishing a logical progression, or citing adequate authority. Speak candidly with your client about the appellate court's disdain for such an approach. Never waste time and space arguing obvious or noncontroversial points (e.g., "the burden of proof on a motion for summary judgment is on the moving party"). Avoid boring the reader by putting a weak argument early in the brief; leave it until the end or, better yet, omit it entirely. The best briefs are short and clear; they cover only the critical issues in the appeal.

(d) *Misstating facts.* Never exaggerate or omit pertinent facts to make them more favorable to the client. Don't dramatize facts with hyperbole. A sentence such as this one might be acceptable in a third-rate novel: "It was a dark and stormy night when John Doe recklessly decided to drive without headlights and without windshield wipers, not caring that an innocent young bicyclist, intent on reaching home, was sharing the rain-drenched road." But it is not acceptable in a brief. A more straightforward approach is advisable: "One night last fall, John Doe was driving home in the rain. His headlights and windshield wipers did not work. Regardless, Doe drove west down Fibble Road around 10:30 P.M. and struck Richard Roe, who was riding his bicycle in the westbound lane." Never ignore pertinent facts, even those that work against your client. Your opponent will make sure that the court hears about them (e.g., "Roe was legally intoxicated and cycling down the middle of the wrong lane against oncoming traffic"). Egregious misstatements of fact are sanctionable; in any event, they are wholly counterproductive.

(e) *Misstating the law.* Never misstate the law, as by omitting authority that contradicts a position you would like to take. Lawyers are required to know the law and are duty-bound to cite adverse authority. Citing that authority is your best opportunity to argue against its applicability. If you let your opponent raise it first—or, worse, leave it for the court to raise—you'll not only have to argue against it but also have to explain why you didn't cite it. Another serious fault is citing authority that doesn't support the argument or incorrectly stating what the law is. The consequences of misstating the law may include sanctions, disciplinary actions, and malpractice lawsuits.

(f) *Exhibiting disrespect.* No matter how you feel personally toward the court, the opposing party, or the opposing counsel, you must always disagree respectfully. Disrespect is shown, among other ways, by the use of colloquialisms and slang; insulting language; overusing italics, boldface type, and underlining; and using "scare" quotes. Attacking the court's or an opponent's integrity instead of arguing the case's merits is never effective.

19.4 Study effective briefs.

(a) *Models.* Model briefs are relatively easy to find. Although some older texts contain well-written briefs, recently published books are the best resources because the briefs are usually shorn of legalese and written in plain English. An especially good collection is *The Great Advocates Legal Briefs* (Steven D. Stark ed., 1994). *See also* Bryan A. Garner, *Legal Writing in Plain English* 182–95 (2001); Linda Holdeman Edwards, *Legal Writing* 377–86 (1996).

(b) *Guidance.* Three useful guides are Bryan A. Garner, *The Winning Brief* 413–33 (1999); *Appellate Practice Manual* (Priscilla Anne Schwab ed., 1992); and Frederick Bernays Wiener, *Briefing and Arguing Federal Appeals* (rev. ed. 1967) (reprinted with a new introduction in 2001).

(c) *An example.* The following appellee's brief, written by a distinguished Louisiana practitioner, addresses a question of constitutionally protected rights. It was the winning brief in the appeal.

> "The best minds of any profession are never guilty of jargon, except when they are very tired. Pedestrian minds are drawn towards it automatically and to the most frightening extent. Jargon, one could suggest, is the natural weapon of highly paid people with very little of any value to say."
>
> —*Kenneth Hudson*

IN THE

LOUISIANA SUPREME COURT

FOR THE STATE OF LOUISIANA

DOCKET NO. 2000-C-2812

BERNARD POITIER, ET AL.,
Plaintiffs/Respondents,

vs.

PARISH OF DEBEVOISE,
Defendant/Petitioner.

Opposition to Debevoise Parish's Application for Supervisory Writs
from the Third Circuit Court of Appeal
Docket No. 99-01334

Brief for Respondents

RICHARD P. KENNEDY (#7788)
P.O. Box 3243
309 Polk Street
Lafayette, LA 70502-3243
Phone: (337) 232-1934
Fax: (337) 232-9720

Attorney for Bernard Poitier, et al.

Table of Contents

i

Table of Authorities

Cases

iii

iv

Constitutions, Statutes, and Rules

v

Poitier's Brief Opposing Debevoise Parish's Writ Application and Explaining Why the Third Circuit Correctly Ruled That the 1996 Substantive Amendment to Louisiana Revised Statute 13:5106(B)(1) Does Not Apply Retroactively to a 1991 Accident

Reasons for Denying the Writ

Under Louisiana Supreme Court Rule X, § 6, the Poitiers oppose Debevoise Parish's writ application. Despite the Parish's attempts to argue the contrary, the Third Circuit's decision is consistent with court rulings on the same routine legal issues since 1855, and its decision does not conflict with any decision by the Louisiana appellate courts, this Court, or the U.S. Supreme Court on the same legal issue. This Court should thus deny the Parish's writ application.

Issue

Because a 1985 damages-cap statute was unconstitutional, a plaintiff could recover unlimited general damages from a public entity both when Poitier was injured in 1991 and when he sued in 1992. Not until 1996 did the legislature limit those damages to $500,000. Since 1855 the courts have refused to retroactively apply a substantive law—such as one limiting the recovery of general damages—to divest a person of a vested property right. Should this Court now reverse a 150-year-old precedent?

Answer

No, because the retroactive application of a substantive law that divests or limits a person's vested property right violates the due-process clauses of both the United States and the Louisiana Constitutions. Louisiana courts have steadfastly refused to commit the constitutional error that the Parish here urges. The Parish offers this Court no legally acceptable reasons why it should now reverse this 150-year-old precedent. Such a decision

1

would create chaos by ushering in a new era in which constitutionally vested rights were rendered meaningless and unprotected.

Actions of the Lower Courts

The district court rejected the declaratory-judgment petition that the State of Louisiana and the Parish filed asking it to find that the 1996 amendment to § 5106(B)(1) imposing a $500,000 statutory cap on general damages in suits against the State and its entities applied retroactively. The district court held that the 1996 amendment was a substantive law, and that the legislature had not made it retroactive.

The State did not join with the Parish in appealing the district court's ruling. The Third Circuit unanimously affirmed the district court's ruling for three reasons. First, the 1996 amendment is a substantive law as it affects a person's vested property right. Second, the legislature did not expressly make the law retroactive. Third, the wording "all cases" as used in the 1996 amendment is not a legislative or constitutional term that signifies legislative intent to apply a substantive law retroactively. One circuit panel member noted an additional reason for denying the Parish's appeal: the retroactive application of a law that divests a person of a vested property right is unconstitutional.

Summary of the Facts

The narrow issue here is whether the Third Circuit and the trial court correctly denied the Parish's motion for declaratory judgment asking the lower courts to apply a 1996 substantive amendment retroactively to a June 1, 1991 motor-vehicle crash at a rural Debevoise Parish intersection formed by a State road and a Parish road. Poitier contends

2

that the crash happened because dense plant growth in front of the stop sign prevented his seeing the sign until after passing the vegetation. By then it was too late for him to stop, and the crash happened as a southbound vehicle on the State road struck Poitier's westbound truck in the intersection, causing his pickup truck to overturn. Because of injuries suffered as a result of the accident, Poitier became a quadriplegic.

When this 1991 crash happened and when in 1992 the Poitiers sued the State and the Parish, no valid law limited the amount of general damages that a party could recover from the State, its agencies, or its political subdivisions.

Argument and Authorities

A. A law that retroactively divests a person of a vested property right violates the due-process clauses of the United States and the Louisiana Constitutions.

1. This bedrock principle has been applied consistently in this state since 1855.

In nearly 150 years Louisiana courts have never retroactively applied a law that deprived a party of a vested property right. In 1855 the court held in *Municipality No. One v. Wheeler & Blake* that "retrospective laws in civil matters do not violate the Constitution, unless they tend to divest vested rights or to impair the obligations of contracts."[1] Just seven months ago, in *Walls v. American Optical Corp.*,[2] this Court held that an amendment to Louisiana Revised Statute 23:1032 extending tort immunity to executive officers applied only to claims that arose after the amendment became effective because the parties had a

---

[1] 10 La. Ann. 745 (1855).

[2] 740 So. 2d 1262, 1268–69 (La. 1999).

3

vested property right to sue the executive officers before the amendment and because the negligent act giving rise to the claim happened before the amendment.

Numerous modern authorities follow the 1855 precedent. For example, in *Lott v. Haley*, this Court refused to retroactively apply Louisiana Revised Statute 9:5628—a limitations statute—to a claim that arose before this law was enacted because "to do so would divest plaintiff of his vested right in his cause of action in violation of the due process guarantees under the state and federal constitutions."[3] As a result, the medical-malpractice plaintiff, who had sued more than three years before the new limitations statute became effective, was not bound by that later-enacted limitations period because the statute disturbed a preexisting right.

Of similar effect was *Gilboy v. American Tobacco Company*,[4] in which this Court held that the legislature's elimination of a theory of recovery from the State's Products Liability Act—abolishing the category of things unreasonably dangerous per se—altered a substantive right and thus did not apply retroactively. Two years later, in 1993, this Court again refused to apply a substantive statute retroactively, this time holding that a 1989 amendment to Louisiana Revised Statute 23:1103 was not retroactive because that statute abolished the employee's right to recover general damages and created a right in the employer's favor to be paid out of any damages the employee recovered in a third-party suit.[5]

---

[3] 370 So. 2d 521, 524 (La. 1979).

[4] 582 So. 2d 1263, 1264–65 (La. 1991).

[5] *St. Paul Fire & Marine Ins. Co. v. Smith*, 609 So. 2d 809, 822 (La. 1993).

4

2. Recent decisions of this Court continue to rely on the same principle.

This Court soon had yet another opportunity to reaffirm this principle, holding in *Aucoin v. State*[6] that amendments to Louisiana Civil Code Articles 2323 and 2324 were substantive and nonretroactive because they shifted liability obligations, which changed the amount of recoverable damages. In particular, this Court refused to retroactively apply a 1996 amendment to Article 2324(B), which adopted pure comparative fault, to a 1990 accident that would have reduced the Department of Transportation and Development's liability from 50% to 15%; the amendment was found to be substantive in that it changed the amount of recoverable damages.

The same broad holding obtained in such other cases as *Segura v. Frank*[7] ("[E]ven where the legislature has expressed its intent to give a substantive law retroactive effect, the law may not be applied retroactively if it would impair contractual obligations or disturb vested rights."); *Graham v. Sequoya Corp.*[8] (refusing to retroactively apply a statutory amendment giving parties the right to contract for fees exceeding the standards set by the Code of Professional Responsibility because suit was filed before the statute became effective); *Burmaster v. Gravity Drainage District No. 2*[9] ("Where an injury has occurred for which the injured party has a cause of action, such cause of action is a vested property right which is protected by the guarantee of due process."); and *Terrebonne v. South*

---

[6] 712 So. 2d 62, 67 (La. 1998).

[7] 630 So. 2d 714, 721 (La. 1994).

[8] 478 So. 2d 1223, 1226 (La. 1986).

[9] 366 So. 2d 1381, 1387 (La. 1978).

5

Lafourche Tidal Control Levee District[10] ("[T]he Legislature simply cannot take away an existing cause of action based upon substantive rights which had clearly been granted by the legislature during the preceding session and had become vested on the effective date of the legislation.").[11]

From this long and unbroken line of cases, certain immutable legal principles may be adduced:

- Both the United States and the Louisiana Constitutions prohibit the retroactive application of a substantive law that deprives a person of a vested property right or impairs a contractual obligation.[12]

- "Once a party's cause of action accrues, it becomes a vested property right that may not constitutionally be divested."[13]

- A cause of action accrues when the party has the right to sue.[14]

- An amendment that changes the amount of damages is a substantive law.[15]

---

[10] 445 So. 2d 1221, 1224 (La. 1984)

[11] Circuit courts, too, have applied the rule against retroactivity to a substantive law. *See, e.g.*, *Jamison v. Hilton*, 721 So. 2d 494, 497 (La. Ct. App. 1998), *writ denied*, 730 So. 2d 871 (La. 1999) (refusing to retroactively apply a statute barring a plaintiff's suit against the state unless the plaintiff requested that the petition be served within 90 days after filing suit); *Batiste v. Capitol Home Health*, 699 So. 2d 395, 398 (La. Ct. App. 1997) (refusing to retroactively apply a 1995 amendment giving an employer 60 days to pay a claimant's medical bills to a 1993 accident, a time when the law required payment within 14 days, because the 14-day rule was a "vested constitutional right.").

[12] U.S. Const. amend. XIV, § 1; U.S. Const. art. I, § 10 cl. 1; La. Const. art. I, § 2; La. Const. art. I, § 23; *Cole v. Celotex Corp.*, 599 So. 2d 1058, 1063 n.15 (La. 1992); *Segura*, 630 So. 2d at 733.

[13] *Cole*, 599 So. 2d at 1063; *see also Walls*, 740 So. 2d at 1268–69 (La. 1999); *Aucoin*, 712 So. 2d at 67.

[14] *Terrebonne*, 445 So. 2d at 1224; *Cole*, 599 So. 2d at 1063; *Abate v. Healthcare Int'l, Inc.*, 560 So. 2d 812, 819 (La. 1990).

[15] *Aucoin*, 712 So. 2d at 67; *Socorro v. City of New Orleans*, 579 So. 2d 931, 944 (La. 1991); *St. Paul Fire & Marine Ins. Co.*, 609 So. 2d at 817.

6

- "An injured party's cause of action is a vested property right which is protected by the guarantee of due process."[16]
- The parties' rights and duties are determined when the suit is filed.[17]
- Even when the legislature expressly states that a substantive law applies retroactively—which, as explained below, is not true here—the courts refuse to do so if its retroactive application disturbs a vested right.[18]

3. The Parish offers this Court no reason to abandon this ancient principle.

Though the Parish cannot and does not point to any contrary authority, it is surprising that its brief to this Court fails to cite (much less to distinguish) any of these controlling precedents. And the Parish offers no reason for this Court to abandon this precedent.

Both the Louisiana Revised Statues and the Louisiana Civil Code prohibit the retroactive application of a substantive law absent a contrary legislative expression.[19] But this Court has never wavered from its prohibition against even the express retroactive application of a substantive law if it disturbs vested rights or impairs contractual obligations.[20] The reason for this bedrock legal principle is simple: the courts cannot give substantive laws retroactive effect without implicating the due-process and contract clauses of the United States and the Louisiana Constitutions.[21]

---

[16] *Davis v. Willis-Knighton Med. Ctr.*, 738 So. 2d 1191, 1194 (La. Ct. App.), *writ denied*, No. 99-C-2712, 1999 WL 12044756 (La. Dec. 10, 1999) (citing *Burmaster*, 366 So. 2d at 1387).

[17] *Graham*, 478 So. 2d at 1226.

[18] *Segura*, 630 So. 2d at 721; *Long v. Ins. Co. of N. Am.*, 595 So. 2d 636, 639 (La. 1992) (quoting *Plebst v. Barnwell Drilling Co.*, 148 So. 2d 584, 588 (La. 1963)).

[19] La. Rev. Stat. Ann. § 1:2 (West 1987); La. Civ. Code Ann. art. 6 (West 1993).

[20] *See Keith v. U.S. Fid. & Guar. Co.*, 694 So. 2d 180, 183 (La. 1997).

[21] *Burmaster*, 366 So. 2d at 1387.

7

Thus, this Court does not have to waste its valuable time addressing the Parish's two red-herring issues: (1) whether an unconstitutional 1985 general-damages-cap law was viable in 1991 because it was not until 1993 that this Court declared the law unconstitutional; and (2) whether the 1996 amendment to § 5106(B) applies retroactively, because the Parish knows that it is a substantive law that diminishes a party's pre-1996 vested property right to fully recover his general damages. Consequently, this Court need only follow its 150-year-old precedent in denying the Parish's writ application and affirming the lower courts' decisions holding that this 1996 substantive amendment creating a $500,000 general-damages cap does not apply retroactively to a 1991 motor-vehicle crash.

And as discussed in the following sections, this Court has still more reasons to deny the Parish's writ application.

B. Louisiana did not have a general-damages cap until 1996.

1. This Court held in 1993 and 1994 that the legislature's 1985 attempts to limit general damages and prejudgment interest in suits against public entities violated the 1974 Constitution.

Louisiana's 1974 Constitution—which provides in Article I, § 1 that government originates with the people and is founded on their will alone—placed no limit on general damages. Because the legislature thus lacked constitutional authority to limit the State's liability on its own, this Court held that the legislature unconstitutionally passed two laws in 1985.

In 1993, this Court held in *Chamberlain v. State* that the amendment to Louisiana Revised Statute 13:5106(B), imposing a $500,000 cap on general damages awarded in suits

8

against the State, its agencies, and its political subdivisions, was unconstitutional because it contravened the Constitution's Article XII, § 10 proscription against sovereign immunity.[22]

The next year, relying on *Chamberlain*, this Court held in *Rick v. State* that the legislature had unconstitutionally enacted Louisiana Revised Statute 13:5112(C), limiting prejudgment interest to 6% on judgments against state entities, because this law also violated the Constitution's prohibition against sovereign immunity.[23]

It is against this backdrop that Poitier asks for nothing more than reaffirmation of what this Court has already decided: that the 1995 and 1996 laws creating a general-damages cap are substantive laws that are not retroactive.

2. A 1995 constitutional amendment permits the legislature to limit general damages on existing and future claims in suits against public entities. But in 1999 this Court held that this permissive, non-self-executing amendment requires that the legislature clearly and expressly state if the general-damages cap applies retroactively.

By 1995 the legislature realized that it needed a constitutional amendment before it could limit general damages and change the legal interest rate for judgments against the State and its political subdivisions. Reacting to *Chamberlain*, the people amended constitutional Article XII, § 10(C); only then was the legislature free to validly reenact Louisiana Revised Statute 13:5106(B).

A constitutional amendment and two laws thus became effective on November 23, 1995. First, amended constitutional Article XII, § 10(C) provided that the legislature *may* limit the amount of recoverable damages in suits against the State and its political

[22] 624 So. 2d 874, 888 (La. 1993).

[23] 630 So. 2d 1271, 1277 (La. 1994).

9

subdivisions to *existing as well as future claims*.[24] Second, contingent upon the passage of this constitutional amendment, the legislature amended Louisiana Revised Statute 13:5106(B) to create a $750,000 general-damages cap, and Louisiana Revised Statute 13:5112(C) to provide for 6% prejudgment interest.

After the 1995 vote of the people, the legislature now had constitutional permission to retroactively impose a general-damages cap on judgments against the State and its political subdivisions. But the Second Circuit Court refused, in *Holt v. State*,[25] to retroactively apply the 1995 general-damages cap to a 1985 automobile accident because the legislature did not make the 1995 amendment applicable to existing claims and because *Chamberlain* had held that the 1985 statutory cap was unconstitutional.

Then in May 1999, a unanimous Supreme Court further clarified the effect of the constitutional amendment by holding in *Jacobs v. Town of Bunkie* that the language and functions of Article XII, § 10 (B) and (C) were not self-executing and thus required the legislature to provide supplemental legislation to limit the liability of the state or any public entity.[26] As this Court noted, subdivision (C) uses permissive language: "the legislature by law *may* limit . . . the . . . liability of the state."[27] *Jacobs* narrows the focus to whether the legislature, in its 1996 amendments to § 5106, clearly and expressly made that substantive law retroactive.

---

[24] La. Const. art. XII, § 10.

[25] 671 So. 2d 1164, 1174 (La. Ct. App.), *writ denied*, 675 So. 2d 1080 (La. 1996).

[26] 737 So. 2d 14, 19 (La. 1999).

[27] *Id.* at 18 (emphasis added).

10

3. In 1996 the legislature amended § 5106(B) to impose a $500,000 general-damages cap and to create a medical reversionary trust.

The legislature amended § 5106, effective in May 1996, in two respects. First, it amended subsection (B)(1) to reduce the general-damages cap from $750,000 per person per accident to $500,000 total per accident. Second, it added subsections (B)(3) and (4), creating a reversionary trust and derivative claims, respectively. Although the Parish proclaims—with no citation to any authority—on page 19 of its brief that the 1996 amendment was done "[i]n response to calls that the 1995 damages cap should be made to apply to all cases," this Court should summarily reject this unsupported claim. Nothing, including the wording itself, suggests that the legislature chose or did not choose any particular language in going from the 1995 to the 1996 amendment in "response" to some outcry that the State's damages exposure should be minimized before as well as after the fact.

Under well-settled law, a cause of action arises when the negligent or tortious conduct causes injury.[28] Because Poitier's cause of action arose in 1991, the issue is no more complicated than whether the 1996 amendatory $500,000 statutory aggregate cap applies retroactively to an accident that occurred five years earlier.

[28] *Abate*, 560 So. 2d at 819; *Lemaire v. Est. of Harrington*, 701 So. 2d 484, 485–86 (La. Ct. App. 1997), *writ denied*, 709 So. 2d 785 (La. 1998).

11

C. An unconstitutional law is void *ab initio*: it is not a law, it confers no rights, and it imposes no duties.

1. The Parish's argument that a general-damages cap existed in 1991 is unsound.

The Parish posits an unusual thesis for its argument that a general-damages cap existed in 1991 to support its contention that the 1996 amendment to § 5106(B)(1) applies to this 1991 crash. The incorrect syllogism goes like this:

Major Premise: An otherwise unconstitutional law is constitutional until the date on which the Supreme Court declares it unconstitutional.
Minor Premise: This Court did not declare the 1985 damages-cap law in suits against public entities[29] unconstitutional until *Chamberlain* in 1993, two years after Poitier's crash.
Conclusion: The unconstitutional 1985 $500,000 damages cap applies to Poitier's 1991 crash.

Understandably, the Parish cites no authority for its proposition, and this Court can quickly dispose of this curious argument. First, *Chamberlain* merely confirmed what Article XII, § 10(A) of the 1974 Constitution made clear: sovereign immunity does not exist in Louisiana. Second, nearly 60 years ago this Court negated the Parish's argument in *Flournoy v. First National Bank of Shreveport.*[30] In dealing with unconstitutional tax legislation, *Flournoy* quoted from a United States Supreme Court decision in holding that:

> An unconstitutional act is not a law; it confers no rights; it imposes no duties; it affords no protection; it creates no office; it is, in legal contemplation, *as inoperative as though it had never been passed.*[31]

---

[29] Effective September 6, 1985, the legislature amended Section 5106(B)(1) to impose a $500,000 general-damages cap in suits against public entities. *See Dubois v. State Farm Ins. Co.*, 571 So. 2d 201, 206 (La. Ct. App. 1990), *writ denied*, 575 So. 2d 367 (La. 1991).

[30] 3 So. 2d 244 (La. 1941).

[31] *Id.* at 248 (emphasis added) (quoting *Norton v. Shelby County*, 118 U.S. 425, 442 (1886)); *Vieux Carre Prop. Owners & Assocs., Inc. v. City of New Orleans*, 167 So. 2d 367, 371 (La. 1964) (*citing City of New Orleans v. Levy*, 64 So. 2d 798 (La. 1953)).

12

That constitutional-law rule applies here with equal vigor. The Parish's implausible argument must suffer the same fate as did the *Flournoy* unconstitutional tax law, because the Parish simply cannot breathe life into a law that this Court has declared unconstitutional. In sum, no general-damages cap existed in 1991; the 1985 cap was a legal nullity.

In refusing to apply the 1985 general-damages cap to a 1987 accident, *Chamberlain* made it clear that constitutional Article XII, § 10(C) provides that the State is not immune from tort damages and that "[l]imiting recoverable tort damages thus flies directly in the face of the constitutional proscription that the state waive sovereign immunity from liability for injury to person or property."[32] This Court continued, "[W]hen immunity has been abolished, *decreasing recovery from full compensation to a maximum ceiling partially resurrects immunity*."[33]

The Parish thus wrongly asserts that Poitier was burdened by a 1985 general-damages cap that this Court later ruled unconstitutional; taken together, *Chamberlain* and Louisiana law on the effect of unconstitutional laws are far more than the mere nuisance that the Parish would implicitly have them be. And the Parish wrongly asserts that the 1996 law merely reaffirmed an unconstitutional 1985 general-damages cap.

---

[32] 624 So. 2d at 883 (internal quotations omitted).

[33] *Id.* at 884 (emphasis added).

13

2. In 1993 when *Chamberlain* held that the 1985 general-damages cap was unconstitutional, the Poitiers' claim was pending.

Apparently the Parish misconstrues the narrow exception to the general rule that an unconstitutional law is void. *Flournoy* recognized that the general rule cannot apply to a final decision because "'[t]he past cannot always be erased by a new judicial declaration.'"[34] The Poitiers concede that had their case become final before the *Chamberlain* decision and had the issue of the unconstitutionality of § 5106(B)(1) not been raised—something the Parish assumes that Poitier would not have done[35]—and had this Court imposed the general-damages cap, then Poitier would have been bound by that decision. But this rank speculation does not apply to the facts here. This is a pending case, and Poitier contends that no general-damages cap applies to this 1991 crash.

This is precisely what the First Circuit decided in *Magee v. Landrieu*,[36] in which the issues were whether *Chamberlain*'s anti-cap decision and *Rick v. State*'s[37] anti-prejudgment-interest limitation applied to pending actions. Following an earlier Supreme Court decision, *Magee* held that both *Chamberlain* and *Rick* applied to the pending claims because no final judgment had been rendered on the dates on which those decisions were rendered. In the court's own words, "[T]he holding in *Chamberlain* is applicable to any and all judgments that were not final, definitive and executory as of the date of rendition of

---

[34] 3 So. 2d at 249 (quoting *Chicot County Drainage Dist. v. Baxter State Bank*, 308 U.S. 371, 374 (1940)).

[35] Parish Brief at 9–10. This is not only purely speculative but also wrong: Poitier indeed contends that the general-damages cap does not apply to this 1991 crash, and there is no reason to suppose that he would, pre-*Chamberlain*, have meekly acceded to the statute's obvious unconstitutionality.

[36] 653 So. 2d 62, 64 (La. Ct. App.), *writ denied*, 654 So. 2d 319 (La. 1995).

[37] 630 So. 2d at 1277.

14

Chamberlain, September 3, 1993. The same is true for the holding in *Rick*, which had a rendition date of January 14, 1994."[38]

The courts consider three factors in deciding whether a decision should be applied retroactively.[39] First, the courts do not retroactively apply a decision that establishes a new legal principle, either by overruling clear past precedent on which the litigants may have relied or by deciding an issue of first impression whose resolution is not clearly foreshadowed. This factor does not apply here because *Chamberlain*, in declaring the 1985 act unconstitutional, simply upheld the 1974 Constitution's sovereign-immunity prohibition. Second, the courts weigh the merits and faults in each case by looking to the history of the rule in question, its purpose and effect, and whether retrospective application will further or retard its operation. Again, applying *Chamberlain* retroactively furthers the meaning of the 1974 Constitution's waiver of sovereign immunity. Third, the courts weigh the inequity that a retroactive application may impose. Again, the inequity in failing to retroactively apply *Chamberlain* would be to deprive Poitier of a vested property right, something prohibited by the due-process clauses of both the federal and state constitutions.

The Parish tries for two equity-like arguments in suggesting that the Poitiers' only expectation when suing in 1992 could have been to recover $500,000, based on the 1985 cap; and that vast liabilities might ensue if this Court affirms the decisions below. As for the first, what the Poitiers expected was that the legislature would adhere to the Constitution; since it did not, a rational litigant would expect that in *some* case—whether

---

[38] *Magee*, 653 So. 2d at 68.

[39] *Lovell v. Lovell*, 378 So. 2d 418, 421–22 (La. 1979); *Magee*, 653 So. 2d at 66.

15

his or someone else's—this Court was bound to eventually undo an unconstitutional law.[40] The "vast liabilities" argument similarly fails as a point of equity: the Poitiers' case is bound to be one of only a few still pending that were filed when an unconstitutional statute was technically on the books but had not yet been declared to be unconstitutional.

The Court's holding in *Chamberlain* that the 1985 general-damages cap was unconstitutional applies to Poitier's 1991 crash. Because the 1985 cap was void, it did not exist in 1991.

3. Contrary to the Parish's argument, the 1985 general-damages-cap law was not a "defect" and Poitier is not seeking a "windfall."

Undaunted, the Parish would have this Court believe that the 1985 general-damages-cap law was problematic simply because of a "defect" in Louisiana's Constitution.[41] *Chamberlain* did not use the word "defect" to declare the 1985 act unconstitutional. Rather, it classified the law as unconstitutional because it violated the 1974 Constitution's prohibition against any limitation on the State's waiver of sovereign immunity. The Parish correctly notes that the people have the right to amend the Constitution,[42] and they did that in late 1995, by amending Article XII, § 10(A) to give the legislature permission to limit the State's liability. (The vote could, of course, have gone the other way, a possibility that the Parish implicitly ignores by characterizing the 1985 law as merely based on a defect.) Even in the face of *Chamberlain*, the Parish contends that Poitier seeks a "windfall"[43]—yet

---

[40] *Chamberlain* was already pending when the Poitiers sued.

[41] Parish Brief at 7, 9, 10.

[42] *Id.* at 8.

[43] *Id.* at 7.

16

it is hardly a windfall to assert a constitutional right to recover full general damages unencumbered by an unconstitutional 1985 law or by a 1996 substantive law that constitutionally cannot apply retroactively to deprive Poitier of a vested right to recover his full damages.

Interestingly, the Parish cites *Walls v. American Optical Corp.*,[44] from which Poitier quotes because it nicely summarizes his position that his right to recover his full damages vested when he was injured in 1991:

> Once a party's cause of action accrues, it becomes a vested property right that may not constitutionally be divested. Therefore, statutes enacted after the acquisition of such a vested property right . . . cannot be retroactively applied so as to divest plaintiff of his vested right in his cause of action because such a retroactive application would contravene the due process guarantees.[45]

Having acknowledged this constitutional proposition, the Parish then concedes that Poitier's right vested on June 1, 1991—the date on which he became a quadriplegic.[46]

To conclude, this Court should reject the Parish's arguments because they would require the Court to:

- find that *Chamberlain* merely found that the 1985 general-damages-cap act was a "defect," thus ignoring this Court's holding that the act was unconstitutional;
- ignore the minor "defect" of its 1993 declaration that the 1985 general-damages-cap law was unconstitutional and to now apply the unconstitutional 1985 law to this 1991 crash; and
- overturn a 150-year-old constitutional proposition that an unconstitutional act is void *ab initio*.

---

[44] 740 So. 2d 1262.

[45] *Id.* at 1268–69 (internal citations omitted).

[46] Parish Brief at vii, 5.

17

Conclusion

The outcome of the Parish's writ application rests on eight legal doctrines, all of which show that the Parish's position is folly:

- Both the United States and the Louisiana Constitutions prohibit the retroactive application of a substantive law that deprives a person of a vested property right or impairs a contractual obligation. So even when the legislature expressly states that a substantive law applies retroactively, the courts refuse to do so if its retroactive application disturbs a vested right.
- Once a party's cause of action accrues, it becomes a vested property right that may not constitutionally be divested.
- A cause of action accrues when the party has the right to sue.
- An amendment that changes the amount of damages is a substantive law.
- An injured party's cause of action is a vested property right that is protected by the guarantee of due process.
- The parties' rights and duties are determined when the suit is filed.
- The 1996 amendment to § 5106(B) imposing a $500,000 general-damages cap is a substantive law.
- The word "all" is not a term that the legislature uses to clearly signal its intent to apply a substantive law retroactively.

The Parish cannot avoid the simple fact that since 1885 Louisiana courts have steadfastly refused to apply a substantive law retroactively if it deprives a party of a vested property right. A damages claim is a vested property right. A law limiting a party's damages recovery is a substantive law. In 1991, when Poitier became dead from the neck down in a motor-vehicle crash, the State imposed no lawful limitation on general damages in suits against public entities. The Parish has not given this Court one reason to overturn a

18

nearly 150-year-old rule prohibiting the retroactive application of a law that deprives a person of a vested property right.

Surely this Court has more pressing business than to take the time to affirm yet again such a bedrock, unremarkable rule of law. It should therefore deny Debevoise Parish's petition for writ of certiorari.

Respectfully submitted,

RICHARD R. KENNEDY (#7788)
P.O. Box 3243
309 Polk Street
Lafayette, LA 70502-3243
Phone: (337) 232-1934
Fax: (337) 232-1905
Attorney for Bernard Poitier, et al.

19

Verification

STATE OF LOUISIANA

PARISH OF DEBEVOISE

BEFORE ME, the undersigned authority, personally came and appeared Richard R. Kennedy, who, after being duly sworn, did depose that he is the attorney for the Poitiers in the above-captioned matter; that all facts contained in the foregoing original brief are true and correct to the best of his knowledge and belief; and that he has served a copy of this original brief on the following parties by depositing the same in the United States mail, postage prepaid, and properly addressed as follows:

Mr. Frank Insko
Attorney at Law
P.O. Drawer 4527
Debevoise, LA 70509
Attorney for the Parish of Debevoise

Mr. Sean Dancer
Attorney at Law
P.O. Drawer 2603
Debevoise, LA 70502
Attorney for the State of Louisiana

Ms. Norma Dauplaise
Attorney at Law
P.O. Box 868
Calais, LA 70821
Attorney for the State of Louisiana, Through the Department
of Health and Hospitals

____
RICHARD R. KENNEDY

SWORN TO AND SUBSCRIBED before me this 21st day of March, 2000.

____
NOTARY PUBLIC

20

§ 20
Contracts

20.1 Understand the main goals of a contract.

(a) *Creating a legal relationship.* A contract, the most general type of transactional document, creates reciprocal duties between the parties. It may be anything from a lease to a license to a land sale to a settlement. A lawyer drafting a contract or advising a client about a contract must remember the simple truth that whenever someone asks someone else to sign a document, the signer may someday regret having signed. The contractual terms matter most if that day ever comes. While a contract may begin a relationship with which all the parties are pleased, and close a deal about which they are optimistic, the drafter must look toward the chance that the satisfaction and optimism may fade. The document must serve well in that future day as well as in the present.

(b) *Readability and unmistakability.* On the one hand, a contract should be readable so that the parties will understand their rights and duties. On the other hand, it must be unmistakable in its meaning, since whenever a disagreement arises the parties will have a conscious or unconscious incentive to interpret the contract in their favor. Unlike most documents, contracts can be subjected to willful perversions of meaning. So the wordings must be so clear that they foreclose frivolous positions about what they mean.

20.2 Think about the specific goals of your contract.

(a) *Accuracy, completeness, and precision.* As a drafter, you must understand exactly what the parties wish to accomplish. This means that you must truly understand the practical character of the business transaction. You must express this accurately, completely, and precisely.

(b) *Protecting the client.* You must foresee situations that your client has not necessarily thought about. If the relationship sours, or if goods turn out not to be as represented, or if one of the parties becomes bankrupt, what then happens? The central question is always the same: How can you protect the interests of your client in advance? The answers to this question (there will always be more than one answer) will vary from contract to contract, but it is precisely the question that you will have to pose again and again. In a publishing agreement in which you represent the author, what happens if the publisher goes out of business? What happens with later editions if the author dies? Are the heirs protected, and for how long? Can you retain the copyright in your client's name (as opposed to granting it to the publisher)? Can you have escalating royalties after the sale of a few thousand copies? Can you negotiate a commitment from the publisher to promote the book and related computer products? Depending on the type of contract you work on, the provisions that you need to think about require great creativity and insight.

(c) *Getting the deal done.* Although you want to protect your client's interests, you will never be able to reduce your client's risk to zero. Undertaking contractual obligations always entails some element of risk. You must allow your client, after receiving your advice, to make business judgments about the level of acceptable legal risk. If you draft an agreement that is so lopsided that the other party scoffs at it or (worse) gets offended by it, you have failed in an essential element of good drafting. Even though your draft will invariably protect your client more than the other side, you should always approach the deal with an eye toward reasonableness and the type of business relationship that your client hopes to cultivate. It is an immature transactional drafter who always begins with the most extreme positions. A good deal is good for both parties at the inception; the contract fixes the deal so that if the context changes, the parties' interests are defined.

20.3 Avoid the common faults of contracts.

(a) *Patchwork style.* Contracts are often the product of many generations of drafters, each of whom had a slightly different style. Duties are often inconsistently stated (*shall, shall have the duty to, agrees to, is required to, must, will, understands that it is her sole responsibility to, is to, promises to,* etc.). Sometimes as many as four ways of stating a duty will appear on a single page. The modern drafter must reconcile these inconsistencies, preferably using ordinary English (either *will* or *agrees to*).

(b) *Inconsistent use of "shall."* Although every drafter seems to have heard that *shall* is a mandatory word, contracts frequently include as many as four or five meanings of the word. Sometimes it is indeed mandatory (*the employee shall send notice*); sometimes it means "may," especially after a negative (*neither party shall disclose*); sometimes it means "is entitled to" (*the corporate secretary shall be reimbursed for all expenses*); sometimes it is merely a future-tense verb (*if any partner shall become bankrupt*); and courts have often held that it means "should." If you want to use *shall* as a mandatory word, be sure that everywhere it appears, *must* would work just as well.

(c) *Density.* Wall-to-wall type is offputting, both to lawyers and to clients. Yet it has become all too common among legal drafters. Ensure that you have set out lists in subparts whenever you can so that readers will get through your provisions with greater ease. You will be able to review your own work with greater confidence when you create meaningful white space. See 4.6.

(d) *Awkward numbering systems.* One reason for density is that the drafter has not adopted a workable numbering system. Some documents are sprinkled with Roman numerals (the small ones are called "romanettes"), and these make for awkward tabs once they are set out in separate subparts. For maximal readability and consistency, the following system is recommended:

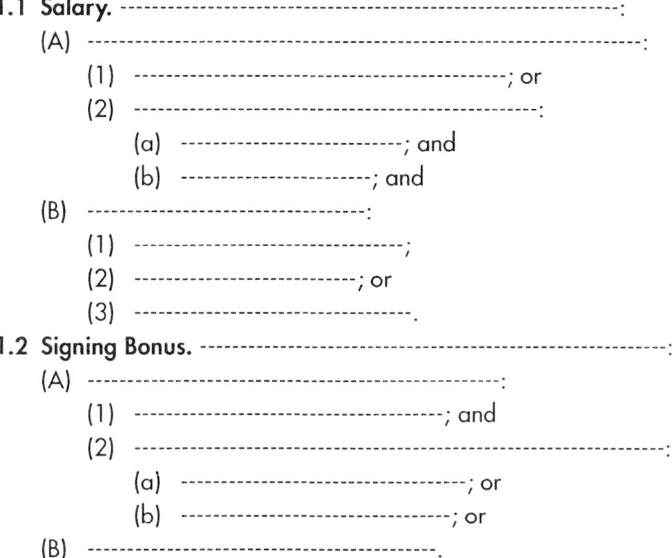

1. **Compensation**
   - **1.1 Salary.** --:
     - (A) --:
       - (1) ---------------------------------; or
       - (2) ---------------------------------:
         - (a) ---------------------; and
         - (b) ---------------------; and
     - (B) ---------------------------:
       - (1) ------------------------;
       - (2) ---------------------; or
       - (3) ------------------------.
   - **1.2 Signing Bonus.** --:
     - (A) ---------------------------------------:
       - (1) ----------------------------; and
       - (2) --:
         - (a) ---------------------------; or
         - (b) --------------------------; or
     - (B) ---------------------------------.

Imposing this kind of numbering system on an old form will typically lay bare both stylistic and substantive problems.

(e) *Uncritical use of forms.* Experienced lawyers know that forms are a better guide to content than they are to form. They will help you think through the kinds of issues that you will need to address, but they will probably be of minimal value in wording the provisions. Inexperienced lawyers sometimes slavishly follow forms (commercial or in-house) and end up not thinking through the issues as penetratingly as they should. Or the lawyers don't stop to think through how a particular boilerplate provision might affect a client with specific requirements and needs.

(f) *Archaisms and legalese.* Many forms are so stuffed with legalisms—such as *witnesseth* (a worthless flourish), *the aforesaid* (as a replacement of *the*), *said* (as another replacement of *the*), and *such* (as yet another replacement of *the*)—that lawyers are afraid to change the forms because they seem to enshrine an untouchable dialect. Lawyers occasionally argue that clients demand forms filled with this archaic jargon, but actual sightings of these clients have never been verified. The better modern forms dispense with the legalese; the provisions are worded more comprehensibly both for lawyers and for clients, and well-drafted plain-English forms more accurately bring about the desired legal relationship than do the old-style forms.

20.4 Study effective contracts.

(a) *Models.* It is useful to consult a formbook to develop an outline of the "deal," to ensure that you have covered all the bases. But then draft the contract yourself, in plain English. Although it is impossible to endorse any formbook because the forms almost invariably need further stylistic work, many useful ideas appear in Peter Siviglia's *Commercial Agreements* (1997–1998) and Robert A. Feldman's *Drafting Effective Contracts* (1996). For a full contract that consistently uses plain-language principles, see Bryan A. Garner, *Legal Writing in Plain English* 196–206 (2001).

(b) *Guidance.* For sound advice on particular elements of contractual drafting, see *Drafting Contracts and Commercial Instruments* (Research and Document Corp. ed., 1971); Carl Felsenfeld & Alan Siegel, *Writing Contracts in Plain English* (1981); Scott J. Burnham, *The Contract Drafting Guidebook* (rev. ed. 1992); and Bryan A. Garner, *A Dictionary of Modern Legal Usage* (2d ed. 1995).

(c) *An example.* The example that follows is a stock-repurchase agreement prepared by a major firm on the West Coast.

> "When words such as *whereby, thereby, heretofore,* and *wherein* creep into your vocabulary, put down your pen, take a few deep breaths, and read your work aloud. Your ear will soon tell you just how awkward and antiquated these phrases are."
>
> —*Gary Blake & Robert W. Bly*

Stock-Repurchase Agreement

This Stock-Repurchase Agreement (the "Agreement"), dated January 31, 2002, is between Fortell Corporation (the "Company") and Jill F. Perlison.

Background

A. Perlison owns 30,000 shares of Common Stock of the Company. She is a party to the shareholders' agreement dated June 11, 1999 between the Company, Joel F. Messerschmidt, individually, and Perlison, and the individual shareholders whose names are set forth on Exhibit A and Exhibit B to that agreement.

B. Perlison is a Severed Stockholder, as defined in the shareholders' agreement. As a result, Perlison is obligated to offer the shares to the Company for repurchase in accordance with § 7 of that agreement.

C. The Company has accepted the offer to repurchase the shares from Perlison.

D. The parties wish to enter into this Agreement to effect the repurchase by the Company of Perlison's shares.

Terms and Conditions

1. **Sale and Purchase of Shares**

   1.1 **Repurchase.** Effective immediately upon the signing of this Agreement, the Company will purchase from Perlison, and Perlison will sell to the Company, all her shares for an aggregate purchase price of $1,500, under the shareholders' agreement and the certificate of value issued in connection with that agreement. Perlison acknowledges receipt of a check for $1,500.

   1.2 **Certificates.** In consideration of the purchase price of $1,500, Perlison will, upon the signing of this Agreement, surrender to the Company for cancellation a certificate representing her shares, together with a duly executed stock power.

1.3 **Shareholders' Agreement.** Performance of this Agreement fully satisfies all obligations under the shareholders' agreement.

2. **Representations and Warranties.**

2.1 **Perlison's Representations and Warranties.** Perlison represents and warrants to the Company as follows:

(A) **Ownership.** Perlison is the beneficial and record owner of the shares, the shares constitute all her shares of capital stock in the Company, and she owns no securities convertible or exercisable for or other rights to acquire capital stock of the Company.

(B) **No Liens.** Perlison has not created any encumbrances or granted any rights in the shares. Upon the Company's repurchase of the shares, Perlison will transfer and deliver to the Company record and beneficial ownership of the shares, free of all encumbrances or restrictions of any kind.

(C) **No Conflicts.** Neither Perlison's signing and delivery of this Agreement nor her consummation of the transactions contemplated by the Agreement conflicts with or violates:

(1) the Company's charter;

(2) any agreement applicable to Perlison; or

(3) any law, rule, regulation, order, judgment, or decree applicable to Perlison or by which any of her property or assets might be affected.

Stock-Repurchase Agreement
January 31, 2002
Page 2

2.2 **Company's Representations and Warranties.** The Company represents and warrants to the Company as follows:

(A) **No Conflicts.** Neither the Company's signing and delivery of this Agreement nor its consummation of the transactions contemplated by the Agreement conflicts with or violates:

(1) the Company's articles of organization;

(2) any agreement applicable to the Company; or

(3) any law, rule, regulation, order, judgment, or decree applicable to the Company or by which any of its property or assets might be affected.

(B) **Authority.** The Company has all necessary power and authority under its articles of organization to sign and deliver this Agreement, to perform its obligations under it, and to consummate the transactions contemplated by it. The signing, delivery, and consummation have been duly and validly authorized by the Company's board of directors. No other corporate proceedings are necessary to authorize this Agreement or to consummate the transactions. The Agreement has been duly and validly signed and delivered by the Company and constitutes a legal, valid, and binding obligation of the Company, enforceable against it by its terms.

3. **Release.** In consideration of the purchase and sale of the shares under this Agreement, Perlison and the Company each release the other (and all related parties, including successors in interest) from all claims, liabilities, and damages of any kind, whether known or unknown, that the releasing party now has or might have against the released party for any reason at all. But this release does not apply to claims that either party may have against the other in connection with this Agreement.

Stock-Repurchase Agreement
January 31, 2002
Page 3

4. **Notices.** Any notice or other communication required by this Agreement must be in writing and must be delivered personally or sent by certified or registered mail, or by overnight courier, postage prepaid, to the following addresses:

If to the Company:	If to Perlison:
Fortell Corporation Attn: General Counsel 555 N. Grand, Suite 1700 Los Angeles, CA 94105	Jill F. Perlison 598 Battery St., Suite 1588 San Francisco, CA 94111

A notice is considered as having been given (1) on the day of personal delivery, or (2) two days after the date of mailing.

5. **Miscellaneous.**

(A) **Choice of Law.** This Agreement is governed by the internal laws of California, without regard to its conflict-of-laws provisions.

(B) **Entire Agreement; Modification.** This Agreement, together with the documents and agreements delivered by its terms and referred to in it, constitutes the entire agreement between the parties pertaining to the repurchase of shares and supersedes all prior and contemporaneous agreements, representations, and undertakings. No supplement, modification, or amendment of this Agreement will be binding unless it is in writing and signed by both parties.

(C) **Waiver.** No waiver of any term of this Agreement constitutes a waiver of any other provision, whether similar or dissimilar. No waiver of any term constitutes a continuing waiver of that term. No waiver is binding unless signed in writing by the waiving party.

(D) **Severability.** If any term of this Agreement is for any reason invalid or unenforceable, the rest of the Agreement remains fully valid and enforceable.

Stock-Repurchase Agreement
January 31, 2002
Page 4

(E) **Binding Effect; Assignment.** This Agreement binds and inures to the benefit of both the parties and their successors and assigns. But the Agreement cannot be assigned without the prior written consent of the other party.

(F) **Headings.** The headings in this Agreement are for convenience of reference only and do not constitute a part of it. The headings do not affect its interpretation.

(G) **Counterparts.** This Agreement may be signed in counterparts, each one of which is considered an original, but all of which constitute one and the same instrument.

Signed: January 31, 2002.

FORTELL CORPORATION

____

By: ____________________________

Title: __________________________

____

JILL F. PERLISON

Stock-Repurchase Agreement
January 31, 2002
Page 5

Word Index

References here are to page numbers.

General Index

References here are to section numbers.